DONATED BY
IAN THOMSON

EUROPEAN COMMUNITY LAW IN THE ENGLISH COURTS

European Community Law in the English Courts

Edited by

Mads Andenas
Director, Centre of European Law, King's College, London

and

Francis Jacobs
Advocate General, European Court of Justice

CLARENDON PRESS · OXFORD
1998

Oxford University Press, Great Clarendon Street, Oxford OX2 6DP
www.oup.co.uk

Oxford New York
Athens Auckland Bangkok Bogotá Buenos Aires Calcutta
Cape Town Chennai Dar es Salaam Delhi Florence Hong Kong Istanbul
Karachi Kuala Lumpur Madrid Melbourne Mexico City Mumbai
Nairobi Paris São Paolo Singapore Taipei Tokyo Toronto Warsaw
and associated companies in
Berlin Ibadan

Published in the United States
by Oxford University Press Inc., New York

First published 1998

British Library Cataloguing in Publication Data
Data available

Library of Congress Cataloging in Publication Data
European community law in the English courts / [edited by] Jacobs and Andenas.
p. cm.
Includes index.
1. International and municipal law—Great Britain.
2. European Union—Great Britain.
I. Jacobs, Francis Geoffrey, 1939– .
II. Andenas, Mads Tønnesson, 1957– .
KD4015.E87 1998 341.242'2'0942—dc21 98–4471

ISBN 0–19–826592–1

1 3 5 7 9 10 8 6 4 2

Typeset by Hope Services (Abingdon) Ltd.
Printed in Great Britain
on acid-free paper by
Biddles Ltd., Guildford and King's Lynn

Contents

C. The Impact on Some Areas of Law

Foreword

BY THE LORD CHIEF JUSTICE,
THE RT HON LORD BINGHAM OF CORNHILL

Almost a quarter of a century has passed since the United Kingdom became a member of the European Community. Politically, our membership has had its ups and downs, with perhaps (until now) more downs than ups. But legally it has been a happier story. British courts have done their best to interpret and apply the law of the Community in cases coming before them; and when in doubt they have not hesitated to seek rulings from the European Court of Justice, loyally giving effect to rulings made. Despite a strong, if recent, tradition of splendid isolation in legal matters, the British courts have with remarkable alacrity recognized and accepted the obligations and implications of a new and very different legal order.

This book is a product of its time. It marks the point which, in the course of its continuing development, Community Law has now reached. It discusses a number of issues which are currently at the centre of controversy. It points the way towards possible future developments. By the range of topics covered, the book makes plain the pervasive influence of Community Law on broad swathes of our economic and social life. Through the medium of our national courts, Community Law has become a central feature of legal life, and it can no longer be seen (as perhaps it once was) as an arcane study pursued by a handful of eccentric lawyers with a taste for the occult.

This is a very interesting book, and a very timely one. The editors are to be congratulated on assembling an outstanding team of judges, practitioners, and academics to address these important, topical, and challenging issues.

The Rt Hon Lord Bingham of Cornhill June 1997

Lord Chief Justice of England
Royal Courts of Justice
The Strand London WC2

Introduction

BY FRANCIS G. JACOBS QC, ADVOCATE GENERAL,
COURT OF JUSTICE OF THE EUROPEAN COMMUNITIES

This book has its origins in two remarkable conferences, held in Oxford and at King's College London. The first, jointly organized by the Bar European Group and King's Centre of European Law, took place in Lady Margaret Hall in March 1996 and was chaired by Sir John Laws and by me. The second was organized by the Centre of European Law in the Great Hall at King's in July 1996 and was chaired by the Lord Chief Justice, Lord Bingham of Cornhill.

The book brings together a number of the papers given at the conferences; in addition some further papers were commissioned from judges, practitioners, and scholars. The authors thus provide a variety of perspectives, and even a refreshing variety of styles.

The book strikingly demonstrates the impact of European Community law on English law, which in recent years has been increasingly significant, and shows how English judges and practitioners have responded to the challenges posed by a new legal system which seems fundamentally different in so many respects from their own.

A number of areas of substantive law illustrate most directly the impact of Community law. Equal rights and equal treatment for men and women, and other areas of employment law, social security and social policy have proved of particular importance. Competition law has had a significant impact. Some aspects of indirect taxation and of intellectual property law now have as their foundation statutes based directly on Community directives such as the VAT directives and the First Trade Marks Directive.

It is of interest to find leading practitioners in specialized fields taking the view that systematic legislation based on Community texts provides in some respects a more satisfactory basis for the law than the piecemeal approach previously adopted in English legislation. Although much of the Community legislation in technical areas is of recent origin, dating from the 1992 single market programme, it is also of interest that where the Court of Justice has had the opportunity to develop a body of case law—as on taxation or on equal pay and equal treatment—the English courts have been able to extrapolate very successfully from the principles laid down in the case law of the Court of Justice.

Perhaps less predictably, Community Law has had an impact on other areas such as criminal law and public law. What has been especially striking has been the perceptible effect of Community law on English law outside the Community context, the most notable example being the assertion by the House of Lords in *M* v. *Home Office*, after *Factortame*, of jurisdiction to grant injunctions against Ministers and other officers of the Crown acting in their official capacity. And mention of the *Factortame* litigation recalls of course the readiness of the House of Lords to give precedence to Community law over Acts of Parliament, thus qualifying the most fundamental principle of the constitution.

Predictable or not, it is of interest also to speculate now, since this book comes twenty-five years after accession to the Community, on which of these developments might or might not have been foreseen then.

One very significant change is the way in which the judiciary, the practitioners, and the universities have adjusted.

In January 1973, when the United Kingdom joined the Community, it cannot be said that the legal profession was in general well prepared for the changes which membership entailed. Apart from pioneering efforts in two or three University law faculties, Community law was an unknown quantity, enshrouded also in the apprehension which often accompanies ignorance.

How different the picture is today, after twenty-five years of membership of the Community—although the changes in the legal scene have been gradual, and indeed many of the most important developments are very recent. Community law is now for practical purposes an essential part of every legal curriculum. Indeed the subject is probably studied more widely, and in more depth, in the United Kingdom than in many other Member States. There are flourishing professional and other legal bodies specializing in promoting the knowledge of Community law. The Judicial Studies Board arranges advanced courses on Community law for the judiciary, and the Civil Service does likewise for the Government Legal Service. Countless visits by students, practitioners, officials, and judges to the Court of Justice and to the other Community institutions have brought greater familiarity with the workings of the institutions—and have shown, perhaps, that these institutions are reasonably open and user-friendly. There are outstanding books and journals.

Although this book is concerned with the impact of Community law in English courts, it should not be assumed that the influence has been entirely in one direction. Examples of great significance can be found in the reverse direction.

Many commentators have noted the contribution of the English notion of natural justice, under the influence of Advocate General Warner, to the development in Community administrative law of 'the right to be heard'. Another general principle of law, that of legal professional privilege, was adopted after successive opinions in the same case by Advocates General Warner and Slynn.

Even more pervasive has been the effect of the European Court's encounter with the English practitioner and with the English legal tradition: the English Bar has unquestionably had an impact on the character of the proceedings in the Court of Justice and given somewhat greater significance to the oral stage of the proceedings; while the common law tradition has perhaps led the Court, as Professor Arnull suggests, to be more explicit in its handling of its previous case law, to the great benefit of clarity and legal certainty.

Could one also suggest that the Court of Justice is, by and large, somewhat more pragmatic, somewhat less dogmatic, in its approach than it was twenty-five years ago? Others must be left to decide—and indeed to judge whether that is progress or the reverse.

It can, however, only be beneficial if legal systems can engage in dialogue with each other, and borrow good ideas, adapt and perhaps improve them. Judges and lawyers who understand another system will also, surely, understand their own system better. These must all be benefits.

There are now even signs of convergence between English law and Community law. But they remain, and will long remain, very different. Different case law techniques, and different approaches to interpretation, are required by English statute law and common law on the one hand and by the legal instruments of Community legislation and by the case law of the Court of Justice on the other hand.

It can, I think, no longer be assumed that all points of difficulty which may arise in the courts of the Member States can be referred to the Court of Justice for a preliminary ruling. As the reach of Community law has expanded over the years—and even if political choice, or the principle of subsidiarity, imposes restraints on future expansion—it will increasingly be necessary for the national courts to take responsibility for ensuring the correct application of Community law.

The making of this book comes at a time which may be seen, in retrospect, as a turning-point: a time at which the national courts assumed an even greater role as, in effect, Community courts. The book also provides assurance that they will be equal to the task.

Table of Cases

PART A

Giving Effect to Community Law in English Courts

1

Critics of the Court: a Reconsideration

BY THE RT HON LORD SLYNN OF HADLEY

This book is concerned with Community law in English courts. Since a great deal of that law is to be found in judgments of the European Court it is not inappropriate to have in mind some of the criticisms which have been made in recent times of that Court and to consider to what extent they are well-founded. No human institution is infallible or perfect and therefore the Court is perfectly capable of making mistakes. It is no less to be expected today that the work of judges is subject to public discussion and criticism. Such criticism should, however, be well-founded in fact and balanced in assessment if it is to be valuable.

Some of these criticisms are that the Court has been too interventionist in ways different from those intended by the signatories to the Treaty of Rome, has increased its powers in a manner which reduces the power of national courts and, in a word, has been too federalist in its approach. One hears remarks such as that 'it is time that the wings of the Court should be clipped'.

The starting point for some of this criticism seems to be the early decisions of the Court in *Van Gend en Loos*[1] decided in 1963 and *Costa* v. *Enel*[2] decided in 1964. In the former the Court recognized that 'The Treaty is more than an agreement which merely creates mutual obligations between the contracting States'. It said 'The Community constitutes a new legal order of international law for the benefit of which States have limited their sovereign rights, albeit within limited fields and the subjects of which comprise not only Member States but also their nationals'. By looking at the spirit and the general scheme of the Treaty the Court recognized the supremacy of Community law over national law and ruled that even a subsequent inconsistent national law could not prevail against a provision of the Treaty. In *Costa* v. *Enel* the Court recognized that some provisions of the Treaty created direct effect on the legal relations between Member States and their nationals so that the latter could require national courts to protect individual rights given by the Treaty.

These two decisions, beyond doubt, have been crucial to much that has followed and all those who have been concerned in the development and

[1] [1963] ECR 1. [2] [1964] ECR 585.

practice of Community law recognize and accept the importance of the principles laid down in them. The principles of direct effect and the precedence or supremacy of Community law have formed the basis of the structure which has emerged from decisions on a case by case basis. Those who criticize say that there is no reason why national courts and, in particular, supreme courts should be required to bend the knee to the European Court on issues of the interpretation and validity of Community legislation and of the interpretation of the Treaty.

These root and branch criticisms seem to me to undermine the whole concept of the Community where, if the rule of law is to mean anything, there must be uniformity in interpreting and applying legislation throughout the Member States. I can see no way in which a Common Market or a European Community can be built unless the law applicable in the Community is uniformly applied. That makes it necessary that the decisions of the European Court, whose overriding function set out in Article 164 of the Treaty is to 'ensure that in the interpretation and application of the Treaty the law is observed', should be applicable throughout the Community. The only way to achieve such uniformity was to give decisions of that Court precedence over decisions of national courts and national legislation, to make national legislation subject to legislation of the Community, even national legislation adopted subsequent to the adoption of the rules of Community law. That is what the Court did and that is precisely what Parliament did for the United Kingdom when it enacted the European Communities Act in 1972. There Parliament accepted that Community law was to be given full effect. This was recognized by the House of Lords in Lord Bridge's speech in the *Factortame* case.[3] For my part I see no reason why in the future these fundamental principles should be any less necessary than they have been in the past, or that they should now be in some way modified. Far from the European Court of Justice having taken a wrong turn in holding that some rules of European Community law can be relied on in national courts its decisions have been of considerable benefit to individual citizens and trading corporations.

Has the Court been too creative, too federalist, 'ceaselessly imperialist' in its approach?

Certainly the Court has taken decisions which have profoundly influenced the development of the Community and strengthened it.

Those who criticize the Court on this basis point to the fact that the Court has recognised that Directives can sometimes be relied on against a Member State even where the Directive has not been incorporated in the legislation of that State. It has recognized the existence of a right to damages against State which has failed to implement Directives thereby

[3] [1991] 1 AC 603.

causing loss to the citizen. It has limited the retroactive effect of judgments so that only the litigant who establishes his claim in the particular proceedings and other litigants who had already commenced proceedings can take advantage of the decision without others being allowed to rely upon it. It has recognized a jurisdiction not expressly conferred by the Treaty as, for example, where the Parliament has been allowed to challenge acts of the Council or the Commission. It has ruled that it alone can hold Community legislation to be invalid even if national courts can hold it to be valid and it has required national courts, so far as possible, to interpret earlier national laws in the light of later unimplemented Directives.

I do not for a moment say that the Court has taken decisions which are not debatable, which are so clearly right that they cannot be criticized. But that is not the question. The question is whether the Court has gone beyond what the Treaty provides, whether in advancing a form of union not contemplated by the Treaty or in restraining activities which the Treaty clearly permits. The question is not whether the Court has in a particular case taken a decision of which one disapproves. The test is whether in reaching its decision the Court has exceeded its jurisdiction. If it does the Court can be justly criticized.

But the mere fact that a Court recognizes new principles of law or modifies existing ones does not mean that it has exceeded its jurisdiction even if some people do not like the principles adopted. In the common law system supreme courts frequently develop the law by new principles and new rules and I imagine that civil law courts do the same even if in a different way and in a different context. The Warren Court in the United States after the Second World War was clearly creative on constitutional issues and the House of Lords itself not infrequently develops new steps in the law. One only has to look at *Donoghue and Stevenson*[4] where Lord Atkin said that in English law 'there must be, and is, some general conception of relations giving rise to a duty of care of which the particular cases found in the books are but instances'. On that basis the present law of negligence began with a new formulation adopted by the House of Lords. Justice Cardozo in the United States said that the judicial process 'in its highest reaches is not discovery but creation'.

It was quite plainly intended from the beginning and was perhaps even inevitable that the European Court would develop new rules and new principles. The Treaty was not a detailed code which judges simply had to apply and there was no body of precedents which they could simply follow.

It seems to me that the Court was bound and certainly entitled to have regard to the nature of the Treaty and the context in which the various

4 [1932] AC 562.

provisions were to be found—the task of the Community set out in Article 2, the activities of the Community set out in Article 3 and the general principles set out in Articles 5–7 were all part of the context in which the Court's task of interpreting the Treaty and legislation had to be formed. In particular factual situations the Court was required to put flesh on the bare bones of the Treaty and on Regulations which were often expressed in terms where alternative interpretations were possible or where their application in particular effectual situations was not obvious. I do not consider that in reaching decisions such as those to which I have referred the Court exceeded its jurisdiction. The particular decisions of principle may well be debatable but it seems to me that on any view they flow from an interpretation of the Treaty which is wholly tenable.

The Court's decision in regard to the non-implementation of Directives illustrates the balance that has to be struck. Thus it was clear that Directives were to be treated in a different way from Regulations. Article 189 of the Treaty made it abundantly plain that Regulations could have direct effect—they were to be 'of general application (. . .) binding in [their] entirety and directly applicable in all Member States'. The Treaty, however, provided that a Directive 'shall be binding as to the result to be achieved upon each Member State to which it is addressed but shall leave to the national authorities the choice of form and methods'. The Court accepted, by following the common law concept of estoppel, that if a State had not given effect to a Directive it could not rely on its own failure to defeat a citizen's claim under the Directive which ought to have been adopted. It has, however, refused to give direct effect as between citizens or companies where the estoppel concept was irrelevant since the citizen was not responsible for the failure to adopt the Directive. It may well be that this distinction ought to be removed. It has always seemed to me, however, that if it is to be removed the Article of the Treaty ought to be changed by the Member States. I do not think that it would have been right for the Court to depart from the language of the Treaty in a way that has sometimes been advocated. The Court's recent affirmation of this distinction seems to be entirely correct.

Similarly the decision of the Court that a State may be liable to pay compensation where in breach of its duty it has failed to implement Directives so that loss is caused to the citizen, seems to be equally within the Court's jurisdiction and indeed the principle had been foreshadowed in earlier cases as far back as the case of *Humblet* v. *Belgium*,[5] a case under the European Coal and Steel Treaty where it was said that if a State had adopted a measure in contravention of Community law it must rescind the measure and 'make reparation for any unlawful consequences which may

[5] [1960] ECR 559.

have ensued'. I have no doubt that the effect of this decision has still to be worked out. Refinements will be necessary. Causation needs to be explained. The concept of damages may need to be elaborated in this area. The Court will have to consider to what extent a State can mount defences against a claim where a Directive has not been adopted.

I do not deal with all these cases in detail in the interests of time and space but I do not think that they show that the Court has exceeded its jurisdiction or has adopted a federalist approach contrary to the provisions of the Treaty itself. It seems to me that the Court has sought to do what the Treaty required it to do. I certainly never saw myself as one of a unanimous group of committed federalists conspiring to push federation beyond the limits laid down by the Treaty. If we had been such, a great deal of the hard-headed discussion in thrashing out judgments within the framework of the Treaty could have been avoided. Instead we sought to decide in accordance with the Treaty and the object and purpose of the legislation.

It has been said further that the Court gives retroactive judgments thereby changing the intention at the time it was made of those who agreed to the legislation. It seems to me that this is a misunderstanding of the judicial process. The Court has to construe the legislation and if it finds that it has a certain meaning that must be the meaning which it always had. That may mean in the result that transactions which occurred previously had taken place on a basis different from that which the Court finds to be the real interpretation. In no sense is this a legislative process. It is a normal process of interpretation which courts are called on to perform regularly. If those who make the delegated legislation do so in terms which are not clear, or which are capable of more than one meaning, then there can be no surprise if a court adopts one meaning rather than another as being that which necessarily is to be taken in the context of the delegated legislation. If the Commission or the Council do not like the decision of the Court they are entitled, of course, to adopt new legislation for the future. To give, however, the Commission or the Council power to make retroactive changes in order to overrule a decision of the Court seems to me to be a violation of the rule of law which constitutionally should not be allowed.

Conversely the Court has been criticized by some for imposing limitations on the effect of its judgments. Thus in a case where an air hostess challenged a particular practice in her company[6] it was held that the effect of the judgment should only apply in her case and in the case of other people who had already commenced proceedings. Similarly in the case of students who challenged a demand for fees to be paid which were

[6] *Defrenne* v. *SABENA* [1976] ECR 455.

discriminatory on the ground of nationality[7] the Court limited the effect of its decision as to the discriminatory practice to the applicants in the case and to others who had already commenced proceedings. This means that those who had not commenced proceedings could not benefit from the Court's ruling as to the proper interpretation or effect of what had been written or done. The Court does this relatively rarely and only in cases where it considers that the limitation is required in the interests of stability and of not upsetting transactions long since past. Some of the cases which came before the Court would have had a disastrous effect on the finances of the university or employer concerned if it had to re-open its treatment of all its staff for many years past. This is a practice to be followed in exceptional circumstances but it is one which it seems to me can, in appropriate circumstances, be justified. On any view I do not consider that what is done can be described as a 'legislative' activity.

The Court is also criticized because of its composition and the way in which it works. It has been said in this country that only persons who have had experience as judges in the supreme court of their Member State should be eligible to be appointed to the European Court. That would have excluded every British nomination so far! I think that it is important that the Court should have on it a substantial number of members who have either practised the law for a long period or sat as judges for a long period or a combination of the two. The Treaty, however, contemplated that the catchment area for judges should be wider. They must be persons who were qualified for appointment to the highest judicial offices in their respective countries or 'who are jurisconsults of recognised competence'.

The practice in States differs and this must be respected in the selection of judges and advocates-general in the European Court. It comes as a surprise to an English lawyer that someone who is a jurisconsult of recognized competence but who is not qualified for appointment to the highest judicial office in his country should be eligible for appointment to the European Court. The aim of this was clearly to allow Member States to nominate professors of law experienced in Community law to be appointed. It also allows the appointment of others such as administrators who have had considerable legal experience and standing. I believe that in this area of the law, which is new to Member States joining the Community from time to time, it is right that professors of law should be eligible since when a new Member State joins there will be no judges who have had judicial experience of Community law and there may be few, if any, lawyers who have had experience in the practice of Community law. It is a specialized subject and I think justifies the appointment of jurisconsults of recognized competence. It is, however, no less important that there

[7] *Blaizot* v. *University of Liège* [1988] ECR 379.

should be a substantial number of those with judicial experience and those with experience in practice on the Court.

The lack of dissenting judgments is also seen as a matter for criticism. It is quite true that judgments of the European Court are collegiate and anonymous and no-one knows precisely what any individual judge thinks. There is in my view much to be said in favour of having individual judgments whether they are in agreement or whether they are in dissent. Individual judgments agreeing with the result for different reasons can often contribute new material in the development of the law. So can dissenting judgments although it seems that a major reason for not having dissenting judgments in the first place was that advocates-general should be appointed to give an individual opinion which might well be different from that given by the Court itself. Individual judgments have the advantage that the judge can express firmly and without having to produce a compromise text the opinions which he holds.

On the other hand it is clear that if five individual judgments are given all on a different basis but achieving the same final result there may be doubt as to what is the real ratio decidendi of the case. Moreover continental lawyers feel that the authority of the Court is reduced if the decision given is a majority and not a collegiate judgment. They also fear that if judges are allowed to dissent there will be a tendency for them to ride hobby-horses and they might always have an eye to what will be thought at home of their judgments. I doubt whether any of these reasons is valid but I do recognize that deliberation in search of a consensus may itself have advantages in that judges do not adopt polarized positions from the beginning. It may well be that a unanimous judgment does give a stronger air of authority, contrary to my view.

I regard the issue as a balanced one. I am sure that the Court as presently constituted would not be in favour of adopting dissenting or individual opinions but it seems to me that the question should be kept under consideration and that in time it may be felt that the Court's authority is such that dissenting opinions could be accepted. I have always felt that it might be possible to adopt a system whereby there was one majority opinion and one minority opinion when those disagreeing with the majority could combine to produce the various reasons why they could not accept the majority decision without individual views being specified. However this is something to be considered in the future.

There are many other areas where the function and the activities of the Court can be reconsidered and where amendments can be introduced. Thus it seems to me that Article 173 should be amended to give wider possibilities for natural and legal persons to challenge the legality of Community acts by which they, or the groups which they represent, are affected. I think that it will be necessary with time to consider the present method of nominating judges. Should there be one for each country even when we have twenty-five Members of the Community? If so, should the full Court consist of twenty-five judges or should there be a limited number of, say, eleven judges with the possibility of two full courts of eleven Members? Alternatively, should we consider introducing an electoral college to which each State would make a nomination from whom the college, perhaps consisting of the Minister of Justice or the President of the Supreme Court of each Member State, could select an agreed number of Members of the Court, such as nine or eleven Members.

Is it still necessary that supreme courts should be obliged to send questions which have to be decided in the cases before them to the European Court? Is the relaxation of the rule set out in the Treaty which the Court itself has adopted sufficiently clear and workable? Could supreme courts now with greater experience not be relied on to arrive at a solution which is *'communautaire'*? I feel myself that the time has come when the final courts with considerable experience should be encouraged to take decisions in areas where they feel reasonable confidence that they are right although I think that the CILFIT[8] test is quite unworkable if taken literally. If it were found that supreme courts were diverging from the principles of Community law then we should investigate whether the Commission should not have a power similar to that of the Attorney-General in criminal cases in this country. It seems to me that it would be perfectly possible to devise a scheme by which if a supreme court, or several supreme courts, were going down a wrong path that the Commission should be in a position to refer a question to the Court for them to lay down the right principle without necessarily affecting the decisions in cases already taken by supreme courts. In this way the law could be kept on the right lines for the future.

I think myself that great care has to be taken in relation to the provisions of Title VI of the Treaty. There it was clearly intended that some matters would be dealt with by Conventions adopted by the Member States to deal with the matters specified in the title and in particular Article K3. For this reason it was agreed that the Court should not have jurisdiction unless the Convention specified that the Court should have jurisdiction to interpret the provision of the Convention and to rule on any disputes regarding the application of such provisions. It is easy to understand the reason why these matters were to be dealt with on an inter-State basis. Many of the matters covered involve questions of policy and co-ordinated administrative action. For some of these there is no necessary role for the European Court and no doubt any disputes could be dealt with in national courts or perhaps even, in an extreme case, in the International Court of Justice at

[8] *CILFIT Srl. and Lanifico de Gavardo Spa* v. *Ministry of Health* [1982] ECR 3415.

The Hague. On the other hand some of the Conventions are likely to have a potentially important effect on individual rights and even liberty which could be harmfully affected by a wrongful interpretation or application of the newly made Convention. It seems to me that such Conventions ought to be interpreted and applied on a uniform basis in the different Member States. This to my mind inevitably means that there should be a central court or tribunal to give a final ruling to be followed by courts and administrative agencies of all the Member States. I think that it is important to consider each Convention on a case-by-case basis and where there is a risk of individual rights being affected by a misapplication of the Convention or a misinterpretation of its terms that the court should be given jurisdiction.

It is obvious also that the delays which occur at the Court, which the Court itself has sought on many occasions to reduce with some success, will have to be kept constantly under review but I have no doubt that the members of the Court are very conscious of the disadvantages of long delays in dealing with the matters which come before the Court.

There may be lots of room for self-questioning, for improvements or modification. That is inherent in any human institution. However, it seems to me important not to lose sight of the fact that a strong and independent Court of Justice is an essential part of the structure of the European Union and any reforms should be directed towards that.

2

Giving Effect to Community Law

BY THE HON MICHAEL BELOFF QC,
PRESIDENT OF TRINITY COLLEGE, OXFORD; BENCHER OF GRAYS INN;
JUDGE OF THE COURT OF APPEAL OF JERSEY AND GUERNSEY[1]

In this chapter I explore the fora in which Community law may be enforced, the criteria which determine the appropriate forum, the merits and demerits of such criteria: and possible reforms.

Where to Start: Luxembourg or England?

The choices of forum lie between the following four. First the two Community courts. The Court of First Instance (CFI) is the forum in which to start actions under Article 173 which allows for judicial review of Community acts (essentially an action for an order for certiorari), or Article 175 which deals with the failure of a Community institution to act (essentially an action for an order of mandamus). Appeals may be brought to the Court of Justice (ECJ), likewise under Article 173 or Article 175. This is the system for Community Judicial Reviews. Actions may also be brought by way of complaint to the European Commission in Brussels, providing a third forum. The fourth forum may be in the English courts through applications for judicial review or in the context of a private action. This may or may not result in a reference to the ECJ pursuant to Article 177.

The question of which forum is the most appropriate one in any one particular case will depend:

- on the type of issue raised and
- on the identity of the potential applicant.

Importantly, national courts do not have the power to quash Community Acts, although they can consider such measures and conclude that they are completely valid. In *Foto-Frost*,[2] the ECJ held that the requirement of uniformity, the necessary coherence of the system of judicial protection

[1] The author wishes to thank Marie Demetriou, Barrister at 4–5 Gray's Inn Square for her help with the preparation of this chapter.

[2] Case 314/85 *Foto-Frost*, 1987 ECR 4199 affirmed recently by the ECJ in Case C–27/95 *Woodspring DC* v. *Bakers of Nailsea Ltd* [1997] 2 CMLR 266.

established by the Treaty, and the procedural advantages enjoyed by the ECJ, all justified that exclusivity. It said,

15. On the other hand, those courts do not have the power to declare acts of the Community institutions invalid. As the Court emphasised in the judgment of 13 May 1981 in Case 66/80 *International Chemical Corporation* v. *Amministrazione delle Finanze* [1981] ECR 1191, the main purpose of the powers accorded to the Court by Article 177 is to ensure that Community law is applied *uniformly* by national courts. That requirement of uniformity is particularly imperative when the validity of a Community act is in question. Divergences between courts in the Member States as to the validity of Community acts would be liable to place in jeopardy the very unity of the Community legal order and detract from the fundamental requirement of legal certainty.

16. The same conclusion is dictated by consideration of the necessary coherence of the system of judicial protection established by the Treaty. In that regard it must be observed that requests for preliminary rulings, like actions for annulment, constitute means for reviewing the legality of acts of the Community institutions. As the Court pointed out in its judgment of 23 April 1986 in *Parti écologiste 'les Verts'* v. *European Parliament*[3], 'in Articles 173 and 184, on the one hand, and in Article 177, on the other, the Treaty established a complete system of legal remedies and procedures designed to permit the Court of Justice to review the legality of measures adopted by the institutions'.

17. Since Article 173 gives the Court exclusive jurisdiction to declare void an act of a Community institution, the coherence of the system requires that where the validity of a Community act is challenged before a national court the power to declare the act invalid must also be reserved to the Court of Justice.

18. It must also be emphasised that the Court of Justice is in the best position to decide on the validity of Community acts. Under Article 20 of the Protocol on the Statute of the Court of Justice of the EEC, Community institutions whose acts are challenged are entitled to participate in the proceedings in order to defend the validity of the acts in question. Furthermore, under the second paragraph of Article 21 of that Protocol the Court may require the Member States and institutions which are not participating in the proceedings to supply all information which it considers necessary for the purposes of the case before it.[4]

Actions brought by individual applicants to challenge Community Acts under Articles 173 and 175 must be brought in the CFI. Appeal lies to the ECJ on points of law. The locus standi rules under Articles 173 and 175 as interpreted by the European Courts draw a sharp distinction between Member States and Community institutions ('privileged applicants') and individual applicants ('non-privileged applicants').

While a Member State (or Community institution) has unrestricted standing to challenge every type of reviewable Community act and has no

[3] Case 294/83, [1986] ECR 1339. [4] At p. 4231.

need to establish a particular interest in the matter,[5] Article 173 provides that such applicants, 'natural or legal', may bring actions to challenge only of:

- a decision addressed to the applicant;
- a decision which is in the form of a regulation and is of direct and individual concern to the applicant (i.e. a disguised decision);
- a decision addressed to another person (i.e. than the applicant) which is of direct and individual concern to the applicant e.g., in competition cases to grant an exemption from the prohibition in Article 85 of the Treaty in relation to anti-competitive acts.

Under Article 173, genuine legislative acts cannot be challenged by individuals and administrative acts only by those to whom they are addressed and by those who are affected by them in a special way much as if they were equally addressed.[6]

Lord Slynn has explained that 'the right to challenge legislation is, in a sense, of a constitutional as well as administrative kind and it was thought right that the prime movers should be the institution and the Member States. The individual's rights should be more limited.'[7]

There are difficulties about satisfying these criteria falling within the following three broad categories:

(1) The issuing of decisions addressed to individuals is not by any means common practice in every area of Community law but only in the areas in which the Commission has an active enforcement role such as competition[8] or State aids.[9]

(2) As to decisions which are formally but not substantially regulations, the case law is complex. Regulations are legislative and applied to groups defined in the abstract by reference to objective legal or factual situations: decisions are applicable to a limited number of persons who are defined or identifiable. But the test is, as so often, easier to state than to apply.[10]

There were some indications that the first limb of a two-pronged test itself, which, it should be noted, is itself two-pronged ('direct and

[5] See Lewis *Remedies and the Enforcement of EC Law*, (1996) p. 252.

[6] Neuwahl, 'Article 173, Paragraph 4 EC: Past, Present and Possible Future' (1996) 21 ELR 17.

[7] *Judicial Review of Community Administrative Acts*, The Exeter Lecture in European Community Law (1985), p. 6.

[8] Where the Commission can fine offending companies, see, Lewis, *op. cit.* p. 11.

[9] Where an individual company is recipient, see Lewis *op. cit.* p. 260.

[10] See e.g., Greaves 'The Nature and Binding Effect of Decisions under Article 189 EC', (1991) 21 ELR 3.

individual concern') might become redundant. In *Codorniu* v. *Council*[11] the ECJ said

> Although it is true that according to the criteria in the second paragraph of Article 173 of the Treaty the contested provision [i.e., a regulation] is, by nature and by virtue of its sphere of application, of a legislative nature in that it applies to the traders concerned in general, that does not prevent it from being of individual concern to some of them.[12]

However, still more recently,[13] a Spanish trade association sought to rely on *Codorniu* to challenge a directive on the financing of health inspections and controls of fresh meat. It argued (i) that the relevant part of the directive merely replaced an earlier decision which it would have had standing to challenge (ii) that *Codorniu* establishes that the normative nature of a provision does not prevent it being of individual concern. The CFI held that there was no provision in Article 173 for individuals to challenge directives. The justification for this is that the judicial protection of individuals is sufficiently assured by national courts which review the transposition of directives into national law.

(3) Applicants may have a substantial interest in a decision addressed to another person or a disguised decision and be directly concerned in the sense of being immediately affected in their legal position by it (i.e. without the intervention of discretionary exercise of power by a third party).[14] They may yet be denied standing to challenge it because of the height of the hurdle of 'individual concern' set by the ECJ and the inconsistency and paucity of reasoning in their judgments.

The seminal case on the meaning of 'individual concern' is *Plaumann*.[15] In that case an importer of clementines was held not to have standing to challenge a Commission decision addressed to the German government refusing to authorize the government to suspend duties on imported clementines. The ECJ held that 'persons other than those to whom a decision is addressed may only claim to be individually concerned if that decision affects them by reason of certain attributes which are peculiar to them or by reason of circumstances in which they are differentiated from all other persons and by virtue of these factors distinguishes them individually just as in the case of the person addressed.'

[11] Case C–309/89 *Codorniu* v. *Council*, [1994] ECR 853. The applicant challenged a regulation which was in truth a regulation, and which stipulated that the term *cremant* should be reserved for sparkling wines of a particular quality coming from France or Luxembourg. The judgment may represent new liberalisation in this area of the law.

[12] At para. 19, p. 1886.

[13] Case T–99/94 *Asocarne* v. *Council* [1994] ECR II–84.

[14] See Neuwahl *op. cit.* 1.6.

[15] Case 25/62 *Plaumann & Co.* v. *Commission* [1963] ECR 95.

The Court stated that 'the applicant is affected by the disputed Decision as an importer of clementines, that is to say, by reason of a commercial activity which may at any time be practised by any person and is not therefore such as to distinguish the applicant in relation to the contested Decision as in the case of the addressee.'

It is noteworthy that this conclusion was reached against the background of the Court's self-direction that the provisions of the Treaty regarding the right of interested parties to bring an action must not be interpreted restrictively!

This test has since been applied in numerous cases with the result, inter alia, that:

- producers of isoglucose were denied standing to challenge a Regulation concerning production of isoglucose even though there are only a very few producers of this product and the number was unlikely to increase since substantial capital investment was necessary and some of the technology involved was protected by patents;[16]
- the only importer of Chinese brushes in the Benelux countries was denied standing to challenge a decision addressed to the three Benelux countries banning imports into those countries of Chinese brushes;[17]
- a firm of wine merchants asked the Commission whether Community law prohibited the use of certain German words to describe wines produced in Hungary and Yugoslavia. The Commission replied that it did not. The firm then took steps to import the wines but the Commission subsequently passed a regulation prohibiting the use of the terms in question. The firm brought proceedings to annul the regulation but the Court held it lacked locus standi.[18]

In the areas of anti-dumping, competition and state aids, the case law is more logical and more liberal.

Complainants have locus standi. Other parties which have played a part in the Commission's enforcement procedure also have standing provided their position in the market was significantly affected.[19]

In state aids cases, it was not sufficient to be an individual recipient, and in dumping it was not sufficient to be a general importer. But the ECJ has

[16] Case 101/76 *KSH* v. *Council and Commission*, [1977] ECR 797.

[17] Case 231/82 *Spijker* v. *Commission*, [1983] ECR 2559.

[18] Case 147/83 *Binderer* v. *Commission*, [1985] ECR 257. And see, recently, Case T–47/95 *Terres Rouges Consultant SA* v. *Commission* [1997] 9 ECM 14.

[19] Case 26/76 *Metro* v. *Commission*, [1977] ECR 1875; Case 169/84 *COFAZ* v. *Commission* [1986] ECR 391. See also Case T–528/93 *Metropole Television* v. *Commission* [1996] 5 CMLR 386 and contrast Case T–87/92 *Kruidvat* v. *Commission* where a much stricter approach was taken by the CFI which held inadmissible an action challenging a Commission decision upholding a selective distribution system from which the applicant was excluded.

extended this approach to a limited extent. In *Extramet*,[20] it ruled that an importer *could* challenge an anti-dumping regulation as he was also the end-user of the product that was subject to the anti-dumping duty. His business depended to a very large extent on those imports, and he would have difficulty in obtaining alternative supplies in the light of the small number of manufacturers of the product and the fact that the sole Community producer was its main competitor. It has been remarked that the Community procedures had been abused by Extramet's competitor in order to push Extramet out of the market and that in the circumstances of the case not allowing Extramet standing would have amounted to a denial of justice.[21]

Lewis has written:

> Rationale. These three categories of cases indicate that the two broad grounds for recognising individual concern is *either* a degree of identification of the individual concerned, that is some indication that the measure is dealing with the *specific* circumstances of an individual's case, *or* the grant of some specific right (to complain or participate in procedures) *coupled* with the fact that the decision affects the legitimate interests of that person. Those two criteria could be broadened to harmonise with the general run of cases so that the essential features of individual concern (and also the features that mark a measure out as a decision not a regulation) are an element of identification or the existence of some specific legislative right coupled with adverse affect and that generalisation of these criteria 'would offer some prospect of creating a unified principle governing standing'.[22]

It is a consummation devoutly to be wished!

It is instructive to contrast the European approach with that in domestic judicial review under Order 53(3)(7) where an applicant for judicial review must have a 'sufficient interest in the matter to which the application relates'. In *R* v. *Inland Revenue, ex p. National Federation for the Self Employed*[23] Lord Diplock[24] in effect suggested that only a busybody would be outlawed; although one judge's busybody may be another's public-spirited citizen or, indeed, vice versa. But mutatis mutandis, locus standi is per se but rarely a bar to modern judicial review; and then usually so *only* when others present before the court can legitimately raise the same issue of public law.

Even the concept of a person 'directly affected'—more linguistically akin to the Community law test—deployed in the same regime to discriminate between the compulsory objects of service of the proceedings and the others[25] has been loosely interpreted, although the focus is the impact of the Court's decision, not the decision of the public body under

[20] Case C–158 *Extramet Industrie SA* v. *Council*, [1991] ECR 2501.
[21] Neuwal, *op. cit.* pp. 26–7.
[22] See, Lewis, *op. cit.*, p. 260.
[23] [1982] AC 617.
[24] At p. 643.
[25] Order 53 rule 5(3).

challenge. In *ex parte Megarry*[26] it was held that the tobacco company's potential defendants in negligence actions brought by ex smokers were not 'directly affected' by a challenge by the ex smoker to a decision of the Legal Aid Board to deny them public funds to litigate it; and emphasis was placed on the qualifying adjective 'directly'. However, in *R* v. *TIC ex parte Virgin*[27] all the disappointed franchise applicants, who failed to obtain leave in their own right, came before the court in the guise of 'directly affected' persons, and ended up—albeit unsuccessfully—in making a full range of submissions potentially as damaging to the applicant as they were to the respondent. This broad commercial and elastic interpretation of the concept of being 'directly affected' may not survive the decision of the House of Lords in *R* v. *Liverpool City Council, ex parte Muldoon*[28] where it was stated by Lord Keith, 'that a person is directly affected by something connotes that he is affected without the intervention of any intermediate agency.'

Some have canvassed relaxation of both the procedural and the substantial fetters of individual challenge to Community acts under Article 173. They have suggested extending the range of Community acts to be challenged to include, for example, Directives. They have also suggested a test for locus equivalent to that of the English Courts' sufficiency of interest. Underlying the reforms is a sense that right of access to the Courts, guaranteed after all by Article 6 of the ECHR, ought not to be unnecessarily confined; a perception that legal certainty is promoted if potentially invalid acts are susceptible of challenge earlier rather than later; and a feeling that there is a paradox that the more people who are harmed by a Community act, the less susceptible it is to review.[29]

Ranged against the philosophers are the pragmatists. They see such reforms as leading to mass litigation with individual farmers challenging e.g., beef bans. They are concerned that what is sauce for individuals must necessarily be sauce for interest groups. The floodgates argument is as potent on mainland as in offshore Europe: 'Economic actions are quite eager to challenge such Community acts when their annulment may mean the construction of their business profits as well as the repayment of any sums unduly paid under an illicit Community measure.'[30] It is feared too that uncertainty would ensue when a measure is under challenge. And they worry that widening access to the ECJ will cause local knowledge and application of EC law in domestic courts to atrophy.

As Professor Arnull has pointed out:

[26] [1994] COD 468. [27] [1996] EMLR 318. [28] [1996] 1 WLR 1103.

[29] See e.g., Tripley, *Greenpeace, Euro JR: and locus standi*, [1996] JR 257.

[30] Neuwahl, *op. cit.* p. 18.

6. The relationship between Article 173 and Article 177

The standing requirements imposed on private applicants by Article 173 are to some extent mitigated by the possibility of contesting the validity of Community acts in the national courts with the use of the Article 177 reference procedures. The jurisdiction of the national courts to rule on the validity of Community acts derives from Article 177 of the Treaty, which empowers (and sometimes requires) national courts and tribunals to ask the Court of Justice for preliminary rulings on the validity of Community acts where that issue needs to be decided before judgment can be given. The question of the validity of a Community act typically arises before a national court where the alleged illegality of the act forms the basis of a challenge to a national measure which purports to implement it.[31]

Neuwahl observes that further implementing or other acts taken by Community institutions (or other non-action) on the basis of an illegal regulation can be challenged in cases pending before the Court of Justice, or example, under Articles 173, 177 or 175, on the grounds of invalidity of the underlying regulations.[32]

In my view, however, liberalization is particularly pressing in view of proposals for increasing the scope of Community law. The Report of the Court of Justice asks

> whether the right to bring an action for annulment under Article 173 . . . which individuals enjoy only in regard to acts of direct and individual concern to them, is sufficient to guarantee for them effective judicial protection against possible infringements of their fundamental rights arising from the legislative activity of the institutions.

The Intergovernmental Conference should grant locus standi to *individuals* in actions against all Community measures having legal effects which are both addressed to them or by which they are otherwise directly and individually affected, and individuals should be treated as individually affected if prima facie any of their rights under Community law have been infringed, the effective protection of which must be undertaken by the European Court of Justice.

England

The national court is presently the only proper place to start for an applicant who wishes to do any of the following:

- challenge a Directive;
- challenge a Regulation (which is *not* a disguised decision);
- invoke a right arising out of a provision of the Treaty or subsidiary of EC legislation;

[31] [1995] CMLR 7 at 40. [32] Neuwahl, *op. cit.* pp 18–19.

- assert that an English measure purporting to implement Community law has not done so properly;
- challenge English law on the ground that it does not comply with Community law;
- sue the Government in damages for non-compliance with Community law.

An action which is initiated in England may end up in Luxembourg as a result of a preliminary reference being made to the ECJ pursuant to Article 177. Such a reference is mandatory (1) in the event that the applicant is seeking to challenge the validity of a measure of Community law (*Foto-Frost*),[33] and (2) where a case reaches the court of last resort and the interpretation of Community law is not acte clair. The complexities of what is a Court of last resort in UK context, where there is a contingent right to appeal in the House of Lords was vividly exposed in *Chiron* v. *Murex*.[34]

In his 1992 Hamlyn Lectures, *Introducing a European Legal Order*, Lord Slynn said

> The Court, often to the surprise of American lawyers, has no power to 'call in' questions of Community law arising in litigation before the national judge [and the parties have no right to insist on a reference] so that some important questions may not reach the Court. On the other hand, persistent refusal by national courts of last resort to refer questions would amount to a breach of the Treaty, though it is unlikely that the Commission would apply to the Court for a declaration that a Member State was in breach of its obligation except in an extreme case. In such a case it seems likely that the Member State would have shown in other ways its intention to disregard Community law.[35]

In my view, however, this is a serious lacuna in the judicial supervision by the ECJ of national courts. Developed jurisdictions such as the United Kingdom and the United States acknowledge the need for an unsuccessful party to have the right to petition the highest court in the land for judicial redress. It is increasingly indefensible that such a right should be denied under the Treaty to European citizens, the more so because the European Convention of Human Rights already incorporates just such a mechanism. Maybe the Vienna Protocol enabling direct access for individuals to that Court could form a model for an amendment to the Protocol on the Statute of the Court of Justice.

I suggest that this, or a future, Intergovernmental Conference should consider a leave to refer mechanism as an amendment to Article 177, enabling parties to proceedings in the court of last instance to petition

[33] Case 314/85 *Firma Foto-Frost* v. *Hauptzollamt Lubeck-Ost*, [1987] ECR 4199.
[34] [1994] FSR 187; [1995] FSR 309.
[35] Lord Slynn of Hadley, *Introducing a European Legal Order* (1993) p. 10.

directly the ECJ, sitting in three judge chambers. Only through such a process will parties seeking to rely upon EC law rights have the necessary guarantee of a fair and informed hearing.

There have been suggestions that Article 177 proceedings should be restricted to appellate court or supreme court jurisdiction. Substantial costs and time are frequently saved by making an early reference under Article 177, rather than waiting until the national appeal processes have been exhausted.

The same can be said in respect of suggestions that the CFI should have a role in Article 177 proceedings. Paragraph 13 of the ECJ's Report highlights the undesirability of such a reform: 'such a system is not appropriate for preliminary ruling procedures both because it would be likely to lead to unacceptable procedural delays and because it would raise problems as to the authority of judgments given at first instance and as to identification of the parties entitled to lodge an appeal.'

It is important to appreciate that in most cases an action initiated in England will be decided in England without recourse to Luxembourg. The English courts are now more willing to be the final arbiters of issues of Community law and have recently reached decisions with far-reaching consequences without seeking the ECJ's endorsement: notwithstanding the cautionary words of Bingham J in *Samex*[36] and as Sir Thomas Bingham MR in *Else*.[37] The 'complete confidence' counselled by Lord Bingham of Cornhill LCJ is found more frequently than before, especially with Lord Slynn in the saddle in the House of Lords.

A notable illustration may be taken from the field of employment law. *Equal Opportunities Commission* v. *Secretary of State for Employment*[38] concerned provisions in the Employment Protection (Consolidation) Act 1978 that part-time workers had to be in continuous employment for five years to qualify for unfair dismissal and redundancy payment under the Act while for full-time workers the qualification period was two years. The Equal Opportunities Commission claimed that the effect of these provisions was to discriminate against women in conflict with Article 119 of the Treaty of Rome, the Equal Pay Directive and the Equal Treatment Directive. Relying on *Factortame*, the House of Lords made a declaration that the provisions at issue were incompatible with Community law.

There are two peculiarities about the decision in the Equal Opportunities case.

The first is that, out of a range of procedural points that the author and Stephen Richards, the Treasury devil took on behalf of the Secretary of State—the one that we declined to take—that the challenge was simply out of time, is the single one that commentators believe may have been

[36] [1983] 1 All ER 1042 at 1055. [37] [1993] QB 534 at 545.

[37] *R* v. *Secretary of State for Employment, ex parte EOC*, [1995] 1 AC 1.

viable—and in subsequent cases e.g., the *Eurotunnel case*,[39] there has been dispute as to whether the decision itself was *per incuriam* as far as this point was concerned.

The second is that there is no trace in the speech of Lord Keith of the main argument that was advanced on behalf of the Secretary of State. We suggested that to have domestic law declared incompatible with Community law at the suit of a non-directly affected party was to collapse the boundary between the direct effect and the non-direct effect of EC measures. If an applicant was employed by a statutory state entity, we conceded that she could rely on EC law as overriding inconsistent domestic law, or in its own right. If she was otherwise employed in the private sector, she could not do so, and a Member State's failure to implement EC law was repressible only at the suit of the Commission in proceedings under Article 169. There was a third option (although we made no concession at that time in the pre-*Factortame No. 3*[40] era) by a *Francovich*[41] claim for damages for non-implementation. The House of Lords simply swept the submission under the carpet.

Oddly enough the robust stance taken by the House of Lords vis-à-vis inadequacy of the Secretary of State's evidence of justification for the discrimination may prove to have been a case of a domestic court being more European than the ECJ. The recent discrimination case of *Nolte*[42] seems to show the ECJ according a wider margin of appreciation to legislative schemes.

Either—or?

In the event that an applicant satisfies the standing requirements under Article 173 does he have an unfettered choice between starting an action in Luxembourg and starting it in England and then seeking a preliminary reference? The ECJ's decision in *TWD*[43] indicates that the practical answer to this question is no.

In *TWD* the Commission held aid which Germany had granted to a company to be incompatible with the common market and thus repayable. The German government informed the company of this, and told it that the Commission's decision could be challenged under Article 173. The company did not do so, but sought instead to raise the legality of the decision in an action in the German courts. The ECJ held that no indirect challenge was possible in this instance; to allow indirect challenge would be to allow the circumvention of the strict two month time limit within

[39] Unreported, 17 Feb. 1995.

[40] [1996] QB 404.

[41] Case C–6–9/90, [1991] ECR I–5357.

[42] Case C–317/93, [1995] ECR I–4625.

[43] Case C–188/92 *TWD Textilwerke Deggendorf GmbH* v. *Germany*, [1994] ECR I–833. See also, Case C–178/95 *Wiljo* v. *Belgium* [1997] 1 CMLR 627.

which actions must be brought under Article 173.[44] It would also be incompatible with 'requirements of legal certainty'[45]

One can see how the particular characteristics of the state aids regime may have prompted this ruling. An undertaking which the Commission decides is in unlawful receipt of aid has a clear financial incentive to delay challenging the decision for as long as possible. This is clearly undesirable and the ECJ's insistence that undertakings in such a position must be held to the two-month time limit under Article 173 seems wholly warranted.

The scope of application of *TWD* and, in particular, the issue of whether it applies wherever an applicant in fact has standing under Article 173, or is limited to circumstances where either he is the addressee of a decision or has been expressly informed of his right to proceed under Article 173, was recently addressed by the ECJ in *Accrington Beef*.[46] The Court held that in circumstances where 'it is not obvious that an action by the applicants under Article 173' would have been admissible, the applicants were entitled to bring an indirect challenge before the national court.

While the *TWD* decision may be said to promote legal certainty from the point of view of reinforcing the time limit under Article 173, it also gives rise to a paradoxical result. In effect it means that individual applicants which satisfy the strict standing test of Article 173 (and therefore certainly have very concrete interests at stake) are subject to a two month time limit. Applicants which do not satisfy the standing rules (and may sometimes have less concrete interests) are subject only to domestic law time limits which in most cases are more generous in bringing their challenge.

A litigant who is unsure whether or not it satisfies the standing test in Article 173 may, thus, be placed in a position where he feels he has to initiate both Article 177 and Article 173 actions simultaneously in order to avoid (i) the waste of time and money which would result from initiating an Article 173 application only to be excluded because of lack of standing, or (ii) the danger of the ECJ ruling an Article 177 reference inadmissible on the ground that the litigant ought to have proceeded via Article 173. This precaution was recently taken by the National Farmers' Union in its challenge to the Commission ban on the sale of British beef.

The effectiveness of Community Law

If one wishes to invoke a Community law right (as opposed to challenge a measure of Community law) the national court is the appropriate forum.

[44] Paras. 16–18.

[45] Para. 17.

[46] Case C–241/95 *R* v. *Intervention Board for Agricultural Produce ex p. Accrington Beef*, [1997] 1 CMLR 675.

There are various ways in which such a right may be made effective. There may simply be a national measure correctly implementing the relevant Community rules.

If not, all or some of the following may be employed to give effectiveness:

- direct effect;
- indirect effect;
- action for damages.

The complexity of the route to effectiveness will depend inter alia on the form of Community law on which one seeks to rely.

Most straightforward of all is where a national measure correctly implements the relevant Community rule. In such a case, of course, it should be remembered that although one is relying on a measure of national law, its Community pedigree may result in the application of principles which would have no place in a purely English law context. Of great significance in this regard is for instance the Community law principle of effective remedies which may result in a more generous remedy attaching to the right than to analogous 'pure English law' rights.[47]

Provisions of the Treaty may be relied on if they are directly effective, see *Van Gend en Loos*.[48] The conditions for direct effect initially imposed by the ECJ were that the provision in question must be clear, unconditional, containing no reservation on the part of the Member State, and not dependent on any implementing measure.

The broad approach taken by the ECJ to the direct effect of Treaty provisions is illustrated by its decision in *Defrenne*[49] which held that Article 119 was directly effective despite the imprecision of the obligation imposed by the principle that men and women should receive equal pay for equal work. Further, it held that it was directly effective in proceedings against a private party (horizontal direct effect) as opposed solely in proceedings against an emanation of the state (vertical direct effect), even though Article 119 is addressed to Member States.

Matters are also straightforward where the right is contained in a Community regulation. Article 189 of the Treaty provides that, in the case of a regulation, the measure 'shall be binding in its entirety and directly applicable in all Member States.' This language envisages that regulations will immediately become part of the domestic law of the Member States and accordingly be subject to direct reinforcement by national courts. This

[47] Case 14/83 *Von Colson and Kamann* v. *Land Nordrhein-Westfalen* [1984] ECR 181 (compensation for sex discrimination under German law).

[48] Case 26/62 *Van Gend en Loos*, [1963] ECR 1.

[49] Case 43/75 *Defrenne* v. *Societe Anonyme belge de Navigation Airenne*, [1976] ECR 455.

has been emphatically confirmed by the ECJ.[50] Indeed the ECJ has discouraged the use of national implementing measures in respect of regulations as it is concerned that, by taking steps to transpose a regulation into national law, a Member State might obscure the fact that the provision was one of Community law. This could have adverse consequences for the Community since the particular qualities of Community law such as supremacy, adequate remedies for breach, and different methods of interpretation, might be ignored.[51] The same is not true of Directives, although the BT case[52] shows the danger in trying to translate a tightly drawn directive into different language.

While all regulations are directly applicable, not all regulations are directly effective. To have direct effect regulations must be sufficiently precise and must not be too conditional.

The position of directives under the Treaty is rather different. According to Article 189 a directive 'shall be binding as to the result to be achieved, upon each Member State to which it is addressed, but shall leave to the national authorities the choice of form and methods.' The provisions of a Directive thus leave certain discretionary options open to Member States; eventual implementation need not be uniform in every Member State.

These factors did not deter the ECJ from holding that Directives may be directly effective, as a spur to timeous and correct implementation by Member States.

The key case was Marshall[53] in which it was held that:

> Wherever the provisions of a directive appear, as far as their subject matter is concerned, to be unconditional and sufficiently precise, those provisions may be relied upon by an individual against the state where that state fails to implement the directive in national law by the end of the period prescribed or it fails to implement the directive correctly.[54]

On that basis Miss Marshall was able to rely upon Article 5(1) of the Equal Treatment Directive[55] which was interpreted to mean that the dismissal of a woman solely because she has attained or passed the qualifying age for a state pension, which difference under national legislation for men and for women constituted discrimination on grounds of sex contrary to the Directive.

However these conditions have gradually been whittled away by the Court so that it may now be contended that the question of direct effect in respect of Treaty provisions and all other types of Community legislation is essentially a question of justiciability.

[50] Case 39/72 *Commission* v. *Italy*, [1973] ECR 101 (provisions for slaughtering cows).
[51] Case 50/76 *Amsterdam Bulb BV* v. *Produktschap voor Siergewassen*, [1977] ECR 137.
[52] *R* v. *HM Treasury ex p. BT*, [1996] ECR I–1631.
[53] *Marshall No. 1* 1986 1 QB 401.
[54] Para. 46.
[55] Council Directive 76/207/EEC.

In *Banks* v. *British Coal*[56] Advocate General Van Gerven spoke of

> the eminently practical nature of the 'direct effect' test: provided and in so far as a provision of Community law is *sufficiently operational* in itself to be applied by a court, it has direct effect. The clarity, precision, unconditional nature, completeness or perfection of the rule and its lack of dependence on discretionary implementing measures are in that respect merely aspects of one and the same characteristic feature which that rule must exhibit, namely it must be capable of being applied by a court to a specific case.

The European Court has held, most recently in *Faccini Dori*,[57] that Directives are not directly effective as between private parties, that they have no 'horizontal' direct effect. The reasons given for this appear to be based on a combination of two considerations. The wording of Article 189 states that Directives are addressed to and binding on Member States; however this is an unusually 'black letter' approach on the part of the ECJ and is to some extent undermined by its decision to grant horizontal direct effect to Article 119 which is addressed to Member States.

Also considerations of legal certainty seem to play a part. It is thought that private parties are not in a position to ascertain what are their obligations under unimplemented directives. Again this is somewhat unconvincing given the obligation under the TEU to publish directives in the Official Journal.

It is hard to escape the conclusion that political considerations have played a large part in the conservative posture of the European Court of Justice on this issue. In *Dori*, the most recent case in which the Court was asked to rule that Directives could have horizontal direct effect, most Member States intervened. All but Greece argued strenuously that Directives should not have direct effect as between individuals. The motives of Greece in arguing for horizontal direct effect were not entirely clear.

The resistance of the European Court to horizontal direct effect for Directives has led to the unfortunate result that where a plaintiff is in the position of having to rely on a Directive, whether or not it may do so will depend on whom it is suing.

For example, in *P.* v. *S and Cornwall County Council*[58] the ECJ held that the scope of the Equal Treatment Directive should be interpreted as extending to discrimination against transsexuals. The relevant UK legislation, the Sex Discrimination Act 1975, does not extend that far. However, pending amendment of the Sex Discrimination Act, only those transsexuals employed by the state or emanations of the state will have a

56 Case C–128/92 *Banks* v. *British Coal*, [1994] ECR I–1209 at 1237.
57 Case C–91/92 *Dori* v. *Recreb Srl*, [1994] ECR I–3325.
58 Case C–13/94 *P.* v. *S. and Cornwall County Council*, [1996] ECR I–2\43.

remedy in the event of discrimination. It is left to Strasbourg to provide a solution which Luxembourg does not provide.[59]

A mitigating feature has been the expansion by the ECJ of the concept of the state. In order to enhance the applicability of directives notwithstanding their lack of effect between private parties, the ECJ has applied a very broad meaning to 'state' so as to extend the scope of vertical direct effect.

In *Foster* v. *British Gas*[60] the ECJ held that British Gas, which was nationalized at the time relevant to the proceedings, was an emanation of the state and was therefore a body of the kind against which the provisions of the Equal Treatment Directive could be invoked. The ECJ held more generally that:

> a body, whatever its legal form, which has been made responsible, pursuant to a measure adopted by the State, for providing a public service under the control of the State and has for that purpose special powers beyond those which result from the normal rules applicable in relations between individuals, is included in any event among the bodies against which the provisions of a directive capable of having direct effect may be relied upon.[61]

The broad interpretation of the ECJ has been cut down by narrow interpretation of UK domestic courts. The extent to which grant-maintained schools, privatized industries which retain some form of special or exclusive right, NHS trusts and other entities which are in the process of being removed from the public to the private sector are emanations of the state for these purposes is unclear: the same problem arises as to whether a body is a public authority and therefore amenable to judicial review.[62] All emanations of the state must be public authorities: but not all public authorities need be emanations of the state: Here the EC and UK jurisprudence is essentially convergent. The Employment Appeal Tribunal initially held that, in the context of the applicability of the Business Transfer Directive, a voluntary aided school was not an emanation of the state. It reached this conclusion despite its finding that the school was providing a public service and was financed out of state and local education authority funds.[63] The Court of Appeal have now (sensibly) taken a different view.[64] The Court of Appeal in *Doughty* v. *Rolls Royce*[65] concluded that Rolls Royce was not an emanation of the state even though it was 100 per cent state owned.

Whether such decision was correct as a matter of European law is far from clear. The dispositif of the ECJ in *Foster* shows why it was arguably

[59] On the scope of the Sex Discrimination Act, see now *R* v. *Secretary of State for Defence ex p. Perkins* [1991] IRLR 297.

[60] Case C–188/89 *Foster* v. *British Gas plc*, [1990] I–3313.

[61] Para. 20 of the court's judgment.

[62] See Andrew Lidbetter, 'Privatised Utilities and Judicial Review' [1996] JR 249.

[63] *National Union of Teachers* v. *Governing Body of St Mary's Church of England Junior School*, [1995] ICR 317, [1997] ICR 334 (CA).

[64] [1997] EuLR 221.

[65] *Doughty* v. *Rolls Royce*, [1992] IRLR 126.

not. The definition of state bodies was exemplary (not exclusive), see the use of the word 'Includes'. Yet in the *St Mary's* case the Employment Appeal Tribunal recited that it was 'common ground that the requisite criteria for determining the issue of state body or not are 'cumulative not alternative'!

However, the Gordian knot may be cut. Advocates-General Lenz, Van Gerven and Jacobs have all taken a different and more radical view: that Directives should be directly effective against private as well as state bodies. And what the Advocates General think today, the ECJ may think tomorrow.

The ECJ in *Dori* held that direct effect forms only part of the scheme of effectiveness of Community law. Another way in which the ECJ has extended the effectiveness and application of directives is via the principle of interpretation, otherwise known as indirect effect.

Where there is a divergence between national measures and a Directive, the national measures must, as far as it is possible for the national court to do so, be interpreted and applied so as to give effect to the Directive.'[66]

It is clear as a result of the *Marleasing*[67] case that an unimplemented Directive can be relied upon to inform the interpretation of national law in a case between private individuals. This, to some extent, 'cures' the absence of horizontal direct effect.

How far a national court must go to comply with the obligation is still unclear. The ECJ in *Marleasing* stated that national courts must 'in so far as possible' read national law in conformity with a relevant Directive, but in that case itself, the Court held that the Spanish court was precluded from interpreting national law in a way which did not comply with the provisions of the directive in question.

It seems that, up until now, the House of Lords has been prepared to comply with the obligation only partially. The House of Lords has held that, where Parliament has acted to implement a Directive, it is proper for the courts to give a 'purposive' interpretation to the implementing national law in order that it accords with the provisions of the Directive. (See *Pickstone* v. *Freemans*[68] and *Litster* v. *Forth Dry Dock Ltd.*[69]) But where Parliament has not so acted, the House of Lords has refused to construe (or 'distort') British legislation so as to conform with the provisions of a directive.[70] *Duke* is a clear case where a *Marleasing* type of approach would inevitably have led to a different result. The relevant section of the Sex Discrimination Act outlaws its ambit 'provisions in relation to death or retirement'. The issue was whether or not a prescription of a retiring age

66 Case 106/89 *Von Colson* v. *Land Nordrhein-Westfalen*, [1984] ECR 1891.

67 [1990] ECR I–4135.

68 [1989] AC 66.

69 [1989] 2 CMLR 194

70 *Duke* v. *GEC Reliance Ltd [1988]* AC 618: *Finnegan* v. *Clowney Youth Training Programme* [1990] 2 AC 407.

was a provision 'in relation . . . to retirement'. Obviously a provision could not prescribe death; and on the conventional grounds of consistency of language, there was a powerful argument in favour of the proposition that discriminatory retiring ages between men and women were unlawful. It would have required little, if any, verbal manipulation. However, with characteristic moderation and understatement Lord Templeman said that he declined 'to distort the construction of the 1975 Sex Discrimination Act in order to accommodate the 1976 Equal Treatment Directive as construed by the European Court of Justice in Marshall'.

The final principle in the scheme of effectiveness is state liability in damages for breach of Community law. This principle is clearly applicable where a state has failed to implement a Directive timeously[71] and is, therefore, another means of giving Directives effectiveness. In the *BT*[72] case the ECJ to some extent assuaged the fears of Member governments. The Court answered one of the questions of the reference:

> 37. By its fourth question, the Divisional Court seeks to ascertain whether a Member State which, in transposing the Directive into national law, has itself determined which services of a contracting entity are to be excluded from its scope pursuant to Article 8, is required by Community law to compensate that undertaking for any loss suffered by it as a result of the error committed by the State.
>
> 38. It should be recalled, as a preliminary point, that the principle of State liability or loss and damage caused to individuals as a result of breaches of Community law for which the State can be held responsible is inherent in the system of the Treaty (judgments in joined cases C–6/90 and C–9/90 *Francovich and Others* [1991] ECR I–5357 [1992] IRLR 84), paragraph 35, and in joined cases C–46/93 and C–48/93 *Brasserie du Pècheur and Factortame* [1996] IRLR 267, paragraph 31). It follows that that principle holds good for any case in which a Member State breaches Community law (judgment in *Brasserie du Pècheur and Factortame,* cited above, paragraph 32).
>
> 39. In the latter judgment the Court also ruled, with regard to a breach of Community law for which a Member State, acting in a field in which it has a wide discretion in taking legislative decisions, can be held responsible, that Community law confers a right to reparation where these conditions are met: the rule of law infringed must be intended to confer rights on individuals; the breach must be sufficiently serious; and there must be a direct causal link between the breach of the obligation resting on the State and the damage sustained by the injured parties (paragraphs 50 and 51).
>
> 40. Those same conditions must be applicable to the situation, taken as its hypothesis by the national court, in which a Member State incorrectly transposes a Community Directive into national law. A restrictive approach to State liability is justified in such a situation, or the reasons already given by the Court to justify

[71] Cases C–6/90 and C–9/90 *Francovich and Bonifaci* v. *Italy,* [1991] ECR I–5357.
[72] Case C–392/93 *R* v. *Treasury, ex parte British Telecom* [1996] ELR I–1631.

the strict approach to non-contractual liability of Community instructions or Member States when exercising legislative functions in areas covered by Community law where the institution or State has a wide discretion—in particular, the concern to ensure that the exercise of legislative functions is not hindered by the prospect of actions for damages whenever the general interest requires the institutions or Member States to adopt measures which may adversely affect individual interests (see, in particular, the judgments in joined cases 83/76, 94/76, 4/77, 15/77 and 40/77 *HNL and Others* v. *Council and Commission* [1978] ECR 1209, paragraphs 5 and 6 and in *Brasserie du Pècheur and Factortame*, paragraph 45).

41. Whilst it is in principle for the national courts to verify whether or not the conditions governing State liability for a breach of Community law are fulfilled, in the present case the Court has all the necessary information to assess whether the facts amount to a sufficiently serious breach of Community law.

42. According to the case law of the Court, a breach is sufficiently serious where, in the exercise of its legislative powers, an institution or a Member State has manifestly and gravely disregarded the limits on the exercise of its powers (judgments in *HNL and Others* v. *Council and Commission*, cited above, paragraph 6, and in *Brasserie du Pêcheur and Factortame*, paragraph 55). Factors which the competent court may take into consideration include the clarity and precision of the rule breached (judgment in *Brasserie du Pècheur and Factortame*, paragraph 56).

Article 5: Involving the Commission

I have discussed so far how Community law may be invoked in a national court. However, in many cases getting Community law before that court will simply be the first, not the last step towards relying effectively on it. Once Community law is raised, evidential and procedural difficulties may present themselves. It may be that the court feels unable to determine with certainty what the correct interpretation of Community law is. In that case, a preliminary reference may be made to the ECJ under Article 177. More complicated are the difficulties which are raised. The Article 177 procedure is one means by which an English court may engage the assistance of Community institutions in areas which the Commission has its greatest enforcement powers such as competition, state aids and anti-dumping. In such cases, it may often be desirable in the context of national proceedings to invoke the co-operation of the Commission.

Involving the Commission can be seen from two viewpoints. The first is the extent of the Commission's duty to co-operate with national courts. Conversely, there is a duty on national courts to co-operate with the Commission.

The Commission *is* under a duty to co-operate with national courts. This is a consequence of Article 5 of the Treaty which provides that:

Member States shall take all appropriate measures, whether general or particular, to ensure fulfilment of the obligations arising out of the Treaty or resulting from action taken by the institutions of the Community. They shall facilitate the achievement of the Community's tasks. They shall abstain from any measure which could jeopardise the attainment of the objectives of this Treaty.

This was interpreted by the Court of Justice in *Zwartveld*[73] to impose a reciprocal duty upon the Commission to co-operate with national authorities in achieving the objectives of the Treaty of Rome. The Court stated at paragraph 17 of its judgment:

In this Community based on the rule of law, relations between Member States and the Community institutions are governed, pursuant to Article 5 of the Treaty, by a principle of sincere co-operation. This principle not only compels Member States to take all suitable measures to secure the application and effectiveness of Community law . . . but also imposes on the Community institutions mutual duties of sincere co-operation with the Member States.

It continued at paragraph 18:

'This obligation of sincere co-operation by the Community institutions is particularly important because it is owed to the judicial authorities of Member States which are responsible for securing the application of and compliance with Community law in the national legal systems.'

In *Zwartveld* the Court ordered the Commission to disclose documents about inspections which it had carried out to a Dutch magistrate investigating allegations of fraud.

The Commission may give assistance to a court going beyond the provision of relevant documents *Zwartveld*. For example in *Hasselblad* v. *Orbinson*[74] counsel for the Commission appeared as *amicus curiae* to explain the workings of the Commission's procedure in competition matters under Regulation 17/62, an intervention which the then Master of the Rolls, Sir John Donaldson, found 'most helpful'.

The Commission has now issued two Notices on the assistance available in these matters in two of the areas in which it possesses its most important powers, competition and state aid. These are:

- *Notice on Co-operation between National Courts and the Commission in Applying Articles 85 and 86 of the EEC Treaty;*[75] and
- *Notice on Co-operation between National Courts and the Commission in the State Aid Field.*[76]

Both Notices envisage that the Commission may provide a national court with a limited amount of information, falling into three categories:

73 Case C–2/88 *Zwartveld* [1990] ECR I–3365.

74 *Hasselblad* v. *Orbinson* [1985] QB 475. See also, Case T–353/94 *Postbank* v. *Commission* [1997] 4 CMLR 33.

75 OJ 1993 C39/6.

76 OJ 1995 C312/8.

- Procedural information, to enable a court to determine whether a case is pending before the Commission and if so, what stage it has reached. In the competition field the Commission has indicated that it will endeavour to give priority to cases which are the subject of national proceedings if such a case has been suspended pending a Commission decision.
- Information on a point of law, though it would seem this is properly a matter for the Court of Justice by way of Article 177.
- Factual data: statistics, market studies, and economic analyses. However, it is important to appreciate that simply because information is provided by the Commission does not make it admissible in evidence per se. While English law cannot use evidential rules in a way which makes it impossible or excessively difficult for a person to exercise their EC law rights (see, e.g. the *San Giorgio* case[77]) a party will have to demonstrate that as a matter of English law the evidence is admissible. This is not a problem unique to EC law. Objections were successfully raised to the use of material from an MMC Report in *MacCarthy plc* v. *Unichem Ltd*.[78]

The Commission stresses in both notices that, in order to maintain neutrality and objectivity, it can only provide information in response to a request from the court and not from the parties unless they are subject to a court order to provide such information.

Even when a request is made, it is understood that the Commission's response is far from immediate. A wait of six months for an answer is not unusual. Nor is there any guarantee that the Commission will actually answer the question put to them. Even so august a body as the EC Commission is not immune from frailties which affect many administrative bodies.

In summary, the Notices display good intentions by the Commission but are not in practice far-reaching. They are only a first step in creating an effective and integrated procedure between Commission and national courts.

I turn now to the attitude of the English courts in dealing with the Commission. The national court's duty to co-operate with the Commission is expressly contemplated by Article 5 of the Treaty.

In practice, as the Commission's greatest powers exist in the Competition and State Aids fields it is in cases involving disputes in these areas before national courts where the issues have arisen, particularly the former.

The problems have arisen in cases which are the subject of parallel proceedings before national courts and the Commission, for instance, where

[77] Case 199/82 *San Giorgio* [1983] ECR 3595.

[78] Scott J, 24 Nov. 1989, unreported.

national courts are policing competition policy. The risk is that the national court and the Commission could come to different conclusions as to whether an agreement violates Article 85 or an act or omission constitutes abuse of a dominant position contrary to Article 86.[78a]

The High Court sometimes takes the view that the English courts are not the proper forum for the resolution of a complex competition dispute. In *R* v. *MAFF ex p. Dairy Trades Federation*,[79] one reason for the refusal of leave to bring an application for judicial review was the fact that the economic issues relating to an allegation that the successor of the Milk Marketing Board, Milk Marque, was abusing a dominant position in its milk pricing contrary to Article 86 EC were issues which would be more suitably assessed by the Commission than in the High Court.

Where there are parallel proceedings, then the High Court may be faced with an application for a stay to enable the Commission to complete its investigation and reach a decision.[80]

In such a situation, it has been stated by Sir Godfrey Le Quesne QC sitting as a Deputy Judge of the Queen's Bench Division in the *ICS* v. *Institute of Personnel Management*[81] case that there are two cardinal principles:

1. The party invoking the powers of the Court in protection of its legal rights should not be denied access to the Court.
2. A defendant should not be required to argue its case simultaneously in two jurisdictions.

The decision in *MTV Europe* v. *BMG Records (UK) Ltd*[82] of Evans-Lombe J refusing an immediate stay of proceedings on the basis of the Commission's interim Statement of Objections was upheld by the Court of Appeal on 17 July 1995.[83] Rejecting the 'as always engaging argument' of counsel for the Appellant Sir Thomas Bingham MR stated:

> There is . . . nothing which suggests that in a case where the answer is not clear in favour of the plaintiff or the defendant, the national court *must* at once stay the proceedings pending a decision by the Commission. The Court's concern is to avoid inconsistent decisions. There is no ground for seeking to prohibit the preparation of an action for trial so long as it does not lead to a decision in advance of a decision by the Commission.

[78a] In *Iberian UK Ltd* v. *BPB Industries and British Gypsum Ltd* [1997] EuLR 1, Laddie J. avoided such a risk by concluding that it would be an abuse of process to allow the defendant to relitigate in the English Court a Commission decision that had gone against it.

[79] *R* v. *MAFF ex p Dairy Trades Federation*, Dyson J, 20 Oct., unreported.

[80] See also Case C–234/89 *Delimitis & Henniger Bräu AG* [1991] ECR I–935, where the relevant principles are set out.

[81] *ICS* v. *Institute of Personnel Management* 1993, unreported, cited by Evans-Lombe J, in *MTV Europe* v. *BMG Records (UK) Ltd* [1995] 1 CMLR 437.

[82] [1995] 1 CMLR 437, see also *Delimitis*.

[83] [1997] EuLR 100.

If an EC case is unsuccessfully brought in the English courts, a complaint to the Commission may then be an appropriate course of action. The Commission may investigate and if necessary bring proceedings against the Member State for infringement of the Treaty. However, the Commission cannot be compelled to act and so there is no guarantee that action by the Commission will be an adequate remedy for failure by national courts to enforce EC law rights.

In the competition field, the Commission's powers under Regulation 17 enable it to investigate a particular complaint directly against an alleged infringer. The Commission's resources do not enable it to investigate every complaint. However, it is under a duty to consider every complaint (*Demo-Studio Schmidt*[84]) in order that it may assess whether it would be appropriate to open an investigation. In making that assessment, it has stated in its Notice on Co-operation that it will reserve investigations for those cases which have 'particular political, economic or legal significance for the Community.'[85]

In *Bureau des Unions des Consommateurs and National Consumer Council* v. *Commission*,[86] a decision not to investigate a complaint on the basis of lack of Community interest was successfully challenged. The challenge was based, inter alia, on the ground that the Commission had not properly exercised its discretion not to investigate by failing to consider sufficiently carefully the legal and factual issues before it.[87]

The *Automec II*[88] judgment of the Court of First Instance deals only with the limits of the Commission's obligations. In that case, the dispute was essentially contractual and already in the national court and so there seemed no reason why the national court should not consider the competition aspects.

It is therefore important to address the issue of Community interest when making a competition complaint. There are three factors that might weigh with the Commission, beyond any particular political, economic or legal considerations special to the case: (i) the reluctance of a national court to uphold a litigant's EC law rights; (ii) the difficulty in obtaining evidence to prove an infringement under national evidentiary rules; (iii) finally, the difficulty in enforcing a judgment obtained in the court of one Member State throughout the Community.

[84] Case 210/81 *Demi-Studio Schmidt* [1984] 1 CMLR 63.

[85] Para. 14.

[86] T–37–92 *Bureau des Unions des Consommateurs and National Consumer Council* v. *Commission* [1994] ECR II–285.

[87] See para. 45 of the CFI's judgment.

[88] Case T–24/90 *Automec II* [1992] 5 CMLR 431.

Conclusions

The Community legal system remains a curious hybrid. Contrary to what many Eurosceptics assert it is not a federal system with a clearly defined allocation of jurisdictions between federal and state courts.

Rather, the Community legal system rests on the ability and willingness of national courts to handle issues of EC law, if necessary in co-operation with the Court of Justice through the Article 177 reference procedure. The Court of Justice's influence thus pervades the Community's legal order but it is to a large extent dependent upon national courts instigating the procedure.

The European Courts have reserved for themselves two main functions: that of a constitutional court and that of a court of special jurisdiction.

The European Courts' role as a constitutional court is to be found in their exclusive right to declare Community legislation invalid.

The Courts' special jurisdiction exists in their monopoly over challenge by individual litigants to decisions addressed directly an individually to them.

The European Commission's function is also changing. Previously the guardian of individuals' rights where it had power to intervene, it is now concerned only to deal with major issues of policy in the competition sphere, while continuing to attempt to administer the state aids and anti-dumping regimes.

These developments in the European Courts and the Commission have in general placed considerably more responsibility on national courts to address issues of EC law. An individual litigant with EC law rights is increasingly likely to find that the path to vindication of those rights starts in England rather than Brussels or Luxembourg—especially if some Eurosceptic government promoted curtailment of the ECJ's powers! But that is 'une autre histoire'.

3

Indirect Effect of Directives in the Application of National Legislation

BY PROFESSOR P. P. CRAIG, WORCESTER COLLEGE, OXFORD

The primary object of this chapter is to examine the way in which UK courts deal with the doctrine of indirect effect when applying national legislation in cases which have a Community law component. The analysis will be divided into three parts. In the first part there will be a brief critical overview of the arguments which have been advanced as to why Directives should not have horizontal direct effect. This will be followed in the second section by an examination of the way in which the UK courts have interpreted the concept of indirect effect. The leading cases will be analysed, but attention will also be given to the decisions of lower courts, in order that a more rounded picture can be attained. The final section will draw some more general conclusions from this jurisprudence and place them in a broader perspective.

1. Horizontal Direct Effect of Directives: the Arguments

According to Article 189 of the EC Treaty, 'A directive shall be binding, as to the result to be achieved, upon each Member State to which it is addressed, but shall leave to the national authorities the choice of form and methods.'

The application of direct effect to directives has, as is well known, proven to be more controversial than in the context of regulations. This is in part because directives clearly do require further action on the part of the Member States, and because they leave the States with some measure of discretionary choice as to methods of implementation.[1] The reluctance to admit that directives can have direct effect is also in part because while Article 189 states that regulations are directly applicable, this phraseology is not used in relation to directives. The ECJ has nonetheless held that directives are capable of having direct effect and it has used three arguments to justify this conclusion.

[1] For general discussion of direct effect, see Craig and de Burca, *EC Law, Text, Cases and Materials* (1995), Chs. 4 and 5.

There is an argument from *general principle*, the essence of which is that it would be inconsistent with the binding effect of directives to exclude the possibility that they can confer rights. The mere fact that regulations are deemed to be directly applicable, and hence capable of conferring rights, should not, said the ECJ, be taken to mean that other Community norms can never have the same effect.[2] A further argument is derived from Article 177. This Article allows questions concerning the interpretation and validity of Community law to be referred by national courts to the ECJ. From the generality of this provision the Court has concluded that questions relating to directives can be raised by individuals before national courts.[3] The final reason for according direct effect to directives, in some instances at least, is the estoppel argument. Given that the peremptory force of directives would be weakened if individuals could not rely on them before national courts, a Member State which has not implemented the directive 'may not rely, as against individuals, on its own failure to perform the obligations which the directive entails'.[4] Provided, therefore, that the directive is sufficiently precise, that the basic obligation is unconditional and that the period for implementation has passed, an individual can derive enforceable rights from a directive.[5]

While the ECJ has been willing to give direct effect to directives it has, however, also held that they only have vertical as opposed to horizontal direct effect. Treaty articles and regulations give individuals rights which can be used both against the state, vertical direct effect, and against private parties, horizontal direct effect. Directives only have vertical direct effect. The authority for this limitation of direct effect was the *Marshall* case,[6] and the ECJ has more recently reaffirmed its holding on this issue in the *Dori* decision.[7] The doctrine of indirect effect was developed by the ECJ against the backdrop of this denial of horizontal direct effect of directives. However before examining the way in which indirect effect has been applied by the UK courts, it may be helpful to analyse briefly the arguments which have been proffered to justify the ECJ's rulings in *Marshall* and *Dori*.

(a) The Textual Argument

It is appropriate to begin with the reason actually given by the ECJ in *Marshall*. The Court provides a textual Treaty justification for its decision:[8]

2 Case 41/74, *Van Duyn* v. *Home Office* [1974] ECR 1337, para. 12.

3 *Loc. cit.*

4 Case 148/78, *Pubblico Ministero* v. *Ratti* [1979] ECR 1629, para. 22.

5 See, e.g., Case 41/74, *Van Duyn* v. *Home Office* [1974] ECR 1337.

6 Case 152/84, *Marshall* v. *Southampton & South West Hampshire Area Health Authority (Teaching)* [1986] ECR 723.

7 Case C–91/92, *Dori* v. *Recreb* [1994] ECR I–3325. See also, Case C–192/94, *El Corte Ingles SA* v. *Rivero* [1996] 2 CMLR 507.

8 Case 152/84, *Marshall* [1986] ECR 723, para. 48.

Article 189 states that the binding nature of a directive exists only in relation to 'each Member State to which it is addressed', and for the Court it therefore followed that directives were not capable of imposing obligations on individuals. It is, however, questionable to say the very least whether this is a convincing justification for the ECJ's decision.

One line of attack has been to say that this formalist mode of Treaty interpretation does not sit comfortably with the more purposive approach used by the Court in other areas.

This may well be so, but the reasoning used by the Court is challengeable in its own terms. Thus even if we assume a formalist or literalist mode of reading the Treaty the ECJ's reasoning is open to question. The ECJ interpreted the phrase 'Member State to which it is addressed' in Article 189 as meaning that obligations contained in a directive could only be imposed upon a state and not upon an individual. This is a non-sequitur.

Why is this phrase present within Article 189 at all? The answer surely is that it simply captures two essential features of directives: directives do not have to apply to all states, and may therefore be addressed to certain particular states; and it is the state which has the correlative duty to take the requisite measures to achieve the ends stipulated therein. When looked at in this way the wording of Article 189 tells us nothing more than that a State will only be bound if the directive is addressed to it, and then it will have the obligation to take the implementing measures. France, for example, will only be bound by a directive if it is mentioned therein, and if it is so mentioned the French government will then have the obligation to pass the measures needed to attain the ends stipulated. The preceding point may be summarized quite simply as follows: on a natural, literalist interpretation of Article 189 the phrase 'Member State to which it is addressed' speaks to the distinction between states, and not to any distinction between a state and the individuals therein.

The Article provides no indication as to whether obligations could be imposed on individuals through a directive. Now there may be other reasons why such obligations should not be imposed on private parties, but the wording of Article 189 is clearly not determinative of the issue. It is therefore unsurprising that the ECJ should have rejected an analogous argument in the context of Article 119 of the Treaty, holding that although this Article was framed in terms of an obligation on Member States to secure equal pay etc., this did not prevent the imposition of duties on private parties.[9]

[9] Case 43/75, *Defrenne* v. *Sabena* [1976] ECR 455, para. 39.

(b) Publication and the Rule of Law Argument

Another reason which has been proffered as to why directives should not have horizontal direct effect is a classic rule of law argument. Prior to the TEU directives did not have to be published, and therefore it would be wrong in principle for private parties to have obligations imposed on them based upon unpublished norms. There is undoubtedly force in this argument. It would be contrary to the rule of law if individuals could be bound by norms which were not published, and therefore not formally accessible to them. The maxim that ignorance of the law is no excuse is premised on the assumption that the relevant legal norm is at least formally accessible, in the sense of being published. This rule of law argument is, however, not conclusive for two reasons.

On the one hand, even prior to the TEU, it could be met quite simply by stipulating that a condition precedent to the horizontal direct effect of any directive should be that the directive in question was actually published. Many directives were in fact published notwithstanding the absence of any formal legal obligation. The Commission had an interest in doing so, even if there was no formal legal duty, quite simply because it wished to see directives complied with, and such compliance was predicated upon people having the opportunity to become aware of the rules contained within these directives. Thus, even prior to the changes brought about by the TEU, it would, in doctrinal terms, have been simple to stipulate that where it was sought to impose an obligation on a private party flowing from a directive, then, in addition to the normal conditions for direct effect, the directive must in fact have been published.

On the other hand, the force of the publication argument has been undermined by Article 191 of the TEU which does now provide an obligation to publish directives passed pursuant to Article 189b, and also directives which are addressed to all Member States. Most directives of real importance will have to be published for one or both of these reasons. For those directives which do not come within the ambit of Article 191, the argument advanced in the previous paragraph could be used: the fact of publication would be a condition precedent for horizontal direct effect.

(c) The Argument Based upon the Distinction between Regulations and Directives

It has also been contended that to accord horizontal direct effect to directives would render the distinction between regulations and directives meaningless. This was certainly a factor which influenced Advocate General Slynn in the *Marshall* case, who expressly mentioned it in his opinion as a reason for not according horizontal direct effect to directives.[10] It

[10] Case 152/84, *Marshall* [1986] ECR 723, 734.

has also featured strongly in the arguments of Member States who are opposed to the very idea of directives imposing obligations on private parties. This argument could be taken in one of two ways, neither of which is convincing.

It could be argued that by according directives horizontal direct effect this in some way would serve to eliminate the textual Treaty distinction between directives and regulations. The essential distinctions between regulations and directives are that the latter do not have to be addressed to all Member States, and that they leave the addressee the choice of form and method when it comes to implementation. Yet to accord horizontal direct effect to directives has no effect on these distinguishing features whatsoever.

The argument under scrutiny could alternatively have the following meaning. Regulations are said by Article 189 to be directly applicable, and hence operative within national legal systems without the need for any further action by a Member State. No such textual Treaty provision exists in the context of directives. To accept that directives could impose duties on private parties would mean that if a state has not implemented a directive within the requisite time, then a private party could still be subject to the obligations contained therein, provided that the duties were sufficiently clear. In this sense directives would be operative within national legal systems against private parties, without the need for, or interposition of, any action by the Member State. This appears to be what the ECJ had in mind in the *Dori* case. Part of the Court's rationale for rejecting horizontal direct effect was that to do otherwise would be 'to recognise a power in the Community to enact obligations for individuals with immediate effect, whereas it has competence to do so only where it is empowered to adopt regulations.'[11]

There is no doubt an element of truth in this second argument, but it does not, nonetheless, provide a convincing reason against horizontal direct effect.

This is in part because the argument as put would apply equally against vertical direct effect, and yet this has been an accepted part of Community jurisprudence for many years. The doctrinal recognition of vertical direct effect does of course mean that in actions brought against the state the Community is in reality enacting an obligation which takes effect on the expiry of the period for implementation. The justification proffered by the ECJ for this where the state is the defendant, as opposed to a private individual, is the estoppel argument considered earlier.[12] Yet the force of this distinction is considerably weakened once it is acknowledged that the

[11] Above n. 7, para. 24. This same reasoning is repeated in *Rivero*, above n. 7, para. 17.
[12] Case C–91/92, *Dori*, above n. 7, para. 23.

state for these purposes can encompass a whole range of entities which have no power or responsibility for implementing directives.[13]

The other reason why the argument is unconvincing can be explained as follows. It is important in this context not to lose sight of the sequence of events. If horizontal direct effect did exist it would only be needed where the state had failed to implement the directive properly within the required period.[14] In other words, Community law would not be seeking to deprive a Member State of the discretion as to implementation expressly accorded to it by Article 189. The EC clearly wants Member States to enact the necessary measures to render the directive an operative reality throughout the Community. Direct effect of directives, both vertical and, if it were to exist, horizontal, merely provides a fall back, in the sense of stipulating that in the absence of the proper measures at state level, reliance should be able to be placed on the directive itself, even though national measures have not been passed or are insufficient. Even then this would only be possible if the particular obligations were sufficiently precise to meet the general requirements for direct effect.

(d) The Legal Certainty Argument

The final argument which has been advanced against giving horizontal direct effect to directives is that to give such effect to directives would infringe legal certainty. Once again it is important to distinguish different versions of this argument.

The thesis could be that horizontal direct effect would infringe principles of legal certainty since it would subject private individuals to obligations the content of which were vague or uncertain. This version of the argument is easily met. If, as a matter of principle, directives could impose obligations upon private parties, it would still be necessary to prove that a particular obligation was sufficiently certain to give rise to direct effect in accordance with the normal rules for the operation of that doctrine. If the nature of any such duty was too uncertain or vague it would not qualify for direct effect under established Community law jurisprudence.

There is another version of the legal certainty argument which is markedly different. The essence of this thesis is as follows. Private individuals should not be placed in unreasonable doubt concerning the nature of their obligations. Given that directives require national implementing legislation this uncertainty might occur if individuals were required to scrutinize differing texts both at national and Community level in order to find out what the law was.[15] There are two major problems with this reasoning.

[13] Craig and de Burca, above n. 1, pp. 184–9.

[14] If the directive had been properly executed then an action could of course be maintained against a private individual based upon the implementing legislation.

[15] Wyatt and Dashwood, *European Community Law* (3rd ed., 1993), p. 75.

On the one hand, it is not immediately obvious why the objection based upon legal certainty is thought to be relevant in the context of directives when no such objection is raised in the context of the primary Treaty provisions themselves. Many of these articles, such as Article 30, have been used expansively by the ECJ to cover a great variety of situations. These articles have horizontal direct effect and no-one has raised the objection of legal certainty, even though there are often conflicting national norms on precisely the same issue, and even though it may not be easy for an individual to know in advance whether there will in fact be any clash between the requirements of Community law and national law. This is especially so given that the meaning of general Treaty provisions such as Article 30 will often only become clearer in the light of the ECJ's own unfolding jurisprudence.

On the other hand, the argument based upon legal certainty lacks plausibility quite simply because of the doctrine of supremacy. Let us imagine that there is a private party who is faced with inconsistent Community and national obligations, the former being based upon a directive. If directives did have horizontal direct effect the problem of legal certainty set out above is readily resolved. Once it is clear that there is an inconsistency between the two sets of norms the private individual is not faced with any dilemma as to which obligation to adhere to, for the doctrine of supremacy dictates that the Community norm should take precedence. What is particularly paradoxical about this argument is that, as we shall see below, it is the doctrine of indirect effect which really does generate problems of legal certainty.

2. Indirect Effect in UK Courts

(a) Indirect Effect: the Basic Doctrine

One important way in which the force of the *Marshall* limitation has been blunted has been through the development of the doctrine which has become known as indirect effect.

The concept is associated with the important decision in *Von Colson*.[16] The applicants relied upon the provisions of a directive in order to argue that the quantum of relief provided by German law in cases of discrimination was too small. The ECJ held that these provisions were not sufficiently precise to have direct effect. It went on, however, to hold that national courts had an obligation to interpret national law so as to be in conformity with the directive. The purpose of the directive was to provide an effective remedy in cases of discrimination, and if states chose to fulfil this aim through the provision of compensation then this should be

[16] Case 14/83, *Von Colson and Kamann* v. *Land Nordrhein-Westfalen* [1984] ECR 1891.

adequate in relation to the damage which had been suffered. National courts should, therefore, construe their own national law with this in mind.

This principle of construction was applied and extended in *Marleasing*.[17] The case was concerned with Council Directive 68/151 which contained rules on safeguards for the establishment of companies within the Community. The plaintiff claimed that one of the defendant companies had been established 'without cause' and that the purpose behind its establishment was to perpetrate a fraud. The plaintiff sought a declaration that the contract establishing this defendant corporation should be held to be void, and sought to found this claim on a provision of Spanish law. The defendant resisted the claim on the ground that Article 11 of Directive 68/151, which lists the grounds on which the nullity of a company may be ordered, did not include lack of cause among these grounds. The Directive had not yet been implemented in Spain, but the Spanish court nonetheless asked the ECJ whether Article 11 could be said to be directly applicable, so as to preclude a declaration of nullity of a public company on a ground other than one set out in that article.

The action was between private corporations, and the ECJ reiterated its holding that a directive could not, in itself, impose obligations on individuals, citing the *Marshall* case as authority.[18]

However, the ECJ qualified this by drawing on its ruling in *Von Colson*. The Court used the judgment in that case as the foundation for the argument that the authorities of the Member States have an obligation to effectuate the ends stipulated in a directive, and that this obligation is binding on all authorities in the state, including the courts. It followed that in applying national law, whether passed before or after the directive, a national court was required to interpret national law as far as possible so as to be in conformity with the directive. From this it followed that the Spanish court should interpret their national law so as not to order the nullity of a company on a ground not listed in Article 11 of the Directive.

While the ruling of the ECJ preserves its previous position, that there is no horizontal direct effect for directives, its findings on the interpretative duties of the national courts go a considerable way to according directives a measure of 'indirect' direct effect. Thus, although an individual cannot, in a literal sense, derive rights from a directive in an action against another individual, it is possible to plead the directive in such an action, in the manner exemplified by the defendant in the present case. Once the directive has been placed before the national court in this way, then the interpretative obligation derived from *Von Colson*, and built upon in

[17] Case C–106/89, *Marleasing SA* v. *La Commercial International De Alimentation SA* [1990] ECR 4135; [1992] CMLR 305.

[18] *Ibid.*, para. 6.

Marleasing, comes into operation. It has, moreover, been held that this interpretative obligation operates even before the time period for the implementation of the directive has expired.[19] Where the directive does encapsulate precise obligations, and where the national court is so minded to interpret national law in the required fashion, this 'indirect' species of enforcement of a directive as between individuals will have the same results as if the directive had been accorded horizontal direct effect.

Recent developments in the UK jurisprudence cast light on three important issues: the range of bodies which will be deemed to be state authorities and thus susceptible to vertical direct effect; the extent to which our courts are willing to interpret UK national law so as to be in conformity with a directive; and the relationship between direct and indirect effect. These issues will be considered in turn.

(b) Directives, Vertical Direct Effect and the Scope of the State

Indirect effect, and the attendant problems concerning the scope of the interpretative obligation, will only arise if the person against whom the directive is being enforced is a private party. This is because directives are capable of having direct effect against the state or an emanation of the state. This necessarily involves difficult questions as to what constitutes a state authority.[20] The closest which the ECJ has come to producing a general test was in the *Foster* case[21] where it held that: a body whatever its legal form which has been made responsible, pursuant to a measure adopted by the state, for the provision of a public service under the control of the state and has for that purpose special powers beyond those which result from the normal rules applicable to relations between individuals, is included among those bodies against which the provisions of a directive may be relied on.

The ECJ will decide on a case-by-case basis which bodies will be an emanation of the state using this criterion.[22] However, the task will also fall to national courts which can choose to decide the matter for themselves using the test laid down by the ECJ and existing case law as a guide.

In the *Foster* case itself British Gas was, at the date relevant to the proceedings, a nationalized industry, and the decision of the ECJ was given on this basis. The High Court has now held in *Griffin* v. *South West Water Services Ltd.*[23] that a privatized utility can also count as part of the state for the purposes of the *Foster* test. The issue at stake in *Griffin* was whether

[19] Case 80/86, *Officier van Justitie* v. *Kolpinghuis Nijmegen* [1987] ECR 3969.

[20] Curtin, 'The Province of Government: Delimiting the Direct Effect of Directives in the Common Law Context' (1990) 15 EL Rev. 195.

[21] Case C–188/89, *Foster* v. *British Gas plc* [1990] ECR I–3313, para. 20.

[22] For discussion, see Craig and de Burca, above n. 1, pp. 184–9.

[23] (1995) IRLR 15.

South West Water (SWW), a privatized utility, should have to consult with Unison concerning certain collective redundancies, in accord with Directive 75/129. SWW had not recognized Unison. The company did not deny that its plans led to such redundancies, but it did deny that it was a body against which the Directive could be enforced.

Blackburne J disagreed. He found that SWW was a state authority for the purposes of the *Foster* test. It was common ground in the case that SWW did fulfil the 'special powers condition' and the 'public service condition' contained in the *Foster* test. The argument therefore turned upon whether the 'control condition' was met here. Blackburne J held that it was, and reasoned as follows. In determining whether a body provided a public service 'under the control of the State', the question was not whether that body was under the control of the state, but whether the public service was under state control. It was irrelevant in this respect that SWW was a commercial concern, that it did not carry out any of the traditional state functions, and that it was not an agent of the state. The legal form of the body was held to be equally irrelevant, as was the fact that the state did not exercise day-to-day control over the activities of the body. On the facts of the instant case, the statutory provisions and the conditions of SWW's licence indicated that it performed its public service as a water undertaking under the control of the state. It was not necessary to show that the state was able to exercise influence over the body with regard to the subject matter of the relevant provision of the particular Directive.

The ruling in *Griffin* is of real significance, given the number of privatized undertakings which now exist. It will now be possible to plead the obligations contained in directives directly against such companies. Vertical direct effect will apply, and plaintiffs will not have to rely upon the application of the interpretative obligation which constitutes indirect effect. In the event of a clash between a provision of a directive and national law, vertical direct effect, combined with supremacy, will serve to ensure that the directive will be applied.

(c) Indirect Effect in UK Courts: the Scope of the Interpretative Obligation

In those cases where the defendant is not an emanation of the state, or where even though it is, the obligation is not sufficiently clear to give rise to direct effect, the plaintiff will have to rely upon the doctrine of indirect effect.

It will be argued within this section that three different strands in the UK case law concerning the doctrine of indirect effect can be distinguished.

First, where the UK legislation has been passed expressly to implement an obligation contained in a Community directive, then our courts will depart from their normal canons of construction and adopt a more purposive style of interpretation which is designed to effectuate the ends laid down in the directive. *Litster* is perhaps the best known example of this.[24]

Secondly, where the relevant national legislation has not been passed to give effect to duties arising under a directive, and where the wording of the national legislation could not be reasonably read to conform to the directive, then, at least as regards actions between private individuals, the national legislation will continue to be applied. Thus in *Duke*[25] the crucial factor was in part that the relevant national statutes had not been passed to give effect to Community norms. The decision was equally influenced by the fact that these statutes contained express provisions which were held to allow differential treatment in relation to retirement to continue.

The third type of case has the following characteristics: the national legislation has not been enacted with the specific intent of giving effect to a Community directive, but the wording of that legislation is capable of being read so as to conform to the meaning of the directive, even though the meaning so given to the legislation is not that which the UK courts would have given to such legislation as a matter of first impression.

The *Webb* case[26] falls into this third category. In this case the applicant was employed by the defendant employer to replace another employee who had become pregnant and who had been given maternity leave for three months. The employer required W to start work immediately and to undergo six months training before the employee which she was replacing left to have her child in February 1988. Two weeks after starting work W discovered that she too was pregnant. She informed the employer of this fact and was dismissed. W claimed that this dismissal was in breach of the Sex Discrimination Act 1975, section 1(1)(a), the argument being that she had been dismissed on grounds of her sex because she was pregnant.

The House of Lords rejected this argument. It held that although dismissal of a woman because she was pregnant would be unlawful direct discrimination under the 1975 Act, in this particular case there had been no such discrimination because it was W's non-availability during the relevant period which was the really critical factor. A man who would have been unavailable during the relevant period would also have been dismissed and hence there was no discrimination on the grounds of sex. Their Lordships also rejected the claim based on indirect discrimination. They accepted that the possibility of pregnancy meant that more women than men were likely to be unable to satisfy the condition for employment in the instant case, and accepted also that W had suffered detriment because she was unable to comply with the condition. However, it was held that

[24] *Pickstone* v. *Freemans* [1989] 1 AC 66; *Litster* v. *Forth Dry Dock* [1990] 1 AC 546.

[25] *Duke* v. *GEC Reliance* [1988] 1 AC 618; *Finnegan* v. *Clowney Youth Training Programme Ltd.* [1990] 2 AC 407.

[26] *Webb* v. *EMO Air Cargo (UK) Ltd.* [1993] 1 WLR 49.

the needs of the employer to have someone who could cover for the absent employee during her maternity leave outweighed the discriminatory effect of the condition which the employer had imposed.

Lord Keith, who gave their Lordships' judgment, recognized that EC law could, however, be of relevance. The key question was whether the action by the employer might be in breach of Directive 76/207, Article 2(1) which prohibits direct or indirect discrimination on grounds of sex. There was no case absolutely on all fours with the facts of the present case and the ECJ's existing case law at that time showed the difficulty of drawing the appropriate lines as to what did or did not constitute discrimination.[27] Lord Keith acknowledged that the Directive did not have direct effect here because the defendant was not a state emanation, but accepted that it was for the UK courts to 'construe domestic legislation in any field covered by a Community directive so as to accord with the interpretation of the directive as laid down by the European Court, if that can be done without distorting the meaning of domestic legislation'.[28] In formulating the test in this manner Lord Keith drew expressly on the criterion laid down by Lord Templeman in the *Duke* case.[29] Lord Keith made it clear that this interpretative obligation applied irrespective of whether the directive preceded or came after the domestic legislation. His Lordship noted that the obligation was, nonetheless, only interpretative. It only obliged the national court to construe the national legislation in the light of the directive if it was possible to do so. What this meant was that 'the domestic law must be open to an interpretation consistent with the directive whether or not it is also open to an interpretation inconsistent with it'.[30] The House of Lords therefore made a reference to the ECJ to determine whether the facts of the present case would be held to constitute discrimination for the purposes of Directive 76/207. Their Lordships left open the question as to whether they would be able to construe the national legislation to be in conformity with the Directive, should the ECJ decide that the facts of the present case came within it.

The ECJ found for the applicant, holding that Article 2(1) prohibited the dismissal of a person in the circumstances of this case.[31] Termination of a contract on the grounds of pregnancy was in breach of the Directive, and this was so irrespective of the fact that the applicant had herself been employed to replace another employee who was on maternity leave.

We are not concerned with the rights or wrongs of this ruling by the ECJ. It is, rather, the response of the House of Lords when the case was

[27] Case C–177/88, *Dekker* v. *Stichting Vormingscentrum voor Jong Volwassen (VJV-Centrum) Plus* [1990] ECR I–3941; Case C–179/88, *Handels- og Kontorfunktionaerernes Forbund i Danmark* v. *Dansk Arbejdsgiverforening* [1990] ECR I–3979.

[28] [1993] 1 WLR 49, 59.

[29] [1988] AC 618, 639–40.

[30] [1993] 1 WLR 49, 60.

[31] Case C–32/93, *Webb* v. *EMO Air Cargo (UK) Ltd* [1994] ECR I–3567; [1994] 3 WLR 941.

returned to it that is of interest to us here, and the light which this sheds on the approach of the UK courts more generally to the interpretative obligation flowing from the doctrine of indirect effect.

In *Webb (No 2)*[32] the House of Lords did feel able to construe the UK legislation so as to be in conformity with the decision of the ECJ. Lord Keith, who once again gave the unanimous judgment for the House of Lords, reasoned as follows. Section 1(1)(a) of the 1975 Act provided that a person discriminated against a woman in any circumstances relevant for the purposes of any provision of the Act if, inter alia, that person treated her less favourably than a man was or would be treated. It will be remembered that in the earlier proceedings a crucial part of the court's reasoning had been that Ms Webb was not being treated less favourably than a man, because if a man had been unavailable for work during the relevant period then he too could have been dismissed. From this it followed that the reason for unavailability for work was not a relevant circumstance within the meaning of the UK legislation and therefore there was no discrimination on grounds of gender. The question was, said Lord Keith, how to fit the ruling of the ECJ into the terms of the test found in the 1975 Act?[33]

> It seems to me that the only way of doing so is to hold that, in a case where a woman is engaged for an indefinite period, the fact that the reason why she will be temporarily unavailable for work at a time when to her knowledge her services will be particularly required *is* pregnancy is a circumstance relevant to her case, being a circumstance which could not be present in the case of a hypothetical man.

The *Webb* case sheds important light on the way in which the UK courts construe their interpretative obligations. It is indicative of a willingness within this third category of case to interpret national law to be in conformity with Community law. The reasoning process employed by Lord Keith is instructive in this respect. His Lordship was willing to read the 1975 Act in the manner required by the Community Directive and the approach was to determine whether the wording contained in the UK statute could be read so as to accommodate this result. On the facts of the case this proved to be possible, notwithstanding the fact that this interpretation was contrary to that which the House of Lords had originally reached. Viewed in this way *Webb (No 2)* represented the application of the criterion which Lord Keith had himself laid down in the earlier *Webb* case: the domestic law must be open to an interpretation consistent with the directive whether or not it was also open to an interpretation inconsistent with it.

What the case still leaves open is how far the UK courts will be willing to employ this technique in this third category of case in the absence of

32 *Webb* v. *EMO Air Cargo (UK) Ltd (No 2)* [1995] 4 All ER 577; [1996] 2 CMLR 990.

33 [1995] 4 All ER 577, 582. Emphasis added.

specific words within the UK legislation which can be 'locked onto' in order to provide the interpretation which is consonant with that demanded by Community law. The actual reasoning employed by Lord Keith is formalist, in the sense of seeking to find appropriate wording within the UK legislation which will justify an interpretation which is in accord with Community law. What is open to question is how far our courts would be willing to use the more purposive techniques of construction which we have seen employed in the first category, that exemplified by the *Litster* decision, in cases which fall into the third category. This remains to be seen in the light of subsequent case law on this topic.

(d) Indirect Effect in UK Courts: the Relationship between Direct and Indirect Effect

The discussion thus far has focused on the way in which the UK courts have dealt with the interpretative obligation imposed on them by the doctrine of indirect effect. The recent jurisprudence of our courts also reveals a somewhat more worrying trend, which concerns possible confusion over direct and indirect effect. It is this aspect of the topic which will be considered within this section.

The relevant cases are not well known and they have arisen in the tax field. The decision in *Imperial Chemical Industries plc* v. *Colmer (Inspector of Taxes)*[34] may be taken by way of example, and the decision is all the more important in that it was given by the House of Lords. The facts were complex, but the essence of the dispute was as follows. ICI and another company, W, both of which were incorporated in the United Kingdom, formed a consortium, in which ICI participated as to 49 per cent and W as to 51 per cent. The consortium owned all the share capital in CAHH, a holding company, also incorporated in the United Kingdom, and CAHH in turn held 100 per cent of the shares in all but one of its 23 subsidiary trading companies. Four of these subsidiaries were resident in the United Kingdom, six were resident in other Member States of the Community, and the remaining thirteen were resident outside the Community. One of the four UK subsidiaries was CAH and it sought to surrender to ICI certain trading losses, thereby allowing ICI to claim group relief by reference to its 49 per cent holding in the consortium, pursuant to section 258(2) of the Income and Corporation Taxes Act 1970. The Inspector of Taxes refused this claim on the ground that CAHH was not a holding company within the definition provided by section 258(5)(b) of the legislation, because its business did not consist wholly or mainly in the holding of shares of trading companies resident in the United Kingdom. He took this view because only four of the of the 23 subsidiaries of CAHH were resident in the

[34] [1996] STC 352. See also, e.g., *Customs and Excise Commissioners* v. *Wellington Private Hospital* [1995] STC 628.

United Kingdom. This decision was reversed by Millett J and his decision was upheld by the Court of Appeal. The basis of these decisions was that the tax authorities had misconstrued the UK legislation. When the case came to the House of Lords ICI sought to support the decision of the Court of Appeal on the ground that not only was it a correct interpretation of the UK legislation, but also on the ground that the position being argued for by the tax authorities would be in conflict with Articles 52 and 58 of the EC Treaty which enshrine the right of freedom of establishment for companies.

Lord Nolan gave judgment for the House of Lords. He found the issue of construction of the UK legislation a difficult one, but on balance came down in favour of the Crown: construing the provisions of the 1970 Act alone concerning consortium relief, the business of a holding company did have to consist mainly in the holding of shares in UK resident trading subsidiaries in order to qualify for such relief. This construction of the UK legislation made it necessary for his Lordship to advert to ICI's arguments based on Community law. Lord Nolan felt that an Article 177 reference was necessary to resolve this issue. Whether ICI's arguments based on Community law are in fact correct is not our immediate concern, and in any event an answer will be forthcoming from the ECJ in due course.

What is of interest is the way in which Lord Nolan chose to express himself on the general relevance of the Community law argument. He stated that 'there can be no doubt of our obligation to construe the 1970 Act in a manner which avoids conflict with Community law, if such a construction is possible,'[35] and this formulation is repeated in the headnote to the case.[36] Now this may seem to be uncontroversial and to be in line with the general case law considered in the previous section. Further reflection on the facts of the case, and on the nature of the parties, reveals the possibility of confusion between direct and indirect effect.

The case concerned a conflict between a company and the tax authorities where the relevant point of Community law concerned not a directive, but a Treaty article. Either of these factors taken by themselves would, subject to a qualification to be made below, raise the possibility of direct effect of Community law, not indirect effect. The fact that the action was brought against the tax authorities brings it unequivocally within the category of actions against the state, i.e. a vertical case. The fact that the norm of Community law which was invoked was a Treaty article is of relevance since such articles, as opposed to directives, can, in any event, have horizontal direct effect.

The reason why this is of such potential importance is as follows. In cases where the Community norm does have direct effect the language of

[35] *Ibid.*, p. 363. [36] *Ibid.*, p. 353.

construction employed by Lord Nolan does not capture the true extent of the obligation flowing from Community law. If there is a conflict between a directly effective Community norm and a provision of national law then the latter falls. The supremacy of Community law demands this result and this has now been generally accepted by the UK courts.[37] Community law does not merely demand that its norms should be given precedence if UK law can possibly be construed to be in line with the dictates of the Community norms. There are two ways in which one might seek to explain the actual reasoning used by the House of Lords in the *ICI* case.

One line of argument would be that although this was a vertical case, the provision of Community law was not sufficiently precise to be accorded direct effect. If this were in fact so it could serve to explain the usage of the less potent interpretative obligation. While this argument is sound in principle, as exemplified by *Von Colson* itself,[38] it is difficult to rationalize the *ICI* case on this basis: Articles 52 and 58 would almost certainly be regarded as being sufficiently precise to be accorded direct effect in this context, particularly given the nature of the breach of those Articles being alleged by the applicants.

The other way in which one might rationalize the reasoning used by the House of Lords would be as follows. It might be argued that in *any* case where there is a conflict between Community law and national law the first step should always be to determine whether the latter could be made to conform to the former through principles of interpretation and construction; that this technique should be employed even in cases where the Community provision does have direct effect; and that only if such principles of interpretation failed to resolve the conflict would it then be necessary to consider the more drastic solution of declaring the national law to be inapplicable. There is clearly some merit in this approach, avoiding as it does the need to declare inapplicable national laws which could, through the use of interpretation, be reconciled with Community law. This is fine provided that it is then made clear that the interpretative strategy is merely the first step in obviating the discord with Community law, and that if it does not work the national law will still have to fall. Unfortunately, whether it was intended or not, the impression left by the reasoning (and headnote) in the *ICI* case is that the principle of construction captures the entirety of the obligation incumbent on UK courts in such cases. At the very least the case serves to blur the line between the duties imposed on national courts flowing from the doctrines of direct and indirect effect.

[37] *Factortame Ltd* v. *Secretary of State for Transport (No 2)* [1991] 1 AC 603.
[38] Above, n. 16.

3. Indirect Effect: Some Broader Reflections

(a) Indirect Effect: Three Problems

There is little doubt that indirect effect does offer a way to circumvent the holding in *Marshall* itself, or at the least, to reach similar results in many instances, albeit by a different route. There is also little doubt that the interpretative obligation creates real problems of its own.[39] Three such difficulties can be adverted to here.

First, it places national courts in some difficulty in deciding how far they can go in reconciling national legislation with Community norms while still remaining within the realm of interpreting, as opposed to rewriting or overruling national norms.

Secondly, the doctrine of indirect effect raises questions of legal certainty for individuals which are, paradoxically, more problematic than if directives had been given horizontal direct effect. This point was mentioned earlier and requires some further explanation here. In the paradigm case where indirect effect is of relevance there will be an unimplemented Community directive combined with national legislation the content of which differs from the directive. A plaintiff will seek to rely upon the directive against a private defendant, and the latter will have to decide whether to follow the directive or the differing provisions of national law. Which of these norms will ultimately be held to apply will be dependent upon a guess as to how far the national courts might feel able to go in reconciling national law with differently worded Community legislation. This is a matter on which even trained lawyers may well differ, and in advance of the national court's judgment any legal adviser may be able to do no more than offer some rough and ready estimation as to the likely outcome of the proceedings. Compare this to the situation which would prevail if directives did have horizontal direct effect. If this were so then the issue would be markedly different. The private defendant, or the legal adviser, would determine whether there was any inconsistency between national law and the relevant directive. If such an inconsistency did exist then the choice for the private party would be clear: Community law should be followed, supremacy of Community law would operate and national law would be trumped.

Thirdly, the present state of the law has, as Advocate General Lenz pointed out in the *Dori* case, the unsatisfactory consequence that 'individuals should be subject to different rules, depending on whether they have comparable legal relations with a body connected with the State or with a private individual.'[40] This is unfortunate in and of itself. It is all the more

[39] de Burca, 'Giving Effect to European Community Directives' (1992) 55 MLR 215.
[40] Case C–91/92, above, n. 7, para. 51.

so once it is realized that the expansive definition of the state which has been adopted serves to undermine the very argument against horizontal direct effect. The interpretation of the 'state' has been discussed above.[41] While the broad contextual approach taken in the *Foster* case might be unexceptionable for many purposes it is curiously at odds with the very reasoning given for confining direct effect to the state. We have seen that the primary argument employed by the ECJ for restricting the direct effect of directives to the state was a textual one, derived from the wording of Article 189. This argument was critically analysed above, but if one accepts it then surely it should point to a narrow and not a broad definition of the state. Normally the only authorities which have the power to implement a directive will be the organs of central government, not local or regional authorities, and certainly not nationalized or privatized industries. The estoppel argument is therefore misplaced when such bodies are the defendants in litigation.

(b) Indirect Effect, Damages Actions and Risk Allocation

When the possibility that directives might have horizontal direct effect was re-litigated in the *Dori* case a large number of Member States submitted opinions, the great majority of which strongly urged the ECJ not to depart from its holding in *Marshall*. Given this pressure it is unsurprising that the ECJ came to the decision which it did in *Dori*. What was, however, also unsurprising was that the ECJ put a sting in the tail of its judgment. The intervening years between *Marshall* and *Dori* had seen the birth of the *Francovich* principle,[42] under which states could, in certain circumstances, be held liable in damages for losses caused by non-implementation of a directive. It was, therefore, predictable that if the ECJ should reaffirm *Marshall*, and the consequential denial of horizontal direct effect, it would also hold open to plaintiffs such as Ms Dori the possibility that the losses which she had suffered might be recoverable from the state in a *Francovich* damages action. The ECJ did expressly include the possibility of such a damages action as part of its judgment in *Dori*.[43]

The net result of this legal reasoning can be expressed in the following way. If horizontal direct effect were to be recognized then, on the facts of a case such as *Dori*, the plaintiff would be able to rely on the directive against a private defendant, with the consequence that she could rescind the contract which she had entered into. Any loss would be borne by the private defendant who had sold the plaintiff goods covered by the directive. Compare this to the result actually reached in *Dori*. The plaintiff cannot rely on the directive against the private defendant. She may seek to

[41] See above.
[42] Cases C–6 and 9/90, *Francovich and Bonifaci* v. *Italy* [1991] ECR I–5357.
[43] Case C–91/92, above n. 7, paras. 27–9.

persuade the Italian courts to interpret Italian law to be in accord with the directive, pursuant to the doctrine of indirect effect. If this is not possible her only hope is to bring a damages action against the state. This clearly involves extra litigation costs, since there will be a separate action and the plaintiff will have to show that the requisites of state liability in damages are met. More important for present purposes is the fact that if the action is successful then the state will be bearing the financial liability. It will be the state which will shoulder the financial risk, rather than the seller of the goods who was the primary 'wrongdoer' in this scenario.

It might be argued that this is as it should be, given that it was the state which should have implemented the directive but has not done so. This is unconvincing. Directives such as that in issue in the *Dori* case are intended to govern relations between individuals. If losses are to be borne as a result of non-compliance with the directive then these should most naturally fall on the private party, assuming of course that the obligations contained therein were sufficiently precise to give rise to direct effect.

What is, in any event, surprising is the continued opposition of Member States to horizontal direct effect of directives, given the fact that this leaves the state open to the increased possibility of monetary liability. Whatever one thinks about the issues of legal principle considered in the preceding pages, government and politicians normally prick up their ears more quickly when it is made clear that the outcome of legal arguments can have far reaching financial implications. If governments were squarely told that their continued opposition to horizontal direct effect of directives rendered them susceptible to a species of financial liability which could be avoided if such direct effect were held to exist one wonders how many governments might reconsider their position on this topic?

4

Claims for Damages against the State for Breach of Community Law

BY HIS HONOUR JUDGE A. GEDDES

Early in 1996 *The Times*, after evidently not too close a reading of the judgment in *Factortame III*,[1] reported that the European Court had awarded Spanish fishermen £30 million of British taxpayers' money. However, while deploring the decision, they sensibly observed that it would be unwise to shoot the judges, as next time they might be awarding Spanish taxpayers' money to the British. Later that same week Ian Duncan-Smith MP for Chingford, again in *The Times*, urged the government to amend the 1972 European Communities Act 'to stop the ruling applying in British courts'. 'The British people' he added, 'want a British Parliament to denounce injustice and not just talk about it but do something.' Unfortunately he overlooked the fact that the 'something' which he proposed would be contrary to European law and consequently would have to be disregarded by the national courts.

Those are perhaps two of the more sober comments by the press on the judgment on *Factortame III* which was delivered on 5 March 1996 to a chorus of disapproval. This hostile reaction by the media has broadly centred on two topics; that this was an irrational and totally unforeseen decision not justified by the Treaty, and that it has produced a bizarre and unjust result. In my judgment, as I suspect in the judgment of most lawyers, those conclusions are wholly wrong. *Factortame III* is not of course a radical departure from the Court's earlier case law but is a measured step in the process of protecting individual rights, of which *Francovich*[2] forms the most conspicuous milestone, and it is that case which I propose taking as my starting point in considering where the law now stands in relation to the right of individuals to obtain compensation for a breach of Community law by the State.

In *Francovich* the Court, basing itself on Article 5 and on what it found to be inherent in the system of the Treaty, established for the first time, although it had alluded to the principle in earlier cases, that Member

[1] Joined cases C–46/93 and C–48/93 *R* v. *Secretary of State for Transport ex parte Factortame and others* [1996] ECR I–1029. See also the Divisional Court's judgment, [1997] EuLR 475.

[2] Joined cases C–6/90 and C–9/90 *Francovich v. Italian State* [1991] ECR I–5357.

States must make good loss and damage caused to individuals by breaches of Community law for which they can be held responsible. 'The full effectiveness of Community rules' the Court stated, 'would be impaired and the protection of the rights which they grant would be weakened if individuals were unable to obtain redress when their rights are infringed by a breach of Community law for which a Member State can be held responsible.' However the Court made it clear that not every breach would give rise to a claim for compensation; that depends on the nature of the breach of Community law giving rise to the loss and damage. In relation to a failure to implement a directive in due time, which was the subject matter of *Francovich*, the Court laid down three essential preconditions:

(a) the directive concerned must confer rights on individuals;
(b) those rights must be capable of precise identification from the provisions of the directive and,
(c) the failure by the Member State to implement the directive in due time has resulted in the loss claimed.

A provision in a directive will as a general rule confer rights on individuals where on its proper construction it is intended to protect natural or legal persons as regards their health, safety or economic welfare; it is irrelevant if that provision is intended to protect the general interest as well. Examples of directives designed to protect people's health and safety are the Product Liability Directive 85/374/EEC, the Bathing Water Directive 76/160/EEC, and the Drinking Water Directive 80/778/EEC. Examples of directives designed to protect a person's economic welfare can be found in the Doorstep Selling Directive 85/577/EEC, the Timeshare Directive 94/47/EEC and the Consumer Credit Directive 87/102/EEC. Where a provision in a directive is not intended to confer rights on individuals (as for example in the case of many directives designed to protect the environment where human health is not an issue) no such right to compensation will arise even though the State is in breach of its Community obligation such as by failing to implement the directive in due time[3].

The fact that Member States may choose one of a number of possible methods for achieving a result prescribed by a directive does not preclude the possibility of enforcing individual rights before the national courts whose content can be determined sufficiently precisely on the basis of the provisions of the directive alone. So, for example, as was the case in *Francovich*, the fact that Member States are given a degree of discretion as to how they provide a guarantee that the outstanding claims of employees

[3] e.g., Case 380/87 *Enichem Base* v. *Commune di Cinisello Balsame* [1989] ECR 2491 (concerning Directive 75/442 on waste).

will be met in the event of their employer's insolvency, and as to the precise amount of that guarantee, will not affect the precise and unconditional nature of the result required so long as the minimum guarantee required by the directive can be established.

In relation to questions of how any damage was to be assessed, the Court in *Francovich* confined itself to stating that that was a matter for national law subject to the usual caveats that the national rules relating to claims for damages for breaches of Community law must be no less favourable than those relating to similar domestic claims, and secondly they must not be so framed as to make it virtually impossible, or exceedingly difficult to obtain reparation.

Although *Francovich* was solely concerned with the State's failure to implement a directive in due time it clearly contemplated that other breaches of Community law by the State might give rise to a claim for damages. Indeed *Francovich* was followed by the decision in *Miret*[4] where it was held that a failure to implement a directive correctly could, in certain circumstances, give rise to such a claim. But *Francovich* left open a number of other important questions:

- Does the principle that Member States are obliged to make good damage caused to individuals by breaches of Community law for which they are responsible apply to all the organs of the State including the legislature?
- Is an action for damages against the State a residual remedy in the sense that such an action may only be brought where the individual has no other means of asserting the rights conferred on him by Community law, or is its ambit wider?
- What are the necessary preconditions which must be fulfilled before such a claim can arise?
- What are the criteria for quantifying the damage and in particular from what time can damages be claimed?

A. Does the principle that Member States are obliged to make good damage caused to individuals by breaches of Community law for which they are responsible apply to all the organs of the State including the legislature?

The Court came to the conclusion that it does and that it makes no difference whether the breach consists of a failure to act or of a positive illegal act. Nor does it make any difference if the illegal act is of a legislative or administrative nature[5]. So in the joined cases in question, the passing of

[4] Case C–334/92 *Wagner Miret* [1993] ECR I–6911.

[5] See for example the opinion of Advocate General Léger in Case C–5/94 *R* v. *MAFF ex parte Hedley Lomas (Ireland) Ltd* [1997] QB 139 (failure to grant an export licence for live sheep).

the Merchant Shipping Act 1988 containing provisions which were in breach of Article 52EC, and the failure by the German legislature to amend legislation which conflicted with rights conferred by Article 30EC, were both capable of giving rise to an action in damages by individuals who had suffered loss thereby.

In reaching that conclusion the Court based itself on the fundamental principles of the Community legal order, and in particular that rights conferred on individuals must be fully protected, and on the general principles common to the legal systems of the Member States especially as referred to in Article 215EC which provides for the Community's non-contractual liability for damage caused by its institutions or by its servants in the performance of their duties. If the Community has such a duty, argued the Court, then it must be implicit in the Treaty that the Member States do also.

Although the Court nowhere expressly says so it is clear I think that the 'State' in this context has the same meaning as was given to that term by the Court in *Foster and British Gas*.[6] That is to say it will include all the organs of central and local government together with other State controlled bodies as defined by Advocate General van Gerven in that case[7]. The House of Lords has held[8] that an action against the 'State' for breach of its obligations under Community law must be brought against the Attorney General. Although that may be correct when the defendant is an organ of central government it is submitted that the Attorney General would not be the appropriate party where the defendant is an emanation of the State such as a local authority.

B. Is an action for damages against the State a residual remedy in the sense that such an action may only be brought where the individual has no other means of asserting the rights conferred on him by Community law, or is its ambit wider?

It was argued in *Factortame III* that the only reason for the Court permitting a claim for damages against the State in *Francovich* was in order to fill a lacuna in the system for safeguarding the rights of individuals where otherwise individuals would have no means of asserting those rights in the national courts and that therefore in cases where the provision relied upon had direct effect this protection was unnecessary. That argument was rejected by the Court. It pointed out that the right of individuals to rely on directly effective provisions of the Treaty or of subsidiary legislation before their national courts was only a minimum guarantee and was

[6] Case 188/89 *Foster* v. *British Gas plc* (1990) 2 CMLR 833.

[7] See paras 21–2 of his opinion.

[8] *R* v. *Secretary of State for Employment ex parte Equal Opportunities Commission* (1994) 1 All ER 910, the speech of Lord Keith. final para.

not sufficient in itself to ensure full and complete protection. That could only be achieved by providing individuals with the right to claim adequate monetary compensation where in the circumstances this was justified.

C. What are the necessary preconditions which must be fulfilled before such a claim can arise?

The Court accepted that not every breach of Community law by the State which resulted in an individual suffering loss could give rise to a claim for damages by that individual. The breach had to be sufficiently serious to justify that liability. The difficulty the Court faced was how to identify that threshold of seriousness above which an action for damages would lie but below which it would not.

The Court turned for assistance in this respect to its case law concerning the Community's non-contractual liability under Article 215EC, observing that the conditions under which Member States could incur liability for damage to individuals caused by their breach of Community law could not, in the absence of particular justification, differ from those governing the liability of the Community in like circumstance. In other words the protection which individuals derive from Community law cannot vary depending on whether a national or Community authority was responsible for the damage. That case law takes into account when assessing Community liability, particularly when considering its legislative activity, inter alia the complexity of the situations to be regulated, difficulties in the application or interpretation of the Community texts and most importantly the margin of discretion available to the author of the act in question. Where in the legislative context the Community has a wide discretion in the implementation of Community policies (as will generally be the case especially as regards economic policies) the Community will not incur liability unless the institution concerned has 'manifestly and gravely' disregarded the limits imposed by Community law in the exercise of its powers. Advocate General Tesauro in his opinion in *Factortame III* characterized such activity as 'arbitrary' but noted a little ruefully that such are the current restrictions on claiming damages against Community institutions under Article 215 that to date the number of awards made under that Article amounted to just eight. The judgment in *Factortame III* makes it clear that in future the Court is likely to take a less restrictive approach to claims under Article 215 particularly in cases where the Community institution concerned does not have a wide discretion as to the action it can take.

The Court held therefore that where Member States have a similar wide discretion in their implementation of Community law they too will only incur liability in the limited circumstances which apply to Community institutions. The Court observed however that such cases would be rare and that usually Member States are given very little discretion under Community law which almost invariably requires them to achieve a particular result, to carry out a specific act, or to refrain from doing such an act, and where this is so any breach is more likely to exceed the seriousness threshold. Advocate General Tesauro went further and stated that in his opinion the discretion element was the decisive factor irrespective of the rank of the provision infringed or the national measure, whether legislative or executive, which infringes it. However he emphasized that what must be looked at is not the breadth of the State's discretion in a given sector but the breadth of discretion available to it in relation to the individual provision on which the claimant relies. He concluded by stating that 'in all those sectors and with regard to all those provisions which do not give Member States a significant margin of discretion, there must be held to be a liability and an obligation in damages simply on account of the infringement of a Community provision which confers on individuals a right which is precise and whose subject matter is determinable; no other factors may be taken into account.'

Although the Court in its judgment did not state the matter quite so clearly it seems to have accepted that argument. Certainly that was the situation both in *Francovich* and *Dillenkofer*[9] where the Member State was in breach of an obligation to implement a directive into its national law in due time; that was also the case in *Miret* where the State had failed to implement a requirement of a directive which was precise and clear, although it might well be otherwise where the requirement was not clear as was the case in *R* v. *H M Treasury ex parte British Telecom*.[10] It would also usually be the case where the State was in breach of any other Community provisions, including Treaty articles, which are confined to imposing on Member States precise, clearly defined obligations or to refrain from some conduct, which concurrently give rise to a right for individuals.

In every case, the Court held the decisive test for finding that a breach of Community law is sufficiently serious is whether the Member State manifestly and gravely disregarded the limits on its discretion. Some of the factors which the national court may take into account when deciding this issue were enumerated by the Court. They include:

- the clarity and precision of the rule breached;
- the measure of discretion left by that rule to the national authorities;
- whether the infringement and the damage caused was intentional or voluntary;

[9] Joined cases C–178 and 179/94 and C–188 to 190/94 *Erich Dillenkofer and Others* v. *Federal Republic of Germany* [1997] QB 259 (Package Travel Directive 90/3514/EEC).

[10] Case C–392/93 *R* v. *HM Treasury ex parte British Telecom plc* [1996] ECR I–1631.

- whether any error of law was excusable or inexcusable;
- whether the position taken by a Community institution may have contributed towards the omission and,
- the adoption or retention of national measures or practices contrary to Community law.

The Court added that on any view a breach of Community law will clearly pass the seriousness threshold if it has persisted despite a judgment finding the infringement in question to be established, or a preliminary ruling, or settled case law of the Court on the matter from which it is clear that the conduct in question constituted an infringement. However it equally made clear that save in so far as the same may be relevant to the question as to whether the breach is sufficiently serious, it is not necessary to prove 'fault' on the part of the public authority concerned in the sense of a deliberate or negligent act. It is this matter which seems to have incurred the wrath of the UK government which would like an immediate change in the law so that no liability would attach to the State irrespective of the seriousness of the breach unless it is shown that it had not acted in good faith.

As if it was aware that the test it had formulated would be difficult to apply in practice the Court went on to give the national court certain guidance in order to assist it in coming to the right decision in the two joined cases in question. In the case of *Brasserie du Pêcheur* the Court suggested that a distinction could be drawn between the German legislature having maintained in force provisions in its beer purity law prohibiting the marketing under the designation 'Bier' of beers imported from other Member States which in the light of case law in particular *Cassis de Dijon* was manifestly unlawful, and the retention of the provisions of that same law prohibiting the import of beers containing additives the illegality of which arguably did not become clear until the Court's judgment in 1987 in case 178/84 *Commission* v. *Germany*. Whether or not the plaintiff could recover damages in that case would depend on which of those two breaches was causative of his loss. Similarly in the case of *Factortame* the Court drew a distinction between the provisions of the Merchant Shipping Act making registration of fishing vessels subject to a nationality condition and those laying down residence and domicile conditions for vessel owners and operators. The former were manifestly contrary to Community law as constituting discrimination on the grounds of nationality, whereas the latter were only found to be in breach of Article 52EC after the European Court had rejected the UK argument that they were justified in terms of the common fisheries policy. In deciding whether the latter breach was sufficiently serious the European Court suggested that the national court might like to take into account among other things the legal disputes relating to particular features of the common fisheries policy, the attitude of the Commission which made its position known to the United Kingdom in good time, and the assessments as to the state of certainty of Community law made by the national courts in the interim proceedings brought by individuals affected by the Merchant Shipping Act.

D. What are the criteria for quantifying damage and in particular from what time can damage be claimed?

It is for the national court to decide whether there is a direct causal link between the breach and the damage claimed, but that chain of causation can be broken by the claimant failing to mitigate his loss. Although the Court did not specifically deal with the matter, the Advocate General gave as his opinion (paragraph 99, *et seq*) that there could be a failure to mitigate if the injured party failed to make use of legal remedies available to him either to prevent the breach or to claim any damages from a third party. Thus there could be a failure to mitigate if he failed to contest the measure complained of by invoking a provision in a directive which had direct effect; or if he failed to pursue a party against whom he had a remedy under purely domestic law, if such a failure to act was in the circumstances unreasonable.

Once causation has been established it will again be for the national court applying its domestic rules as to liability to decide on all issues relating to the type of damage recoverable and its amount. That rule is however subject to a number of reservations which are necessary to ensure that Community rights are fully protected.

First, the compensation provided by national law for a breach of a Community right must be no less favourable than would be provided for a similar domestic claim, and secondly, the conditions which must be satisfied before compensation is granted must not be such as in practice to make the recovery of damages impossible or excessively difficult.

In relation to the second rule the Court pointed out that restrictions under domestic law as to the non-contractual liability of the State in the exercise of its legislative function may have to be ignored. Similarly any condition that may be imposed by English law on State liability requiring proof of misfeasance in public office must be set aside. In addition compensation for any loss and damage must be commensurate with the loss and damage sustained so as to ensure that the rights of individuals are fully protected. In this context therefore it is not permissible to exclude economic loss; loss of profits are therefore recoverable together with interest thereon. Nor is it permissible to insist that the only compensation recoverable is in relation to damage suffered by the plaintiff over and above that suffered by the community at large; the plaintiff must be compensated for all the damage he has suffered as a result of the breach.

Finally, the Court held that the damages recoverable would be limited to those arising from the date when the plaintiff's cause of action for damages arose. It will be recalled that one of the conditions which must be satisfied before that cause of action can arise is that the breach by the State must have risen above the seriousness threshold. The Court made it clear that it is not necessary for there to be in existence a judgment of the European Court on the infringement in question although that will certainly be determinative, but it is implicit in the Court's judgment that a breach which started off as below the threshold may, in changed circumstances, for example a decision of the national or Community court clarifying the matter, cease to be so. Subject to any reasonable national limitation period it will only be from the latter date that damages can be claimed.

5

Aspects of Liability for the State and Public Bodies in English and Community Law

BY JEREMY LEVER QC, FELLOW AND SENIOR DEAN,
ALL SOULS COLLEGE, OXFORD

Background to the case

In *Three Rivers District Council and Others* v. *Bank of England (No 3)*[1] Clarke J, sitting in the Commercial Court, was concerned with the proper definition of the tort of misfeasance in public office and with the application of the European Community law relating to the non-contractual liability of public bodies of Member States. General readers may be deterred from giving the judgment the attention that it merits, partly because of its length (76 pages) and partly because, being given on a trial of preliminary issues, it proceeds on the assumption that the facts alleged in the reamended statement of claim are true; and the reamended statement of claim, although annexed to the original of the judgment,[2] is not included in the only report of the judgment yet published.

The essential facts

The essential facts alleged by the plaintiffs, many of which were denied by the Bank of England, were as follows:

1. The Bank of Credit and Commerce International SA (BCCI SA) was incorporated in 1972 under the laws of Luxembourg and was in receipt of a banking licence from the Luxembourg banking regulator. It subsequently opened a number of offices in the United Kingdom (more than in any other country). From, at latest, about 1977 it had ceased to carry on any sizeable banking business in Luxembourg and its office in Leadenhall Street, London, had become the principal place of business of the three companies which by then comprised the BCCI Group, namely a holding company, 'BCCI Holdings' (incorporated in Luxembourg), 'BCCI SA' and 'BCCI Overseas', a bank incorporated in

[1] [1996] 3 All ER 558.

[2] Both the reamended statement of claim and the Bank of England's defence, which together run to over 300 pp. of typescript, are annexed to the original of the judgment.

1975 in the Cayman Islands, where it had a banking licence but did not carry on any sizeable local banking business.

2. In 1991 the banking operations of BCCI SA and BCCI Overseas were suspended by the Bank of England (the Bank) and other banking regulators, including those of Luxembourg and the Cayman Islands. The BCCI companies then all became subject to insolvency proceedings in various jurisdictions. BCCI Group and BCCI SA were estimated to have net deficits of US $10 billion and US $6 billion respectively.
3. The Bank was the supervisory authority in the United Kingdom for the purposes of the Banking Act 1979 (the 1979 Act) and the Banking Act 1987 (the 1987 Act).
4. On 12 December 1977 the EC Council enacted the First Council Banking Co-ordination Directive (the 1977 Directive) which provided that Member States should require 'credit institutions' to obtain authorization and that the competent national authorities should grant such authorization where certain specified conditions were satisfied. The 1977 Directive further provided that the national authorities should collaborate closely in order to supervise the activities of credit institutions operating in their territory. The 1977 Directive also provided that the competent national authorities might withdraw an authorization but might do so only where certain specified conditions were satisfied.
5. In October 1979 the 1979 Act came into operation. It was enacted in order to give effect to the 1977 Directive. Its relevant provisions remained in force until October 1987 when they were replaced by provisions of the 1987 Act.
6. On the coming into force of each of the 1979 Act and the 1987 Act, BCCI SA was required to be authorized under them.
7. In October 1979 BCCI SA applied for and was granted authorization under the 1979 Act; by virtue thereof it was deemed to be authorized under the 1987 Act when that Act came into force.
8. As a deposit-taking institution carrying on business within the United Kingdom under a banking name, BCCI Overseas also required similar authorization but it never applied for authorization and was not authorized.
9. The Bank 'knowingly, deliberately contrary to the statutory scheme and hence in bad faith':
   (i) granted BCCI SA authorization under the 1979 Act when, as the Bank knew, the statutory criteria were not fulfilled;

(ii) in so doing, purported to rely on assurances given by the Luxembourg authorities even though the Bank knew that under the 1979 Act it was not entitled to do so and even though no assurances which satisfied the statutory requirements had been given;
(iii) thereafter purported to conclude that it had no discretion or power to revoke BCCI SA's licence after the Bank knew inter alia that the statutory criteria had not been and were not fulfilled and that BCCI SA was conducting its affairs in a way which threatened the interest of its depositors; and/or
(iv) acting on the basis of improper motives, failed to revoke BCCI SA's licence when it knew facts that made it necessary to do so;
(v) continued to rely on assurances given by the Luxembourg authorities when the Bank knew that BCCI SA's principal place of business was in the United Kingdom and not Luxembourg and that the Luxembourg authorities could not provide reliable assurances about BCCI SA;
(vi) permitted BCCI Overseas to carry on an unlawful deposit-taking business in the United Kingdom, on an unsound basis, illegally using a banking name;
(vii) failed to supervise either BCCI SA or BCCI Overseas.

10. Alternatively the Bank acted recklessly in the respects set out above.

11. Further or alternatively the Bank 'frequently and/or seriously and/or repeatedly' violated the requirements of the 1977 Directive which was designed to secure protection in Member States for depositors and potential depositors at banks. Such conduct on the part of the Bank, culminating as it did in the foreseeable collapse of the unsupervised BCCI companies and group, was actionable as misfeasance in public office at the suit of depositors who suffered loss thereby and this was so whether or not the Bank knew of its own wrongdoing.

12. Had the Bank not acted in breach of its duties as alleged above, BCCI SA would not have been authorized under the Banking Acts or its authorization would subsequently have been revoked; and the plaintiffs would not have deposited, and maintained deposits of, money with BCCI SA and would not have lost that money or would have lost less than they did.

13. The losses suffered by the plaintiffs were the likely consequences of the Bank's conduct and precisely such as the imposition of duties on the Bank by the Banking Acts was intended to avoid.

14. Further, to the knowledge of the Bank or as a matter of reckless indifference to it, losses by depositors and potential depositors were the

inevitable or necessary consequence of the Bank's conduct which was calculated to cause depositors and potential depositors harm as a direct, immediate and/or natural consequence; and the Bank must be taken to have intended such consequences.

15. Alternatively, the consequences were foreseeable.

No Claim in Negligence or for Breach of Statutory Duty under the Banking Acts

The plaintiffs recognized that in the light of the decision of the Privy Council in *Yuen Kun-yeu* v. *A-G of Hong Kong*[3] and *Davis* v. *Radcliffe*[4] they could not simply say (absent the effect of the 1977 Directive) that the Bank was in breach of statutory duty under the Banking Acts 1979 and 1987 by failing properly and carefully to supervize BCCI.[5] Moreover section 1(4) of the 1987 Act presented a further obstacle in the way of any ordinary claim for breach of statutory duty since section 1(4) excluded liability on the part of the Bank and its representative 'for anything done or omitted in the discharge or purported discharge of the functions of the Bank under this Act unless it is shown that the act or omission was in bad faith'.

The Preliminary Issues

Clarke J ordered the trial of three preliminary issues, to be determined on the assumption that the facts pleaded by the plaintiffs were true. The three issues were:

(i) Is the Bank capable of being liable to the plaintiffs for the tort of misfeasance in public office?
(ii) Were the plaintiffs' alleged losses caused in law by the acts or omissions of the defendant?
(iii) Are the plaintiffs entitled to recover for the tort of misfeasance in public office as existing or potential depositors?

Misfeasance in Public Office

According to the plaintiffs, it was sufficient for them to prove:

- that the Bank knew that it was acting unlawfully or was reckless as to whether it was or was not acting unlawfully and,
- that, as a result, the plaintiffs suffered loss, provided that they proved that it was reasonably foreseeable by the Bank that, if it acted unlawfully, the plaintiffs might suffer loss as a result (though the plaintiffs

[3] [1988] AC 175. [4] [1990] 1 WLR 821.
[5] See per Clarke J at [1996] 3 All ER, p. 596.

also made various factual allegations of knowledge and recklessness in this regard also: see above).

By contrast, the Bank's case was that, to establish liability on the part of the Bank, the plaintiffs would have to prove:

- that injuring the plaintiffs (or at least some depositors) was an actual purpose of the Bank and/or,
- that the Bank's acts or omissions were aimed at the plaintiffs (or at least some depositors) and/or,
- that the Bank knew that its alleged acts or omissions of misfeasance must inevitably and/or necessarily injure the plaintiffs (or at least some depositors).

Both sides submitted that Clarke J was bound by the decision of the Court of Appeal in *Bourgoin SA* v. *Ministry of Agriculture, Fisheries and Food*,[6] though they differed as to effect of that decision.

Bourgoin

In *Bourgoin*[7] the defendant Minister accepted, for the purposes of determination of the question whether the relevant paragraphs of the statement of claim disclosed a cause of action, that:

- in revoking a licence to import turkeys, the Minister's purpose was to protect English turkey producers from French competition;
- at the time of the revocation, the Minister knew that his act was one which involved the United Kingdom in a breach of Article 30 of the EEC Treaty;
- his act would, and was calculated to, injure the plaintiffs in their businesses; and
- the protection of English turkey producers was not a purpose for which powers were conferred on him by the enabling primary and secondary legislation.

At first instance in *Bourgoin*, Mann J accepted that those facts, if proved, disclosed a cause of action, notwithstanding that there was no allegation that the purpose of the Minister was the infliction of harm upon the plaintiffs; and the question with which Mann J was primarily concerned was whether malice (in the sense of targeted malice) was always required rather than whether knowledge of merely likely rather than inevitable damage would suffice. However on that latter question, Mann J's judgment indicated that the defendant must know that his misfeasance *would* injure the plaintiff and, though Mann J subsequently referred to *'foreseeable*

[6] [1986] QB 716. [7] *supra*.

and actual consequences', Clarke J accepted the argument for the Bank, that Mann J must have meant 'foreseen'.[8]

On this question Clarke J concluded that the judgment of Oliver LJ, with which Nourse LJ and, on this point, Parker LJ agreed, in the Court of Appeal in *Bourgoin* took the matter no further: clearly, as Oliver LJ said, where an official does an act which he knows must necessarily injure the plaintiff, he cannot be heard to say that he did not intend to do so; and that was clearly the position on the facts in *Bourgoin*. That being so, one could not derive from Oliver LJ's judgment (as the Bank sought to do) the further proposition that, in the absence of targeted malice, the plaintiff *must* establish:-

- that injury of the plaintiff was at least a subsidiary actual *purpose* of the defendant and,
- that the defendant must know that his act will *necessarily* cause the loss suffered by the plaintiff.[9]

Thus, the question of whether damage caused by a public officer's misfeasance needs to be actually foreseen by him rather than merely foreseeable does not arise where (or in so far as) the plaintiff relies on what Clarke J describes as the 'first limb' of the tort, that is where the public officer's misfeasance had, as its object, injury of the plaintiff ('targeted malice'); it arises only under the alternative 'second limb' of the tort, that is to say where the officer performs an act which he knows that he has no power to perform which harms the plaintiff. Clarke J concluded that *Bourgoin* is authority for the proposition that, under the second limb, the tort is committed where the officer knows that the plaintiff *will* be injured and that *Bourgoin* is not authority for the proposition that mere foreseeability of such injury will suffice.[10] On the other hand, as Clarke J concluded, *Bourgoin* is not authority for the proposition that nothing less will suffice than actual knowledge that the misfeasance will necessarily cause damage to the plaintiff: to ascertain whether that is so necessitates a review of other authorities.

However, on the question of knowledge in relation to injury for the purposes of the second limb of the tort, most of those authorities were inconclusive, stating at most that, for the purposes of that limb, the defendant must know that he was acting *ultra vires*, without stating what further criteria must be established.

[8] [1996] 3 All ER, p. 568.

[9] See per Clarke J at [1996] 3 All ER, p. 569.

[10] As Clarke J pointed out (at [1996] 3 All ER, pp. 570–572), the view of what *Bourgoin* decided expressed by Taylor J in *R* v. *Home Secretary, ex parte Ruddock* [1987] 1 WLR 1482 was consistent with Clarke J's conclusion, as too was *Gerrard* v. *Manitoba* [1993] 1 WWR 182 (Manitoba CA).

Northern Territory v. *Mengel*

The most important case decided on the topic since *Bourgoin* was the decision of the High Court of Australia in *Northern Territory* v. *Mengel*.[11] In that case the plaintiffs (the Mengels) suffered loss because of the action of two government livestock inspectors whose action was without any statutory or other authority but who were held not to have acted negligently. At first instance the Mengels succeeded on only one of the causes of action on which they relied, namely the innominate tort of the nature of an 'action for damages upon the case' available to 'a person who suffers harm or loss as the inevitable consequence of the unlawful, intentional and positive acts of another'.[12] In *Northern Territory* v. *Mengel* the High Court of Australia held that there was no such tort. Amongst the other causes of action then considered by the High Court of Australia was the tort of misfeasance in public office.

In *Northern Territory* v. *Mengel*, the majority of the High Court of Australia reaffirmed that that tort required that *either* there should be an intention to cause harm *or* the officer concerned should knowingly or at least recklessly, but not merely negligently, have acted in excess of his powers; if the latter, the majority thought that *Bourgoin*[13] indicated that the damage should be foreseeable—in Clarke J's judgment, a misunderstanding of *Bourgoin*.[14] In any event the majority of the High Court of Australia thought that mere foreseeability was not enough: the officer must have known that his *ultra vires* act was 'calculated in the ordinary course to cause harm' or must have acted with 'reckless indifference to the harm that is likely to ensue'.

It follows that, on Clarke J's view of *Bourgoin*, the majority of the High Court of Australia differed from the Court of Appeal only in that they stated that recklessness was to be equated with intention and knowledge in relation to both absence of lawful authority and the damage-causing nature of the misfeasance.

On these points the minority in the High Court of Australia did not differ from the majority, though Brennan J did say that, if the officer was recklessly indifferent to the injury which the impugned conduct was calculated to produce, then, whether or not the damage *actually* caused was foreseeable, he was liable no less than if he acted with malice towards the plaintiff or with knowledge that the act would or was likely to or would probably cause the plaintiff the injury that he in fact suffered. Deane J said much the same thing.

[11] (1995) 69 ALJR 527.

[12] *Beaudesert Shire Council* v. *Smith* (1966) 120 CLR 145 as characterised by Lord Diplock in *Lonrho Ltd* v. *Shell Petroleum Co Ltd* [1982] AC 173, p. 187.

[13] See n. 7, *ante*.

[14] See n. 6, *ante*.

Clarke J's definition of the tort

Clarke J summarized the authorities that he had, to that point in his judgment, reviewed, as follows:[15]

- The second limb of the tort is distinct from the first.[16]
- Both limbs require 'an invalid, unauthorized or unlawful act (or perhaps an omission) on the part of a public officer in the exercise of his public duty as such public officer which causes damage to the plaintiff'.[17]
- '[To] establish the first limb the plaintiff must prove malice on the part of the officer, that is an actual intention to injure the plaintiff'.[18]
- To establish the second limb of the tort, it is sufficient for the plaintiff to prove that the defendant had 'actual knowledge that [he] had no power to do the act complained of and that the plaintiff will suffer loss as a result but that "mere negligence, however gross" was not enough; nor was it sufficient to show only that loss was merely foreseeable'.[19]
- A public officer who wilfully shuts his eyes to the obvious, or while suspecting that his act is beyond his powers and/or that his act will probably cause damage to the plaintiff (or a class of persons of whom the plaintiff is a member) wilfully and recklessly fails to make such inquiries as an honest and reasonable man would make (so that the officer's recklessness can be equated with malice such as to make his conduct an 'abuse of powers') is to be treated as having actual knowledge of the matter in question.[20]

Clarke J then reviewed a large number of earlier English and Commonwealth authorities and textbooks and concluded that they did not vitiate the propositions of law that he had formulated on the basis of the later authorities.

European Community Law

The plaintiffs contended that European Community law was relevant in two ways:

- the Bank was, the plaintiffs alleged, in breach of the duties imposed by the 1977 Directive; and,

[15] [1996] 3 All ER pp. 578–582. His own summary of his conclusions, 'unless bound by authority to reach a different conclusion, and subject to the question whether the plaintiff must prove the infringement of a legal right', are set out at [1996] 3 All ER, p. 582; and see also p. 583 as to omissions, as distinct from positive acts. With regard to infringement of a legal right, Clarke J's conclusion was, in effect, that, of course, a plaintiff had to have *locus standi* (see his comment on *Ashby* v. *White* at [1996] 3 All ER, p. 586); and see under the heading '*Legal right*' at [1996] 3 All ER, p. 593.

[16] [1996] 3 All ER, p. 578. [17] *Ibid.* [18] *Ibid.* [19] *Ibid.* [20] *Ibid.*

- whether or not the plaintiffs could rely on a breach of the 1977 Directive, if the tort of misfeasance in public office was not wide enough to give them an effective remedy on the assumed facts of the case, it should be modified in order to do so.

The plaintiffs' direct reliance on breach of the 1977 Directive

Clarke J's judgment records that it was the plaintiffs' contention that the 1977 Directive had direct effect in the United Kingdom (so far as complaints against the Bank as a public body were concerned) and that they were entitled to rely on its terms in the English courts to obtain damages against the Bank.

The plaintiffs' primary case was that the United Kingdom had discharged its obligations under the Directive by enacting the Banking Acts 1979 and 1987 and that since the Directive gave the plaintiffs a right to damages, so must the Acts.

The plaintiffs' alternative case was that, if the Acts did not have that effect, the plaintiffs nevertheless had the right because of the direct effect of the Directive. The plaintiffs accepted, as Clarke J understood it, that they could succeed under this part of their claim only if:

- EC law had conferred rights on the plaintiffs;
- as a matter of EC law, breach of those rights sounded in damages in an action brought before a national court; and,
- the Bank had infringed those rights.

The privy council decisions on the liability of banking supervisory authorities

In this connection, the decisions of the Privy Council in *Yuen Kun-yeu* v. *A-G of Hong Kong* and *Davis* v. *Radcliffe*[21] were relevant in a number of respects:

- The statutory banking supervisors in those cases, as in the case of the Bank under the Banking Acts, had no day-to-day control of the supervised institutions and therefore no power to prevent fraud.
- The immediate cause of the loss suffered by depositors with a bank that failed because of fraud perpetrated by its management was the fraud of the managers.
- The exercise of the powers and performance of the duties of a banking supervisor involve the balancing of many different and possibly conflicting factors in the interest of the public generally and of both existing and future depositors.

[21] See nn. 3 and 4 *ante* and text thereto.

The nature of the breaches complained of by the plaintiffs

Clarke J observed that 'somewhat curiously' the plaintiffs did not contend that, as a result of the 1977 Directive, the Banking Acts must be treated as giving the plaintiffs a right against the Bank to damages whenever a plaintiff suffered loss as a result of breaches of the duties imposed on the Bank by the Acts but contended only that the plaintiffs had actionable rights if the Bank 'flagrantly and/or seriously and/or repeatedly' violated the terms of the 1977 Directive.

A possible inconsistency in the plaintiffs' case

Clarke J further drew attention to an apparent inconsistency in the plaintiffs' approach: they accepted that, by enacting the Banking Acts, the United Kingdom had given proper effect to the 1977 Directive. But they recognized that, as a matter of construction in accordance with English law, those Acts did not entitle the plaintiffs to sue the Bank for breach of statutory duty. Yet they argued that they were entitled to recover damages from the Bank for breach of duty, albeit only where the breach was flagrant, serious and/or repeated. Clarke J concluded: 'It follows, as I see it, that if the plaintiffs are to succeed they must do so by reliance on the Directive itself'.[22] Yet it is difficult to see how the plaintiffs *could* rely on the Directive itself if the plaintiffs' concession that the Banking Acts properly implemented the Directive was correct, for, as Clarke J pointed out, accepting what the Bank called its 'implementation point':[23] 'Once a directive has been correctly implemented there is no question of direct effect because, by definition, effect has already been given to it (see *Felicitas Rickmers-Linie KG & Co.* v. *Finanzamt für Verkehrsteuern, Hamburg*, Case 270/81 [1982] ECR 2771).'

On Clarke J's following analysis the problem was effectively resolved thus:

(i) the 1977 Directive did not confer, or require Member States to confer, on depositors a right to compensation from their national supervisory authorities in any circumstances; therefore

(ii) (a) the fact that the Banking Acts did not confer any such right on depositors (in the absence of bad faith) did not involve any failure by the United Kingdom correctly to implement the 1977 Directive (itself a bar to a claim by the plaintiffs directly under the Directive) and

(b) even apart from the implementation point, depositors had never even potentially had a claim to compensation under the terms of the Directive itself (another bar to a claim under the Directive itself).

[22] [1996] 3 All ER, p. 604. [23] [1996] 3 All ER, p. 603.

The question that did not need to be addressed

For this reason Clarke J did not need to address the question that would have arisen if he had found that:

- the Directive required Member States to confer on depositors a right to compensation from their national supervisory authorities in the event of breach by the latter of a duty that the Directive imposed or required to be imposed on them; and,
- in breach of the Directive, the United Kingdom had failed to confer such a right on depositors.

In those circumstances would depositors have had a right under EC law to compensation from the *British Government* if the depositors could have established the existence of the conditions for State liability for failure correctly to implement a directive[24] (in which case a plea that the alleged breach was flagrant, serious and/or repeated would have been relevant)? Could the depositors have sued the Bank, pleading that it was an organ of the State and as such should be treated as being in the same position as that in which it would have been had the Directive been correctly transposed into national law (in which case a plea that the alleged breaches were flagrant, serious and/or repeated would seem to be irrelevant)? Those questions are considered further below.

The conditions for reliance on the 1977 Directive

The Bank, as well as taking the 'implementation point' referred to above, contended that at least the following conditions needed to be satisfied if the plaintiffs were to be entitled to rely on the 1977 Directive:

- that the provision or provisions of the 1977 Directive relied on by the plaintiffs unconditionally and sufficiently precisely identified the plaintiffs as persons on whom the relevant provisions conferred rights (the 'eligible plaintiff point'): *Becker* v. *Finanzamt Munster Innenstadt;*[25] *Francovich* v. *Italy;*[26] *R* v. *International Stock Exchange, ex parte Else* [1993] QB 534 (CA);
- that these provisions unconditionally and sufficiently precisely identified what exactly the right conferred on the plaintiffs was (the 'contents points'); (*Francovich, supra*); and,
- that the provisions unconditionally and sufficiently precisely identified a right to damages, i.e., that the award of compensation was the

[24] See *Kirklees MBC* v. *Wickes Building Supplies Limited* [1993] AC 227, p. 283 per Lord Goff.
[25] Case 8/81 [1982] ECR 53.
[26] Joined Cases C–6/90 and C–9/90 [1991] ECR I–5357.

required sanction for infringement of the right (the 'damages points'); *von Colson & Kamann* v. *Land Nordrhein-Westfalen*[27]).

Clarke J accepted the plaintiffs' contention that the fact that a directive has more than one aim or objective does not prevent its being relied upon by an individual whose interests are also intended to be protected; but that did not answer the anterior question, which was one of purposive interpretation, namely whether the relevant provisions of the Directive were intended to give rise to rights that were to be enforceable by that person at all: *Hurd* v. *Jones (Inspector of Taxes)*;[28] *Banks (HJ) & Co. Ltd.* v. *British Coal Corp*.[29] The Bank contended that the purpose of the 1977 Directive was simply to harmonize the measures for the control of credit institutions in Member States throughout the Community. Although Clarke J found that the underlying purpose of the proposed system as harmonized was the protection of savers by the protection of their savings, that alone did not mean that the Directive conferred enforceable rights on savers. To arrive at that conclusion would have necessitated finding a provision in the body of the Directive that was intended to confer such rights on identifiable individuals and that had been infringed: the recitals to a directive could not in themselves confer rights on anyone.

The provisions of the 1977 Directive on which the plaintiffs relied in particular were:

- Article 3: the duty of the national supervisory authorities to authorize credit institutions, subject to, and subject to only, certain specified conditions;
- Article 7: the duty of the national supervisory authorities to collaborate closely in order to supervise the activities of authorized institutions (as distinct from a duty to supervise); and,
- Article 8: the power of the national supervisory authorities to withdraw authorization in, but only in, certain specified circumstances.

Clarke J rejected the plaintiffs' argument that the fact that provisions of the Directive imposed duties upon supervisory authorities *for the benefit of* depositors and potential depositors in itself implied that depositors and potential depositors had *enforceable rights* against those authorities because otherwise depositors' and potential depositors' *interests* would not be effectively protected:[30] the 1977 Directive could easily have provided for,

[27] Case 14/83 [1984] ECR 1891.

[28] Case 44/84 [1986] ECR 29, para. 47.

[29] Case C–128/92 [1994] ECR I–1209 per Mr A. G. Van Gerven, p. I–1237.

[30] *Cf.* per Leggat LJ in *R* v. *International Stock Exchange, ex parte Else* [1993] QB 534, p. 554 to the effect that an argument similar to that here advanced by the plaintiffs in *Three Rivers DC* v. *Bank of England* involved a non sequitur.

but did not provide for, the creation of such rights.[31] Indeed the 1977 Directive did not even create a duty to supervise; and the United Kingdom therefore could not be criticized either for failing to include such a duty in the 1979 Act or for restricting any liability of the Bank for failure to supervise cases of bad faith in section 1(4) of the 1987 Act. Moreover there were very good policy reasons for not conferring rights on savers or other creditors of credit institutions as against supervisory authorities[32] (and the plaintiffs had been somewhat equivocal as to precisely which categories of creditors were allegedly granted rights[33]).

The present case was thus to be contrasted with *Francovich*[34] where the only way in which the Directive there in issue could be performed was by requiring the provision of a guarantee to pay the amounts due to identifiable persons. Similarly in *von Colson* and *Marshall*[35] the Directives in issue, which included remedies provisions, were found to require full compensation to be given to identifiable persons. By contrast, the 1977 Directive did not require any compensation to be given to any relevant person. Lastly, as was agreed between the parties in *Else*[36] in relation to the directive that was there in issue, a directive may have (vertical) direct effect in the sense that one or more of its provisions confer rights on *particular persons* without any of the provisions of the directive conferring rights on *other persons*. Therefore the fact that Article 13 of the 1977 Directive might confer a directly enforceable right on a credit institution that was wrongly refused authorization was no indication that the 1977 Directive was intended to confer rights on other individuals.

Clarke J considered the judgments of the European Court of Justice in a number of other cases and concluded that none of them supported the proposition that, however liberally construed, the 1977 Directive was intended (any more than the 1979 Act was intended) to confer, whether on existing or future depositors, trade counterparties or other creditors, rights of action in damages against supervisory authorities; and he derived assistance from the Opinion of Advocate General Tesauro in

[31] The fact that the only remedies provision in the 1977 Directive, namely Article 13, did not give savers, or anyone else, a right to damages was a further pointer, but no more than a pointer, to the conclusion that the Directive was not intended to confer on savers rights which were actionable against the supervisory authorities for breach of duty: see [1996] 3 All ER, p. 618; and see *von Colson & Kamann*, cited at n. 28 above and Case C–271/91 *Marshall* v. *Southampton and South West Hampshire Area Health Authority (No 2)* [1993] ECR I–4367.

[32] See the text above following the reference to *Yuen Kun-yeu* v. *AG of Hong Kong* and *Davis* v. *Radcliffe* cited at n. 22 above.

[33] *Cf. R* v *International Stock Exchange, ex parte Else* [1993] QB 534 where the difficulty of identifying precisely the class of persons on whom rights should be held to have been intended to be conferred was one of the grounds on which a directive was held not to have direct effect.

[34] Cases C–6/90 and C–9/90 *Francovich* v. *Italy* [1991] ECR I–5357.

[35] Cited at n. 31 above.

[36] Cited at n. 33 above.

Joined Cases C–178/94, 179/94 and C–188/94 to C–190/94 *Dillenkofer* v. *Germany* (the judgment of the ECJ in that case—given on 8 October 1996—being still awaited when Clarke J. gave judgement—see further below).

On the issue of whether plaintiffs could rely on any of the provisions of the 1977 Directive as having direct effect, Clarke J expressed his overall conclusion as follows:[37]

It follows from the above that the plaintiffs are not entitled to succeed against the Bank as the result of the direct effect of the Directive. The plaintiffs say that that conclusion displays a narrow common law approach which is out of step with the approach of the European Court. In my judgment, that is not so. Some directives confer rights and some do not. The question is whether this Directive does so. I do not think that it does or was intended to do so.

Francovich

Francovich[38] exemplified State liability where:

- the State failed to implement a directive and although
- the directive did not have direct effect, nevertheless
- a private person was entitled to claim against the State compensation for the loss that the State's failure to implement the directive had caused him.

In the *Three Rivers DC* case, the Bank contended that the plaintiffs could not rely on *Francovich* for four reasons:

(i) the plaintiffs did not allege inadequate implementation of the 1977 Directive;
(ii) the defendant was the Bank not the United Kingdom;
(iii) the plaintiffs could not show that the provisions of the 1977 Directive on which the plaintiffs sought to rely entailed the grant of rights to them;
(iv) nor could the plaintiffs show that the contents of those rights were sufficiently defined by the 1977 Directive.

Clarke J concluded that for the same reasons as those given in relation to direct effect, the Bank's 'eligible plaintiff point' ((iii) above) and its 'contents points' ((iv) above), which effectively also embraced the Bank's 'damages point' precluded reliance by the plaintiffs on *Francovich*.

Effect of EC Law on the Common Law

The last way in which the plaintiffs put their case in *Three Rivers DC* was on the basis that the jurisprudence of the European Court of Justice[39]

[37] [1996] 3 All ER, p. 621.

[38] See n. 35, *supra*.

[39] Opinion of Mr A. G. Leger in Case C–5/94 *R* v. *Minister of Agriculture, Fisheries and Food, ex parte Hedley Lomas (Ireland) Ltd* [1996] All ER (EC) 493, paras. 141, 164, and 169; Opinions of Mr A. G. Tesauro in Joined Cases C–46/93 and C–48/93 *Brasserie du Pêcheur SA* v. *Germany*

showed that the common law tort of misfeasance in public office was too narrow and should be broadened.

Clarke J concluded that the jurisprudence in question showed that where a claim is brought

(i) against an emanation of the State under a directive that has direct effect and that has not been implemented or
(ii) against the State under the principle in *Francovich*[40] or
(iii) against a State for breaches of Community law under the principles enunciated in *Brasserie du Pêcheur*,[41] including a failure properly to transpose a directive,

the test of liability is different from either of the tests that are to be applied when the plaintiff relies on the tort of misfeasance in public office in a purely domestic UK context.

It was unnecessary to consider whether liability based on EC law, of the kinds considered above, was properly to be classified as

(a) a species of misfeasance in public office in which new tests were to be applied; or
(b) a claim for damages for breach of duty imposed by EC law or for the infringement of a right conferred by EC law.

Those questions did not arise in the *Three Rivers DC* case since the plaintiffs first needed to establish a relevant right, which they had failed to do.

Answers to the Preliminary Issues on the assumed facts

Issue 1: Was the Bank capable of being liable to the plaintiffs for the tort of misfeasance in public office?

Provisional Answer: Not unless the plaintiffs amended to plead that the Bank knew (or were in the relevant sense reckless as to whether) the managers or operators of BCCI would probably act fraudulently and that the plaintiffs would therefore probably suffer loss as a result of the Bank's act or omission.

Issue 2: Were the plaintiffs' alleged losses caused in law by the acts or omissions of the Bank?

Provisional Answer: The alleged losses were not capable in law of being caused by the acts or omission of the Bank unless the Bank knew,

and *R* v. *Secretary of State for Transport, ex parte Factortame Ltd* [1996] QB 404, paras. 7 and 74, and in Case C–392/93 *R* v. *HM Treasury, ex parte British Telecommunications plc* [1996] All ER (EC) 411; and the judgments of the ECJ in *Brasserie du Pêcheur, supra,* at para. 40.

[40] See n. 39, *supra*.

[41] See n. 40, *supra*.

(i) that a loss such as the loss that occurred was probable in the absence of remedial measures and,
(ii) that remedial measures were not being taken and
(iii) that remedial measures would not be taken in the future and that some plaintiffs would probably suffer loss.

Issue 3: Are the plaintiffs entitled to recover for the tort of misfeasance in public office as existing or potential depositors?

Provisional Answer: In principle yes, if a plaintiff proved that he had suffered a loss as a result of misfeasance as defined earlier in the judgment: the famous statement of Cardozo J in *Ultramares Corporation* v. *Touche*[42] that a defendant should not be exposed to 'liability in an indeterminate amount for an indeterminate time to an indeterminate class' was inapplicable to liability for misfeasance in public office.

Dillenkofer v. *Germany*

The European Court of Justice gave judgment in Joined Cases C–178/94, C–179/94 and C–188/94 to C–190/94 *Dillenkofer* v. *Germany* [43] on 8 October 1996, i.e., after Clarke J had given judgment in the *Three Rivers DC* case. *Dillenkofer* concerned Council Directive 90/314/EEC of 13 June 1990 on package travel, package holidays and package tours. The Directive required the organizer and/or retailer to provide sufficient evidence of security for the refund of money paid over and for the repatriation of the consumer in the event of insolvency. Germany was some eighteen months late in implementing the Directive. The plaintiffs in the main proceedings were purchasers of package travel who suffered loss as a result of the insolvency of the operators from whom they had brought their package travel after the Directive should have been implemented in Germany and before it was in fact implemented.

The judgment of the European Court of Justice confirms that complete failure by a Member State to implement a directive within the prescribed time limit (what French lawyers call '*carence*') constitutes per se a manifest and grave disregard of the limits on its discretion. As confirmed by the recitals to the Directive, the purpose of the relevant provision of the Directive was to protect consumers and although that provision simply required organizers to provide sufficient evidence of security and did not expressly confer on consumers a right to such security, the provision was to be construed as granting package travellers rights guaranteeing the

[42] (1931) 174 NE 441, quoted by Lord Keith in *Yuen Kun-yeu* v. *AG for Hong Kong* cited at n. 22 above.
[43] [1997] QB 259.

refund of money that they had paid over and their repatriation in the event of the organizer's insolvency; and the content of those rights was established by the Directive with sufficient precision. While national courts were always entitled to inquire whether the injured person had shown reasonable care to avoid his loss or damage or to mitigate it, the fact that a package traveller paid an organizer the whole price in advance rather than availing himself of a right to pay no more than 10 per cent of the total before obtaining documents of value did not constitute contributory negligence.

Thus in *Dillenkofer*, *Francovich*-type liability was held to exist since the Directive in issue was interpreted as conferring with sufficient precision, albeit by implication, defined rights on identifiable persons such as the claimants were. The European Court of Justice may in due course be called upon to determine how far, if at all, the interpretation of the Package Travel Directive casts light on how the 1977 Directive on the co-ordination of banking laws is to be interpreted. Clarke J's view was that the wording and purpose of the two Directives were in very different terms and that, while he could well understand the conclusion of the Advocate General in *Dillenkofer*, which subsequently the Court effectively followed, he, Clarke J, derived no real assistance from *Dillenkofer* in deciding the question that he had to decide, namely whether the 1977 Directive was intended to confer rights on private persons.

General observations

National governments and other 'organs' of the State are today entrusted with the performance of a vast range of functions. In the course of performing those functions, they are often likely to prejudice the interests of private individuals; and the prejudice will often be foreseeable. Sometimes in such cases their actions are arguably unreasonable: examples in the fields of taxation, town and country planning, the bringing of criminal prosecutions and foreign relations spring readily to mind. Nevertheless we recognize that in general the prejudice thereby suffered by private persons, though it may sometimes have been unreasonably inflicted upon them, is a price that has to be paid for government and that the general prejudice that would result from anarchy would be immeasurably worse: therefore compensation for the prejudice suffered in such cases is the exception rather than the norm.

It has also to be borne in mind that, in so far as exceptions are made to the norm, the expense ordinarily falls on the general body of taxpayers or ratepayers, many of whom may be less well-off, overall, than the person who is claiming compensation from the public body for prejudice that the claimant has suffered by reason of that body's action or inaction. This helps to explain why in the United Kingdom we attempt to remedy exceptional hardship through social payments and benefits rather than through a general system of State compensation in those cases where individuals have suffered misfortunes whether as a result of acts or omissions of public bodies or otherwise.

Thus, English law has defined rather narrowly the liability of public officers and bodies for misfeasance in public office, as is evident from the judgment of Clarke J in the *Three Rivers DC* case with which much of this chapter has been concerned. Because the conditions that a plaintiff who relies on that tort must satisfy are so rigorous, plaintiffs have increasingly sued in the tort of negligence and/or for breach of statutory duty save where, as in the *Three Rivers DC* case, there was clear authority that such an alternative claim does not lie. A discussion of the liability of public authorities for negligence would fill not just a chapter but a volume which would probably require to be published in loose leaf form to facilitate its frequent updating. In a recent judgment of 9 February 1997 in *W* v. *Home Office*[44] (no potential liability on the part of immigration officers for negligent detention of persons under the Immigration Act 1971), Lord Woolf MR reviewed a number of authorities and articulated the applicable principles in relation to where the boundaries should be drawn for holding public authorities liable in negligence. The judgment shows that there are many situations in which carelessness in the performance of a public duty or the exercise of a public power does not give rise to liability to pay compensation for loss caused by that carelessness. The further working out of the relevant principles can be expected to exercise the Courts for some time to come: *cf.* the even more recent judgments of the Court of Appeal of 14 March 1997 in *Capital & Counties plc* v. *Hampshire County Council*[45] where it was held that fire brigades have no duty to answer calls and no duty of care in relation to the discovery of fires and attending to their extinguishment but they do have duty of care in relation to what they do in the course of fighting a fire, e.g., in switching off a sprinkler system.

From the standpoint of EC law somewhat different considerations from those that are relevant under national law apply to the imposition of civil liability on Member States and domestic public bodies to pay compensation to private persons for prejudice suffered by the latter as a result of action or inaction on the part of the former in breach of EC law. From the standpoint of the Community, it is desirable in principle (in the English sense) that there should exist private law sanctions that private persons can enforce to reinforce the public law duty of Member States to comply with EC law, including their duty correctly to implement directives within the prescribed time. The non-implementation of a directive within the pre-

[44] CA, *The Times*, 14 Mar. 1997

[45] [1997] 3 WLR 331.

scribed time is per se a substantial and inexcusable breach of EC law; and if the directive was intended to confer on private persons valuable rights, it is not surprising that EC law should require the Member State that is guilty of the inexcusable default to compensate such private persons for the loss caused to them in consequence: see *Dillenkofer, supra*.

Where the Member State implements a directive but does so incorrectly, the question of its liability is determined by the same considerations as apply in other cases of breach of EC law by a Member State, effectively:

- whether the Member State's breach was substantial and inexcusable (which cannot here simply be presumed as it can in the case of straightforward failure to implement the directive all) and, if so
- whether the injured claimant is a person to whom EC law grants (or the incorrectly implemented directive intended that there should be granted) a right to compensation enforceable by such persons in the national courts.

But to the second of those two questions, broadly similar policy considerations will often be relevant to those that apply in circumscribing the liability, under national law, of States and public authorities to private persons who have suffered loss as a result of 'public' action or inaction.

Once an injured claimant has established his status as a person given, or intended to be given, under EC law a legal right infringement of which sounds in damages (which is entirely a matter of EC law), the national courts must treat the claim no less favourably than they would treat a comparable claim for breach of a national law where the claim is brought by a person with the requisite status under national law; and in such circumstances, even if the national court would not recognize such a claim for breach of national law (e.g., because under English law neither the tort of misfeasance in public office nor that of negligence could be relied upon) the national court must grant reparation for the breach of EC law if it was sufficiently serious and there was a direct causal link between the breach and the damage sustained by the injured claimant.

A second policy consideration which arises at the level of EC law where:

- a Member State has not implemented or has incorrectly implemented a directive, provisions of which were intended to confer legally enforceable rights on private persons;
- because of the State's default, such persons do not enjoy the national law right that implementing measures ought to have conferred, but do not confer, upon them; and
- a private person is prejudiced by an act or omission of the State or a public authority in respect of which the directive intended that he should enjoy legal rights.

In such circumstances EC law (rather like the English rules of Equity) effectively treats as done that which ought to have been done and itself confers on the private person in question the intended right against the State or public authority in question: the 'vertical' direct effect of the directive enables such persons to vindicate their rights in the national courts.

The equation of public authorities to Member States for this purpose is entirely understandable at the level of EC law for two reasons. First, the application of EC law in this respect cannot be allowed to depend upon the precise allocation by Member States of public functions, powers, and duties as between central and local government and other public authorities within the Member State. Secondly, a Member State and its organs must not be allowed to be placed in a better position by reason of failure by the Member State duly and correctly to implement directives than had the Member State done so.

But a serious and as yet unresolved problem arises in the following kind of situation. A Member State may incorrectly but excusably implement a directive in a particular way. Local authorities and other public bodies may then conduct their affairs on the basis of the national measure; in so doing their conduct can clearly not be characterized as inexcusable any more than can the conduct of the Member State; yet, because of the doctrine of vertical direct effect, they may find themselves saddled with the cost of liabilities for breach of duties that ought to have been imposed on them by the implementing measures but were not so imposed because of the (excusable) default of the Member State. The cost will then fall on local ratepayers or other limited classes of persons. Moreover, the problem thus identified does not go away even if the local authority or other public body was guilty of 'flagrant and/or serious and/or repeated' breaches of the directive, correctly interpreted (as the plaintiffs claimed was the case in *Three Rivers DC* v. *Bank of England, supra*): in the hypothesized circumstances the local authority or other public body will (*ex hypothesi* reasonably) have conducted its affairs by reference to the national implementing measure (which it will have supposed had superseded the directive) and not by reference to the provisions of the directive. It would not seem satisfactory that in such circumstances, while central government could not be successfully sued for breach of EC law, the cost of the non-compliance resulting from the error of central government should fall on a more limited class of persons.

6

Injunctions and Damages against the State for Breach of Community Law—a Legitimate Judicial Development

BY PROFESSOR DERRICK WYATT QC, ST EDMUND HALL, OXFORD

It is well established that the exercise of Community rights before national courts has as a corollary the requirement that national procedures and remedies ensure a certain minimum standard of effective protection for such rights. It is the purpose of this chapter to comment on developments in the case law of the Court of Justice as regards injunctions and damages against the State. I will also comment on a broader question; that of the legitimacy of the European Court's development of the law of remedies in these fields. That is to say, the question whether the Court of Justice has acted properly and within its jurisdiction as a Court, charged with the duty of upholding the rule of law, as opposed to improperly, in the sense of having exceeded any reasonable construction of the remit afforded to it by the EC Treaty.[1]

The basis of the jurisdiction of the Court of Justice to authorize and require national courts to make certain national remedies available against the State, and indeed to adjust those national remedies as appropriate, is the doctrine of direct effect. The legitimacy of the development of that doctrine has itself not gone unquestioned, in particular as regards the direct effect of unimplemented or improperly implemented directives.[2] In my view, the development of the doctrine of direct effect of provisions of the Treaty, and provisions of directives, was a legitimate, though not inevitable, inference from the text of the Treaty. It was always obvious

[1] For recent 'sceptical' assessments of the role of the Court of Justice, see Sir Patrick Neill, QC, *The European Court of Justice: A Case Study in Judicial Activism*, evidence submitted to the House of Lords Select Committee on the European Communities, Sub-committee on the 1996 Inter-Governmental Conference, *1996 Inter-Governmental Conference, Minutes of Evidence, House of Lords, Session 1994–95*, 18th Report, p. 218; T. Hartley, *The European Court, Judicial Objectivity and the Constitution of the European Union*, (1996) 112 LQR 95. For a well considered assessment from a somewhat different perspective, see Tridimas, *The Court of Justice and Judicial Activism* (1996) 21 EL Rev. 199.

[2] The case law of the Court of Justice on the direct effect of directives has been ignored or criticized by national courts, see e.g., *Cohn-Bendit* [1979] Dalloz Jur. 155 (Conseil d'Etat); *Kloppenburg*, judgment of 25 April 1985, (Bundesfinanzhof), (1985) 10 EL Rev. 303.

from the wording of Article 189 of the Treaty that Regulations were in effect Community statutes capable of being invoked with immediate effect before national courts. It has been the direct effect of Treaty Articles and Directives which has given rise to controversy. The strongest textual inference of the direct effect of Treaty Articles to which reference is made by the Court of Justice in *van Gend en Loos*[3] is that derived from Article 177 of the Treaty. In relevant part Article 177 provides for the Court of Justice to give preliminary rulings on the interpretation of the Treaty, and on the validity and interpretation of the acts of the institutions. The text implies, at the very least, that in principle individuals may invoke, before national courts, Articles of the Treaty, and acts of the institutions. It would surely have been significant if Article 177 had confined the jurisdiction of the Court to ruling on the interpretation and validity of *regulations*; but it did not. Article 177 at the very least leaves open the possibility that directives (and indeed decisions), as well as regulations, might have some legal consequences when pleaded before national courts. The possibility that those legal consequences might have been held to be confined, e.g., to providing guidance to national courts for the interpretation of national rules implementing directives does not render illegitimate the Court's actual conclusion; *viz.*, that unimplemented or improperly implemented directives might in appropriate cases impose obligations upon the Member States analogous to those imposed by provisions of the Treaty.

Between 1963 and 1976 the doctrine of direct effect was developed in a series of preliminary rulings by the Court of Justice concerning in particular Articles 30, 48, 52, 59, 85, 86, 95 and 119.[4] During this same period directives were held capable of having direct effect. It is trite law that where there is a right there must be a remedy. And indeed it can only be regarded as inevitable that national courts would seek to link the new rights derived from Community law with the remedies available under national law. In 1976 the Court of Justice, in two significant preliminary rulings (*Rewe* and *Comet*[5]) laid down three principles applicable in cases where individuals invoked Community rights before national courts:

- it is for the national legal system to determine the courts and tribunals and procedures and remedies available to secure enforcement of directly effective Community rights;

[3] Case 26/62 *Van Gend en Loos* v. *Nederlandse Administratie der Belastingen* [1963] ECR 1. The Court of Justice makes the point on Article 177 *a propos* directives in Case 9/70 *Franz Grad* v. *Finanzamt Traunstein* [1970] ECR 825, at p. 837, para. 6.

[4] See, in general, Wyatt and Dashwood, *European Community Law*, Sweet and Maxwell, 1993, 3rd ed., pp. 58 *et seq.*

[5] Case 33/76 *Rewe-Zentralfinanz* [1976] ECR 1989; Case 45/76 *Comet* v. *Produktschap* [1976] ECR 2043.

- those national procedures and remedies must not be less favourable than those available to enforce similar national rights;
- the national procedures and remedies must not make the enforcement of Community Law impossible in practice.

Those principles represented a deduction from the text and scheme of the Treaty, and in particular Article 5 of the Treaty, with which it is difficult to take issue. In 1980, commenting on *Rewe* and *Comet*, I expressed the following view: 'The application of the principles referred to, would, it seems, prohibit a national court from refusing an effective remedy to an individual who had initiated legal proceedings against the state, based on Community law, on the ground that national law precluded such a remedy being awarded against the state.'[6] The above proposition was advanced by me with specific features of English law in mind. One was Section 21 of the Crown Proceedings Act 1947, which provides that in civil proceedings no injunction be granted against the Crown or an officer of the Crown. It seemed to me at the time to be reasonably clear that this feature of English law—a blanket unavailability of injunctive relief against the Crown—could infringe the principle in *Rewe* and *Comet* that the application of national remedies should not make the exercise of Community rights impossible in practice.

The above proposition was of course to be tested in the *Factortame*[7] case. The Court of Justice made no direct reference to the rulings in *Rewe* and *Comet*, preferring to rely upon its judgment in the *Simmenthal*[8] case, which emphasized the incompatibility with Community law of judicial practices which might prevent, even temporarily, Community rules from having direct force and effect. Application of the principle of English law excluding injunctive relief (*in casu* interim injunctive relief), was held to be incompatible with Community law where that rule was the sole reason for an English court refusing such relief.

The Court of Justice in *Factortame* did not address the question of the *criteria* to be applied in granting or withholding interim injunctive relief. The Court proceeded on the basis that since the sole ground for the House of Lords refusing relief appeared to be the provision of English law precluding such relief against the Crown, addressing the question of the criteria to be applied in granting or withholding relief would have been superfluous.

In two subsequent cases, *Zuckerfabrik*[9] and *Atlanta*,[10] the Court of Justice

[6] Wyatt and Dashwood, *Substantive Community Law*, Sweet and Maxwell, 1980, p. 45.

[7] Case C–213/89 *Factortame* v. *Secretary of State for Transport* [1990] ECR I–2433.

[8] Case 106/77 *Simmenthal* v. *Amministrazione dello Stato* [1978] ECR 629.

[9] Cases C–143/88 and C–92/89 *Zuckerfabrik Süderdithmarschen and Zuckerfabrik Soest* [1991] ECR I–415.

[10] Case C–465/93 *Atlanta Fruchthandelsgesellschaft mbH and others* v. *Bundesamt fur Ernährung und Forstwirtschaft* [1995] ECR I–3761.

did have cause to examine the criteria applicable to the grant of injunctive relief by national courts in cases involving the application of Community law. In these cases, interim injunctive relief was sought in national proceedings in circumstances in which the effect would have been to suspend the application of EC Regulations. In the first place, the Court of Justice holds that where an individual relies upon Community law, the conditions for interim relief must be the same, whether the individual challenges the compatibility of national legal provisions with Community law, or the validity of secondary Community legislation, because in each case the claim is based upon Community law itself. Secondly, the Court addresses the circumstances in which a national court may suspend a Community act pending a ruling by the European Court on the validity of that act.

It will be recalled that in *Foto-Frost*[11] the Court of Justice held that while a national court did not have jurisdiction to invalidate a Community act (such jurisdiction being reserved to the Court of Justice), different considerations applied if an applicant sought to suspend a Community act pending a ruling on invalidity by the European Court. In that case the Court had not specified with precision the circumstances in which a national court could suspend a Community act, and had not indicated whether those circumstances were defined by Community law or by national law. It might be said that such a question could be left entirely to national law. But in Member States in which interim relief would be readily granted against the administration the practical consequence could be the paralysis of a Community legal regime resulting from the suspension of the relevant Community legislation.

Community law of course makes provision for interim relief in direct actions before the Court of Justice for the judicial review of Community acts, pursuant to Articles 173, 185 and 186. In such actions the Court of Justice will suspend the act in question where there is a prima facie case, and urgency resulting from the likelihood of irreparable damage to the applicant. This is balanced against the possibility of irreparable damage to the Community should the act be suspended but the applicant's case fail. The requirement of a prima facie case is not onerous. The question posed is this: can it reasonably be asserted that the plea is without foundation? If the answer is no, there is a prima facie case, and the Court moves on to urgency and balancing.[12]

In *Zuckerfabrik* and *Atlanta,* the Court draws an analogy with the test under Articles 185 and 186 EC for interim relief in direct actions before the Court. But it substitutes a different preliminary hurdle. Instead of the

[11] Case 314/85 *Foto-Frost* v. *Hauptzollamt Lubeck-Ost* [1987] ECR 4199.

[12] Case T–29/92 R *SPO v Commission* [1992] ECR II–2161, para. 34; Joined Cases C–239/96 R and C–240/96 R *United Kingdom* v. *Commission,* Order of 24 Sept. 1996, paras. 51–3, and 61.

prima facie case requirement, in the sense in which that is meant in this context, the Court holds that a national court must be satisfied that *serious doubts* exist as to the validity of the Community act in question. Thus the national court must make a preliminary assessment of the merits, which goes farther than establishing factors likely to cast doubt on the the conclusions reached by the Community authority.[13] The approach urged on national courts by the Court of Justice in the above cases is not far distant from the approach of the House of Lords in *Factortame* when the reference came back after the ruling of the European Court. The House of Lords applied the normal *American Cyanimid* principles. This latter case had substituted for the prima facie test as it is understood in English law the lesser hurdle of a serious case to be tried. But in *Factortame* the merits creep back at the stage of considering the public interest. Lord Goff says: '[T]he court should not restrain a public authority by interim injunction from enforcing an apparently authentic law unless it is satisfied, having regard to all the circumstances, that the challenge to the validity of the law is, prima facie, so firmly based as to justily so exceptional a course being taken.'

In *Atlanta,* a propos the balancing stage, the Court of Justice stresses the Community interest, and the need for the national court to take into account the cumulative effect which would arise if a large number of courts were also to adopt interim measures for similar reasons.

The conditions laid down in these cases represent both a minimum standard for the judicial protection of individuals, and a minimum standard of protection for the public interest in the form of the uniform force and effect of Community law. Moreover, since the Court emphasizes that the same considerations apply when individuals challenge national law on the basis of Community law, it seems that Community law affords the same protection to national law challenged on the basis of Community law as it affords to acts of the institutions whose validity is challenged before national courts. It is to be noted that the Court of Justice applies by analogy the Community rules which apply in comparable direct actions before the Court of Justice, while devising a more rigorous test of the merits for the national judge than applied to the European judge. This latter feature no doubt reflects a certain lack of confidence in the ability or willingness of the national judge to take sufficient account of the Community interest at the balancing stage. So the merits must be strong before the question of balancing arises.

Does the Court of Justice go too far in this respect, bring about, in effect, a *harmonization* of interim relief which should only properly be achieved by measures such as Directive 89/665[14]—the remedies directive in the

[13] See n. 12.

[14] OJ 1989 L 395/33; reprinted in Rudden & Wyatt, *Basic Community Laws*, OUP, 1996, 6th ed.

field of public procurement? I do not think so. It would have been wholly inadequate for the Court of Justice simply to say that national courts must be entitled to grant interim relief, even as against Community acts, but then go on to leave the legal issues arising from this pronouncement entirely to national law. The result would in practice have been to create unworkable disparities between the practice in different Member States, since in certain Member States the ready availability of interim relief in proceedings for judicial review of administrative action could paralyse relevant elements of the Community legal system in that State, while in other Member States more restrictive principles of national law could leave the Community regime with full force and effect. But the conclusion is not simply a policy driven imperative. It is based on legal principle. If individuals have rights, they must have remedies, and it is inevitably for the Court of Justice to identify remedies under national law which give full force and effect to those rights. But the individual's right is the administration's obligation, whether the administration is the Community administration or the national administration. The Court of Justice could not avoid determining the criteria applicable to interim relief, because the content of a right cannot be divorced from the scope of the remedies which protect that right. Once the Court embarks upon the task of delimiting the scope of the remedies which protect a right, the process is one of judicial inference from texts which are sometimes silent and sometimes ambiguous. The Court of Justice may be said to be right or wrong about the way in which it resolves particular cases. But in this field it has surely acted properly as a court fulfilling the task allotted to it under the Treaty.

The possibility of the best qualified judges drawing different inferences from texts in the field of injunctive relief is of course illustrated by developments in the United Kingdom. In *Factortame* the House of Lords took the view that Section 31 of the Supreme Court Act 1981 did not have the effect of amending the prior law on the lack of availability of interim injunctive relief against the Crown. As Lord Bridge said: 'It is impossible to construe S.31 of the 1981 Act except in the light of the relevant preceding history.'

That history led to the conclusion that interim injunctive relief was not available against the Crown. Yet in *M* v. *Home Office*[15] the House of Lords took a different view. I refer to this difference of judicial opinion to make a modest point. Texts may allow the judge more than one possibility. And the selection of the appropriate possibility involves analysis of grammar, history, principle, and a sense that some directions are more worth travelling than others. This latter consideration, the judge's sense of direction, is to be gleaned from the entire framework of rules and principles relevant to the case in hand, and may legitimately take account of how well,

[15] [1994] 1 AC 377; [1993] 3 All ER 537 (HL).

in a practical sense, one solution rather than another fits into that framework.

In 1991 the Court of Justice took a bold decision. The judgment in *Francovich*[16] indicated that the total failure of a Member State to implement a directive could result in damages, where the directive was intended to confer rights on individuals, and the failure caused loss. This judgment caused a minor legal earthquake, perhaps comparable to that caused by the ruling of the House of Lords in *Donogue* v. *Stevenson*.[17] Trying to avoid the deceit of hindsight, I looked back on my own speculation on the future of damages liability in Community law, as I recorded it in the past. In 1982 an article in the European Law Review examined the possibility of a direct damages action against a Member State before the European Court. *En passant*, I noted: 'Furthermore, the direct effect of Community law entails the duty of State courts to utilize such procedural rules and remedies available to them under national law to safeguard the rights of individuals. The integrity of the Community system of judicial remedies might therefore reinforce the inference drawn from the texts in restricting a damages action to an action before national courts.'[18] In the second edition of Wyatt and Dashwood's *Substantive Community Law*, published in 1987, after considering the case law to date and the text of Article 5 of the EC Treaty, I expressed the view that, '[I]t would seem to follow that in some cases at least a right to compensation in accordance with national law constitutes an adjunct to the direct effect of rules of Community law.'[19] The point is not that I was in any sense expecting *Francovich*. The point is that it can be said in 1996 without any affectation that the concept of rights derived from Community law unattended in any case at all by the requirement of a remedy in damages has been regarded by many lawyers for a good number of years as close to inconceivable. In *Bourgoin* v. *MAFF*,[20] long before *Francovich*, a majority of the Court of Appeal, in response to arguments advanced on behalf of MAFF, drew a parallel between Community liability under Article 215(2) EC and state liability for breach of directly effective provisions of the Treaty. In this way the Court of Appeal foreshadowed the approach of the European Court in its later case law. In *Zuckerfabrik* and *Atlanta* the Court drew a parallel between a national action for judicial review of the administration in its application of Community rules, and a direct action against a Community institution based on Article 173. The Court used this analogy to assist it in defining the scope of national remedies against the State when the State was chal-

16 Cases C–6/90 and C–9/90 *Francovich and others* v. *Italian Republic* [1991] ECR I–5043.
17 [1932] AC 562; [1932] All ER Rep. 1.
18 Wyatt, *New Legal Order, or Old?* (1982) 7 EL Rev. 147 at 161.
19 Wyatt and Dashwood, *Substantive Community Law*, Sweet and Maxwell, 1987, p. 57.
20 [1985] 3 All ER 585.

lenged in its application of Community law. A decade after *Bourgoin* the specific analogy relied upon by the Court of Appeal in that case was to provide the basis for the Court's articulation of the scope of the rights of individuals to damages for breach of directly effective Treaty provisions.

After *Francovich* academic literature sought to plot the future course of damages liability in Community law. A consensus emerged favouring the conditions for state liability being based on the conditions for Community liability under Article 215(2) EC.[21] This would mean that where a Member State enacted legislation in the exercise of a wide discretion as to the choice of policy to be adopted, there could only be liability if the state acted in manifest and grave disregard of a superior rule of law for the protection of the individual. When *Factortame III* and *Brasserie du Pêcheur* were considered by the Court of Justice,[22] the real legal question for the Court of Justice was the standard of liability which it would set. It will be recalled that in *Factortame* United Kingdom rules had sought to reserve the British flag for vessels owned by British nationals. Spanish fishermen asserted infringement of their right of establishment under Article 52. In *Brasserie* German rules had in effect excluded from the German market beer produced other than in accordance with the German pure beer rules. A frustrated exporter of beer to Germany claimed violation of Article 30 on the free movement of goods. The Court of Justice drew a parallel between liability of the State, and liability of the Community under Article 215(2) EC. Where national authorities have a wide discretion, comparable to that of the Community in implementing Community policies, the conditions under which the state may incur liability must in principle be the same as for the Community. Both the United Kingdom and Germany had a wide discretion in adopting the national rules in question, and accordingly would be liable only if three conditions were satisfied:

- the rule of law must be intended to confer rights on individuals;
- the breach must be sufficiently serious;
- there must be a direct causal link between breach and damages.

As regards the seriousness of the breach, the test for liability is whether the Member State (or the Community in the case of Community liability) has manifestly and gravely disregarded the limits on its discretion. The factors which the national court might take into consideration in assessing the seriousness of the breach included:

[21] Indeed, in the *Factortame III/Brasserie* litigation, the Irish, Dutch and UK governments argued for the application by analogy of the court's case law on Article 215(2) if liability arose in a case such as that in issue.

[22] Joined Cases C–46/93 and C–48/93 *Brasserie du Pêcheur SA* v. *Federal Republic of Germany; R* v. *Secretary of State for Transport ex parte Factortame Ltd and others* [1996] ECR I–1029; [1996] 1 CMLR 889.

- the clarity and precision of the rule breached;
- the measure of discretion left by that rule to national and Community authorities;
- whether the infringement and damage caused were intentional or involuntary;
- whether any error of law was excusable or inexcusable.

The Court held in these cases that the European Court cannot substitute its own assessment for that of the national courts, which have sole jurisdiction to find the facts and to characterize the breaches of Community law at issue. But the Court stated that it might be helpful to indicate a number of circumstances which the national court might take into account. The Court of Justice in effect gives advice to the national courts as to how to characterize the breaches in question. I consider that the Court of Justice was wrong to do this. The national courts are in a far better position to do so in all the circumstances of the cases in question. I find one passage in the judgment in *Factortame/Brasserie* particularly unfortunate. The Court states:

> The decision of the United Kingdom legislature to introduce in the Merchant Shipping Act 1988 provisions relating to the conditions for the registration of fishing vessels has to be assessed differently in the case of the provisions making registration subject to a nationality condition, which constitutes *direct discrimination manifestly contrary to Community law,* and in the case of the provisions laying down residence and domicile conditions for vessel owners and operators.[23] [emphasis added]

I consider this observation to be unjustified. The United Kingdom proceeded on the basis that the equal treatment requirement of Article 52 had no application to the registration of fishing vessels. If a Member State erroneously considers that it is no more discriminatory to deny merchant vessel registration to a non-national than it is to deny a passport to a non-national, the discrimination in question can only be said to be manifestly contrary to Community law if the error of law as to the sphere of application of the Treaty is manifestly wrong. The position in this regard taken by the United Kingdom in the *Factortame* proceedings was shared by other Member States, and although it was held to be wrong, it is seriously arguable that it was not manifestly wrong. I do not consider that the view of the United Kingdom authorities at the time was manifestly wrong. There was much doubt about the matter at the time. It is important to avoid the vice of hindsight.

After *Factortame III/Brasserie* came *British Telecom*.[24] This case was a variant on *Francovich*. Whereas the latter case involved the total failure to

[23] *Ibid.*, para. 61

[24] Case C–392/93 *R* v. *HM Treasury ex parte British Telecommunications plc* [1996] ECR I–1631; [1996] 2 CMLR 217.

implement a directive, *British Telecom* involved a *mis*implementation of a directive by the United Kingdom, which had adopted rules implementing a directive which in a certain respect failed properly to give effect to the directive. In *Francovich* the mere failure to implement attracted liability. Would the mere misimplementation of a directive equally attract liability, or would the manifest and grave disregard test developed in *Factortame III/Brasserie* apply? The Court adopted the latter solution. The Court does not quite justify this by saying that Member States enjoy a discretion in implementing directives (though Article 189 refers to the choice of means open to Member States in implementing directives). Rather, the Court, referring to its reasoning in *Factortame III/Brasserie*, and to the conditions applicable in circumstances where Member States enjoy a discretion in making legislative decisions, goes on to say:

> Those same conditions must be applicable to the situation, taken as its hypothesis by the national court, in which a Member State incorrectly transposes a Community directive into national law. A restrictive approach to State liability is justified in such a situation, for the reasons already given by the Court to justify the strict approach to non-contractual liability of Community institutions or Member States when exercising legislative actions in areas covered by Community law where the institution or State has a wide discretion—in particular, the concern to ensure that the exercise of legislative functions is not hindered by the prospect of actions for damages whenever the general interest requires the institutions or Member States to adopt measures which may adversely affect individual interests.[25]

The Court went on to exonerate the United Kingdom from liability for misimplementing the provision of the directive in question.

> In the present case [the provision in issue] is imprecisely worded and was reasonably capable of bearing, as well as the construction applied to it by the Court in this judgment, the interpretation given to it by the United Kingdom in good faith and on the basis of arguments which are not entirely devoid of substance . . . That interpretation, which was also shared by other Member States, was not manifestly contrary to the wording of the directive or to the objective pursued by it.[26]

This approach surely strikes the right balance between the legal protection of individuals and the leeway which must in a practical world be given to the law-maker.

The final case on damages to be treated in this chapter appears to adopt somewhat dubious reasoning. It is *Hedley Lomas*.[27] The facts may be briefly rehearsed. The plaintiff in the national proceedings was an exporter of sheep for slaughter to Spain. The United Kingdom Ministry of Agriculture

[25] *Ibid.*, at para. 40.

[26] *Ibid.*, at para. 43.

[27] Case C–5/94 *R* v. *Ministry of Agriculture, Fisheries and Food ex parte Hedley Lomas (Ireland) Ltd* [1996] ECR I–2553; [1996] 2 CMLR 391, [1997] QB 139.

Fisheries and Food refused to issue licences for the export to Spain of live animals for slaughter on the ground that their treatment in Spanish slaughterhouses was contrary to an EC Directive on stunning of animals before slaughter. The plaintiff sought damages before an English court for breach of Article 34 EC, which prohibits restrictions on exports. The English court referred certain questions to the Court of Justice on inter alia the extent to which the United Kingdom authorities could rely upon Article 36 EC (which allows derogation from Article 34 on various grounds including the welfare of animals) in circumstances where a harmonizing directive had made provision for the animal welfare, but the United Kingdom authorities considered that that directive was not being enforced in the Member State to which the animals were being exported. The Court held that recourse to Article 36 is no longer possible where Community directives provide for harmonization of the measures necessary to achieve the specific objectives which would be furthered by reliance upon that provision. I would note that this holding, while sound, does not but perhaps should refer to the difficulties of interpretation which arise in determining whether a harmonization directive is a measure of exclusive harmonization, leaving no scope for further unilateral action by Member States, or a measure of partial harmonization which does not exclude further unilateral action by Member States. The point is significant, since the Advocate General took the view that the Directive was a partial measure of harmonization and that recourse to Article 36 was not excluded. On the question of damages liability, the Court noted that where a Member State enjoyed a wide discretion, it would only be liable for a sufficiently serious breach of a rule of law for the protection of the individual. As regards the question of the seriousness of the breach in the case in point, the Court stated: 'where, at the time when it committed the infringement, the Member State in question was not called upon to make any legislative choices and had only considerably reduced, or even no, discretion, the mere infringement of Community law may be sufficient to establish the existence of a sufficiently serious breach.'[28]

The above formulation appears to express a corollary of a principle that in cases where a Member State has a wide discretion, a serious breach must be established to establish a basis for damages liability. The corollary is that if there is not a wide discretion, then it may not be necessary to establish a serious breach; the way the Court puts it is to say that if there is little or no discretion then the breach may per se be serious. But the difficulty arises in a case where a Member State proceeds, and proceeds reasonably, on the basis that it has a wide enough discretion for unilateral action, but is held to be wrong *as to the existence of the discretion*. In such a

[28] *Ibid.*, at para. 28.

case, according to *Lomas*, it seems that liability follows from the breach, and there is no room to argue that the error as to the existence of the discretion was an excusable error of law. The point is relevant in *Lomas* because the United Kingdom took the view, favoured by the Advocate General, that the directive in issue had not wholly excluded Member State competence, and that recourse could be had to Article 36 because the directive in question had not in fact been implemented in the Member State to which the animals had been exported. While these errors might not have been excusable, it would have been preferable to have decided the case on the basis that that the United Kingdom was manifestly wrong in thinking that it had competence to act, rather than on the basis that because the United Kingdom was in fact wrong about its competence to act, it had forfeited the right to argue the excusability of the errors of law which it had made. A well-founded, albeit wrong, assessment that a State enjoys a discretion to act consistently with Community law ought in principle to provide a defence to a damages action. Indeed, this latter approach seems more in line with that taken in *British Telecom*. If a justifiable error of law in implementing a directive is a good defence to an action for damages, why is not a justifiable error of law in taking action under Article 36 which furthers the animal welfare aims of an EC directive equally a good defence to a claim for damages? My objection to the reasoning in *Lomas* may be overcome if one emphasizes the word *may* in the Court's judgment—the mere infringement of Community law *may* be sufficient to establish a sufficiently serious breach where the Member State in question is not called upon to make any legislative choices and had only considerably reduced or even no discretion. In such a case it will be an up-hill struggle to show that an error is excusable, but the argument is not excluded. On that reading of *Lomas* I would be content.

Does the Court go too far in developing damages liability in *Factortame III/Brasserie* and the cases which followed? Germany thought so, and argued as much. The Court published the report for the hearing in *Factortame III/Brasserie* (the report is normally considered an internal document). The following summary of the position of the German government appears in the Report for the Hearing:

> . . . The German Government further states that an extension of Community law by judge-made law going beyond the bounds of the legitimate closure of lacunae would be incompatible with the division of competence between the Community institutions and the Member States laid down by the Treaty, and with the principle of the maintenance of institutional balance. The institutions having legislative competence, in particular the Council and the Parliament, cannot be excluded from the establishment of a general right to compensation, which requires democratic legitimisation. Furthermore, such a principle requires an alteration of the

Treaty entailing financial implications which also necessitate the consent of the national parliaments.[29]

The Court of Justice specifically responds to this challenge to its competence to declare the rights of individuals to secure compensation for breach of directly effective Community rights. The Court states:

Since the Treaty contains no provision expressly and specifically governing the consequences of breaches of Community law by Member States, it is for the Court, in pursuance of the task conferred on it by Article 164 of the Treaty of ensuring that in the interpretation and application of the Treaty the law is observed, to rule on such a question in accordance with generally accepted methods of interpretation, in particular by reference to the fundamental principles of the Community legal system and, where necessary, general principles common to the legal systems of the Member States.

. . .

The principle of the non-contractual liability of the Community expressly laid down in Article 215 of the Treaty is simply an expression of the general principle familiar to the legal systems of the Member States that an unlawful act or omission gives rise to an obligation to make good the damage caused. That provision also reflects the obligation on public authorities to make good damage caused in the performance of their duties. In any event, in many national legal systems the essentials of the legal rules governing State liability have been developed by the courts. . . [30]

To me, the Court's judgments in *Francovich* and *Factortame III/Brasserie* were bold, yet represent a principled and legitimate development of the law. They were bold in the way that *Donogue* v. *Stevenson* was bold. This case law of the Court, and the Court's legal method, should strike chords with the common lawyer. It is interesting to recall the defence of Lord Diplock in *Home Office* v. *Dorset Yacht Co. Ltd*[31] of the role of the judges in developing the law of tort (in a case, interestingly enough, which involved an extension of the liability of the State):

The justification of the courts' role in giving the effect of law to the judges' conception of the public interest in the field of negligence is based on the cumulative experience of the judiciary of the actual consequences of lack of care in particular instances.[32]

From such a perspective, the European Court is certainly well qualified to develop the law of State liability. It sees at first hand and in all shapes and forms the consequences of failure by the Member States to comply with Community law. The Article 177 procedure brings the European Court, by express invitation, into the thick of actions pending before the national

[29] Report for the Hearing, para. 32.
[30] *Ibid.*, paras. 27–30.
[31] [1970] AC 1004.
[32] *Ibid.*, p. 1058.

courts. As often as not the cause of action arises from the allegation that the State has failed to meet its responsibilities under Community law. The questions for the Court of Justice are in substance, does this or that party have a *right* in Community law, and if so must that right be given effective judicial protection? It is the instinct of judges, whether they sit on the Strand or in Luxembourg, to see that rights are protected by effective remedies. It is an instinct which should not in itself attract criticism and if that instinct continues to give impetus to a principled development of the law, on a case-by-case basis, then any alleged divergence between the 'European' method, and the common law method, may shrink to vanishing point.

7

Judicial Review and the Role of the English Court in European Community Disputes

BY CLIVE LEWIS, BARRISTER, 4/5 GRAY'S INN SQUARE, VISITING RESEARCH FELLOW, CENTRE OF EUROPEAN LAW, KING'S COLLEGE LONDON

Introduction

The requirements of European Community law have brought about changes in the way that the English courts carry out their tasks in the exercise of their judicial review jurisdiction and further changes may well be necessary. In judicial review, the English courts traditionally exercise a limited supervisory role over the actions of the administration to ensure that they act in accordance with the requirements of public law. The prime responsibility for exercising power and deciding what ought to be done lies with the administrative decision-maker. The courts are concerned with ensuring that a decision-maker properly interprets the law, does not infringe one of the recognized public law principles governing the exercise of discretionary power (such as not having regard to irrelevant matters or not rigidly fettering the exercise of a discretion) and follows a fair procedure in reaching a decision.[1] The courts also exercise a large measure of self-restraint in procedural terms. They rarely engage in fact-finding exercises in judicial review and usually proceed on the basis of affidavit evidence only (even if a question of precedent fact or other factual dispute arises). Cross-examination and discovery are rarely ordered.[2]

Many cases involving individuals or others relying on rights derived from Community law fall within the realm of judicial review as they involve challenges to the actions of public bodies. The traditional limits on the role of the court will, in certain circumstances, need to be modified in order to accommodate the requirements of European Community law. The English court will need to engage in a greater scrutiny of certain administrative decisions and legislation to ensure that they do not breach

[1] See, generally, the standard text books such as De Smith, Woolf and Jowell, *Judicial Review of Administrative Action* (1995) and Wade and Forsyth *Administrative Law* (1997).

[2] *R* v. *Secretary of State for the Environment ex p. Islington LBC*, The Independent, 6 Sept. 1991. See, generally, Lewis *Judicial Remedies in Public Law* (1992) at pp. 255–8.

the requirements of Community law. That in turn may involve the court changing its approach to procedure and evidence on judicial review.

The Role of the Domestic Court

In broad terms, the obligation on the domestic court is to ensure the full and effective protection of rights derived from Community law.[3] That obligation manifests itself, however, in a number of different ways. In some instances, the task of the judicial review court in a case with a European Community dimension will not differ in essence from its usual task. In one recent case,[4] for example, the question arose as to whether the Secretary of State could have regard to economic considerations, as well as ornithological criteria, in deciding whether to designate an area as a Special Protection Area for birds under the Birds Directive. That issue involved construing the Birds Directive to determine whether economic considerations were matters to which the Secretary of State could have regard. That is, in essence, very similar to one of the tasks usually performed by a judicial review court, namely, determining whether on a proper construction of the legislation conferring a discretionary power, a particular consideration is a relevant one which the decision-maker may take into account in deciding whether to exercise the power (albeit that construction of a directive may involve a different approach to construction of domestic legislation).

A court may also have to consider whether the provisions of primary legislation are compatible with Community law. Again this may involve no more than interpreting the domestic instrument and measuring it against the relevant Community instrument to determine if it is compatible with Community law. The essence of the exercise is one of the interpretation of a legal instrument and is similar to situations where the courts have to determine whether subordinate legislation is *ultra vires* any domestic legislation. The principles of interpretation that the courts apply may differ, for example, because national courts are under an obligation to attempt to interpret national law wherever possible to accord with Community law. Furthermore, the fact that the English courts are engaging in the exercise of reviewing legislation and may have to disapply legislative provisions which restrict the enforcement of directly effective Community law rights is, of course, an entirely novel constitutional development. The consequences of review are in the process of being worked out, for example, whether the courts may grant a declaration that a provi-

[3] Case C–213/89 *R* v. *Secretary of State for Transport ex p. Factortame (No 2)* [1991] ECR I–3905 ; Joined Cases C–6/90 and C–9/90 *Francovich* v. *Italian Republic* [1991] ECR I–5357. See generally Lewis *Remedies and the Enforcement of European Community Law* (1996), ch. 5.

[4] Case C–44/95 *R* v. *Secretary of State for the Environment ex p. Royal Society for the Protection of Birds* [1997] 2 WLR 123.

sion of national law is incompatible with Community law in a case involving applicants without directly effective rights.[4a] The actual intellectual exercise in which the courts are engaged does not, however, place undue strain on the traditional English approach to judicial review.

There are instances where it has been argued that the role of the court goes further than merely reviewing to ensure that the legislation is compatible with Community law or that a decision-maker has complied with his obligations. It is sometimes argued that the court must itself take the substantive decision and exercise the relevant discretion or perform the task required by the Community instrument. The issue usually arises in the following way. Community law may confer responsibility for a particular task on the competent national authority. That may be an administrative authority. It will, of course, have to ensure that it properly interprets the relevant Community law and acts in accordance with it. Its actions will be subject to judicial review if it does not. Subject to that, the exercise of the discretion ought to be left to that body which is, under national law, the competent authority. Thus, the Directive on medicinal products requires such products to be authorized by the competent authority of the Member State (the Licensing Authority in England). The Directive sets out the various requirements that the product must satisfy in order to be licensed. The competent authorities are required to revoke an authorization if it proves harmful or therapeutic efficiency is lacking or in other specified circumstances but cannot revoke except on the grounds set out in the Directive. That system clearly places primary responsibility for taking the decision to revoke on the administrative authorities (subject always to judicial review by the courts to control the interpretation of the directive and observance of other relevant Community principles). The court would not be responsible for deciding whether the decision is correct or incorrect on its merits (i.e., whether the product is harmful or lacks therapeutic efficiency). The Divisional Court so interpreted the respective role of the court and the licensing authority in *Upjohn* v. *Licensing Authority*. The Court of Appeal, however, considered that it was arguable that on a true construction of the Directive, a person had a right to place a product on the market and could not have its authorization refused or revoked unless it was demonstrated objectively to the satisfaction of national court that a ground of revocation was made out. It was not enough for the competent authority to have been satisfied even if it had made no error of law in its decision. As the Directive had direct effect, no law of the Member State (including the principles limiting the role of the court in judicial review) could restrict the power and duty of the courts to investigate whether the decision of the licensing authority was or was not objectively correct. Consequently, the Court of Appeal referred various questions to the European Court of Justice to determine whether the national

[4a] See *R.* v. *H. M. Treasury ex p. Shepherd Neame Ltd* The Times, February 2, 1998

court was obliged to decide whether the decision to revoke was correct.[5] With respect, that decision appears not to distinguish adequately between the principle of direct effect and the construction of the Directive. Direct effect means that the rights conferred by a Community instrument may be relied upon and enforced in a national court. The scope and content of the rights are derived from the Community instrument itself. If the instrument confers responsibility on a competent authority (which may be a national administrative authority) then the substantive decisions are for that competent authority (subject to acting in accordance with Community law properly interpreted). Direct effect is not a means of transferring the substantive decision from the competent authority to the courts: it is a means of ensuring that the rights conferred by the Directive are respected by the competent authority (and policed, where and to the extent necessary, by the courts).

Real difficulties, however, arise in other areas. Community law may impose prohibitions or confer rights on individuals but the prohibition or right may not be absolute or unqualified. Member States may be permitted to derogate from the prohibition or obligation in specified circumstances and subject to normal Community principles such as proportionality and observing fundamental human rights. The classic examples are Article 30 to 36 and Article 119 of the Treaty of Rome. Article 30 prohibits quantitative restrictions on imports and measures having an equivalent effect. Article 36 permits the imposition of restrictions on certain specified grounds. Further, Article 30 may apply to national provisions which affect both domestic and imported goods, unless the national measure pursues a legitimate objective, justifiable under Community and is proportionate in that it does not impose greater restrictions than necessary to achieve that legitimate aim.[6] Article 119 guarantees equal pay for equal work and legislative provisions which derogate from that are only permissible if they are based on objectively justified grounds unrelated to discrimination on grounds of sex and the measures correspond to a necessary aim of its social policy and are suitable and requisite for achieving that aim. It is in these areas where the basic decision lies with the legislature or the decision-maker but where that decision is subject to greater scrutiny than would be usual in a purely domestic law judicial review that the courts have had to adapt their role to the requirements of Community law.

The Approach of the Courts

The English courts considering whether action is a permissible derogation from Community law will normally have to engage in the following tasks. First, it must identify the aim of the domestic legislation. That will nor-

[5] *Upjohn Limited* v. *The Licensing Authority* unreported 26 Oct. 1995 (leave to appeal has been refused by the House of Lords).

[6] See, e.g., Case 145/88 *Torfaen Borough Council* v. *B & Q* [1989] ECR 3851.

mally involve consideration of the domestic statute to determine, from its terms, what its aims were. In addition, it may be necessary to adduce evidence indicating the mischiefs which the legislation was introduced.[7] This may include committee reports or other reports by commissions prepared as a prelude to the introduction of the legislation.[8] It is unclear whether the courts would permit the use of extracts from Hansard setting out the speeches made during the parliamentary debate. The court will have regard to ministerial statements made when laying draft regulations before Parliament which are intended to meet Community law obligations.[9] It is uncertain whether the court will use such material for the broader purpose of determining what were the aims of the legislation.[10]

Having determined what are the aims of the domestic legislation, the English court can then consider whether the aims are ones permitted under Community law. This may involve deciding whether the aim falls within an express derogation such as Article 36 or whether it is a legitimate aim recognized by the European Court as one that is capable of being pursued by a Member State. That may involve referring the question of whether Community law permits acting for that purpose to the European Court or the national court may seek to answer the question itself. In *R* v. *Coventry City Council ex p. Phoenix Aviation*,[11] for example, the Divisional Court ruled that a decision to prohibit exporters of veal calves from using a local authority owned airport to export veal (which may have been in breach in Article 34 of the Treaty of Rome) could not be justified on the grounds that to allow such exports might result in fierce protests and resulting public order and security problems. The court ruled that such considerations did not fall within the 'public order' exception in Article 36.

Secondly, the national court will normally have to consider questions of proportionality. This is a much more complex task. The precise scope of the proportionality requirement and the degree of scrutiny required may differ depending on the context. There is some indication, for example, that in areas legitimately regarded as social policy matters for the Member States, it has a broad margin of discretion in choosing the measures capable of achieving that aim. In other areas, involving fundamental Community principles, the Member State may have less room for manoeuvre.

The concept of such review is relatively novel in England. It raises issues as to the correct approach to be adopted and as to the evidence required or

[7] *R* v. *Goldstein* [1983] 1 WLR 151, p. 155.

[8] *Fothergill* v. *Monarch Airlines* [1980] 2 All ER 696, p. 706.

[9] *Pickstone* v. *Freemans plc* [1989] AC 66.

[10] See dicta of Hoffman J at first instance in *Stoke-on-Trent CC* v. *B & Q plc* [1991] 1 Ch. 48. See also, the decision in the House of Lords in *Melluish* v. *BMI No (3)* [1994] 3 WLR 1032 which seeks to restrict the use of Hansard, although that case did not involve any Community law dimension.

[11] [1995] 3 All ER 66.

permissible in reaching such decisions. In one case,[11a] Hoffman J considered the proper test for review in cases involving questions of whether legislation adopted for an aim recognized by the European Court as legitimate was also proportionate. There he was considering whether legislation prohibiting trading on Sunday (an acceptable social and cultural aim[12]) was disproportionate in that its effects on trade exceeded what was necessary to achieve that aim. He considered that this involved balancing competing interests which was primarily a matter for the legislature and the role of the court was limited to determining whether the view reached was one that a legislature could reasonably hold. He concluded that the duty of the court was only to inquire whether the legislative compromise was one that a reasonable legislature could adopt. At that stage in the development of Community law, that test, and in particular the language used to describe the test, would not have been appropriate. In questions of proportionality, the court has to determine whether the measure adopted is suitable and necessary. The generally accepted view was that this required the court itself to make some assessment of the relationship between the effects of the measure, the aim to be achieved, and the possibility of the use of other, less restrictive measures. Member States may have a broad measure of discretion as to the choices to be made and that may influence the national court both in terms of its assessment of proportionality and the type of evidence it considered was necessary to justify a measure but it is unlikely to remove the obligation of the court to make its own assessment. The Advocate General in *Stoke-on-Trent*[13] expressly criticized the test adopted by Hoffman J and indicated that the court could not automatically accept the view of the legislature nor limit itself simply to considering the reasonableness of the legislative choice. The House of Lords, which had referred the matter to the European Court, had asked on what criteria and by reference to what factual or other evidence the courts were to assess the question of proportionality in the context of Sunday trading. The European Court considered that it did not need to answer that question as the European Court had itself decided that limits on Sunday trading were not incompatible with Community law.[14] Since that decision, however, the European Court has indicated that a more relaxed degree of judicial scrutiny might be suitable, at least in certain fields, as discussed below.

[11a] *Stoke-on-Trent* v. *B & Q plc* [1991] Ch 48 for a similarly relaxed approach in the context of administrative decisions, see *R.* v. *Chief Cunstable of Sussex ex p. ITF* [1997] 3 WLR 132 now on appeal to the House of Lords.

[12] See case 145/88 *Torfaen Borough Council* v. *B & Q* [1989] ECR 3851.

[13] Case C–169/91 *Stoke-on-Trent* v. *B & Q plc* [1993] AC 900, p. 939, para. 27.

[14] *Ibid.*, and see its earlier decisions in case C–312/89 *Conforama* [1991] ECR I–997; Case C–332/89 *Marchandise* [1991] ECR I–1027.

The House of Lords returned to the difficult question of the role of the court in *R* v. *Secretary of State for Employment ex p. Equal Opportunities Commission*.[15] There, the House of Lords had to consider legislation laying down different qualifying requirements for eligibility for certain employment rights for part-time and full-time workers. Part-time workers working less than 16 hours a week had to work for five years whereas those who worked more than 16 hours a week only had to work for two years in order to be able to claim a right not to be dismissed unfairly and a right to redundancy pay. The greater majority of workers working more than 16 hours a week were men and the greater majority working for less than 16 hours were women. The legislation was therefore indirectly discriminatory unless it could be objectively justified on grounds other than sex. The House of Lords considered that the question was whether the means chosen to meet the policy were suitable and requisite for achieving that aim. They pointed out that the original justification for the rule was that part-time workers were less committed than full-time workers and that the purpose was to ensure that the legislation struck a 'fair balance' between the rights of employees and employers. Those justifications had been abandoned by the time the matter came to court. The justification then advanced was that the legislation sought to increase the availability of part-time work which was a beneficial social aim. The House considered the suitability of the legislation and whether it was requisite to achieve the aim. As to suitability, the House of Lords was able to deal with that by reasoning alone. The legislation was said to be suitable because it reduced the cost of employing part-time workers; that could not be considered a suitable measure as a matter of law as a similar result could follow from paying a lower hourly rate to part-time workers which was normally a breach of the principle of equal pay. In considering whether the legislation was 'requisite', the House had regard to the affidavit evidence filed for the Secretary of State but that was said not to include any factual material demonstrating the correctness of the Department's views that differing qualifying threshold for part-timers led to more part-time work. The House also considered the applicant's evidence which consisted largely of one report from the House of Commons and one from the House of Lords which revealed there was a diversity of view as to the effect of different qualifying thresholds on part-time employment. They also considered statistics from other Community countries on part-time employment where there were no thresholds. The House concluded that, on the material before them, there was no objective justification for the different thresholds and ruled that the national legislation in question was incompatible with Community law.

[15] [1995] 1 AC 1.

The *EOC* provides a useful example of the kind of scrutiny that may be necessary in determining the compatibility of legislation although a number of difficult and important questions remain. The case is a reminder to any department sponsoring legislation of the need to offer, at the very least, some form of evidence capable of justifying the legislation. Part of the difficulties faced by the Department in the *EOC* case appeared to stem from the fact that the original justification for the legislation had changed and either there was no material supporting the new justification, or if there was, it was not produced. In purely domestic judicial review, this may not be a problem. It is recognized that Parliament is supreme and the courts would not begin to question the reasons or the justification for legislation. In the case of administrative decisions, the courts will normally only consider whether the view that the decision-maker has taken is irrational and whether there was some material before the decision-maker on which he could base his decision. The court will not go beyond that to inquire into questions of justification and may be (and often is) satisfied by even relatively limited evidence. In policy matters, the courts would normally accept a priori reasoning as to the desirability of a particular course of action and would not normally consider the need for factual or other evidence. In cases with a European Community dimension, the respondent department will, in the light of the *EOC* judgment, need to give consideration to placing material before the court justifying its conclusion. The range of such material could, of course, be quite wide depending on the subject matter. It is not difficult to envisage questionnaires, statistical evidence, expert reports and comparisons with other countries all featuring in affidavit evidence. Another difficulty, not yet considered by the courts, is whether it should order discovery, so that documents indicating that the proposed legislation or course of action will not necessarily achieve the relevant aims should be disclosed. In general, the English courts are reluctant to order discovery in judicial review cases and, in relation to particular documents (such as advice from civil service or cabinet papers[16]), such documents may be protected from disclosure by public interest immunity. It is not difficult to envisage a situation where an applicant will argue that, unless he can obtain access to particular documents, neither he nor the court will be able properly to determine whether the United Kingdom is acting in accordance with Community law and, therefore, any rule or practice of national law restricting or preventing the disclosure of certain information is contrary to Community law. The fate of such a claim before the English courts and the European Court of Justice is difficult to predict.

[16] See, e.g., *Air Canada* v. *Secretary of State for Trade and Industry (No 2)* [1983] 2 AC 394; *Burmah Oil Co Ltd* v. *Governor and Co. of the Bank of England* [1980] AC 1090.

The question remains as to whether there are any instances where no 'evidence' in the sense of factual material needs to be adduced to justify legislation which, prima facie would conflict with Community law unless it pursued a legitimate aim and was proportionate. The *EOC* case makes an interesting contrast with the subsequent decisions of the European Court in *Nolte*[17] and *Megner*.[18] There, German social security legislation excluded part-time workers from the social security system. This meant that they did not qualify for certain benefits and employers did not have to pay contributions in respect of such workers. The German government relied, inter alia, upon social policy and employment policy aims. The social policy aims appeared to include the fact that the present scheme was predicated on exclusion from benefits together with exemption for employers from paying contributions and, if benefits had to be paid, the social security scheme in its present form (with no contributions being paid) could not operate. The employment policy aims arose from the fact that exemption from contributions for employers was attractive and if this financial advantage were withdrawn, there might be a loss of full-time or part-time jobs. Further, the German government argued that there might be an increase in unlawful employment and a rise in circumventing devices (such as falsely claiming that persons were self-employed). The European Court observed that in the current state of Community law, social policy was a matter for the Member States. Consequently, it was for Member States to choose the measures capable of achieving the aim of their social and employment policy and in exercising that competence, the Member States have a broad margin of discretion. The European Court then noted that the social and policy aim relied upon were unrelated to sex and 'the national legislature was reasonably entitled to consider that the legislation in question was necessary in order to achieve that aim'.

The *Nolte* and *Megner* decisions certainly lay greater emphasis on the broad scope of legislative discretion. The European Court appeared prepared to proceed on the basis of a priori reasoning as to whether the justifications advanced by the German government were acceptable, rather than scrutinizing the evidence for such justifications. The cases of course, came to the European Court by way of Article 177 references for a preliminary ruling. The European Court does not exercise a fact-finding jurisdiction in Article 177 cases. Nevertheless, the European Court did rule that the measures were not discriminatory because the legislature was reasonably entitled to consider that the legislation was necessary to achieve a social policy aim. In that respect, the European Court appeared to go beyond its normal role on Article 177 references of answering the

[17] Case C–317/93 *Nolte* v. *Landesversicherunganstalt Hannover* [1996] IRLR 325.

[18] Case C–444/93 *Megner and Scheffel* v. *Innungkrankenkasse Vorderpfalz* [1996] IRLR 236.

questions of European Community law and leaving the national court to apply these to the facts as found by it. The European Court appears to have assumed the task of adjudicating on compatibility from the information before it. In that case, there must be a strong argument that national courts faced with similar problems are entitled to adopt a similar approach and proceed on the basis of simply assessing whether the legislature was reasonably entitled to take the view it did.

It is, as yet, uncertain whether the *Nolte* and *Megner* decisions represent a significant departure in terms of the role of the courts in considering questions of compatibility of national legislation and Community law. In particular, it is unclear whether the decision is limited to considering objective justification in the context of indirectly discriminatory legislation or whether it applies generally in any area where there is a question of assessing proportionality. It is likely to apply only to legislative measures and it is not likely to apply to other types of administrative measures such as individual decisions or policy decisions short of legislation. It is, however, too early to predict whether these cases represent a more relaxed approach to judicial scrutiny of national legislation applicable generally to cases involving questions of justification or proportionality or whether they are (or will be) limited in some way.

Criminal Matters

Particular problems have arisen in the context of criminal legislation which is alleged to be incompatible with Community law. Such matters will come before the magistrates court or the Crown Court. One problem here is that the prosecutors would rarely have access to all the relevant material and evidence to put before the court in relation to enable it to determine in any full sense whether the legislation is compatible and in particular whether the measure goes further than is necessary to meet its aims. There is the prospect of an appeal by way of case stated (from the magistrates court, or from a Crown Court following an appeal to that court).[19] The case-stated procedure involves the court simply stating the facts as found by it. It would not normally record the evidence. Even if it did, that would not solve which arises when the lower court has not been given the sort of information that the relevant department of state would provide if it were a party to the proceedings. There is a real need to find some way in which there could be co-operation between the lower criminal courts and the High Court to enable an authoritative ruling, based on

[19] There is an appeal from the Crown Court to the Court of Appeal (Criminal Division) in a case first tried on indictment before the Crown Court. There may be a greater chance that, if relevant evidence was produced, it would be recorded or otherwise available on an appeal. The difficulty is often that the prosecutor would not have had access to the evidence in the first place.

all relevant evidence, to be obtained in a case where there is a serious issue as to the compatibility of national law with Community law. One obvious model would be to develop a sort of domestic 'reference for a preliminary ruling'. A magistrates court could refer the question of compatibility to the High Court which could join as a party the relevant sponsoring department and give directions as to the filing of evidence. It would then give one ruling on the compatibility question. Such a system would also have the merit that, in practice, criminal courts throughout the country would rely on such a ruling and would not normally seek to depart from it and determine for themselves whether the legislation was compatible.

PART B

General Principles of Community Law in English Courts

8

Interpretation and Precedent in European Community Law

BY ANTHONY ARNULL, WRAGGE PROFESSOR OF EUROPEAN LAW, UNIVERSITY OF BIRMINGHAM*

Statutory interpretation and precedent are the poor relations of the English legal curriculum, all too often taken for granted or dismissed as dull and uninspiring. Those attitudes are doubly unjustified when it comes to Community law, for in that context both subjects take on a special interest for English lawyers.[1] That is because the approach of the Community Courts[2] to these matters differs in several major respects from that of most courts in the common law world.

Methods of Interpretation

Let us look first at the methods of interpretation employed by the Community Courts.[3] In its White Paper issued on the eve of the 1996 intergovernmental conference, the UK government observed: 'There is concern that the ECJ's interpretation of laws sometimes seems to go beyond what the participating Governments intended in framing these laws.'[4] That observation echoes a comment by the Warden of All Souls College, Oxford, Sir Patrick Neill QC: 'The methods of interpretation adopted by the ECJ appear to have liberated the Court from the customarily accepted discipline of endeavouring by textual analysis to ascertain the meaning of the language of the relevant provision.'[5] To what extent is the criticism implicit in those remarks justified?

* This is a revised version of the paper I presented at the conference at King's College, London on 6 July 1996. I am grateful to those who took part in that conference, to my colleague Jeremy McBride and to Professor John Usher for their comments on some of the issues discussed. The usual disclaimer applies.

[1] For useful introductions, see Manchester, Salter, Moodie, and Lynch, *Exploring the Law: The Dynamics of Precedent and Statutory Interpretation* (1996), pp. 68–112; Weatherill and Beaumont, *EC Law* (2nd ed., 1995), pp. 166–84.

[2] That is, the European Court of Justice (ECJ) and the Court of First Instance (CFI).

[3] The approach of the English courts to the interpretation of Community provisions, or of national provisions with Community antecedents, will be touched on only briefly.

[4] 'A Partnership of Nations' (Cm 3181), para. 37.

[5] See 'The European Court of Justice: a case study in judicial activism', a memorandum submitted to the House of Lords Select Committee on the European Communities (HL Paper 88, Session 1994–5, 18th Report), p. 218 at p. 244.

(i) General Considerations

In order to form an objective assessment of the Court's methods of interpretation, it is necessary to take account of 'the characteristic features of Community law and the particular difficulties to which its interpretation gives rise,' as the Court itself put it in *CILFIT* v. *Ministry of Health*.[6] In that case, the Court underlined three features in particular:

(a) Community legislation is drafted in several languages. The different language versions are all equally authentic and may have to be compared;
(b) Community law uses terminology which is peculiar to it. Legal concepts do not necessarily have the same meaning in Community law as in the laws of the Member States;
(c) every provision of Community law must be placed in its context and interpreted in the light of the provisions of Community law as a whole. Regard must be had to the objectives of Community law and to its present state of development.

This does not mean that the Court takes no account of the wording of the provision it is called upon to interpret. Sometimes the Court will conclude that the ordinary meaning of the words used can be applied. In *Marshall I*[7] and *Faccini Dori*,[8] for example, the Court said that directives were not binding on individuals because Article 189 of the Treaty, which describes the characteristics of the legislative acts which the political institutions are empowered to adopt, only says that they are binding on Member States. In *Netherlands* v. *Reed*,[9] the Court said that Article 10(1) of Regulation 1612/68, which confers on the 'spouse' of a migrant worker the right to install him or herself in the territory of the host State, did not extend to unmarried partners.

But there are two reasons why the wording cannot always be treated as decisive. One, mentioned by the Court in *CILFIT*, is the multi-lingual nature of Community law. In *R* v. *Bouchereau*, that factor was overlooked by the UK government when it sought to rely on the use of the same term in the English text of separate provisions of a Community directive. The Court observed:[10] 'A comparison of the different language versions of the

[6] Case 283/81 [1982] ECR 3415, paras. 17–20.

[7] Case 152/84 [1986] ECR 723.

[8] Case C–91/92 [1994] ECR I–3325. See also Case C–192/94 *El Corte Inglés* v. *Blásquez Rivero* [1996] ECR I–1281.

[9] Case 59/85 [1986] ECR 1283.

[10] Case 30/77 [1977] ECR 1999, para 13. See also Case 29/69 *Stauder* v. *Ulm* [1969] ECR 419; Case 9/79 *Koschniske* v. *Raad van Arbeid* [1979] ECR 2717. More recent judgments in which reference is made to different language versions of a provision include Case C–298/94 *Henke* v. *Gemeinde Schierke*, judgment of 15 Oct. 1996; Joined Cases C–283/94, C–291/94 and C–292/94 *Denkavit and Others* v. *Bundesamt für Finanzen*, judgment of 17 Oct. 1996; Case C–64/95 *Lubella* v. *Hauptzollamt Cottbus*, judgment of 17 Oct. 1996; Case C–72/95 *Kraaijeveld* v. *Gedeputeerde*

provisions in question shows that with the exception of the Italian text all the other versions use different terms in each of the two articles, with the result that no legal consequences can be based on the terminology used.'

Another reason why a literal approach is often inappropriate concerns the way in which many Community provisions are drafted. Lord Denning put the point with his usual clarity in *Bulmer Ltd* v. *Bollinger SA*.[11] The Treaty, he said,

> lays down general principles. It expresses its aims and purposes. All in sentences of moderate length and commendable style. But it lacks precision. It uses words and phrases without defining what they mean. An English lawyer would look for an interpretation clause, but he would look in vain. There is none. All the way through the Treaty there are gaps and lacunae. These have to be filled in by the judges, or by Regulations or directives. It is the European way . . . Likewise the Regulations and directives.

The point was reiterated by Bingham J (as he then was) in *Customs and Excise* v. *ApS Samex*:[12] 'The interpretation of Community instruments involves very often not the process familiar to common lawyers of laboriously extracting the meaning from words used but the more creative process of applying flesh to a spare and loosely constructed skeleton.'

Thus, depending on the circumstances, the Court may give priority to factors other than language, such as the objectives of the provision concerned (so-called 'teleological interpretation') and its legal context. These factors were treated as decisive in *Bouchereau*,[13] where the Court declared: 'The different language versions of a Community text must be given a uniform interpretation and hence in the case of divergence between the versions the provision in question must be interpreted by reference to the purpose and general scheme of the rules of which it forms a part.'

In the case of provisions contained in the Treaty, the teleological method is facilitated by its preamble and opening provisions, which set out the principles on which the system it establishes is based. The body of the Treaty is also peppered with articles explaining the purpose of more detailed provisions.[14] As for Community acts, these are required by Article 190 of the Treaty to 'state the reasons on which they are based'. 'So they start off with pages of preambles, "whereas" and "whereas" and "whereas" ', as Lord Denning put it in *Bulmer* v. *Bollinger*.[15] It therefore comes as no surprise to find that the Court has made extensive use of the teleological and contextual approaches, not only to resolve divergences between different language versions but also to confirm interpretations

Staten van Zuid-Holland, judgment of 24 Oct. 1996; Joined Cases C–267/95 and C–268/95 *Merck and Others* v. *Primecrown and Others*, judgment of 5 Dec. 1996.

[11] [1974] Ch 401, 425.

[12] [1983] 1 All ER 1042, 1056.

[13] *Supra*, para. 14. See also *Primecrown*, *supra*, para. 22.

[14] See e.g., Arts. 39, 110, and 117 EC.

[15] *Supra*, p. 426.

suggested by the wording,[16] to clarify ambiguity and to fill in gaps in the legal framework. It would be quite wrong to suggest that the Court pursues some hidden agenda of its own in its approach to questions of interpretation. If there is an agenda pursued by the Court, it is one set by the authors of the Treaties and by the Community legislature.

(ii) Interpreting the Treaty

A good illustration of the methods employed by the Court is the famous *Van Gend en Loos* case.[17] There the Court was asked whether Article 12 of the Treaty, which concerns the elimination of customs duties between Member States, might have direct effect, that is, confer rights on individuals which the national courts had to uphold. The Treaty is silent on the question of its relationship with domestic law. In order to resolve that question, the Court therefore said it was 'necessary to consider the spirit, the general scheme and the wording' of the Treaty.[18] As to its spirit, the Court inferred that the objective of the Treaty was to create 'a new legal order of international law for the benefit of which the states have limited their sovereign rights . . . and the subjects of which comprise not only Member States but also their nationals.' Turning to the general scheme of the Treaty, the Court observed that an essential element of the customs union on which the Community was based was the prohibition of customs duties and charges having equivalent effect. That prohibition was laid down in a part of the Treaty entitled 'Foundations of the Community'.[19] As for the wording of Article 12, the Court pointed out that it contained 'a clear and unconditional prohibition' which was not qualified by any reservation making its implementation dependent on national legislation. The Court therefore concluded that 'Article 12 must be interpreted as producing direct effects and creating rights which national courts must protect.'

The contrary view, that the effect of the Treaty in the national legal systems should have been left to depend on the constitutional law of the country concerned, would have fatally undermined the common market. Had the effect of the Treaty been determined by national law, it would have had direct effect in some States but not in others. It is plain that the common market could not have functioned properly on that basis. This

[16] See e.g., Case C–260/90 *Leplat* [1992] ECR I–643; Case C–84/95 *Bosphorus Hava Yollari AS* v. *Minister for Transport, Energy and Communications, Ireland* [1996] 3 CMLR 257.

[17] Case 26/62 [1963] ECR 1.

[18] Cf. Case 53/81 *Levin* [1982] ECR 1035, para. 9, where the Court said that, in order to determine the meaning of two terms which had not been expressly defined, it was appropriate 'to have recourse to the generally recognized principles of interpretation, beginning with the ordinary meaning to be attributed to those terms in their context and in the light of the objectives of the Treaty.'

[19] The Treaty no longer contains a part with that title. Art 12 is now to be found in Title I of Part Three, which is entitled 'Community Policies'. This does not reflect any diminution in its importance.

was acknowledged in *Costa* v. *ENEL*,[20] where the Court made explicit what was implicit in *Van Gend en Loos*, namely that Community law took precedence over inconsistent provisions of national law. The Court observed that 'the law stemming from the Treaty, an independent source of law, could not, because of its special and original nature, be overridden by domestic legal provisions, however framed, without being deprived of its character as Community law *and without the legal basis of the Community itself being called into question*' (emphasis added).

In *Van Gend en Loos*, the Treaty was silent on the question the Court had been called upon to resolve. A case in which the natural meaning of an express provision of the Treaty was overridden on the basis of pressing contextual and teleological considerations is *Foto-Frost* v. *Hauptzollamt Lübeck-Ost*.[21] There the Court held that national courts have no jurisdiction to declare acts of the Community institutions invalid, even though the terms of Article 177 EC might have suggested the contrary. The Court emphasized that the purpose of that article was to ensure that Community law was applied uniformly by national courts. The requirement of uniformity, it said, was 'particularly imperative when the validity of a Community act is in question. Divergences between courts in the Member States as to the validity of Community acts would be liable to place in jeopardy the very unity of the Community legal order and detract from the fundamental requirement of legal certainty.'

That conclusion, based on the objectives of the preliminary rulings procedure, was supported by the system of judicial protection established by the Treaty. The preliminary rulings procedure, along with the action for annulment, constituted a means of reviewing the legality of acts of the Community institutions. Since the Court had exclusive jurisdiction in annulment proceedings to declare such acts void, 'the coherence of the system requires that where the validity of a Community act is challenged before a national court the power to declare the act invalid must also be reserved to the Court of Justice.'[22] The Court evidently took the view that the opposite result would have been so damaging to the Community system that it could be produced only by language a good deal clearer than that of Article 177.

Both *Van Gend en Loos* and *Foto-Frost* also illustrate the Court's general aversion to *a contrario* reasoning to resolve questions of interpretation.[23] In

[20] Case 6/64 [1964] ECR 585, 594.

[21] Case 314/85 [1987] ECR 4199, paras. 16–17. See also Case 294/83 *Les Verts* v. *Parliament* [1986] ECR 1339.

[22] This rule is relaxed where the national court is asked for interim relief: see Joined Cases C–143/88 and C–92/89 *Zuckerfabrik Süderditmarschen* v. *Hauptzollamt Itzehoe* [1991] ECR I–415; Case C–465/93 *Atlanta Fruchthandelsgesellschaft I* [1995] ECR I–3761, discussed further below.

[23] This is one of the reasons why the Court's reasoning in *Faccini Dori*, *supra*, is widely considered unconvincing.

the former, the Court rejected the view that the fact that Article 12 only expressly imposed an obligation on the Member States in any way implied that their nationals could not benefit from that obligation.[24] In the latter, the Court refused to accept that, because Article 177 enabled national courts (other than those of last resort) to refer to the Court of Justice questions on the validity of Community acts, it had settled the question whether such courts could themselves declare Community acts invalid.

(iii) Methods of Interpretation in Public International Law

It would be a mistake to think that the Court's approach to the interpretation of the Treaty is especially unorthodox. According to Article 31(1) of the Vienna Convention on the Law of Treaties, '[a] treaty shall be interpreted in good faith in accordance with the ordinary meaning to be given to the terms of the treaty in their context and in the light of its object and purpose.' That is not a bad summary of its approach in the cases mentioned above. Article 31 of the Vienna Convention was mentioned by the Court in its first Opinion[25] on the compatibility with the Treaty of the draft agreement establishing a so-called European Economic Area (or EEA) extending certain provisions of Community law to the EFTA States and to Liechtenstein. It was the intention of the authors of the agreement that its substantive provisions should be interpreted and applied in the same way as the corresponding provisions of Community law. To that end, identical language had where possible been used. However, the Court pointed out that this was not in itself enough: 'The fact that the provisions of the agreement and the corresponding Community provisions are identically worded does not mean that they must necessarily be interpreted identically.'[26] Referring to the Vienna Convention, the Court noted that the objectives of the Community and the context in which they were pursued differed from those of the agreement, which merely created rights and obligations between the Contracting Parties and did not provide for the transfer of sovereign rights. It followed, the Court said, 'that homogeneity of the rules of law throughout the EEA is not secured by the fact that the provisions of Community law and . . . the corresponding provisions of the agreement are identical in their content or wording.'[27] There could be no clearer illustration[28] of the importance attached by the Court to the objectives and context of a provision in establishing what it means.

As a supplementary means of interpretation, Article 32 of the Vienna Convention envisages recourse to the preparatory work (or *travaux*

[24] See also Case 43/75 *Defrenne* v. *SABENA* [1976] ECR 455, para 31.

[25] Opinion 1/91 [1991] ECR I–6079. [26] Para. 14. [27] Para. 22.

[28] See also Case 270/80 *Polydor* v. *Harlequin Record Shops* [1982] ECR 329; Case 104/81 *Hauptzollamt Mainz* v. *Kupferberg* [1982] ECR 3641. Cf. Case C–163/90 *Administration des Douanes et Droits Indirects* v. *Legros and Others* [1992] ECR I–4625.

préparatoires) of a treaty in order to confirm the meaning resulting from the application of Article 31 or remove ambiguity or absurdity. This is not a method which has commended itself to the European Court of Justice. As H Kutscher, formerly a Judge at the Court, has explained:[29]

> The Court cannot rely on preparatory work which provides a history of how the Treaties came into being. In so far as any such preparatory work exists at all—essential questions were obviously only discussed and decided within working groups—it has in any case not been published. Documents which are not generally accessible must, however, be ruled out as aids to interpretation for constitutional reasons.

Some *travaux préparatoires* concerning the Treaties have found their way into the public domain, but only via unofficial avenues. This is a further factor which would seem to preclude reliance on them by the Court. In any event, it has been observed that 'Resort to *travaux préparatoires* seems inappropriate in respect of the Treaties, because their authors set in motion a process of economic and political integration whose course and outcome could not be foreseen in detail.'[30]

It is sometimes suggested that the interests of the Member States are accorded less weight in European Community law than in public international law. In a memorandum on the European Court of Justice submitted to the intergovernmental conference by the United Kingdom in July 1996, it was even proposed that a protocol should be added to the EC Treaty providing that 'when faced with more than one possible interpretation of provisions of Community law, the Court shall, unless there is a clear contrary intention, prefer the interpretation which least constrains the freedom of the Member States.' The philosophy underlying that proposal is not rigidly adhered to in public international law and is incompatible with the very nature of the Community legal order, which the Court has said entails a limitation of the sovereign rights of the Member States and whose beneficiaries include individuals.[31] Moreover, it underestimates the extent to which the Court has sought in appropriate cases to protect the interests of the Member States.[32] If there is any truth in the suggestion that it gives those interests less weight than other international

[29] See 'Methods of interpretation as seen by a judge at the Court of Justice' in Reports of a Judicial and Academic Conference (Luxembourg 1976), p. I–21.

[30] Wyatt and Dashwood, *The Substantive Law of the EEC* (2nd ed., 1987), p. 93. See also Brown and Kennedy, *The Court of Justice of the European Communities* (4th ed., 1994), pp. 307–11.

[31] See the *Van Gend en Loos* case and Opinion 1/91, *supra*.

[32] See e.g., Opinion 1/94 on the World Trade Organisation [1994] ECR I–5267; Opinion 2/92 on the Third Revised Decision of the OECD on national treatment [1995] ECR I–521; Opinion 2/94 on the accession of the Community to the European Convention on Human Rights [1996] ECR I–1759.

tribunals,[33] its approach may be justified by the unprecedented degree of economic and political integration contemplated by the Treaties on which the European Union is based.

(iv) Interpreting Community Acts

In principle the Court takes a similar approach where it is called upon to interpret an act of one of the Community's political institutions. However, the Court may give less emphasis to the objective of a provision and to its legal context where there is a detailed legislative scheme, such as those that have been laid down in the fields of social security and agriculture.[34] Indeed, where the legislature has made its intentions clear through the use of detailed provisions, the Court may feel bound to acknowledge the results which the provisions concerned were designed to produce. Thus, in a series of cases,[35] the Court struck down successive Council regulations designed to curb milk production on the ground that they failed to respect the legitimate expectations of a particular class of producers. The Court's decisions exposed the Community to substantial claims for compensation[36] and severely hampered the Council's attempts to achieve an objective which was in itself entirely legitimate. However, as Advocate General Jacobs observed in the *Dowling* case:[37]

> . . . the Court did not feel itself able to interpret those provisions in such a way as to bring them into conformity with Community law. It seems to me that the Court was unable to do so because the intention of the legislation, however defective, was abundantly clear, and there was accordingly no occasion to depart from the literal meaning of the provisions in which it was expressed. Since the intention of the legislator was inconsistent with a general principle of Community law, the Court had no choice but to declare invalid the provisions which gave effect to that intention.

[33] For the approach of the European Court of Human Rights, see Matscher, 'Methods of interpretation of the Convention', and Golsong, 'Interpreting the European Convention on Human Rights beyond the confines of the Vienna Convention on the Law of Treaties?', in Macdonald, Matscher and Petzold (eds.), *The European System for the Protection of Human Rights* (1993), chs. 5 and 8 respectively; *cf.* the Separate Opinion of Judge Fitzmaurice in the *Golder* case, Series A, No. 18, 1 EHRR 524. On the interpretation of treaties generally, see Brownlie, *Principles of Public International Law* (4th ed., 1990), pp. 626–32; Jennings and Watts (eds.), *Oppenheim's International Law*, vol. I (9th ed., 1992), pp. 1266–84.

[34] By contrast, the Court has relied extensively on the teleological and contextual methods in interpreting the Community's detailed VAT legislation: see Farmer and Lyal, *EC Tax Law* (1994), pp. 89–90.

[35] Case 120/86 *Mulder* [1988] ECR 2321; Case 170/86 *von Deetzen* [1988] ECR 2355; Case C–189/89 *Spagl* [1990] ECR I–4539; Case C–217/89 *Pastätter* [1990] ECR I–4585.

[36] See Joined Cases C–104/89 and C–37/90 *Mulder and Others* v. *Council and Commission* [1992] ECR I–3061.

[37] Case C–85/90 [1992] ECR I–5305, 5320–2.

Where legislation is less precise,[38] its objectives and context will assume greater prominence. In *P* v. *S and Cornwall County Council*,[39] the Court was asked whether a Directive on equal treatment for men and women was infringed if a transsexual was dismissed for a reason related to his or her change of sex, or 'gender reassignment'. It was argued before the Court that the answer to that question was no, at least if it appeared that the employee concerned would have been dismissed regardless of his or her sex prior to the gender reassignment operation. The Court rejected that argument. It observed that the Directive simply gave expression to the principle of equality, 'one of the fundamental principles of Community law'. It added that 'the right not to be discriminated against on grounds of sex is one of the fundamental human rights whose observance the Court has a duty to ensure.' The Court concluded: 'the scope of the directive cannot be confined simply to discrimination based on the fact that a person is of one or other sex. In view of its purpose and the nature of the rights which it seeks to safeguard, the scope of the directive is also such as to apply to discrimination arising . . . from the gender reassignment of the person concerned.' Such discrimination, the Court said, was based essentially on that person's sex.

Another technique which the Court sometimes uses is the comparative analysis of the laws of the Member States on a given problem in order to find the solution which is best adapted to the needs of the Community. An example is *A M & S Europe Ltd* v. *Commission*.[40] There, having examined the position in the Member States, the Court accepted that a limited doctrine of legal professional privilege applied in EC competition cases, notwithstanding the silence of the relevant provisions on the matter.[41]

Sometimes Member States or Community institutions[42] make statements, which may be recorded in the Council minutes, when a measure is adopted about what they consider its scope to be. Whether or not they are made public, such statements cannot affect the objective meaning of the measure. In *Antonissen*,[43] a case concerning the free movement of workers,

[38] Even relatively detailed legislation may leave crucial questions unresolved: see e.g., the attempts of AG Lenz and the Court to establish the requirements of Directive 89/552 on television broadcasting (OJ 1989 L 298, p. 23) in Case C–222/94 *Commission* v. *United Kingdom* [1996] 3 CMLR 793 and Case C–11/95 *Commission* v. *Belgium*, judgment of 10 Sept. 1996.

[39] Case C–13/94 [1996] 2 CMLR 247. Cf. Case 184/83 *Hofmann* v. *Barmer Ersatzkasse* [1984] ECR 3047; Case C–249/96 *Grant* v. *SW Trains*, judgment of 17 Feb. 1998.

[40] Case 155/79 [1982] ECR 1575. See also Case 374/87 *Orkem* v. *Commission* [1989] ECR 3283.

[41] Cf. Case C–84/94 *United Kingdom* v. *Council* [1996] 3 CMLR 671 concerning Directive 93/104 on the organization of working time (OJ 1993 L 307/18), where AG Léger referred to Danish law in interpreting Art. 118a EC, which originated in a proposal made by the Danish government at the IGC preceding the Single European Act: see para 42 of the Opinion.

[42] See e.g., the accompanying statements entered in the minutes of the Council when Reg. 4064/89 on merger control was adopted, [1990] 4 CMLR 314.

[43] Case C–292/89 [1991] ECR I–745. See also Case C–25/94 *Commission* v. *Council*, judgment of 19 Mar. 1996, para. 38; Hartley, 'Five forms of uncertainty in European Community law' [1996] CLJ 265, 274–8.

the High Court asked the Court of Justice 'what weight if any is to be attached by a court or tribunal of a Member State to the declaration contained in the minutes of the meeting of the Council when the Council adopted Directive 68/360?' The Court replied:[44] 'Such a declaration cannot be used for the purpose of interpreting a provision of secondary legislation where, as in this case, no reference is made to the content of the declaration in the wording of the provision in question. The declaration therefore has no legal significance.' Similarly, in *Denkavit and Others* v. *Bundesamt für Finanzen*,[45] the Court stated: 'Expressions of intent on the part of Member States in the Council . . . have no legal status if they are not actually expressed in the legislation. Legislation is addressed to those affected by it. They must, in accordance with the principle of legal certainty, be able to rely on what it contains.'

(v) Concluding Remarks

Much of what has been said so far may seem to offer little help in resolving concrete problems. That is in the nature of the subject, which is concerned more with maxims and aids than with rules or principles. There are, however, two principles of a somewhat more precise nature which should be mentioned for the sake of completeness. The first is that derogations from general provisions are normally interpreted strictly.[46] This principle has been applied not only to provisions of the Treaty, such as Articles 36[47] and 48(3),[48] but also to those contained in Community acts.[49] Secondly (and some of this may seem obvious), the Court has said that:[50]

[44] Para. 18. Declarations published when the Treaties were signed or on the occasion of later amendments may be of greater significance, especially when endorsed by all the Member States: see Schermers, 'The effect of the date 31 December 1992' (1991) 28 CMLRev 275; *cf.* Toth, 'The legal status of the declarations annexed to the Single European Act' (1986) 23 CMLRev 803.

[45] Joined Cases C–283/94, C–291/94 and C–292/94, judgment of 17 Oct. 1996, para. 29.

[46] It is not always clear which provision lays down the general rule, which the derogation: see AG Léger's Opinion in Case C–84/94, *supra*, para. 36 *et seq*, where the relationship between Art. 118a EC, and Art. 100a(1) and (2) EC, is discussed. The point is dealt with by the Court at paras. 11 and 12 of the judgment (Art. 118a not to be interpreted strictly).

[47] See e.g., Case 95/81 *Commission* v. *Italy* [1982] ECR 2187, para. 27. See also *Primecrown*, *supra*, para. 23. But *cf.* the line of cases beginning with Case 120/78 *Rewe* v. *Bundesmonopolverwaltung für Branntwein* ('Cassis de Dijon') [1979] ECR 649, which effectively introduced a new class of derogations from Art. 30 EC, the so-called mandatory requirements, in the case of non-discriminatory national restrictions on imports.

[48] See e.g., Case 30/77 *Regina* v. *Bouchereau* [1977] ECR 1999, paras. 31–5. But even where the derogations contained in Art. 48(3) are not relevant, the Court has accepted that restrictions on the free movement of persons are permissible where they pursue a legitimate aim compatible with the Treaty and are justified by pressing reasons of public interest: see e.g., Case C–19/92 *Kraus* v. *Land Baden-Württemberg* [1993] ECR I–1663, para. 32; Case C–415/93 *URBSFA and Others* v. *Bosman and Others* [1995] ECR I–4921, para. 104.

[49] See e.g., Case 222/84 *Johnston* v. *Chief Constable of the RUC* [1986] ECR 1651, para. 36; Case C–450/93 *Kalanke* [1995] ECR I–3051, para. 21.

[50] Case C–61/94 *Commission* v. *Germany*, judgment of 10 Sept. 1996, para. 52. See also Case C–135/93 *Spain* v. *Commission* [1995] ECR I–1651, para. 37.

When the wording of secondary Community legislation is open to more than one interpretation, preference should be given as far as possible to the interpretation which renders the provision consistent with the Treaty. Likewise, an implementing regulation must, if possible, be given an interpretation consistent with the basic regulation . . . Similarly, the primacy of international agreements concluded by the Community over provisions of secondary Community legislation means that such provisions must, so far as is possible, be interpreted in a manner that is consistent with those agreements.

There is no doubt that striking the right balance between the various considerations mentioned above is a difficult task for any national court, whatever its origins.[51] English courts on the whole have a good record in applying provisions of Community law when there is a line of decisions of the Court of Justice to guide them.[52] Where they are asked to interpret such provisions in the absence of guidance from Luxembourg, their task is a much more difficult one.[53] It is for that reason that Sir Thomas Bingham (as he then was) has on more than one occasion drawn attention to the advantages enjoyed by the Court of Justice in deciding questions of Community law and encouraged national courts to make a reference if they have any real doubt about the answer.[54]

Precedent

Let us turn now to the question of judicial precedent in Community law. This is a question which needs to be approached from a number of different angles.[55]

(i) The Court of Justice

The first concerns the extent to which the Court of Justice considers itself constrained to follow its own decisions. The general position may be stated very simply: the Court of Justice is not bound by its previous

[51] The difficulties facing English courts in particular were acknowledged by Lord Denning in *Bulmer* v. *Bollinger, supra,* at pp. 425–6.

[52] See e.g., *Pickstone* v. *Freemans plc* [1989] 1 AC 66; *Litster* v. *Forth Dry Dock Co Ltd* [1990] 1 AC 546; *R* v. *Secretary of State, ex p EOC* [1994] 2 WLR 409. For a recent discussion of the approach which should be adopted to the interpretation of *English* legislation in cases with a European element, see *Three Rivers DC* v. *Bank of England* (No 2) [1996] 2 All ER 363 (QBD).

[53] A notorious example of misinterpretation of a Treaty article by an English court is the decision of the Court of Appeal in *Henn and Darby* [1978] 1 WLR 1031. The error was corrected by the House of Lords following a reference to the Court of Justice: see [1980] 2 WLR 597.

[54] See the *Samex* case, *supra*; *R* v. *Stock Exchange, ex p Else* [1993] 2 WLR 70. It is ironic that in the latter case the Court of Appeal felt that it could with complete confidence resolve the point of Community law at issue and that the decision of the judge at first instance to refer the point to the Court of Justice should be quashed.

[55] See Arnull, 'Owning up to Fallibility: Precedent and the Court of Justice' (1993) 30 CMLRev 247.

decisions but in practice it does not often depart from them. A doctrine of binding precedent on common law lines would have been entirely inappropriate in what was originally a court of first and last resort, many of the decisions of which could only be changed by amending the Treaties, a lengthy process requiring the agreement of all the Member States and ratification by each of them in accordance with their respective constitutional requirements. It was therefore imperative that the Court should have the power to change the direction of its case law and to depart from its previous decisions, particularly in cases with important constitutional implications.

The general position is exemplified by the extent of the freedom enjoyed by the national courts of the Member States to request preliminary rulings from the Court of Justice under Article 177 EC. Since the Court of Justice is not bound by its own previous decisions, the national courts are not precluded from taking that step merely because the point of Community law at issue has already been dealt with by the Court of Justice.[56]

A corollary of the absence of a doctrine of binding precedent in Community law is that the distinction between the ratio decidendi of a judgment of the Court and its obiter dicta loses much of its significance.[57] The distinction is important in the common law because it is only the ratio of a case which is capable of binding other courts in the future.[58] However, in principle everything that is said in a judgment of the Court of Justice expresses the Court's opinion and is therefore capable of having the same persuasive force.[59]

This point may be illustrated by the decision in *Marshall I*,[60] where the Court held that directives were not in themselves capable of imposing obligations on individuals, that is, of producing horizontal direct effect. That decision was reached in proceedings in which the appellant was seeking to enforce a Directive against a public authority. It was therefore not strictly necessary for the Court to decide whether directives could be enforced against individuals, but this factor had no effect on the status of

[56] See Joined Cases 28, 29, and 30/62 *Da Costa* v. *Nederlandse Belastingadministratie* [1963] ECR 31; Case 66/80 *International Chemical Corporation* v. *Amministrazione delle Finanze dello Stato* [1981] ECR 1191, para. 14; *CILFIT* v. *Ministry of Health, supra*, paras. 14 and 15; *Faccini Dori, supra*.

[57] See further Toth, 'The Authority of Judgments of the European Court of Justice: Binding Force and Legal Effects' (1984) 4 YEL 1 at pp. 36–42; Cross and Harris, *Precedent in English Law* (4th ed., 1991), pp. 1718. *Cf.* Koopmans, '*Stare decisis* in European Law' in O'Keeffe and Schermers (eds.), *Essays in European Law and Integration* (1982), 11 at pp. 22–4.

[58] See further Cross and Harris, *op. cit.*, ch. II.

[59] See AG Roemer in Case 9/61 *Netherlands* v. *High Authority* [1962] ECR 213 at p. 242. *Cf.* the Opinion of AG Warner in Case 112/76 *Manzoni* v. *FNROM*, [1977] ECR 1647 at pp. 1661–3.

[60] Case 152/84 [1986] ECR 723.

the Court's judgment on that point and it has been followed in a number of subsequent cases, notably *Faccini Dori*.[61]

Occasionally, however, the Court seeks to distinguish a case on which a party has sought to rely. In order to perform this exercise, the Court has to establish what the previous case, properly construed, in fact decided. This process is analogous to that of identifying the ratio of a judgment given by a common law court. An example is *CIRFS* v. *Commission*,[62] where the applicants challenged the validity of a Commission decision to the effect that aid which the French government was proposing to grant to a company called Allied Signal did not have to be notified to the Commission. The case turned on the scope of a code agreed by the Commission with the Member States on the circumstances in which aid in the field of synthetic fibres had to be notified. The French government and Allied Signal argued that the code merely laid down guidelines setting out the practice which the Commission intended to follow and that the way in which the code was interpreted by the Commission and the Member States could not be challenged by a third party. The Court's decision in *Deufil* v. *Commission*[63] was cited in support of that view. However, the Court said that the two cases could be distinguished:[64] *Deufil* was concerned with the question whether an aid code was capable of derogating from the provisions of the Treaty, whereas the question in *CIRFS* was whether such a code could bind the Commission and the Member States. The reasoning adopted in *Deufil* was not therefore applicable.

Of course, like all courts the Court of Justice tries to be consistent in the decisions it reaches. Thus, in proceedings under Article 177 in which the Court is asked to rule on a point it has already dealt with, it will, in the absence of any suggestion that the previous case was wrongly decided, simply repeat its earlier ruling.[65] Indeed, where a question referred to the Court for a preliminary ruling is 'manifestly identical to a question on which the Court has already ruled', the Court is empowered by Article 104(3) of its Rules of Procedure to give its decision by reasoned order in which reference is made to its previous judgment.

It might be said that the general approach of the Court of Justice is not dissimilar to that which, following the 1966 Practice Statement,[66] now prevails in the House of Lords. However, that would be to underestimate

[61] *Supra*. See also Case 80/86 *Kolpinghuis Nijmegen* [1987] ECR 3969, para. 9; Case C–221/88 *Busseni* [1990] ECR I–495, para. 23.

[62] Case C–313/90 [1993] ECR I–1125.

[63] Case 310/85 [1987] ECR 901.

[64] See para. 34 of the judgment in *CIRFS*.

[65] See e.g., Case C–350/89 *Sheptonhurst Ltd* v. *Newham Borough Council* [1991] ECR I–2387, where the Court repeated its ruling in Case C–23/89 *Quietlynn Ltd* v. *Southend Borough Council* [1990] ECR I–3059. *Cf.* Joined Cases C418/93 etc. *Semeraro Casa Uno and Others*, judgment of 20 June 1996.

[66] [1966] 1 WLR 1234.

the influence on the Court's practice of its civil law origins. In the civilian tradition, the judge is merely the mouthpiece of the law:[67] judicial decisions are not a formal source of law and judges do not feel compelled to analyse or reconcile earlier judgments in the manner of the common law judge.[68] Indeed, for many years the Court rarely referred in its judgments to its previous decisions, even when repeating a passage verbatim. Perhaps under the influence of the common law, where it has been acknowledged at least since the time of Dicey that judges do make law,[69] the Court of Justice now deals more fully with previous cases in its judgments. But the analysis remains superficial and selective by the standards of English courts. The reader of its judgments will be struck by the fact that previous decisions are frequently only cited by the Court where they support its argument. Authorities which point the other way are sometimes not mentioned at all, sometimes presented as if they support the line the Court has chosen to take.[70]

There are signs in some recent decisions of a growing willingness on the part of the Court to confront the implications of earlier case law. In *HAG II*,[71] the Court for the first time expressly overruled one of its own previous decisions. Following the advice of Advocate General Jacobs, the Court in that case abandoned the much-criticized doctrine of common origin laid down in *HAG I*,[72] which limited the circumstances in which the owner of a trade mark in one Member State could restrain imports of products legally bearing the mark in another Member State. Advocate General Jacobs stated that, if he was to be followed, 'the Court should in my view make it clear, in the interests of legal certainty, that it is abandoning the doctrine of common origin laid down in *HAG I*.' He went on: 'That the Court should in an appropriate case expressly overrule an earlier decision is I think an inescapable duty, even if the Court has never before expressly done so.' In the Advocate General's view, to depart from *HAG I* without

[67] See Montesquieu, *De l'esprit des lois*, Livre XI, Chapitre 6: 'Mais les juges de la nation ne sont . . . que la bouche qui prononce les paroles de la loi; des êtres inanimés qui n'en peuvent modérer ni la force ni la rigueur.' The English rendition is taken from para. 165 of the Opinion of AG Léger in the case on the working time directive, *supra*.

[68] See Brown and Kennedy, *op. cit.*, pp. 343–4.

[69] See Dicey's *Lectures on the Relation between Law and Public Opinion in England during the Nineteenth Century* (1926), Lecture XI of which is entitled 'Judicial Legislation' and the Appendix to which contains an extensive note (at pp. 483–94) on 'Judge-Made Law'. In that note, it is suggested (at p. 483) that the existence of judge-made law is due in part to the doctrine of precedent. Lord Reid once described the suggestion that judges do not make law as a fairy tale: see 'The Judge as Law Maker' (1972–3) XII JSPTL (NS) 22.

[70] See e.g., Case C–358/89 *Extramet* v. *Council* [1991] ECR I–2501, where Court failed to acknowledge that its conclusion on the admissibility of the action represented a departure from its earlier case law. *Cf.* Case 302/87 *Parliament* v. *Council* ('Comitology') [1988] ECR 5615; Case C–70/88, *Parliament* v. *Council* ('Chernobyl') [1990] ECR I–2041.

[71] Case C–10/89 *CNL-Sucal* v. *HAG GF* [1990] ECR I–3711.

[72] Case 192/73 *Van Zuylen* v. *HAG* [1974] ECR 731.

abandoning the doctrine or to seek to rationalize such an outcome on some other ground 'would be a recipe for confusion'. The remarks of Advocate General Jacobs seem to have produced the desired result, for the Court said that it considered it 'necessary to reconsider the interpretation given in [*HAG I*]'.[73] The remainder of the judgment makes it clear that the doctrine of common origin no longer forms any part of the Court's case law on intellectual property, a result subsequently confirmed in the *Ideal Standard* case.[74]

In a subsequent case concerning the scope of Article 30 EC, *Keck and Mithouard*,[75] the Court also departed from previous case law, but it did so less candidly. The Court stated that it considered it 'necessary to re-examine and clarify its case-law on this matter' and concluded, 'contrary to what has previously been decided', that certain types of national legislation which might appear to hinder imports were nonetheless compatible with the Treaty. Unlike *HAG II*, however, the Court did not make clear precisely what it was overruling. The effect of its judgment was therefore to leave the status of its previous decisions on the matter unclear. While a willingness to depart from previous decisions which are producing unsatisfactory effects is wholly desirable, it is imperative that, when the Court decides to take that course, it explains clearly which of its previous decisions are no longer to be treated as authoritative.

The criticism which this aspect in particular of the *Keck* ruling attracted[76] seems to have produced an effect. In *Cabanis-Issarte*,[77] a social security case,[78] the Court made it clear that an earlier ruling[79] was to be regarded as confined to its facts and that a series of specified later cases based on it were no longer good law. The Court went on to limit the temporal effect of its judgment in order to 'preclude legal situations being called into question which have been definitively settled in accordance with the Court's previous case law, whose scope is limited by this judgment.'[80] The ruling in *Cabanis-Issarte* represented a courageous attempt by the Court to correct what it saw as a wrong turning in its earlier case law.

[73] At para. 10.

[74] Case C–9/93 *IHT Internationale Heiztechnik* v. *Ideal Standard* [1994] ECR I–2789.

[75] Joined Cases C–267 and C–268/91 [1993] ECR I–6097.

[76] See e.g., Gormley, 'Reasoning renounced? The remarkable judgment in *Keck and Mithouard*' (1994) EBLR 63, 66; Reich, 'The "November revolution" of the European Court of Justice: *Keck, Meng* and *Audi* revisited' (1994) 31 CMLRev 459, 471.

[77] Case C–308/93 [1996] 2 CMLR 729.

[78] The case concerned the right of a widow of a migrant worker to rely on the principle of equal treatment laid down in Art. 3(1) of Regulation 1408/71 (see OJ 1983 L 230, p. 6).

[79] Case 40/76 *Kermaschek* v. *Bundesanstalt für Arbeit* [1976] ECR 1669.

[80] Para. 47. Cf. *Primecrown, supra*, where the Court refused to depart from the rule in Case 187/80 *Merck* v. *Stephar and Exler* [1981] ECR 2063.

(ii) The Court of First Instance

The establishment of the CFI raised two further questions about the status of judicial precedents in Community law: (a) is the CFI bound by its own previous decisions; and (b) is it bound by the decisions of the Court of Justice? The answer to the first question is that, like the Court of Justice itself, the CFI is not strictly bound by its own decisions but that it endeavours to be consistent. The second question needs to be explored at somewhat greater length in order to discover the answer.

A common lawyer might be tempted to say that, because the Court of Justice is hierarchically superior, its rulings ought to bind the CFI in the interests of legal certainty and the coherence of the law.[81] A more technical argument might be based on Article 51 of the EC Statute of the Court, according to which one of the grounds on which appeal lies to the Court against decisions of the CFI is 'infringement of Community law by the Court of First Instance'. It has been argued that '[t]he precedents set by the Court are, of course, part of Community law, so that where these are clear and consistent the lower court would regard itself as bound to follow them at risk of its decision being set aside on appeal. Only in the presence of unclear or conflicting decisions of the higher court would it feel free to decide the matter as it thought fit.'[82]

On the other hand, it might be said that the decisions of the Court are *not* a source of law in themselves, but merely illustrations of the way in which the law has in the past been applied. In the absence of any written rule to the contrary, the case law of the Court should of course be treated as influential, but it would not be in keeping with the civilian tradition for the CFI to regard it as strictly binding. More importantly, it might seem improbable that the Court of Justice would ever uphold an appeal on the sole ground that its own case law had not been followed. The Court would surely be more likely to ask whether the CFI has reached the right result, itself qualifying any of its own previous decisions which seem to stand in the way.[83]

In practice, the CFI makes extensive reference to the Court's case law in its judgments and clearly considers it highly persuasive. However, where the CFI believes it is liable to produce adverse results, it has not hesitated to look for ways of avoiding it. Indeed, since it heard its first case in 1989, the CFI's attitude to the case law of the Court has become increasingly robust.

An early case in which the CFI demonstrated its readiness to distinguish inconvenient rulings of the Court of Justice was *BASF and Others* v.

[81] *Cf.* Slynn, *Introducing a European Legal Order* (1992), pp. 165–6.
[82] Brown and Kennedy, *op. cit.*, p. 351.
[83] See Arnull, *op. cit.*, p. 263.

Commission,[84] where the applicants sought the annulment of a Commission decision relating to a proceeding under Article 85 of the Treaty in the PVC sector. One of the grounds put forward by the applicants was that the Commission had infringed the first paragraph of Article 12 of its own Rules of Procedure,[85] which provided that '[a]cts adopted by the Commission, at a meeting or by written procedure, shall be authenticated in the language or languages in which they are binding by the signatures of the President and the Executive Secretary.' The Commission sought to rely on the judgment in *Nakajima* v. *Council*,[86] where the Court of Justice said that 'the purpose of the rules of procedure of a Community institution is to organize the internal functioning of its services in the interests of good administration.' According to the Court of Justice, it followed 'that natural or legal persons may not rely on an alleged breach of those rules since they are not intended to ensure protection for individuals.'

Notwithstanding the apparently general terms of that ruling, in *BASF* the CFI took the view that it was limited in scope:

> The Court [of First Instance] considers that that judgment must be interpreted as meaning that it is necessary to distinguish between those provisions of an institution's Rules of Procedure whose infringement may not be relied upon by natural and legal persons because they are concerned solely with the internal working arrangements of the institution and cannot affect their legal situation and those whose infringement may be relied upon because, as is the case with Article 12 of the Commission's Rules of Procedure, they create rights and are a factor contributing to legal certainty for such persons.

The CFI went on to find that the contested measure was vitiated by such serious defects that it was to be considered nonexistent. The Commission then appealed to the Court of Justice,[87] which set aside the conclusion of the CFI that the measure was non-existent. However, without referring to its decision in *Nakajima*,[88] it declared that '[a]uthentication of acts referred to in the first paragraph of Article 12 of the Commission's Rules of Procedure . . . constitutes an essential procedural requirement within the meaning of Article 173 of the EEC Treaty breach of which gives rise to an action for annulment.'[89] Since the Commission had failed to authenticate the contested decision in accordance with the requirements laid down in its Rules of Procedure, the Court concluded that the decision should be annulled.[90]

[84] Joined Cases T–79/89 etc. [1992] ECR II–315. *Cf.* more recently Case T–353/94 *Postbank NV* v. *Commission*, judgment of 18 Sept. 1996, para. 70.

[85] OJ, English Special Edition, Second Series VII—Institutional Questions, p. 9, as amended by Commission Decision 75/461, OJ 1975 L 199, p. 43.

[86] Case C–69/89, [1991] ECR I–2069, paras. 49 and 50.

[87] Case C–137/92 P *Commission* v. *BASF and Others* [1994] ECR I–2555.

[88] But see the Opinion of AG Van Gerven at pp. 2598–605.

[89] Para. 76.

[90] In a subsequent case, the Court cited its rulings in *Nakajima* and *BASF* as if they were consistent: see Case C–58/94 *Netherlands* v. *Council*, judgment of 30 April 1996, para. 38.

Perhaps emboldened by that episode, the CFI subsequently appeared to depart from the decision of the Court of Justice in *Dutch Books*[91] that Community law did not require the Commission to divulge the contents of its files to the parties in competition cases. In *Solvay* v. *Commission* and *ICI* v. *Commission*, the CFI described access to the file as 'one of the procedural safeguards intended to protect the rights of the defence' and declared that '[r]espect for the rights of the defence in all proceedings in which sanctions may be imposed is a fundamental principle of Community law which must be respected in all circumstances . . . '[92] Again, in *Kotzonis* v. *ESC*,[93] the CFI expressly stated that the case law of the Court of Justice on the effect of a provision of the Staff Regulations 'ought to be reconsidered' and went on to depart from it. The CFI has also displayed a marked reluctance to follow the lead given by the Court in *Codorniu* v. *Council*[94] by relaxing the standing conditions which natural and legal persons must satisfy in order to bring proceedings under Article 173 EC for the annulment of Community acts.[95]

Perhaps the clearest statement to date of the attitude of the CFI to the case law of the Court of Justice is to be found in a dumping case, *NMB France and Others* v. *Commission*.[96] In that case (*NMB II*), the applicants sought the annulment of a series of Commission decisions concerning the refund of antidumping duties collected on certain imports of ball-bearings originating in Singapore which had been fixed at too high a rate. According to the applicants, the method used by the Commission to calculate the amount of the refunds was unlawful. A curious feature of the case was that, before the CFI acquired jurisdiction in dumping cases, the applicants had already brought an unsuccessful action before the Court of Justice (*NMB I*)[97] for the annulment of Commission decisions on the refund of anti-dumping duties they had paid on the same product from the same origin. The decisions contested in *NMB II* related to different periods but the arguments advanced by the applicants were essentially the same as those previously rejected by the Court.

The Commission argued that the second action constituted an abuse of procedure, in that the applicants were in reality seeking to challenge the

[91] Joined Cases 43 and 63/82 *VBVB and VBBB* v. *Commission* [1984] ECR 19, para. 25.

[92] Case T–30/91 [1995] ECR II–1775, para 59, and Case T–36/91 [1995] ECR II–1847, para. 69, respectively. In both cases, the contested decision was annulled. See Moore, (1996) 33 CMLRev 355.

[93] Case T–586/93 [1995] ECR II–665, para. 92.

[94] Case C–309/89 [1994] ECR I–1853.

[95] See e.g., Case T–489/93 *Unifruit Hellas* v. *Commission* [1994] ECR II–1201; Case T–472/93 *Campo Ebro and Others* v. *Council* [1995] ECR II–421; Case T–96/92 *CCE de la Société Générale des Grandes Sources and Others* v. *Commission* [1995] ECR II–1213; Case T–12/93 *CCE de Vittel and Others* v. *Commission* [1995] ECR II–1247. Cases T–96/92 and T–12/93 are discussed by Arnull at (1996) 33 CMLRev 319.

[96] Case T–162/94, judgment of 5 June 1996 (Second Chamber, Extended Composition).

[97] Case C–188/88 *NMB and Others* v. *Commission* [1992] ECR I–1689.

judgment of the Court in *NMB I*. The Commission was supported by a federation representing European bearing manufacturers, which maintained that the second action constituted a 'disguised appeal against the first judgment.'[98] However, the CFI held that the second action was admissible, declaring:[99] 'It must be borne in mind at the outset that the Court of First Instance is only bound by the judgments of the Court of Justice, first, in the circumstances laid down in the second paragraph of Article 54 of the Statute of the Court of Justice of the European Community, and, secondly, pursuant to the principle of res judicata.'

Article 54 of the Statute is concerned with the consequences where an appeal to the Court against a decision of the CFI is upheld. One of the options open to the Court is to refer the case back to the CFI for judgment. When that option is exercised, the second paragraph of Article 54 states that the CFI 'shall be bound by the decision of the Court of Justice on points of law'. In the interests of completeness, the CFI might also have mentioned Article 47 of the Statute. According to that provision, where the Court finds that an action which has been brought before it falls within the jurisdiction of the CFI, it must refer the action to the CFI, which 'may not decline jurisdiction'. In other words, the CFI is bound by the finding of the Court of Justice that the former Court has jurisdiction to hear the action.

However, neither Article 47 nor Article 54 of the Statute was relevant in the circumstances of *NMB II*, so the CFI went on to consider whether the status as res judicata[100] of the judgment of the Court of Justice in *NMB I* rendered the second action inadmissible. The CFI observed: 'It is settled case-law that this can be the case only if the proceedings disposed of by the judgment in [*NMB I*] were between the same parties, had the same purpose and were based on the same submissions as the present case . . . those conditions necessarily being cumulative.'[101] The CFI pointed out that the second action concerned 'different, later decisions relating to other quantities [of ball-bearings] and import periods and reimbursements of different amounts.'[102] It followed that the status of the judgment in *NMB I* as res judicata could not affect the admissibility of the second action. The CFI went on to note that, although the complaints put forward in the second action largely coincided with those advanced in *NMB I*, there were nonetheless significant differences: the international legal context had changed and the Community had adopted a new basic regulation on protection against dumping. The second action could not therefore be considered 'a mere replication'[103] of the first. Moreover, one of the applicants in *NMB II* had not been involved in *NMB I*. It followed, said the CFI, that 'this

[98] Para. 31 of the judgment in Case T–162/94. [99] Para. 36.

[100] See further Toth, *The Oxford Encyclopaedia of European Community Law*, vol. I (1990), pp. 464–7.

[101] Para. 37 of the judgment in *NMB II*. [102] Para. 38. [103] Para. 39.

action is entirely admissible and that the Court of First Instance must therefore examine its merits. In so doing, it should take account simultaneously of the judgment in [*NMB I*] and of the new issues raised by these proceedings'.[104] After a detailed examination of the grounds put forward by the applicants, the CFI dismissed the action as unfounded.

The judgment in *NMB II* confirms the indications given by earlier cases that the CFI does not consider itself bound by decisions of the Court of Justice except in certain exceptional and clearly defined circumstances. Those decisions are treated by the CFI merely as persuasive, although the more there are in support of a given proposition, the less likely the CFI will be to depart from them.

(iii) National Courts

What effect do decisions of the Community Courts produce in the national courts of the Member States?[105] The short answer to that question seems to be that national courts—whether or not they are covered by the third paragraph of Article 177—are not entitled to depart from such decisions without making a reference to the Court of Justice.

It is clear that a preliminary ruling delivered by the Court of Justice is binding on the court which made the reference.[106] Such a ruling is probably also binding on other courts.[107] It may as a result obviate the need for a further reference to be made: in *International Chemical Corporation* v. *Amministrazione delle Finanze dello Stato*,[108] the Court said that 'although a judgment of the Court given under Article 177 of the Treaty declaring an act of an institution, in particular a Council or Commission regulation, to be void is directly addressed only to the national court which brought the matter before the Court, it is sufficient reason for any other national court to regard that act as void for the purposes of a judgment which it has to give.' The *International Chemical Corporation* case was concerned with preliminary rulings on *validity*, but there is no doubt that national courts are also entitled to follow preliminary rulings on the *interpretation* of Community provisions. In addition, national courts may apply judgments given by the Court in direct actions. In the *CILFIT* case, it was acknowledged that any previous decision of the Court, whether given in a refer-

[104] Para. 41. The CFI referred to Joined Cases 311/81 and 30/82 and Case 136/82 *Klöckner Werke* v. *Commission* [1983] ECR 1549 and 1599 respectively, para. 5.

[105] See generally Toth, 'The Authority of Judgments of the European Court of Justice: Binding Force and Legal Effects' (1984) 4 YEL 1.

[106] Case 29/68 *Milchkontor* v. *Hauptzollamt Saarbrucken* [1969] ECR 165, paras. 2–3.

[107] See Hartley, *The Foundations of European Community Law* (3rd ed., 1994), p. 301; Jacobs in Andenas (ed.), *Article 177 References to the European Court—Policy and Practice*, at p. 30. The point is not entirely free from doubt: see the discussion in Anderson, *References to the European Court* (1995), at pp. 307–15.

[108] Case 66/80 [1981] ECR 1191, para. 13.

ence for a preliminary ruling or in a direct action, may remove the obligation to make a reference which the third paragraph of Article 177 imposes on national courts of last resort. It follows that other national courts may properly decline, in the exercise of their discretion, to make a reference where the point at issue has already been dealt with by the Court of Justice. However, it was emphasized in *CILFIT*[109] that national courts remain free in such circumstances to ask for a preliminary ruling. This is clearly a possibility of which advantage should be taken if a national judge wishes to depart from the case law of the Court of Justice.

The capacity of previous rulings of the Community Courts to bind national courts was underlined in *Atlanta Fruchthandelsgesellschaft I*,[110] where the Court of Justice considered the circumstances in which national courts are entitled to suspend, on an interim basis, national measures adopted in implementation of Community acts the validity of which is disputed. It was held that national courts were obliged, under Article 5 of the Treaty, to respect any decisions the Court of Justice or the CFI might have given on the validity of the contested act or on an application for interim measures where interim relief had been sought at Community level. In the circumstances of *Atlanta*, the Court had refused such an application by a Member State[111] and subsequently upheld the validity of the contested act.[112] It followed that, in the absence of any new considerations, a domestic court was not entitled to suspend a national measure adopted to give effect to it.

What is the status of decisions of domestic courts on questions of Community law? Article 177 confers on inferior national courts a discretion either to refer to the Court of Justice questions of Community law they are called upon to resolve or to decide such questions for themselves. That discretion, being granted directly by the Treaty, cannot be fettered by the decisions of superior national courts. Thus, in *Rheinmühlen*[113] the Court of Justice made it clear that 'a rule of national law whereby a court is bound on points of law by the rulings of a superior court cannot deprive the inferior courts of their power to refer to the Court questions of interpretation of Community law involving such rulings.' Similarly, rulings of superior national courts on questions of Community law cannot deprive inferior courts of their power to decide such questions for themselves. In other words, a ruling on a question of Community law given by a national court,

[109] Para. 15. See also *International Chemical Corporation, supra*, para. 14.

[110] Case C–465/93 [1995] ECR I–3761. See also Case C–68/95 *T Port GmbH & Co KG* v. *Bundesanstalt für Landwirtschaft und Ernährung*, judgment of 26 Nov. 1996.

[111] See Case C–280/93 R *Germany* v. *Council* [1993] ECR I–3667.

[112] See Case C–280/93 *Germany* v. *Council* [1994] ECR I–4973; Case C–466/93 *Atlanta Fruchthandelsgesellschaft II* [1995] ECR I–3799. (The latter case was decided on the same day as Case C–465/93.)

[113] Case 166/73 [1974] ECR 33, para. 4.

whatever its status, can never be anything more than persuasive.[114] So an industrial tribunal is not bound by a decision of the House of Lords on a point of Community law, although if the tribunal were minded to depart from such a decision a reference to the Court of Justice would normally be appropriate.

The principles discussed in this section are reinforced for English courts by section 3(1) of the European Communities Act 1972, according to which questions of Community law which arise in legal proceedings in the United Kingdom must either be the subject of a reference for a preliminary ruling or be determined in accordance with the principles laid down by the Community Courts.

[114] See Brown and Kennedy, *op. cit.*, p. 354; Jacobs in Andenas (ed.), *op. cit.*, p. 30.

9

The Application of General Principles of Community Law by English Courts

BY THE RT HON LORD JUSTICE SCHIEMANN

Introduction

There is now a good deal of political controversy about the European Court of Justice (ECJ), and what it is up to. So let me first make a few points about the nature of the judicial process in a context which has nothing whatever to do with the European Union.

The sources of the general principles[1]

When an English court is faced with a legal problem it seeks to solve it by looking at the statutes and the Common Law as recorded in the cases. Usually, once the facts are found, the answer, relying on those sources, is manifest. But what if neither the statutes nor binding precedent provides an answer to the question posed by the parties? This is a question regularly faced by all courts although since the doctrine of binding precedent does not apply to the House of Lords it faces them more often. The fact of the matter is that, even if the statute is not clear or the case before the court is one not covered by the statute the court still has to come up with a judgment and in so doing a certain amount of judicial law making is clearly involved whatever the language used in the judgments. This is not gratuitous judicial activism. It is an ineluctable part of the task of providing a decision. The court has to solve the problem. In doing so it inevitably looks around for some sort of inspiration to help it come to a conclusion as to what the law ought to be. Where does the court look for inspiration?

The English judge's instinctive first reaction to what is a new problem to him is to look around to see how similar problems have been tackled by others. He looks at the case law in related fields and he may look at the statute law in those fields. He will try to express something which, when

[1] Useful textbook references in this context are: Schermers and Waelbroek, *Judicial Protection in the European Communities* (5th ed., 1992) pp. 42–165; Brown and Kennedy, *The Court of Justice of the European Communities* (4th ed., 1994) Ch. 15; Schwarze, *European Administrative Law* (1992); Wyatt and Dashwood, European Community Law (3rd. ed., 1993) pp. 88–103.

read by others, will strike them as the just and proper solution to the conundrum in question. He will know that their reaction will, in part, be conditioned by the results of and reasoning in past cases and, in part, by conceptions of justice formed by other sources. One desideratum in any legal system is that all courts should answer the same problem in the same way. He will consider whether a proposed solution coincides with his sense of what is a desirable solution from the point of view of society as a whole but he will ask himself 'Will others agree or am I wholly out of step with what other judges would do?'

Having decided how to resolve the problem before him, he must then decide how to express the justification for his decision. In England the tradition in the courts' judgments has been to argue by analogy, stating that the solution to the problems posed by the present case are implicit in the solution found in the past to what are perceived by the judge as being similar cases. To a degree, as I have indicated, this echoes the reality of the situation. To a degree, this way of expressing the justification for the decision has traditionally been adopted in order to let the litigant feel that what he has heard is not his particular judge making up the law on the hoof but rather his particular judge declaring what any other judge would also have declared.

Just as in England the court sometimes has to deal with legal problems to which there is no clear answer in the statute law or in the case law, so the ECJ also has to deal with questions, either substantive or procedural, to which the words of the Treaties and any relevant directives and regulations do not provide any solutions. The ECJ also can not just walk away. On the other hand, it is acutely conscious that there is political opposition to overt law making by the Court. What happens in practice is not very dissimilar to what has happened here over the centuries. The Court starts by looking at the equivalent of the statute law material—the Treaties. Although by now there is a fair amount of ECJ case law, originally the ECJ could not look at any previous case law of its own because there was not any. So it looked at what appeared to be the principles behind the laws and legal practices of the various Member States in order to seek inspiration for a solution which would commend itself. The Court consists of eminent lawyers from the Member States and has considerable research facilities of its own. Its procedures allow for an input from each Member State's traditions and it takes time to consider and synthesize these traditions. Anyone interested in getting a feel for the methodology of the Court would enjoy reading the opinions of Advocate General Tesauro in the joint cases *Brasserie du Pecheur SA* v. *Germany* and *R* v. *Secretary of State for Transport, ex p. Factortame and Others*,[2] of the same Advocate General in *P*

[2] [1996] ECR I–1029.

v. *S*[3] and of Advocate General Leger in *R* v. *MAFF ex parte Hedley Lomas (Ireland) Ltd.*[4] The first considers the circumstances in which a Member State could be held liable for loss and damage caused to an individual as a result of a legislative act involving breaches by the State of Community Law; the second considers whether the principle of non-discrimination on grounds of sex has application to transsexuals and the third has a wide ranging review of state liability for wrongful legislative action. The opinions are full of quotations from the European Treaties, Regulations and Directives, ECJ case law, National Constitutions, national statutes, the case law in various Member States, writings in legal journals in various countries, the European Convention on Human Rights, proceedings in the European Parliament and so on, quite apart from citations from the US Supreme Court. All these are considered by the Advocate General and he then propounds his own views as to what if any general principles of Community law are applicable. It is perhaps worth noting AG Leger's comment in *Hedley Lomas* at paragraph 100:

> From this I conclude that, as far as state liability for legislative action is concerned, there are no general principles which are *truly common* to the member states. The principles established by the Court in relation to Article 215 of the Treaty have, in fact, been those laid down by the systems of domestic law most protective of individuals suffering damage through legislative action.

The court's judgments in these cases were in accord with the views expressed by the Advocate Generals but much more succinct.

One can crudely summarize the situation by saying that the general principles of Community law have evolved under the pressure of having to reach decisions in relation to matters not expressly covered by the Treaties and that those principles are extrapolated from the Treaties and from currents of thought in the legal systems of Member States as at the time of the decision. It should be remembered that this country and Eire chose not to enter the Communities when they were first set up with the result that the search for legal principles in the first years of the Communities took place largely outside the common law within the legal systems of countries which had more in common with each other than any of them had with the common law. In consequence there are times when the English legal community is rudely surprised by what it is told is a principle common to the legal systems of all Member States.

What is a self-evident truth to a French lawyer is frequently not a self-evident truth to an English lawyer, and vice versa. For instance most continental lawyers would react with incredulity to the following quotation from the judgment of Laws J in *R* v. *London Borough of Ealing, ex p. Parkinson*:[5] 'A public body condemned by the court as having acted

[3] [1996] ECR I–2143. [4] [1996] ECR I–1553. [5] [1996] COD 232.

irrationally, unfairly or illegally is not thereby rendered liable in damages.' The Community recognizes no such principle; on the contrary as innumerable cases show.

The Application of the General Principles of Community Law in the English Courts

There is a conceptually clear distinction between, on the one hand, cases in which, by virtue of the European Communities Act, the English courts are *bound* to take into account the general principles of Community law and, on the other hand, cases where there is no Community element. In the past, those brought up without the benefit of Community jurisprudence have tended only to look to it where it was directly applicable. What has happened over the years is, first, that the field of Community activities has expanded with the result that the general principles are directly applicable over a wider area. Secondly, lawyers have become more familiar with Community law and so a Community point is more frequently argued. Thirdly, those who have become familiar with the general principles have obtained inspiration from them in solving problems which have no Community law element.

This seems to me eminently sensible. All the Member States face rather similar problems and tensions in our politico-legal systems. For instance the tension between merits and legality. We all recognize that the wisdom of a policy is not for the court or Council of State and yet we all recognize that outrageous decisions must be susceptible to some sort of control. So we all face the difficulty of identifying the degree of control which is appropriate. Some talk of irrationality or of failure to take into account relevant considerations; others of lack of proportionality; yet others point out that for the administrator to fail to take into account a lack of proportionality betrays a failure to take into account a relevant consideration.

Our law is playing a part in the formulation of the general principles of Community law. Those general principles are in turn a component of our law. Traditionally when developing one area of the law the judges have always drawn inspiration from other areas. The process is well described in *R* v. *Knuller*[6] where Lord Simon of Glaisdale said this:

> It is in general the difference between mature and rudimentary legal systems that the latter deal specifically with a number of particular and unrelated instances, whereas the former embody the Law in comprehensive, cohesive and rational general rules. The Law is then easier to understand and commands a greater respect. Fragmentation, on the other hand, leads to anomalous (and therefore inequitable) distinctions and hedging legal rules around with technicalities that are only within the understanding of an esoteric class.[7]

[6] (1973) AC 435. [7] at 492.

I therefore think it likely that over the years there will be a fair amount of cross fertilization. As the cases to which I am about to turn demonstrate, the process is under way but hesitantly and patchily. That again is just what you would expect given that it is less than a quarter of a century since we joined the Communities, and given that the commanding heights of our legal system have during much of this time been occupied by those not familiar with Community law and given stare decisis.

What then are the General Principles of Community Law?

In a chapter of this length it seems sensible to pick out those principles the application of which may surprise the English lawyer. There are many others—such as the right to be heard before a decision is made, the absence of an obligation of self-incrimination, the concept of res judicata and that of non-retroactivity of penalties—which are very similar to those we are used to.[8] Sometimes one comes across a principle—the principle of primacy referred to by AG Leger in *R* v. *MAFF, ex p. Hedley Lomas* is a case in point—where one does not recognize the phrase but does recognize the concept, namely that Community law trumps national law. In consequence, rather as one may talk prose without knowing it, it is easy to find oneself applying what are general principles of Community law without being conscious of this fact. This is just what one would expect given the origin of the general principles of Community law. All the Member States have a common Western European heritage of thought and so our ideas of justice are likely to have much in common.

Before turning to those principles of present interest I make three preliminary observations.

1. As Steyn LJ observed in *R* v. *Home Secretary ex parte Adams*[9] 'It is a principle of Community Law that rights under Community Law must be protected by an effective means of resort to Judicial Review'. A failure to protect those rights can render the state liable in damages to the individual.'[10]
2. It will be obvious from what I have said so far that there is every likelihood that more principles will emerge as occasion demands.
3. One should note that cases frequently arise when several principles are of relevance and not infrequently these will conflict among themselves leaving the court to decide which should be given priority. This priority ranking may in itself be elevated into a principle.

[8] 'It is a general principle common to the legal systems of the member states that the injured party must show reasonable diligence in limiting the extent of the loss or damage, or risk having to bear the damage himself,' para. 85 of the ECJ judgment in *Brasserie du Pecheur*.

[9] [1995] All ER (EC) 177.

[10] at 189.

The Principles which I propose to highlight are those listed by Schermers under the headings, Fundamental Human Rights, Equality, Legal Certainty, and Fair application of the law. Recent case law here and in Luxembourg makes it sensible to look at Human Rights and Equality first in Luxembourg and then here and thereafter carry out the same compare and contrast exercise in relation to Legal Certainty and Fair application of the law.

Fundamental Human Rights and Equality in Luxembourg

The ECJ stated in *the Second Nold case*[11] that 'international treaties for the protection of human rights on which the Member States have collaborated or of which they are signatories, can supply guidelines which should be followed within the framework of Community Law.' It has frequently referred to the European Convention and to the findings of the Strasbourg Court as evidencing Common principles of Community law. The phraseology used is often similar to that used in *Defrenne*:[12] 'respect for fundamental human rights is one of the general principles of Community law the observance of which [the court] has a duty to secure.'

The principle of equality provides that situations are not to be treated differently unless differentiation is objectively justified. There are provisions in the Treaty and the directives which forbid specific types of discrimination—discrimination based on nationality or on sex are examples—but the Court has worked out a much wider principle. An interesting recent example of this is *P* v. *S*. This case concerned a transsexual manager of an educational establishment who was dismissed because he intended to undergo gender reassignment. It was submitted that the Equal Treatment Directive had no application since female transsexuals were treated in the same way as male transsexuals and since the Directive was couched in terms of the man/woman dichotomy. The ECJ, following the opinion of the Advocate General, rejected this argument, stating:

> The principle of equal treatment 'for men and women' to which the Directive refers in its title, preamble and provisions means . . . that there should be 'no discrimination whatever on grounds of sex'. Thus the Directive is simply the expression, in the relevant field, of the principle of equality, which is one of the fundamental principles of Community law.
>
> The right not to be discriminated against on grounds of sex is one of the fundamental human rights whose observance the Court has a duty to ensure.
>
> Accordingly, the scope of the Directive cannot be confined simply to discrimination based on the fact that a person is of one or other sex. In view of its purpose and the nature of the rights which it seeks to safeguard, the scope of the Directive

[11] [1974] ECR 507. [12] [1978] 1366 at 1378.

is also such as to apply to discrimination arising . . . from the gender re-assignment of the person concerned.

To tolerate such discrimination would be tantamount, as regards such a person, to a failure to respect the dignity and freedom to which he or she is entitled, and which the Court has a duty to safeguard.

Fundamental Rights and Equality in England

The ECJ decision in *P* v. *S* can be compared and contrasted with a case decided by the Court of Appeal four months earlier: *R* v. *Ministry of Defence, ex p. Smith.*[13] One of the issues there was whether the discharge of the applicants on the ground that they were of homosexual orientation amounted to a breach of the Equal Treatment Directive (76/207/EEC). It was held by the Court of Appeal that it did not. Thorpe LJ put the matter thus: 'any common sense construction of the Directive in the year of its issue leads in my judgment to the inevitable conclusion that it was solely directed to gender discrimination and not to discrimination against sexual orientation.' Sir Thomas Bingham MR took the same view. Counsel had attempted to rely for the purpose of construing the Directive on Article 26 of the International Covenant on Civil and Political Rights. This starts: 'all persons are equal before the law and are entitled without any discrimination to the equal protection of the law.' Sir Thomas rejected the relevance of the Covenant and decisions under it. I do not know whether the principle of equality, as later formulated by the ECJ in *P* v. *S*, was advanced as an applicable principle to the court.

So far as human rights were concerned the court reiterated the received view that the Convention could not be enforced as such in our courts. Since the court took the view that the Directive had no application, no Community principles fell to be applied. However, it is noteworthy that the court accepted the following proposition from David Pannick, QC:

> The Court may not interfere with the exercise of an administrative discretion on substantive grounds save where the court is satisfied that the decisison is unreasonable in the sense that it is beyond the range of responses open to a reasonable decision maker. In judging whether the decision maker has exceeded this margin of appreciation the human rights context is important. The more substantial the interference with human rights, the more the court will require by way of justification before it is satisfied that the decision is reasonable in the sense outlined above.

When considering whether any human rights were in play the court looked at the European Convention. This approach is close to that of the ECJ.

[13] [1996] 2 WLR 305.

The Appeal Committee of the House of Lords, which included Lord Slynn, refused leave to appeal. That refusal was after the delivery of the Advocate General's opinion in *P* v. *S* but before the ECJ's decision. I understand that the AG's opinion was not referred to by the parties.

I add by way of postscript that Sedley J recently gave leave to move for judicial review in another homosexual case based on the Directive. He took the view that, in the light of *P* v. *S*, it was arguable that the Court of Appeal's decision in the *Ministry of Defence* case could no longer stand.

Legal Certainty and Fair Application of the Law in Luxembourg

The essence of the principle of legal certainty is that the application of the law to a specific legal situation must be predictable and it underlies the approach of Community law in a variety of contexts. AG van Gerven in *Coloroll Pension Trustees* v. *Russell*[14] put it thus:

> . . . in deciding to limit the scope of a judgment in time the Court is guided by two considerations: a general principle of legal certainty inherent in the Community legal order and a concern to prevent serious problems from arising, through unrestricted retroactive application of the judgment, in respect of legal relationships established in good faith.
>
> The fact that the principle of legal certainty forms part of the Community legal order is sufficiently well known. In essence, the Court is prepared, on account of special circumstances, to avoid calling in question legal relationships established in the past, notwithstanding the fact that there are grounds for this under a clarifying ruling which the Court has given in the meantime. It appears from its case law that the Court recognises the good faith, or the legitimate expectation, of the parties concerned or of the member states as such a special circumstance if the retroactive application of the judicial decision involves serious problems for the parties or the member states.[15]

These considerations influenced the Court in its famous judgments not only in *Defrenne*[16] and *Barber*[17] and its most recent judgments in *Brasserie du Pecheur SA* v. *Germany* and *Factortame III*.

The principle of legal certainty underlies the Community legal order in various, sometimes overlapping, contexts. For present purposes, I refer only to the doctrine of legitimate expectation. This doctrine, stemming from German law, has been widely and flexibly applied. Wyatt and Dashwood[18] happily summarize it thus: 'those who act in good faith on the basis of the law as it is or seems to be should not be frustrated in their expectations.' However, as Schermers points out: 'The protection of legitimate expectation is not a compelling principle which always takes priority. It will yield to overriding considerations of public interest.'

[14] [1994] ECR I–4389.
[15] paras. 14 and 15 of the opinion.
[16] [1978] ECR 1365.
[17] [1990] ECR I–1889.
[18] at p. 91.

Waelbroeck[19] has identified from the ECJ's case law various conditions which hedge about the application of the principle:

The commercial operation for which protection is claimed must be irrevocable. The legal rule which caused the expectation must definitely lead to the result expected : a chance is not enough.
The benefit for which protection is claimed must be a foreseeable result of the previous rules. The protected interest must be worth protection.
The change in legislation should not be foreseeable at the moment when the operation for which protection is claimed was performed.
Transitional provisions of the new legislation must be insufficient.

Proportionality is an aspect of the principle of the fair application of the law which is often invoked in Luxembourg (and, incidentally, in Strasbourg). This principle in essence requires that the means used by the authorities must be in proportion to their purpose. In England the principle is sometimes stated as being encapsulated in the phrase :'You must not use a sledgehammer to crack a nut.'

A recent example of the application of the principle is *Skanavi*.[20] The Greek Mrs Skanavi had taken up residence in Germany in order to run a furniture business. She was stopped in Germany while driving. She had a valid Greek driving licence but had failed to exchange it for a German one within a year of becoming resident in Germany as she was required to do under German law. She was charged with driving without a licence. The ECJ held that: 'Treating a person who has failed to have a (driving) licence exchanged as if he were a person without a licence, thereby causing criminal penalties, even if only financial in nature, such as those provided for in the national legislation in question in this case, would be disproportionate to the gravity of that infringement in view of the ensuing consequences.'

Legal Certainty and Fair Application of the Law in England[21]

The influence of the ECJ decisions is illustrated in some comments I made in an a case in the Court of Appeal, *Percy* v. *Hall*.[22] In *Percy* it was argued that certain byelaws which governed an airfields were void for uncertainty. The applicants had been arrested while on the airfield pursuant to powers on the face of it given by the byelaws. We in fact held that the byelaws were not void for uncertainty. But we had heard many submissions on the basis that they **were** void. I ventured to say the following:

It has been commonplace in our jurisprudence, as Simon Brown LJ points out, to speak of a basic principle that an ultra vires enactment is void ab initio and of no

[19] Reference given at Schermers p. 67. [20] [1996] ECR I–929.
[21] See P. P. Craig, *Administrative Law* (5th ed.) pp. 409 ff.
[22] [1996] 4 All ER 523 at 545.

effect. This beguilingly simple formulation, as is widely acknowledged, conceals more than it reveals. Manifestly in daily life the enactment *will* have had an effect in the sense that people will have regulated their conduct in the light of it. Even in the law courts it will often be found to have had *an* effect because the courts will have given a remedy to a person disadvantaged by the application of the ultra vires enactment to him or because a decision, binding on the parties thereto, has been rendered on the basis of the apparent law or because some period of limitation has expired making it too late now to raise any point on illegality.

The policy questions which the law must address in this type of case are: whether any and if so what remedy should be given to whom against whom in cases where persons have acted in reliance on what appears to be valid legislation. To approach these questions by rigidly applying to all circumstances a doctrine that the enactment which has been declared invalid was 'incapable of ever having had any legal effect upon the rights and duties to the parties' seems to me, with all respect to the strong stream of authority in our law to that effect, needlessly to restrict the possible answers which policy might require. For instance, in the context of the present case had we held the Byelaws to be invalid, as it seems to me a sensible answer might be that no remedy should be given against the policeman who acted in good faith but that a remedy should be given against a Secretary of State who put into circulation invalid byelaws with the perfectly foreseeable consequence that policemen would act on the assumption that they were valid. We are not required in the present case to decide whether that is the answer given by our law as it stands. I merely give it as a possibility.

It may be that, in the development of the law, future cases will draw on that part of our law which is applicable to cases containing a European Community element which shows a considerable amount of flexibility in dealing with this question. There are now many cases which examine the conflict which an *ex tunc* declaration produces with the principles of legal certainty, acquired rights and legitimate expectation.

Proportionality is a controversial doctrine here. As Steyn LJ put it in *Adams*[23] at page 191:

Although the proportionality principle is part of our law through Community Law it seems to us that the explanation of the principle are not in harmony . . . As English judges it seems to us that explanation of the principle span a spectrum of views from a narrow doctrine not essentially very different from Wednesbury unreasonableness to a de novo review of the administrative decision. On the other hand, there may be better explanations placing the principle between these extremes. Even in respect of proportionality there may be a margin of appreciation.

The fourth question referred to the ECJ in *Adams* reads: 'What are the precise requirements of the principle of proportionality in a case such as the present which, in relation to limitations on rights of free movement, involves freedom of speech and national security.'

[23] [1995] All ER (EC) 177.

Proportionality has not yet been officially received in the non-European part of English law. However note again what the court accepted in the *Ministry of Defence* case:

In judging whether the decision maker has exceeded this margin of appreciation the human rights context is important. The more substantial the interference with human rights, the more the court will require by way of justification before it is satisfied that the decision is reasonable in the sense outlined above.

Legitimate expectation is increasingly referred to in judicial review proceedings which have nothing to do with the European Treaties. Just as one would expect, concepts which are useful legal tools are beginning to be used outside their original context. Thus the approach to Human Rights in the context of irrationality in the *Ministry of Defence* case is very similar to the approach to proportionality sometimes taken by the ECJ.

An interesting example of this process of reception is the judgment of Sedley J in *R* v. *MAFF, ex p. Hamble Fisheries*.[24] He was there concerned with whether there could be an enforceable expectation of a substantive, as opposed to a merely procedural, benefit. Let me cite bits of it:

I turn therefore to the question which has been most heavily fought over in these proceedings: did the Applicant have a legitimate expectation that an exception would be made for fishermen in its position? It has been debated before me almost entirely in terms of the jurisprudence of the Court of Justice of the European Community. Neither counsel submits that there is any material difference between this body of Law and the domestic law of England and Wales.[25]

What matters, therefore, in the Common Law both of the European Community and of Britain, is whether (in Professor Schwarze's words) the Applicant can demonstrate 'An expectation which is worthy of protection'. While the phrase may have lost something in what is generally an excellent translation, it pinpoints the question begged by the Common Law concept: what makes an expectation legitimate?[26]

At page 731 of the judgment we find an answer to this question:

Legitimacy in this sense is not an absolute. It is a function of expectations induced by government and of policy considerations which militate against their fulfilment. The balance must in the first instance be for the policy-maker to strike; but if the outcome is challenged by way of Judicial Review, I do not consider that the Court's criterion is the bare rationality of the policy-maker's conclusion. While policy is for the policy-maker alone, the fairness of his or her decision not to accommodate reasonable expectations which the policy will thwart remains the Court's concern . . . To postulate this is not to place the Judge in the seat of the Minister. As the foregoing citations explain, it is the Court's task to recognise the constitutional importance of ministerial freedom to formulate and to re-formulate policy; but it is equally the Court's duty to protect the interests of those individuals whose

24 [1995] 2 All ER 723. 25 at p. 724. 26 at p. 728.

expectations of different treatment has a legitimacy which in fairness out-tops the policy choice which threatens to frustrate it.'

This approach was thereafter described as heretical by the Court of Appeal in *R.* v. *Secretary of State ex p. Hargreaves* [1997] 1 All ER 397.

Conclusion

The Judge's reasoning is an indication of the process of the cross-fertilization of Community law by our law and of our law by Community law. The General Principles of Community law repay study. There are cases where the English judge is bound to take into account the General Principles of Community Law. This field has expanded and will continue to do so. Lawyers will continue to make better use of the General Principles as they become more familiar with them. It is to be expected that as judges, and those arguing the cases before them, become familiar with the general principles in this way, they will obtain inspiration from these principles, also in cases where they are not bound to take them into account. This, as I have set out above, is a natural extension of techniques used by our judges when solving problems.

10

*A Sense of Proportion**

BY THE RT HON LORD HOFFMANN

I have chosen proportionality as my subject because it is one of those principles used to demarcate the line between the powers of the judiciary on the one hand and the executive and the legislature on the other. It marks the boundary between constitutional law and political discretion and has a tendency to be somewhat controversial. But before I explain what the principle of proportionality means, I want to set the scene by describing the context in which it arises.

By way of introduction therefore, I shall touch upon three topics. First, I shall describe the problems involved in judicial control of the exercise of power by the other two branches of government. Secondly, I shall try to explain why, despite the fact that the United Kingdom has no written constitution, its principles of judicial control do not in practice differ from those applied in countries like the United States or Ireland which have constitutionally guaranteed human rights. Thirdly, I shall give a brief sketch of what those principles are.

There can hardly be a more important function for the judiciary than controlling the exercise of power of the State. In a democratic society it is the courts which hold our political masters to the terms of the social contract under which they govern. The judicial power to review the acts of the executive and in some cases the legislature and to declare invalid any wrongful exercise of power is the most fundamental aspect of that complex notion which we call the rule of law. It is however also one of the most delicate tasks which a judge can have to perform. Judges have always to remember that their function is to enforce the law of the land and the principles of the constitution and that, subject only to the laws, government is entrusted to the elected representatives of the people. The boundary between the application of legal principle and the exercise of political discretion is often hard to draw. It is, however, for the judges to say where it lies. They have to bring to this task not only analytical skills as lawyers but also what I can only describe as political sensitivity. By this I do not mean that they must temper decisions to political expediency. The courts must

* This is the text of the third John Maurice Kelly Memorial lecture delivered in University College, Dublin on 19 November 1996 and published by the Faculty of Law 1997. The introductory passage of the lecture is omitted here.

be fearless in holding the government to the law whether its earns them praise or abuse. But the constitution is a living thing: it has to be applied to real people, with human failings but also with human values. On the one hand it has to remembered that the business of government is difficult and that one cannot expect all decisions to be taken with calm deliberation or perfect foresight of their consequences. Politicians and civil servants complain, and sometimes with good cause, that judges do not understand the realities of the world in which they have to work. On the other hand, it must also be recognized that a democratic society is based upon values which accord to everyone certain basic rights which must be respected not only by government but also by the elected representatives of the majority. It is the function of the courts to protect these rights against even the most well-intentioned invasion.

The basic rights which judges must enforce are not necessarily precisely the same in every democratic society. In particular, the importance which is attached to different rights and the hierarchy which determines which should take precedence over another will depend very much upon the history and culture of the nation. Some basic rights are not compatible with each other and compromises have to made. Complete freedom of expression is not compatible with protection of the privacy and dignity of the individual; liberty in full measure is not compatible with equality and so on. In some countries, there is a broad consensus on such issues.

The values of a people, the importance which they attach to one right as against another are often moulded by the injustices which its members have suffered in the past; a society which has made a new start after a regime of religious oppression will attach great importance to freedom of religion; one which has suffered under a brutal and arbitrary dictatorship will value above all the dignity of the individual. It is easy to recognize examples in various European countries. And in addition to these national differences there are changes within a single society from one period to another. In the United Kingdom, for example, the 1960s were a watershed in social values. A decade which saw the decriminalization of attempted suicide and homosexual acts between adults, the abolition of capital punishment, the reform of the divorce laws, and the passing of legislation to prohibit racial and sexual discrimination is evidence of more than a hyperactive legislature. It represented an important shift in attitudes to the proper relationship between the individual and the State; to the division between individual freedom and the power of the State to intervene for the protection of the rights of others. But no one would suggest that a country in which attitudes on such matters were somewhat different was on that account any less democratic.

All these distinctions, sometimes subtle, sometimes rather less subtle, between different nations and different eras, have to be taken into account by judges deciding on the constitutional limits of State action. I may also say that the high degree to which decisions on State power must be specific to a particular society at a particular time makes me doubt the wisdom of entrusting these matters to international tribunals such as the Court of Human Rights at Strasbourg.

I pass then to my second preliminary subject, which is the peculiar position of the United Kingdom. We have, at least for the moment, a sovereign legislature which is untrammelled by any formal legal requirement that it should respect basic human rights. There is a certain amount of academic debate, in which one or two of my colleagues have perhaps unwisely joined, as to what would happen if Parliament decided to test the theory to destruction and pass legislation so undemocratic as to destroy the social contract upon which the principle of parliamentary sovereignty itself was based. I think that one can safely leave that question until the time it arises; perhaps the answer is that a government so hostile to democratic principles would hardly be deterred by a bench of judges saying that they had no power to enforce their will.

The principle of the sovereignty of Parliament might therefore suggest, to someone who knew nothing else about the people of the United Kingdom, that they were a democratic society only in the sense that they entrusted power to the elected representatives of the majority, or strictly speaking, given the system of voting in the United Kingdom, to the representatives of the largest minority party, but that they lacked that other essential element of democracy, namely a set of legal values which protect certain rights of the individual from invasion even by the majority. In fact, of course, this would be wrong. For centuries the principles which protect individual rights have been part of the common law. The American Bill of Rights is based upon the common law. And while in theory these common law rights can be overridden by statute, the fact that they are embedded in the history and culture of the United Kingdom makes the courts assume, when they have to interpret legislation, that Parliament intended to respect them. I write in the conventional way of what Parliament intended because judges usually write as if their task was to decode a message sent to them by the group of people who took part in the legislative act. But a moment's thought will show that this notion contains great difficulties and it might be more realistic to say that the common law of basic human rights is simply the law which English judges apply and that they approach with varying degrees of incredulity, depending on the seriousness of the invasion, any Parliamentary text which could be read as trenching upon those rights. This means that although no judge in the United Kingdom will ever declare an Act of Parliament invalid, his approach to things done or powers exercised under that Act will in practice differ very little from that of a judge applying a written constitution which contains an entrenched declaration of basic rights. In theory the only question in each case is what the Act of Parliament means, but beneath that uniform surface of statutory construction one can, like a geologist, detect the difference between the malleable clay of questions of economic and social policy which are subject to majority rule and the hard igneous rock of basic human rights which resists erosion by everything except the most powerful reasons of State.

I am bound to say, however, that the English theory of parliamentary sovereignty does have some effect on the way in which judicial review is perceived by the people and the press. Because the government in effect controls Parliament, people have difficulty in understanding the distinction between the legislature and the executive. They have even more difficulty in understanding the concept of a hidden landscape of human rights; in fact they tend on the whole not to be enthusiastic about human rights for other people at all. Couple this with a tendency in the press to portray cases on judicial review as football matches and one has the picture, which is assiduously cultivated by politicians as well as newspapers, of permanent conflict between unelected judges and an elected government.

As a third and last preliminary matter, I want to sketch the general principles which English, and I think Irish, courts, presently apply to the review of State action. These principles were encapsulated by Lord Diplock in his celebrated judgment in the *GCHQ* case,[1] when he said that they fell under three heads; illegality, irrationality, and procedural impropriety. Illegality, he said, meant a failure on the part of the decision-maker correctly to apply the law which governs the exercise of his power. This was clearly a justicable question. Procedural impropriety included such matters as bias or not giving someone an opportunity to be heard. The most difficult head to apply is the second, irrationality. Lord Diplock defined it as 'a decision which is so outrageous in its defiance of logic or of accepted moral standards that no sensible person who had applied his mind to the question to be decided could have arrived at it.' The rhetorical thrust of this formulation is intended to emphasize that courts will not easily be persuaded that an exercise of State power otherwise lawful was irrational. Its actual content, with its emphasis on logic and moral standards, is perhaps more doubtful; it has been convincingly criticized by Henchy J in the *Stardust* case[2] on the grounds that, on the one hand, many administrative decisions involve political compromises which will not stand up to logical analysis and are none the worse for that, while the application of moral standards takes the court onto slippery and dangerous ground. In practice, however, English courts have not regarded themselves as bound either by the rhetoric or content of this definition. The

[1] *Council of Civil Service Unions* v. *Minister for the Civil Service* [1985] AC 374.

[2] *The State [Keegan]* v. *The Stardust Victims Compensation Tribunal* [1986] IR 642, 658.

notion of irrationality has been applied in a flexible way, accommodating itself to the hidden landscape of human rights. So, for example, in decisions of general social or economic policy the courts have indeed required a high degree of irrationality. On the other hand, the different approach to cases involving basic rights was made explicit by Lord Bridge in *Brind* v. *Secretary of State for the Home Dept.*,[3] a case on freedom of speech, when he drew attention to the fact that we had no constitution which entrenched the right to freedom of speech but went on to say:

> In exercising the power of judicial review we have neither the advantages nor the disadvantages of any comparable code to which we may refer or by which we are bound. But again, this surely does not mean that in deciding whether the Secretary of State, in the exercise of his discretion, could reasonably impose the restriction he has imposed on the broadcasting organisations, we are not perfectly entitled to start from the premise than any restriction of the right to freedom of expression requires to be justified and that nothing less than an important competing public interest will be sufficient to justify it.[4]

The difficulty for the applicants in the *Brind* case was that the public interest competing with freedom of speech was the security of the State. In the hierarchy of values which the courts apply, the security of the State almost always wins. Judges are understandably very reluctant to take the responsibility for questioning the opinion of executive government as to what the security of the State requires. But the general principle that any invasion of basic individual rights needs a high degree of justification is now well established.

There is, I think, an important lesson to be learned here. The principles of judicial review, the ceaseless struggle to delimit the boundaries which the law has set to the power of the State, cannot be captured even by Lord Diplock in three or four bullet points with single word headings elucidated by a single sentence of explanation. It is a far more subtle and complex subject. Judges tend to support their decisions in a particular case by appropriate rhetoric. In a case in which the court has decided that judicial intervention is inappropriate, there is a temptation to emphasize in the most general terms the reluctance of the courts to intervene. And there is always a tendency to reductionism, to trying to squeeze the diversity of life into single formula which can be made to yield an answer in every case.

This lengthy introduction brings me at last to the principle of proportionality, which was given a fair wind by Lord Diplock in his statement of the law in the *GCHQ* case. After enumerating the grounds of illegality, irrationality and procedural impropriety, he added: 'That is not to say that further development on a case by case basis may not in course of time add

[3] [1991] 1 AC 696. [4] at pp. 748–9.

further grounds. I have in mind particularly the possible adoption in future of the principle of "proportionality" which is recognised in the administrative law of several of our fellow members of the European Economic Community . . .'[5]

Since then, a number of academic writers and counsel in the United Kingdom have been making strenuous efforts to fulfil this rather tentative prophesy. In Ireland too the doctrine may be said, to borrow a phrase from Hogan and Morgan's splendid book, *Administrative Law in Ireland*,[6] to be slouching towards the Four Courts to be born.

It is timely therefore to consider whether it is a rough beast which ought to be expelled or a useful addition to the judicial armoury.

Proportionality was said by Lord Diplock to mean not using a steam hammer to crack a nut.[7] The principle was developed by the Prussian Administrative Supreme Court in the last century for the admirable purpose of controlling the exercise of power by the Prussian police.[8] From these beginnings it has been extended to be a general test for the constitutionality of an exercise of State power and has been taken up as a basic legal principle of the European Community. The Germans, in their Germanic way, analysed the principle of proportionality or *Grundsatz der Verhältnismäßigkeit* into three parts: first, a measure must be suitable for the purpose which the power has been conferred; secondly, it must be necessary, in the sense that the purpose could not have been achieved by some other means which are less burdensome to the persons affected, and thirdly it must be proportional 'in the strict sense', *im engeren Sinn*, that is to say, the burdens which are imposed by the exercise of the power must not be disproportionate to the importance of the purpose which it achieves. An example given in the German literature[9] is a regulation made in the exercise of a power to control smoke pollution which requires factory chimneys to be at least 30 metres high. Such a measure will not be suitable if high chimneys do not in fact have any effect on the amount of smoke pollution which the factory produces; it will not be necessary if the same reduction could have been achieved by a chimney half as high or requiring the use of another cheaper method such as a filtration system and it will not be proportionate in the strict sense if the achieved reduction in smoke pollution is wholly disproportionate to the cost of a high chimney.

I draw attention to certain features of this example. The power in question is being exercised for a narrow and technical purpose, namely to

[5] *Supra*, n. 1, p. 410.

[6] (2nd ed. 1991) p. 515, n. 44.

[7] *R* v. *Goldstein* [1983] 1 WLR 151, 157.

[8] Schwarze, *European Administrative Law* (1992), p. 685: Jakobs, *Der Grundsatz der Verhältnismäßigkeit* (1994), pp. 5, 6.

[9] Maurer, *Allgemeines Verwaltungsrecht* (9th ed. 1994) pp. 225–6.

reduce smoke pollution. Whether high chimneys have this effect and whether something else would work as well or better is again a technical question, capable of being established by evidence. In this example, a decision which offended the principle of suitability or necessity could be comfortably accommodated within English doctrine on the ground that it was irrational. It is the third question: proportionality in the strict sense, which may cause difficulty. And at least one of the difficulties lies in the problem of commensurability: how does one compare the cost to factory owners in marks and pfennigs with the somewhat more imponderable benefits to the local population of breathing cleaner air and not having smuts on the laundry. If the local authority has taken the view that the balance comes down in favour of higher chimneys, it will not be easy for a court to explain why it thinks that the local authority was wrong.

If I may at this stage introduce some autobiography, my own first encounter with proportionality was as a part of European law. It was, to say the least, an unusual experience for an English lawyer. Article 30 of the Treaty of Rome says: 'Quantitative restrictions on imports and all measures having equivalent effect shall . . . be prohibited between Member States'. Article 36 contains a number of exceptions and the Court of Justice has also recognized that Member States may pursue other legitimate objectives like keeping out pornography even if they have the effect of restricting trade across European borders. In each case, however, the Court has said that the principle of proportionality must be observed: the measure affecting Community trade must be suitable to achieve its legitimate purpose; it must be necessary in that the purpose could not have been achieved in a way which did not affect Community trade and it must not be disproportionate. An example of these tests being applied is the *Cassis de Dijon* case.[10] The measure in this case was a German law which prohibited the sale of fruit liqueurs having an alcoholic content less than 25 per cent. This ruled out the French blackcurrant liqueur known as *Cassis de Dijon*, which has by German standards a rather feeble alcoholic content of less than 20 per cent. The Germans said the law was necessary because German shoppers expected liqueurs to be serious alcoholic drinks and would be misled by *Cassis de Dijon*. The Commission said that if the Germans were really worried about people being misled, they could require labels stating the alcohol content. They did not have to ban the sale of the drink altogether. The Court of Justice agreed. Here again, you will notice, the object of the measure is fairly technical and common sense is enough to suggest that alternative measures would do just as well. Indeed, the German argument makes one doubt their bona fides, just as the Court doubted the bona fides of the British government when it claimed that

[10] Case 120/78 *Rewe-Zentral AG* v. *Bundesmonopolverwaltung für Branntwein* [1979] ECR 649.

about six weeks before Christmas it had discovered that French turkeys might harbour some obscure disease which was a danger to the health of the British public: *Commission* v. *United Kingdom*.[11] The Court held that the total ban on the import of French turkeys which the government had imposed failed the test of necessity.

These are fairly straightforward examples of proportionality being applied to cases on restrictions on imports under Article 30. But the case in which I first met it arose out of the prohibition on Sunday trading in the Shops Act 1950, which has since been repealed. For years before its repeal, it was widely disregarded in England, particularly by DIY shops and garden centres, but some local authorities tried to enforce it and the stores hired ingenious lawyers to think up defences. One of these was that a prohibition on Sunday trading was an infringement of Article 30 because it had equivalent effect to a quantitative restriction on imports. This may seem rather strange, because the law simply said that, with certain exceptions, shops had to be closed on Sundays. It did not distinguish between sales of imports and other goods. Nevertheless, the store owners argued that if they could not open on Sundays they would, for example, sell less Dutch bulbs than they otherwise would and the law was therefore equivalent to a quantitative restriction on the import of Dutch bulbs. This knotty question was referred to the European Court, which gave an answer in November 1989.[12] It said that regulating the times at which shops could open was a legitimate area of legislation for Member States. In its characteristic Eurospeak it said: 'Such rules reflect certain political and economic choices in so far as their purpose is to ensure that working and non-working hours are so arranged as to accord with national or regional socio-cultural characteristics, and that, in the present state of Community law, is a matter for the member states.'[13]

However, a prohibition on Sunday trading could infringe Article 30 if the effect on Community trade was disproportionate: as the Court said, 'where the restrictive effects on Community trade which may result therefrom do not exceed the effects intrinsic to rules of that kind'. Whether it did or not was a question of fact to be decided by the national court.

The result of this decision was that magistrates' courts and county courts all over England were asked to decide, as a question of fact, whether the extent to which Sunday trading rules achieved their legitimate objectives was proportionate to their effect on Community trading. Economists, theologians, and others hired by the store owners toured the country to give local magistrates the benefit of their expertise. They found it all very puzzling. The Sunday trading laws were a political compromise which had been put together in 1936. The motives for which they had been

[11] Case 40/82, [1982] ECR 2793.

[12] *Torfaen BC v. B & Q plc* [1990] 2 QB 19.

[13] *Id.*, p. 53.

enacted were extremely muddled: a mixture of Sabbatarianism, trade unionism and the protection of small shopkeepers against big stores. The Act was full of illogical and obsolete exceptions: for example, there was an exception for periodicals but not books, so that one could buy *Playboy* on Sunday but not the Bible. There was very little logic in the scheme of the Act. So the magistrates had the task of first, trying to state the purposes of the Act in a coherent form and then asking themselves whether it restricted Community trade more than was necessary for those purposes. Not surprisingly, they arrived at different answers and so one had a situation in which the Shops Act was contrary to European law in one area but enforceable in another area.

One such case, which was brought in the High Court, came before me.[14] So I was asked to decide whether, for example, the social or religious policies of the Act, such as they were, would be seriously damaged if Dutch bulbs or Italian furniture were added to the list of exemptions. I am afraid that I declined to do any such thing. Such a weighting of imponderables seemed to me a legislative exercise which was quite inappropriate for a judge. I said that the Act involved compromises between competing interests and my only duty was to ask: 'whether the compromise adopted by United Kingdom Parliament, so far as it affects community trade, is one which a reasonable legislature could have reached.'[15]

This way of putting the matter, with its obvious echoes of *Wednesbury* unreasonableness,[16] the origin of the English principle of rationality, raised the hackles of European lawyers. When the House of Lords referred the Sunday trading case back to Luxembourg for a ruling on how the proportionality test was to be applied, I was criticized by the Advocate-General. He said it was for the courts to ensure that any obstacles to free movement of goods observe the limits laid down by Community law and not confine themselves to deciding whether the national legislature could reasonably have adopted the provisions in question.[17]

I suspect, however, that my real sin was to have used the wrong terminology. What I should have said was that the UK legislature should be allowed a substantial margin of appreciation in ensuring that working and non-working hours were so arranged as to accord with national or regional socio-cultural characteristics. A reference to a margin of appreciation is the phrase which European lawyers use when they recognize that the application of a concept like proportionality or indeed any other form of judicial review is taking them into areas of politics and administration which judges are not equipped to handle.

[14] *Stoke on Trent CC* v. *B & Q plc* [1991] Ch. 48. [15] *Id.*, p. 69.

[16] *Associated Provincial Picture Houses Ltd* v. *Wednesbury Corporation* [1948] 1 KB 223.

[17] *Stoke-on-Trent CC* v. *B & Q plc* [1993] AC 900, 944–5.

For example, the Court of Justice decided recently[18] that a directive prescribing a maximum 48 hour working week could be made under Article 118a of the Treaty as a requirement to improve the health and safety of workers. The United Kingdom had argued that the Directive lacked proportionality because health and safety could be improved by less sweeping and restrictive measures. The Court stated the conventional principles of proportionality: the means which the Directive employs must be suitable for the purpose of achieving the desired objective and must not go beyond what is necessary to achieve it. The Court then went on to say:[19]

> As to judicial review of those conditions, however, the Council must be allowed a wide discretion in an area which, as here, involves the legislature in making social policy choices and requires it to carry out complex assessments. Judicial review of the exercise of that discretion must therefore be limited to examining whether it has been vitiated by manifest error or misuse of powers or whether the institution concerned has manifestly exceeded the limits of its discretion.

The Court has said the same thing on many previous occasions. It is a piece of boilerplate text regularly bolted into the Court's judgments: in my first draft of this chapter, I had taken a similar passage from a case on the Common Agricultural Policy.[20] For my part, I can see no daylight between this test and the English concept of irrationality as it would be applied to a case involving the exercise of a similar discretion in the field of economic and social policy. In each case, not involving any question of fundamental human rights, the overriding concern of the Court is not to become involved in policy choices but to confine itself to ensuring that the decision complies with fairly undemanding standards of irrationality.

The most determined effort to persuade an English court to accept proportionality as a freestanding principle of judicial review was by Lord Lester of Herne Hill QC in the *Brind* case.[21] This case, which I have already mentioned, concerned the ban on Sinn Fein or IRA members being shown speaking on television, as opposed to being quoted or having actors speak their words. The Government claimed that the interference with freedom of speech was a modest one and that it was justified in the interests of the security of the State—an interest which, as I mentioned, almost invariably trumps other interests. Lord Lester argued that even if the rule could not be said to be irrational under traditional doctrine, the court should invalidate it on the grounds that the infringement of freedom of speech was disproportionate to the contribution it made to State security.

Lord Lowry's attitude to proportionality was rather like that of the Caliph of Baghdad to the books in the library of Alexandria: either they

[18] Case C–84/94 *UK* v. *Council of the European Union*, [1996] ECR I–5755.
[19] Para. 58.
[20] *Société RU-MI* v. *FORMA* [1982] ECR 4167, 4190.
[21] *R* v. *Secretary of State for the Home Department, ex parte Brind* [1991] 2 AC 696.

said the same as the Koran and should be burned as superfluous or they said something different and should be burned as heretical. If proportionality offered a wider scope for judicial review than the traditional principle of irrationality, it must by definition involve the court deciding questions which the law entrusted to the executive. Lord Ackner agreed and the other Law Lords expressed no view.

An analysis of the cases in England in which there has been or might have been some reference to proportionality tends in my view to bear out Lord Lowry's opinion. Of course there may be cases in which the best way to explain why a decision is, in the English or Irish sense irrational, is to point out that its effects are disproportionate. There are decisions, for example, as to the imposition of penalties, where the essence of rationality is to show a sense of proportion. For example, the case of Mr Hook,[22] who in 1976 was deprived of his livelihood as a street trader by Barnsley Borough Council because one afternoon, emerging from the pub, he peed in a quiet corner of the street, is sometimes cited as the first swallow heralding the arrival of the principle in English constitutional law. The Court of Appeal quashed the decision on the grounds that the penalty was excessive. It seems to me, however, that no reference to German scholarship is needed to justify such a decision as a correction by the court of the Council's complete lack of common sense. Likewise cases of interference with fundamental human rights frequently raise what can accurately be described as questions of proportionality. The Articles of the European Convention on Human Rights which declare that various basic rights may be abridged only on certain grounds and only so far as is necessary in a democratic society, carry with them a built-in requirement of proportionality and English courts, as we have seen from Lord Bridge's speech in *Brind*, apply the same principles as a matter of common law.

On the other hand, an argument on proportionality was expressly rejected by the House of Lords in *Tesco Stores Ltd* v. *Secretary of State for the Environment*,[23] a case on town and country planning. Sainsburys had been granted planning permission to build a supermarket at Witney in Oxfordshire, greatly to the annoyance of Tesco, who had been refused. A condition of the grant of planning permission had been that Sainsburys should enter into a planning agreement by which they undertook to provide various infrastructural benefits, such as a contribution to a new link road to relieve congestion in the centre of the town. These benefits were in general terms related to the development: for example, the supermarket was undoubtedly going to add to the traffic. But Tesco complained that the benefits provided by Sainsburys were disproportionate to any environmental disadvantages of the scheme. The benefits exacted by the planning

[22] *R* v. *Barnsley MBC ex parte Hook* [1976] 1 WLR 1052.

[23] [1995] 2 All ER 636.

authority lacked proportionality and the permission should not therefore be held invalid. The House of Lords said that they could not say whether the benefits were disproportionate without deciding the extent to which the scheme carried environmental disadvantages. This was a question of planning merits which had been entrusted by statute to the planning authority. Unless therefore the benefits were plainly irrelevant to the development, like providing a swimming pool on the other side of town, the court would not intervene.

Tesco was treated by the House of Lords as a pure social policy case, involving no question of human rights and therefore a matter of unfettered discretion. This illustrates the importance of a point which I made earlier, namely the existence of national and cultural differences about the relative importance of various human rights. In the United States, for example, State interference with the right to develop one's land is regarded in principle as a taking of property without compensation, contrary to the Fifth Amendment. Planning conditions are unlawful unless they can be justified on the grounds of necessity and proportionality. In the United Kingdom, this is not the case. The freedom to build whatever one likes on one's land is regarded as having been nationalized, once and for all, by the Town and Country Planning Act 1947: *Westminster Bank* v. *Beverley Borough Council*.[24] A refusal of planning permission gives no right to compensation and decisions on planning permission fall outside the various techniques which the courts use for the protection of human rights.

I hope I have demonstrated from both the jurisprudence of the European Court and the English courts that the argument about proportionality in English law does seem to be over labels rather than substance. Whether the courts ride into battle with proportionality or rationality inscribed upon their banners, the weapons they carry to defend the citizen against the State are much the same. In neither case can the full practical working of the principles which the courts apply be deduced from the single word on the label. Proportionality may sound more encouraging to judicial intervention than rationality, but when one looks at the actual decisions which have come before the courts, judges are no more willing to characterize a decision as lacking proportionality than they are to describe it as irrational.

What then is the future of proportionality in English law? Not, I think, as a new technique for twisting Leviathan's tail or a new tool for picking the lock of a door to judicial review which the courts presently keep shut. Our courts and those in Europe and Germany are engaged in trying to solve substantially the same problems by substantially the same methods.

24 [1971] AC 509.

Proportionality is not a new principle but another and sometimes better way of explaining how we apply our existing principles. It may or may not enable a court to give a more convincing explanation for the way in which it has applied established principles in the particular case. Sometimes, as in the Sunday trading cases, it will be quite inapposite. Sometimes it will be illuminating. But that, I think, is all. Perhaps this outcome is less revolutionary than the protagonists of proportionality expect. But in these matters too, one must have a sense of proportion.

PART C

The Impact on Some Areas of Law

11

Community Competition Law in English Courts

BY THE HON MR JUSTICE HUGH LADDIE

This chapter, which is based upon a lecture given at the conference at King's in 1996, arises out of a decision given by me at an interlocutory stage in *Iberian UK Limited* v. *BPB Industries plc*.[1] That case concerned the extent to which English courts should pay regard to decisions of the Commission in relation to allegations of breach of the competition law under the Treaty of Rome. The views expressed below are, of course, mine alone. In one sense this is a strange chapter to write since it seeks to explain and justify the decision I reached in *Iberian*. As to the first of these objectives, the judgment should do that itself. The latter is somewhat presumptuous. Whether the decision is correct will no doubt be tested in a higher court.[2]

As is well known, a central objective of the Treaty of Rome is the creation of a single undivided market between Member States of the European Union. To that end it contains special provisions relating to the free movement of capital and people. It also contains the wide-ranging competition or anti-trust provisions in Articles 85 and 86. An inevitable consequence of imposing legal restraints on the exercise by individuals or corporations of economic power is that there must be some definition of which exercises of power are to be treated as unacceptable. Someone accused of breaching the standards must be given the opportunity to challenge that assertion and defend himself. This results in one of the significant problems generated by any such system of restraints; the determination of whether there has been a breach is complex and expensive. Anti-trust suits in the United States are notorious for their prolixity and cost. There is no reason to expect the equivalent suits involving the anti-trust provisions of Articles 85 and 86 of the Treaty of Rome to be significantly cheaper or easier. Any attack on anti-competitive behaviour is likely to involve the consideration of detailed economic data. And charges of such behaviour which could lead to the offender being subject to heavy financial penalties and restrictions on his future freedom of action must be expected to be fought with all the resources the offender can muster.

[1] [1997] EuLR 1.

[2] See also the judgment by Tuckey J in *The Coal Authority* v. *J H Banks and Company Ltd* [1997] EuLR n.y.r.

Where the offensive activity consists of the creation of a cartel between manufacturers or vendors designed to restrict competition and keep prices up, there may well be no one who is willing to break ranks. All the actors may benefit from the suppression of competition. Indeed there may be no one outside the club except the eventual consumer and he may not realize that the cartel exists or that it is being used to restrict supplies and inflate prices. Absent an outside agency to intervene on behalf of the consumer, the anti-trust provisions will prove to be of little value. Furthermore, even if there is someone who is, and knows he is, adversely affected by the anti-competitive activities of manufacturers or suppliers in a particular market, he may have insufficient financial strength to take on the perpetrators. It follows that the provision of an independent body to police the competition rules is not only reasonable but essential. Furthermore the existence of an independent body which has special responsibility in an area as potentially complex as competition law means that it can build up the necessary expertise to ensure not only that disputes can be resolved efficiently but that decisions in different cases are as consistent as possible. The fact that the Treaty also envisages the imposition of fines for breach of the competition rules also makes it essential to have an independent policing and enforcement authority. That authority is the Commission.

Directorate General (or DG) IV of the Commission has the power to investigate, bring charges, prosecute, and fine offenders. It can be said to be police, prosecutor, judge, and jury. But it is subject to strict rules imposing obligations on it to act fairly, make clear the charges, look at evidence, hear submissions and give reasoned decisions. Furthermore, its decisions are subject to appeal to the CFI and ECJ. It can investigate alleged breaches of the Treaty either of its own motion or because a complaint is sent to it by a third party. In this respect it exhibits similarities to police investigations of crime in the England. Even if there is a complaint by a third party, the conduct of the investigation and what issues, if any, are pursued are matters for the Commission alone. In reality it is a complete enforcement agency with the dedicated function of ensuring compliance with Articles 85 and 86.

But of course the competition provisions of the Treaty are not only enforced by the Commission. The Treaty of Rome is part of our domestic law. It creates rights and obligations just as a piece of domestic legislation can do. An English company which is prevented from importing from or exporting to the rest of the Union, for example as a result of an anti-competitive clause in a contract, can seek relief from the domestic courts. If his trade is damaged by anti-competitive practices, for example by misuse of patent rights preventing exports of licensed goods from England into Germany, he can not only seek injunctive relief but he may be able to claim damages for breach of statutory duty.

It is therefore said that the national courts and the Commission have concurrent jurisdiction in relation to competition issues. However that is not completely true. They are really separate jurisdictions with a large area where they overlap. Only the Commission has the power to impose fines and it also has exclusive jurisdiction under Article 85(3) to grant exemptions. On the other hand, domestic courts have the exclusive jurisdiction to make orders for compensation in favour of those harmed by offensive commercial activities and the national courts are peculiarly well placed to give injunctive relief, particularly at the interlocutory stage. It follows that in some areas each has exclusive jurisdiction but they share jurisdiction to determine whether there has been a breach of Articles 85 and 86, i.e., to assess the facts and apply the jurisprudence which has been developed under the Treaty. Notwithstanding this sharing of responsibility, there is no doubt that the Commission has built up a body of expertise in anti-trust matters which is unmatched by any national court. The personnel in DG IV are experts in this area.

The existence of the overlapping jurisdiction of the Commission and national courts on competition matters raises an important issue: what is the interrelationship between Commission and those courts? Is there a pecking order? In some cases the alleged victim of offensive trade practice will complain to the Commission as well as making a claim in the national courts. Furthermore the competition provisions of the Treaty can be made a matter of abuse. In the intellectual property field it has been a common strategy for an infringer to raise more or less specious Treaty of Rome defences and to complain to the Commission at the same time so as to ensure that the proceedings in the national courts become expensive and slow while he continues to infringe. It was in the face of that kind of tactic that the late Walton J once said that the Treaty was being used as a 'Pirate's Charter'.

It is the simultaneous consideration of the same competition issues before the Commission and one or more national courts which gives rise to particular problems. Two questions arise: (a) what impact does the existence of Commission proceedings have on the conduct of parallel English proceedings? and (b) what impact should a decision of Commission have on such parallel proceedings?

The impact of the *Existence* of Commission Proceedings on the Conduct of English Proceedings

Even in purely domestic situations, English courts have set their face against subjecting parties to multiple simultaneous proceedings. This is exemplified by cases such as *Thames Launches* v. *Trinity House Corporation*[3]

[3] [1961] Ch 197.

and *Sears plc* v. *Sears, Roebuck & Co.*[4] Normally the approach has been to impose a stay on the 'junior' proceedings. A very similar approach has been adopted by English courts to concurrent competition proceedings before them and the Commission. On a number of occasions our courts have stayed domestic proceedings pending the outcome of proceedings before the Commission. The logistical advantages of this course are clear. The parties are not subject to litigating the same heavy issues before two tribunals at the same time. The costs implications of doing otherwise are too obvious to state.

But that is not the only consideration which makes a stay desirable. There is the issue of consistency. It is useful to bear in mind what the ECJ has said on this subject. In *Stergios Delimitis* v. *Henninger Bräu*,[5] a number of questions had been referred by the Oberlandesgericht Frankfurt am Main to the ECJ. One of them raised the question of the respective powers of the Commission and national courts in the application of Community competition rules. The ECJ said:

> the Commission does not have exclusive competence to apply Articles 85(1) and 86. It shares that competence with the national courts. . . . It now falls to examine the consequences of that division of competence as regards the specific application of the Community competition rules by national courts. Account should here be taken of the risk of national courts taking decisions which conflict with those taken or envisaged by the Commission in the implementation of Articles 85(1) and 86, and also of Article 85(3). Such conflicting decisions would be contrary to the general principle of legal certainty and must, therefore, be avoided when national courts give decisions on agreements or practices which may subsequently be the subject of a decision by the Commission . . .

The same approach was adopted in *MTV Europe* v. *BMG Record (UK) Limited*.[6] In that case the plaintiff, MTV, was the provider of television programmes. It obtained copyright licences for the materials it broadcast from a number of copyright collection societies. It entered into a licence with a number of them but in June 1992 it complained to the Commission that the collection societies' licences and operations breached Articles 85 and 86. A year later they sued a number of companies, including the collection societies, in England for breach of statutory duty. A few months later the defendants applied to stay the High Court proceedings pending final determination of MTV's complaint to the Commission. That matter came before Evans-Lombe J. The primary argument advanced by the defendants was that, absent a stay, there existed 'a potential for conflict between any judgment of this court and the decision of the Commission, or any appeals from it'. The Judge expressed the view:

[4] [1993] RPC 385. This decision was upheld in an unreported decision of the Court of Appeal.

[5] [1991] ECR I–935.

[6] [1997] EuLR 100.

It seems to me that for the court to decide at this stage to press on to judgment, in the light of the proceedings before the Commission, involves the court in coming to the clear conclusion that the final determination of the complaint to the Commission will be decided in favour of MTV. To do otherwise would be to run the risk of conflict with the decision of the Commission, which this court is enjoined to avoid if possible by the Delimitis decision.[7]

On that basis the Judge ordered that there be a stay on the setting down until the determination of the European proceedings. However he allowed the action to proceed up to the point of setting down because that course would involve 'no risk of conflict between a decision of the Court and a decision of the Commission.' It appears from the report that the plaintiff had pointed out that there would be years of delay before the European proceedings, including all appeals, came to an end and it wanted to be in a position to proceed with the trial as soon as possible after the latter proceedings were terminated. Hence it wanted all the pre-trial preparations to proceed without a stay. That was the effect of the Judge's order. The defendants appealed. They wanted a complete stay. The course adopted by the Judge would expose them to the trouble and expense of preparing for trial. They argued in the Court of Appeal that the Judge was obliged to order a full stay. The appeal was unsuccessful. The Court of Appeal neither disapproved of the course adopted by the Judge or his reasoning. It was a reasonable exercise of his discretion. Furthermore the Court of Appeal's analysis of the European authorities is illuminating. Sir Thomas Bingham MR made the following observations:

. . . material rulings of the European Court of Justice are, as I understand them, based on the extreme undesirability of inconsistent decisions as between the Commission, on the one side, and national courts on the other. It is not hard to understand the undesirability of such inconsistency which undermines legal certainty, leaving parties in doubt as to where they stand, and infringes the integrity of the Community legal order.[8]

It seems to me that the effect of that decision is that the national court should generally stay proceedings pending a decision by the Commission in the interests of legal certainty unless the answer to the complaint is clear.[9]

There is, in my judgment, nothing which suggests that in a case where the answer is not clear in favour of the plaintiff or the defendant, the national court must at once stay the proceedings pending a decision by the Commission. The Court's concern is to avoid inconsistent decisions. There is no ground for seeking to prohibit the preparation of an action for trial *so long as it does not lead to a decision in advance of a decision by the Commission.*[10]

That reasoning is, as it seems to me, entirely consistent with earlier authority, but I find nothing in it to suggest that the European Court of Justice was intending to

[7] [1995] 1 CMLR 437, at 449. [8] at p. 105. [9] at p. 106. [10] at p. 108.

forbid national judges, in cases where the outcome was not clear, from allowing the preparation of proceedings to go ahead until a point short of decision. (emphasis added)[11]

It seems that two points come out of this. First, it may be appropriate to continue with the preparation of the case and, secondly, that a fundamental objective is to avoid inconsistent decisions between English courts and Commission. The latter point was also made by Lord Donaldson in *Hasselblad (GB) Ltd* v. *Orbinson*:[12] 'it cannot be right that national courts and Community institutions shall both independently weigh the force of particular evidence with the possibility of inconsistent results'.

However even an application for a stay may raise difficult questions. It may be a tactical device, e.g., by an unmeritorious defendant to put off the day of reckoning, and it may raise questions of what the court should do in the meantime; should there be an interlocutory injunction. The circumstances will vary from case to case but it appears that there will be some situations when the English court may feel almost bound to grant a stay. This is likely to be the case in certain cases where Article 85 is in issue and an application for exemption under Article 85(3) has been lodged with the Commission. Since only the Commission has jurisdiction to grant exemption it may well be that in all but the clearest cases the courts will be constrained to defer considering the issue. That appears to be the view of the Commission as expressed in its 1993 *Notice on co-operation between national courts and the Commission in applying Articles 85 and 86 of the EEC Treaty*.[13]

It must not be forgotten that stays may work injustice. It may be a cliché, but no less accurate for that, that justice delayed is justice denied. A stay may put off the final determination of the issues to the considerable disadvantage of the injured party. In deciding whether a stay should be granted, it should be borne in mind that the Commission is presented with more cases than its budget will allow it to process. Therefore it has to make priorities. In the 1993 *Notice* referred to above, the Commission stated expressly:

> The Commission is obliged to establish priorities. The Commission intends, in implementing its decision-making powers, to concentrate on notifications, complaints and own-initiative proceedings having particular political, economic or legal significance for the Community. Where these features are absent in a particular case, notifications will normally be dealt with by means of comfort letter and complaints should, as a rule, be handled by national courts or authorities.

Therefore a complaint in a trivial matter may not be processed with any speed or at all. How is the national court to react? Once again, the Commission is clearly aware of the problem and in its 1993 *Notice* it says:

[11] at p. 109. [12] [1985] 1 QB 475. [13] OJ 1993 C 39/6.

The national courts may ask the Directorate-General for Competition . . . for information of a procedural nature to enable them to discover whether a certain case is pending before the Commission, whether a case has been the subject of a notification, whether the Commission has officially initiated a procedure or whether it has already taken a position through an official decision or through a comfort letter sent by its services. If necessary, national court may also ask the Commission to give an opinion as to how much time is likely to be required for granting or refusing individual exemption for notified agreements or practices, so as to be able to determine the conditions for any decision to suspend proceedings or whether interim measures need to be adopted. The Commission, for its part, will endeavour to give priority to cases which are the subject of national proceedings suspended in this way, in particular when the outcome of a civil dispute depends on them.

I suggest that this willingness to co-operate should be made use of by national courts so that they are in a better position to know whether a stay, and interlocutory relief, are appropriate. There is, however, a much bigger question which needs to be answered. What happens after the Commission has come to a decision, e.g., that there has been an abuse of a dominant position?

The Impact of a *Decision* of the Commission on Domestic Parallel Proceedings.

It is clear from *Delimitis, MTV,* and *Hassleblad* that the expectation is that once the Commission has made a finding, the domestic court will not come to an inconsistent decision. Otherwise there is not much point in a stay. The natural conclusion is that the decision of the Commission is, at the least, admissible in the national proceedings and, possibly, binding. This was the issue raised in *Iberian.* The facts were simple. An abuse of a dominant position was alleged. This consisted of attempts made by the defendant, BPB, to squeeze out cheaper Spanish plasterboard so as to keep the cost to British customers high. The importer, Iberian, sued for breach of statutory duty. It also complained to the Commission. A stay of the English proceedings was ordered. The proceedings before the Commission were attended by both Iberian and BPB. Large quantities of evidence and documents were deployed and formal documents, equivalent to pleadings, were served. The Commission found that there had been abuse and imposed a very large fine. BPB appealed to the CFI. Again both parties attended (together with intervening Spanish and British governments). Save in one small respect, the appeal was dismissed. BPB then appealed to the ECJ. No one attended before that court and eventually the appeal was dismissed. By this time nine years had passed since the events complained of. The proceedings in England then came back to life. Not surprisingly Iberian wanted to rely on the decisions of the Commission, the CFI, and the ECJ.

BPB said that the decision of the Commission was neither binding or admissible in English court proceedings. It said the same thing about the decisions of the CFI and ECJ except on issues of pure law. Iberian argued the contrary. That was the core of the issue which came before the court as a preliminary point.

The first argument advanced on behalf of Iberian was that, because both parties had appeared and argued the case fully before the Commission, CFI and ECJ, there was an issue estoppel. Issue estoppel has become a term of some precision as explained by Diplock LJ in the Court of Appeal in *Mills* v. *Cooper*.[14] In the House of Lords in *Hunter* v. *Chief Constable of the West Midlands*[15] he said:

> [The issue estoppel] doctrine, so far as it affects civil proceedings, may be stated thus: a party to civil proceedings is not entitled to make, as against the other party, an assertion, whether of fact or of the legal consequences of facts, the correctness of which is an essential element in his cause of action or defence, if the same assertion was an essential element in his previous cause of action or defence in previous civil proceedings between the same parties or their predecessors in title and was found by a court of competent jurisdiction in such previous civil proceedings to be incorrect, unless further material which is relevant to the correctness or incorrectness of the assertion and could not by reasonable diligence have been adduced by that party in the previous proceedings has since become available to him.

This is quite narrow. It requires that there be two *court* proceedings to which there are the same *parties* or their predecessors. In *Hasselblad*, the plaintiff, the well-known manufacturer of high quality cameras, was being investigated by the Commission in relation to alleged breaches of Article 85 and 86. Camera Care Limited was the complainant. A customer, Mr Orbinson, had bought one of the plaintiff's cameras which had then malfunctioned. Mr Orbinson found that the plaintiff refused to service the camera because it was a 'grey import'. He complained by letter of this refusal to the shop from which the camera had been purchased. Camera Care obtained a copy of the letter and sent it to the Commission in support of its complaint. Hasselblad sued Mr Orbinson for libel. It accepted that a defence of qualified privilege might arise but that would depend on the evidence at the trial. Mr Orbinson argued that his letter, as sent to the Commission, was protected by absolute privilege. At first instance, Comyn J held, inter alia, that the Commission was a quasi-judicial body and that documents, such as the letter, voluntarily submitted to it for the purpose of a competition law investigation was absolutely privileged. In

14 [1967] 2 QB 459.

15 [1982] AC 529.

the Court of Appeal, Donaldson MR, with whom O'Connor LJ agreed, held in relation to the procedure of the Commission as follows;

This procedure is wholly dissimilar to that of any court or judicial tribunal operating under the common law system, but I do not think that that is the test. The fact that the Commission quite clearly has regard to the rules of natural justice, as shown inter alia by the procedure which gives the alleged infringer a right to an oral hearing, does not advance the matter, because those who take purely administrative decisions are often required to have regard to those rules. However, the fact that the decision is reached by Commissioners, who have not attended the hearing, on the basis of advice from representatives of the European Community nations, who are not directly concerned, seems to me to show that the Commission is acting in a manner which is dissimilar to that of either civil or common law courts of justice and that its attributes are dissimilar to such courts. This is not a criticism of the Commission and its procedures. It is merely an acceptance that the Commission and its procedures fall into a different category, better labelled as administrative rather than judicial or quasi-judicial.

May LJ, who agreed with the majority on this issue but not on the outcome of the appeal, also said:

Still using English terminology for the moment, I think that the Commission's procedure in investigating alleged infringements of articles 85 and 86 has to be described as administrative rather than judicial or quasi-judicial. Indeed both the Commission itself and the European Court of Justice have clearly taken the same view in the *Fedetab* judgment [1981] 3 CMLR 134 and in the *Pioneer* judgment [1983] 3 CMLR 221, 315.

Similarly in *AKZO Chemie BV* v. *The Commission*[16] the Advocate General expressed the opinion:

Competition proceedings before the Commission are . . . not to be regarded as adversary proceedings between the complainant and the undertaking concerned. The complainant is limited to a role which corresponds to the position under criminal procedure, of a person who reports a matter to the authorities. The competition proceedings themselves are conducted by the Commission.

The Commission, even when hearing competition complaints is not, in my view, a court. It is an administrative tribunal operating under rules which enforce an obligation to meet the requirements of natural justice, e.g., hearing the parties. It appears and appeared to me that if it is necessary to put competition proceedings before the Commission into a pigeonhole, then according to English terminology such proceedings are administrative, not judicial. Therefore I held that issue estoppel did not apply. However in *Hunter* the House of Lords drew a distinction between issue estoppel properly so-called and the wider general principle of *estoppel per rem*

[16] [1986] ECR 1965.

judicatum. The latter was part of the amorphous body of procedural law by which the courts attempt to prevent abuses of process. As Lord Diplock made clear in *Hunter*, the term issue estoppel was only meant to define one particular species of *estoppel per rem judicatum* and was put forward to avoid confusion. It did not pretend to limit the application of res judicata in situations which were outside that definition.

The *Hunter* case was satellite litigation which flowed out of the Birmingham bombing convictions. Six men, including Hunter, were arrested for their alleged participation in an IRA-inspired bombing of a public house. The six were arrested by the police and when they appeared in the magistrates' court some three days later their faces showed injuries consistent with them having been seriously assaulted. During those three days, confessions of guilt were allegedly volunteered by the six. At an early stage in the criminal trial, defence counsel argued that the alleged confessions should be excluded from the trial because they had been obtained by violence or threat of violence by the police. After a lengthy *voir dire*, the trial judge held that the prosecution had proved that the accused had not been assaulted by the police and that the confessions had been given voluntarily. After conviction, all six issued writs against the police and the Home Office seeking damages for assault. The police applied to have the action struck out as an abuse of process. The House of Lords unanimously upheld the decision of the Court of Appeal to strike out but on different grounds. What the House of Lords had to decide was whether Hunter should be allowed to maintain his action and in deciding that it approached the issue as one of broad principle. Thus Lord Diplock said:

> Lord Denning MR and Sir George Baker were also in favour of extending the description 'issue estoppel' to cover the particular example of abuse of process of the court presented by the instant case—a question to which much of the judgment of Lord Denning is addressed. Goff LJ, on the other hand, expressed his own view, which had been shared by Cantley J, that such extension would involve a misuse of that expression. But if what Hunter is seeking to do in initiating this civil action is an abuse of the process of the court, as I understand all your Lordships are satisfied that it is, the question whether it also qualifies to bear the label 'issue estoppel' is a *matter not of substance but of semantics*. (emphasis added)

Approaching the matter as one of principle, it appears and appeared to me that the question to be decided in *Iberian* could be put as follows: 'In all the circumstances of this case should the complainant and investigatee be allowed to open up and dispute in these proceedings the final conclusions of fact or law reached in competition proceedings in Brussels and Luxembourg?'

If the answer to that is in the negative, it does not matter whether it is categorized as a part of the law of res judicata, i.e. that the complainant and investigatee are bound by those conclusions, or as part of the law of abuse of process, i.e., that any attempt by either of them to challenge the conclusions is improper. In either case the same public policy considerations are at work. In considering this broader question it is necessary to have regard both to the realities of what happened in the European proceedings and the special position the Commission holds in relation to Articles 85 and 86. Furthermore it is necessary to bear in mind that we are part of the European system and that we are obliged to meet our obligations under the Treaty of Rome.

The realities of what happened before the Commission were as follows; Because the abuse of dominant position was directed at Iberian's trade (and the trade of one other importer) it was able to claim a legitimate interest within Regulation 17, Article 3(2). It was then involved throughout the European proceedings. It was represented by lawyers, it served what we would call pleadings, it attended the oral hearing before the Commission and it argued in support of its complaint and against the arguments advanced by the BPB. To adopt the words used by C. S. Kerse in paragraph 1.39 of *E.C. Antitrust Procedure*,[17] in these circumstances the proceedings took on an adversarial character. The adversaries were the Commission and Iberian on one side and BPB on the other. The Commission's power to hear parties is embodied in Article 19(2) which provides that it may hear persons other than the investigatee. Article 19(2) also obliges the Commission to hear a person if he shows sufficient interest. The procedure adopted by the Commission is fleshed out in Regulation 99/63. It makes provision for 'pleadings' and written and oral submissions. The regulation in effect obliges the Commission to follow a procedure which complies with what we would call the rules of natural justice. It was said on behalf of Iberian that for all practical purposes the result was that the hearing before the Commission was like a trial and a participating complainant, such as Iberian, is a litigant. The fact that there is a procedure for challenging the decision before the CFI and ECJ is consistent with that characterization.

As against this, BPB raises a number of substantial arguments. It said that proceedings before the Commission are sui generis. They are neither criminal or civil proceedings between the same parties. Procedure which is administrative without the presence of the complainant is not changed into a court proceeding merely because the complainant may be allowed, if he so requests, to intervene and make submissions. The procedure is still one which is essentially between the Commission and the investigatee. The Commission does not pretend to resolve issues of liability as between the investigatee and the complainant.

In deciding the issue I took the view that I had to have regard to the special position of the Commission. I have already mentioned that the

[17] 3rd ed., 1994.

Commission shares jurisdiction with national courts as far as Articles 85 and 86 are concerned. In some areas the Commission's jurisdiction is exclusive. However, even in areas of shared jurisdiction, the Commission does not play a subservient role. On the contrary, there is much to indicate that in these areas the Commission has a most important, and perhaps primary, function as a fact-finder. Competition cases tend to involve complicated factual issues. In view of its special jurisdiction in this area, the relevant department of the Commission (DG IV) has unequalled expertise. The consideration of the relationship between the Commission and national courts was discussed in *Delimitis*. The ECJ said:

> . . . It should be stressed, first of all, that the Commission is responsible for the implementation and orientation of Community competition policy. It is for the Commission to adopt, subject to review by the Court of First Instance and the Court of Justice, individual decisions in accordance with the procedural rules in force and to adopt exemption regulations. The performance of that task necessarily entails complex economic assessments, in particular in order to assess whether an agreement falls under Article 85(3) . . .

I decided that it was against that background that the question of the effect of a Commission decision should be decided. Avoiding inconsistent decisions between the Commission and national courts is now part of our domestic law. Principles of public policy arising under the Treaty of Rome are now our public policy. It is a principle of public policy which, in my view, we must take into account when deciding how to run court proceedings in England. I came to the conclusions that where the parties had indeed argued the case fully, and at very great length, before the Commission (and on appeal from that through two levels of appeal) it would be an abuse of process to allow the loser to relitigate it again before the national court. Even though strangers to the Commission proceedings would be free to challenge the decision, the parties to the proceedings should not. There has to be finality. I decided that both Iberian and BPB were bound.

An alternative way the *Iberian* case was put was that BPB had been found guilty of abuse of a dominant position and it should not be allowed to challenge the correctness of that decision in any court against *any* party. To allow it to assert the opposite of what the Commission found would amount to a collateral attack on the Commission decision.

In his *Rationale of Judicial Evidence* Jeremy Bentham said:

> There is reason for saying that a man shall not lose his cause in consequence of the verdict given in a former proceeding to which he was not a party; but there is no reason whatever for saying that he shall not lose his cause in consequence of the verdict in a proceeding to which he was a party, merely because his adversary was not. It is right enough that a verdict obtained by A against B should not bar the

claim of a third party C; but that it should not be evidence in favour of C against B, seems the very height of absurdity.[18]

Once again the policy considerations which make it so undesirable to permit inconsistent decisions in this most complex and expensive area of litigation, led me to the conclusion that to allow a collateral attack on the Commission decision was also impermissible as a matter of public policy. The result was that BPB could not deny the correctness of that decision in the English proceedings.

I am very aware that to some this may appear unorthodox. As lawyers we are taught to believe that no dispute resolution procedure can be better than that made available through our courts and that all subjects have the right to have their disputes resolved by the courts here. I suspect that lawyers in other countries believe the same about their courts. Of course that somewhat xenophobic view has already been severely undermined by the principles of issue estoppel. We decline to let parties relitigate issues already contested before foreign courts not because we always agree with their decisions or their procedures for reaching them but as a personal fetter on the litigants themselves.

So in the case of the Commission, we should bear in mind that we may not be serving litigants well if we allow re-litigation of issues which have been disposed of by that body in one of its specialist functions. It would be most unfortunate if in every other Member State, decisions of the Commission were binding or persuasive but here they are ignored.

Sooner or later the Court of Appeal, and perhaps the ECJ, will have to decide whether *Iberian* v. *BPB* was rightly decided. But if it is, there are still significant questions which need to be resolved. One strikes me as being particularly important. It will be recalled that in *MTV* both the High Court and the Court of Appeal decided that it was appropriate for full preparation for trial here, including the expensive discovery stage, to proceed and that it was a proper exercise of the discretion to impose a stay only in relation to the trial itself. But if it is right that the parties are bound by the outcome before the Commission, why should those time consuming domestic steps be taken? Put simply, what is the purpose of preparing discovery and evidence for the English proceedings unless it is to seek to come to a decision here which is inconsistent with the Commission decision? In the end I suspect that the courts here will have to grasp the nettle. Granting stays merely puts off the day when the courts will have to decide whose voice should be listened to when parallel competition proceedings are on foot. There is only one reliable way of avoiding inconsistent decisions. It is to have only one decision. As long as the possibility of two (or more) decisions exists, not only is there a risk of inconsistency, but parties within

[18] J. Bentham, *Rationale of Judicial Evidence* (1827).

the EU will be faced with the possibility of multiple expensive proceedings to determine the same issues in accordance with what ought to be the same principles of law arising under Articles 85 and 86. The costs and manpower consequences of that in many cases will be severe and will adversely affect all but the richest litigants. Although we may cherish the independence of national legal systems, the user could be forgiven for thinking that it is an expensive luxury for which he is being made to pay. As the Woolf report reminds us, a system which deprives all but the richest and poorest of full access to the law is not one of which we should be proud.

In addition to this there is another issue which will need to be resolved, namely the question of the admissibility of Commission decisions on competition issues when they arise in proceedings between other parties. Our law is clear. A decision of one court on a factual issue between litigants A and B is not admissible as evidence in proceedings between C and D. It appears that our rule, one of evidence, is perfectly logical, even if the consequence is that the same issue has to be litigated again between C and D. I do not know whether our domestic rule of evidence will be pressed to give way to the public policy considerations set out in *Delimitis*. Only time will tell. I do not see it happening from within. The real question is whether it will be imposed by the ECJ.

12

Reliance on Commission Decisions in National Courts

BY PROFESSOR DAN GOYDER CBE, KING'S COLLEGE LONDON, SOLICITOR, CONSULTANT TO LINKLATERS & PAINES

It is perhaps surprising that, 40 years on from the signing of the Treaty of Rome, important constitutional and jurisdictional issues remain not merely undecided but even without sufficient relevant case law to enable rational assessment or prediction of the way in which such issues should be decided by national or Community courts. It is therefore with some pleasure that lawyers should welcome the judgment of Laddie J in the recent important case of *Iberian* v. *BPB and British Gypsum.*[1] In this case the Judge had to decide whether in the courts of the United Kingdom a litigant could rely on the findings of the European Commission contained in a formal Decision, as well as on subsequent findings of facts by both the court of first instance and European Court of Justice in the course of subsequent appeals to them. If such a question were to be answered by the High Court in the affirmative then the defendant to the litigation would be unable to reopen the questions of fact decided by these tribunals or require them to be proved anew by the plaintiff.

The facts of the *Iberian* case are quite straightforward, though the timetable is an extended one. Between 1984 and 1987 BPB and BG sought to discourage builders' merchants in the United Kingdom from purchasing Spanish plasterboard imported by Iberian, offering them a loyalty rebate and delivery priority so long as they abstained from purchasing any of this imported material. Not surprisingly these practices damaged Iberian's business in the United Kingdom. It therefore complained in 1986 to the European Commission which after investigations eventually issued a decision against BPB and BG on 5 December 1988 finding breaches by both companies of Article 86 in respect of these 'fidelity rebates'. In respect of the abuse of its dominant position in the United Kingdom plasterboard market fines totalling three million ECU were imposed. Appeals by the companies against this decision to the Court of First Instance and from that Court to the European Court of Justice were dismissed, without any reduction in the fines imposed.

[1] [1997] EuLR 1.

However, Iberian understandably still wished to seek damages for their loss of profit in the United Kingdom as a result of the defendants' practices for which the fines had been imposed. This case came before Laddie J on a preliminary issue of law as to whether the defendants could force the plaintiffs to prove their case ab initio; i.e., without reliance on the facts found by the Commission in its decision. Had the Judge accepted the defendants' arguments it would of course have meant that, more than ten years after the commercial practices complained of and after nearly a decade of litigation in Europe, the plaintiff would essentially have to start all over again to prove his case. In the event Laddie J, rejecting the defendants' arguments, adopted what the majority of EC lawyers would have regarded as an appropriate attitude to the case in the light of Article 5 of the Treaty setting out the duties of co-operation between Member States and the institutions of the Community. Laddie J was also, however, to rely on a number of earlier High Court decisions which, without dealing with the points specifically, at least provided him with respectable support, if not binding authority, for his approach. In particular he emphasized in his judgment the importance of *Hasselblad Ltd* v. *Orbison*,[2] where Donaldson MR had explained the desirability in the public interest that the Commission as a 'primary authority of the Community' was not frustrated in carrying out its duties of enforcing Articles 85 and 86'; such frustration would be likely if both national courts and Community institutions insisted on each weighing independently the force of particular evidence, with the evident likelihood of inconsistent results. The key element in Laddie J's assessment of the issues is the importance of consistency between the decisions of the Community institution and those of national courts.

There is of course in existence a Notice published by the European Commission in 1993 dealing with the relationship between Community institutions and national courts on such matters. In his judgment Laddie J does refer to two paragraphs of the Notice, 4 and 5, which contain the following statements:

> The Commission is the administrative authority responsible for the implementation and for the thrust of competition policy in the Community and for this purpose has to act in the public interest. National courts, on the other hand, have the task of safeguarding the subjective rights of private individuals in their relations with one another. In performing these different tasks national courts and the Commission possess concurrent powers for the application of Article 85(1) and Article 86 of the Treaty.

There is however a further paragraph in the notice to which Laddie J does not specifically refer, namely, paragraph 20 which states:

[2] [1986] QB 475.

'The first question which national courts have to answer is whether the agreement, decision or concerted practice at issue infringes the prohibitions laid down in Article 85(1) or Article 86. Before answering this question, national courts should ascertain whether the agreement, decision or concerted practice has already been the subject of a decision, opinion or other official statement issued by the administrative authority and in particular by the Commission . . . Such statements provide national courts with significant information for reaching a judgement, even if they are not formally bound by them . . .

While it is likely true that a mere statement by even a leading official of the Commission would not have any binding effect on a High Court judge, the status of a formal decision (of which there are a mere handful each year) is surely in quite a different category, as indeed the judge acknowledges implicitly in his approach to the relevant decision in the *BPB* case. It is of course relevant that the commercial activities of the defendants under challenge had been litigated to the ultimate degree on appeal from the Commission itself right up to both the superior courts of the Community in Luxembourg; and the argument for giving respect both to the fact finding of those hearings and the application of Article 86 to the facts was overwhelming. A more difficult issue, however, not disposed by the present case, was whether the facts and application of Articles 86 (or indeed Article 85) would likewise have been binding had they not been dealt with between the parties themselves but arose in litigation in between other parties who did not have an opportunity of arguing their viewpoint when the matter between, say, BPB and the Commission was dealt with by the Community institutions. It is of course true under the procedural rules of Regulations 17/62, Article 19, that third parties can be heard by the Commission as intervenors in its cases as well as being free in practice to submit written argument to the Commission and to have access to a limited degree to the file of relevant documents which the Commission holds. It had been hoped that the Court of Appeal, to whom Laddie J's judgment was originally appealed, would provide further guidance and clarification as to how widely the principles of his judgment can be applied, but the plaintiff's claim has now been settled.

The case also raises interesting issues under UK law with reference to the relevant treatment in cases brought by litigants under Article 86, who may wish to make reference not necessarily only to European Community decisions but also to those of relevant UK or other Member State competition authorities. If the practices of which Iberian complained had also been the subject of a public interest finding by the Monopolies and Mergers Commission, as was actually the case,[3] would it have been possible for Iberian to have referred to that report and its relevant findings of fact in its

[3] Cm.1224, published Oct. 1990.

High Court action, or would BPB have been able, in this case, to argue with greater success than before Laddie J that Iberian would have to treat the MMC report as mere 'hearsay'? This policy argument relating to the duty of co-operation under Article 5 of the Treaty would not of course be available to the plaintiff here and the traditional answer of the common law would have been that the MMC report could not have been used in this way, because it was indeed 'hearsay'. Though MMC is a 'statutory authority' within the definition of Article 9 of the 1968 Civil Justice Act, its reports are not 'public records' of a kind contemplated by the exception to the hearsay rule referred to in Article 9(2)(b) of the Act. It has been held that such a phrase only applies to records such as those of births, death, and marriages which are maintained by public officials and are available for inspection by the public. By contrast, although the reports of the Monopolies and Mergers Commission are freely (or rather expensively) available for purchase at HMSO, they are not publicly available for inspection in the same way as such registers.

This was the answer given by Scott J (as he than was) in 1989 when the issue was raised in *Macarthy Plc* v. *Unichem*.[4] Here the plaintiffs had sought to rely in the course of action against Unichem for trading losses, as a result of trading practices by Unichem claimed to be a breach of Article 85, on findings contained in a report of MMC on these practices published in May 1989,[5] as the result of a reference to the MMC by the Director General of Fair Trading whose report had also been published in September 1988. However, because Scott J felt that both reports did not fall within the statutory exception to the hearsay rule he ruled they could not be used by the plaintiffs to ease their task of proof. Their contents were simply not admissible under the long-standing English rules of evidence then prevailing.

However an important change to these rules has now taken place. Under the 1995 Civil Evidence Act, which came into force on 1 November 1996 (some months therefore *after* the judgment of Laddie J in the *Iberian* case) the rule of common law against the admission of hearsay evidence in civil proceedings has been abolished, at least for England and Wales. Procedural rules have been provided in order to prevent any abuse of this new freedom by litigants but there would not now seem to be any reason in principle why a plaintiff seeking civil damages in respect of practices already the subject of a published report of the Director General of Fair Trading or the MMC, or indeed of any other statutory body not already covered by the 1968 statutory exceptions to the hearsay rule (which are expressly preserved) from relying on such reports to the degree that they can be of assistance to it. Clearly such a report would not necessarily carry

[4] 24 Nov. 1989, unreported. [5] Cm 691.

the weight of a formal decision of the European Commission, albeit it is clear that the Commission's decisions are themselves not judicial but of an administrative nature. Nevertheless, the important reform which the 1995 Act has implemented (following on the recommendation of the Law Commission) may well have the beneficial effect of making the bringing of civil proceedings more attractive where parties have suffered loss as a result of restrictive trading practices or abuse of monopoly power. As Vulcan LJ said in *Ventouris* v. *Mountain (No 2)*:[6] 'The modern tendency in civil proceedings is to admit all relevant evidence and the Judge should be trusted to give only proper weight to evidence which is not the best evidence'.

It will be interesting to see if the High Court does in future take up the opportunity given under the 1995 Criminal Justice Act reforms to make the bringing of actions of this kind in civil courts less difficult than they have been in the past, when litigants were prevented by rules of court from referring to reports of statutory bodies that might have proved highly relevant to their cases.

[6] [1992] 1 WLR 887.

13

Damages for Breach of Competition Rules

BY DAVID ANDERSON, BARRISTER, BRICK COURT CHAMBERS,
SENIOR VISITING RESEARCH FELLOW, CENTRE OF EUROPEAN LAW,
KING'S COLLEGE LONDON

Introduction

The competition rules of the EC Treaty have long been the source of some of its most developed jurisprudence. Yet surprisingly, in the light of recent developments in relation to damages against the State, it is generally agreed that there is no simple answer to the question of whether, and if so on what conditions, Community law requires an injured party to be able to sue for damages for breach of Article 85 or 86.[1]

Articles 85 and 86 EC: 'create direct rights in respect of the individuals concerned which the national courts must safeguard.'[2] The direct effectiveness of Articles 85 and 86 is therefore clear. The English courts are prepared to safeguard the rights created by the competition rules, at least up to a point. They recognize that Articles 85 and 86 may be relied on by way of defence (for example to a contractual claim or to a patent infringement action) so long as there is a sufficient nexus between the relief sought by the plaintiff and the alleged contravention of the competition rules.[3] They recognize also that Articles 85 and 86 may be used as the basis for a claim of injunctive relief.[4] Yet some residual uncertainty remains in relation to damages.

The Commission has generally been prepared to assume that damages are already available in Member States for breach of competition law.[5] Perhaps for this reason, it has not thought it necessary to propose

[1] Kerse, *Antitrust Procedure* (3rd ed., 1994) at 10.15; *cf.* Bellamy & Child, *Common Market Law of Competition* (4th ed., 1993) at 10-035; see generally Hoskins, 'Garden Cottage Revisited: the Availability of Damages in the National Courts for Breach of the EC Competition Rules' [1992] 6 ECLR 257.

[2] Case 127/73 *BRT* v. *Sabam* [1974] ECR 51, para. 16.

[3] *Chiron* v. *Murex* [1994] 1 CMLR 410.

[4] *Garden Cottage Foods* v. *MMB* [1984] AC 130; Cutsforth v. Mansfield Inns [1986] 1 All ER 577.

[5] Report on reparation for damage as a result of breach of Arts. 85 and 86 of the EEC Treaty, Collected Studies Series on Competition, No. 1, Commission, Brussels, 1966; Notice on Cooperation between the Commission and national courts on the application of Arts. 85 and 86, OJ 1993 C–39/6.

legislation to ensure the availability of damages or to harmonize the applicable conditions. The field has been left to the courts of the Member States and of the Community.

Those courts, or perhaps more accurately the litigants on whom they depend, have been slow to oblige. Advocate General Léger recently said: 'it is widely accepted that an individual or undertaking may bring an action for damages against another individual or undertaking for breach of a rule of Community law having direct horizontal effect.'[6]

But the only authority he cited for that proposition was a twelve-year-old expression of opinion by a majority of the House of Lords in *Garden Cottage Foods Ltd* v. *Milk Marketing Board*.[7] Their lordships did not expressly decide that damages were available as a remedy; they reached their conclusion without full argument; and Lord Wilberforce dissented in such a way as to leave some limited room for debate both as to the scope of the dictum and as to its correctness.[8]

Advocate-General van Gerven in *Banks*

The best insight as to how the Court of Justice might decide the question of the availability of damages for breach of the competition rules is the opinion of Advocate-General van Gerven in Case C–128/92 *H. J. Banks & Co Ltd* v. *British Coal Corporation* [1994] ECR I–1209.[9] In relation to a case on the borderline of the competition provisions of the EEC and the ECSC Treaties, the English Commercial Court asked, inter alia: 'Does the national court have the power and/or the obligation under Community law to award damages in respect of breach of the said Articles of the ECSC and the EEC Treaties for loss sustained as a result of such breach?' Both the Advocate-General and the Court proceeded on the basis that the ECSC rather than the EEC Treaty applied, but in the Advocate-General's view, similar principles applied to each.[10]

Principle of Liability

The Advocate-General considered that the principle of effective protection required the *Francovich* principle to be applied to actions against private

[6] Case C–5/94 *R* v. *MAFF ex p Hedley Lomas (Ireland) Ltd*, [1996] ECR I–2553.

[7] *Garden Cottage Foods Ltd*.v. *Milk Marketing Board* [1984] ECR 130.

[8] HH Judge Curtis QC in *Merson* v. *Rover Group*, judgment of 22 May 1992 (High Court), after hearing detailed argument on *Garden Cottage* and the approval of the majority's opinion by the Court of Appeal in *Bourgoin* v. *MAFF* [1986] QB 716, found the question of whether damages were available for beach of Art. 85 to be 'not nearly so clear as the plaintiff professes it to be'.

[9] See also Question 2(d) in Case C–18/94 *Hopkins and others* v. *National Power*, [1996] ECR I–2281. The question was not answered by the Court.

[10] Para. 36.

individuals, concluding: 'the national court is obliged in principle, under Community law, to award damages for loss sustained as a result of breach of a directly effective provision of competition law.'[11] He noted that it was for the internal legal order of each Member State to designate the competent courts and lay down the detailed procedural rules for legal proceedings. But in recognition of the modern tendency to lay down the minimum requirements of Community law in that respect, he went on to clarify what he described as the detailed rules for bringing a damages action of this nature, both as to procedure and as to substantive grounds for liability.

Conditions of Liability: Procedure

The detailed *procedural* conditions were as follows:

(a) Every type of action provided for by national law must be available, on the same conditions concerning admissibility and procedure as would apply were it a national law question.
(b) The substantive and formal conditions (e.g., jurisdiction and procedure) may not be less favourable than those relating to similar domestic claims, and may not be so framed as to make it virtually impossible to exercise the rights conferred by Community law.
(c) National rules of evidence must not make it practically impossible or excessively difficult to obtain redress as required by Community law, particularly by means of unreasonable presumptions or rules of evidence or by means of special limitations concerning the form of the evidence to be adduced.
(d) Time limits must be reasonable.[12]

These conditions, which are entirely orthodox in terms of the Court's case law, demonstrate the great inroads that Community law has been making into national civil procedure.

It is interesting to speculate how many of the accretions to the English jurisprudence in cases involving Articles 85 and 86 might be vulnerable on the basis of the procedural conditions set out by the Advocate-General. Some examples, in no particular order, are:

(a) the dictum that breach of the competition rules must be proved to a 'high degree of probability';[13]
(b) the suggestion that Commission decisions, like Monopolies Commission reports, may be inadmissible in evidence before an English civil court;[14]

[11] Paras. 36–45, 62.

[12] Opinion, para. 48.

[13] *Shearson Lehmann* v. *Maclaine Watson* [1989] 3 CMLR 429, per Webster J.

[14] Bellamy & Child, 4th ed., 1993 at 10–47, referring to *Macarthy plc* v. *Unichem Ltd*, judgment of 24 Nov. 1989 (unreported); see now the Civil Evidence Act 1995.

(c) the decision of the House of Lords that section 14 of the Civil Evidence Act may justify the non-disclosure of documents which might expose an undertaking to a risk of a fine by the Commission;[15]
(d) perhaps even the enthusiasm with which courts hearing intellectual property infringement cases have used the rules relating to pleadings in order to frustrate claims of abusive conduct.[16]

The continued existence of such obstacles, real or imagined, to the enforcement of competition law in the English courts demonstrates the timeliness of Advocate-General van Gerven's approach.

Conditions of Liability: Substance

9. The Advocate-General went on to deal with the *substantive* conditions for liability in respect of breach of the competition rules. Anticipating the line taken by the Court of Justice in *Factortame III*[17] he applied the basic Article 215 conditions which he defined as:

(1) the *existence of damage* (mere speculative damage would not be enough; the injured party must show reasonable diligence in mitigating his loss; allowance must be made for the passing on of damage by increased selling prices of the complainant undertaking; economic surveys are an acceptable means of assessing damage; the court must have an unfettered discretion in assessing all the evidence submitted to it);[18]
(2) *a causal link between the damage claimed and the conduct alleged against the institution;*[19] and,
(3) the *illegality of that conduct* (such illegality being established by a mere breach and not requiring proof of fault or of the absence of any ground of exemption contemplated by national law).[20]

To define the substantive conditions of the tort as a matter of Community law would until recently have been highly controversial; and there may still be room for argument as to the nature of the definition and as to the extent of discretion remaining in the national court (may it, for example, insert a test for remoteness of damage in addition to the test of causation?). In the light of *Francovich* and now *Factortame III*, however,

[15] *Rio Tinto Zinc* v. *Westinghouse Electric* [1975] 1 All ER 434, the correctness of which is queried by Bellamy & Child (4th ed., 1993) at p. 666, n. 41.

[16] See e.g., *Ransburg-GEMA AG* v. *Electrostatic Plant Systems Ltd* [1989] 2 CMLR 712; *Chiron* v. *Murex* [1992] 3 CMLR 813 and [1994] CMLR 410.

[17] Case C–48/93; [1996] ECR I–1029.

[18] Opinion, para. 51.

[19] Opinion, para. 53.

[20] Opinion, para. 53: *cf.* Case T–65/89 *BPB Industries plc* v. *Commission*, 1 April 1993, para. 70.

with their delineation of the substantive conditions for liability in actions against public authorities, it would be surprising if the European Court were to shrink from a similar approach when it is next given the opportunity.

As well as improving the effectiveness and consistency of application of Articles 85 and 86, a Community approach to the substantive conditions of liability would have the incidental benefit of rendering largely redundant the debate in England over whether breach of the competition rules should be characterized as breach of statutory duty or as the economic tort of unlawful interference.[21] The debate has seemed an important one because of the different substantive conditions that must be satisfied by a plaintiff raising those different causes of action. To the extent that Community law dictates the conditions, the debate loses its significance. Indeed the approach of the Advocate-General in *Banks* might be said to demonstrate the lonely foresight of Lord Denning who in one of the earliest Community law cases decided in England held that Articles 85 and 86 create new torts or wrongs called 'undue restriction of competition within the Common Market' and 'abuse of dominant position within the Common Market'.[22]

Factortame III

The analysis of the Advocate-General in *Banks* was never considered by the Court in that case, which disagreed on the logically prior point of whether the relevant provisions of the ECSC Treaty had direct effect at all. But that analysis, in particular the use of Article 215 as a starting-point and the absence of any requirement of fault, stands up well to the approach taken by the Court in *Factortame III*. Where a wide legislative discretion is involved, *Factortame III* imports the further requirement of a manifest and grave disregard for the limits on the exercise of the public authority's powers: the Advocate-General was surely right to suggest that no such requirement could be applied in the case of a breach of precise and directly effective competition rules.

Factortame III helps the plaintiff in competition law cases in another way. The Court held that the recovery of loss or damage could not be made conditional on a prior finding by the Court of an infringement of Community law attributable to a Member State, since rights arising for individuals out of directly effective provisions of Community law cannot depend on the

[21] This debate is summarized by Hoskins, *op. cit.* at pp. 260–2. The difficulties inherent in applying to Arts. 85 and 86 the normal English law test for whether damages are available for breach of statutory duty have not been diminished by the decision of the House of Lords in *X* v. *Bedfordshire County Council* [1995] 2 AC 633.

[22] *Application des Gaz* v. *Falks Veritas* [1974] 2 CMLR 75.

Commission's assessment of the expediency of taking action against a Member State pursuant to Article 169 of the Treaty or on the delivery by the Court of any judgment finding an infringement.[23] The same reasoning must presumably apply in relation to damages for infringement of the competition rules: their availability cannot be made dependent upon the Commission having decided to take action against an undertaking.[24]

Factortame III nevertheless leaves questions for the party seeking damages for an infringement of competition law. One such difficulty is the suggestion that the national court may consider the duty to mitigate loss will be satisfied only if the plaintiff has 'availed himself in time of all the legal remedies available to him'.[25] Transposing this to the private law context, does it mean that damages may be denied to the victim of abusive conduct in circumstances when that victim could have, but did not, apply for injunctive relief against the abuser?[26] The availability of damages will, in Community law and English law alike, generally be a reason against the grant of interim relief: it would be hard indeed if the availability of interim relief, by the same token, constituted a reason against the grant of damages.

Summary

The lack of legal certainty relating to the availability of damages for breach of the competition rules has long been a deterrent to UK plaintiffs contemplating damages actions for breach of the competition rules. When it next has an opportunity, it is to be hoped that the Court of Justice will give a lead by confirming the principle of liability for breach and by defining the basic substantive as well as procedural conditions attaching to liability. The approach of the Advocate-General in *Banks* provides a workable model and one which, after *Factortame III*, may prove to be less controversial than it may once have seemed.

[23] Judgment, para. 95.

[24] Except in ECSC cases, where the Commission has sole jurisdiction to find an infringement of Arts. 65 and 66(7), with the result that national courts may not entertain an action for damages in the absence of a Community decision adopted in the exercise of that jurisdiction: Case C–128/92 *Banks* [1994] ECR I–1209, para. 21.

[25] Para. 84.

[26] If so, the duty to mitigate would be far harsher than in England, where it will not generally require the prior commencement of proceedings against the Defendant or even against a third party: *Pilkington* v. *Wood* [1953] Ch 770.

14

The Community Law Impact in Employment Cases

BY THE RT HON LORD JUSTICE MUMMERY

Introduction

In his fragment of autobiography, posthumously published in 1996, Lord Devlin wrote: 'There is no pleasure except in a life of occupation. The essential pleasure in life is to be obtained only from congenial work. That must be the sun that heats the spirit.'[1] That view was shared by Judge Learned Hand about *his* work: '. . . A delectable calling—a pleasure which nobody who has felt it will be likely to underrate.'

Employment in the profession of the law ranks high in the scales of job satisfaction; but no Act of Parliament, no directive of the Council of Ministers supplies congenial occupation (except for lawyers) to 'heat the spirit'; or makes a person happy in his work; or ensures that a person is fit for his occupation or makes a success of it. Employment law, whether made in Westminster or Brussels, has a modest aim: minimum standards of access to work and of terms of work; protection from unfair dismissal; the elimination of discrimination on grounds of sex, race or disability; the improvement of working conditions, such as hours of work and health and safety at work.

Domestic Law

The domestic sources of Employment law are common law—mainly contract, but some tort, too—and statute law, principally the Equal Pay Act 1970, the Sex Discrimination Act 1975, the Race Relations Act 1976, the Disability Discrimination Act 1995 and the consolidating legislation in the Employment Rights Act 1996 and the Industrial Tribunals Act 1996.

Most of the cases invoking statutory protection are brought, and can only be bought, in specialist industrial tribunals, from which an appeal lies on a point of law to the Employment Appeal Tribunal. Both levels of tribunal are distinctive for their tripartite composition, (legally qualified chairman and two lay members) with lay members representative of

[1] *Taken at the Flood* (1996), p. 74.

employers and employees in the majority, even when deciding points of law. Appeals to the Court of Appeal and to the House of Lords on points of law are on the increase, as are applications, justiciable only in the High Court, for judicial review of the legality of employment legislation and decisions of employers in the public sector.

Community Law

Since the European Communities Act 1972 came into force on 1 January 1973, there has been another source of law with a substantial and sometimes determinative impact on the adjudication of employment disputes. Community law is embodied in the Treaty of Rome, in Directives of the Council of Ministers, in Regulations and in the decisions of the European Court of Justice. The rights and obligations created by or arising out of these legal sources often create enforceable community rights recognized and available in law to individuals in legal proceedings in national courts. By virtue of Section 2(1) of the 1972 Act:

> All such rights, powers, liabilities, obligations and restrictions from time to time created or arising by or under the Treaties, and all such remedies and procedures from time to time provided for by or under the Treaties, as in accordance with the Treaties are without further enactment to be given legal effect and used in the United Kingdom shall be recognised and available in law and be enforced, allowed and followed accordingly; and the expression 'enforceable community right' and similar expressions shall be read as referring to one to which this subsection applies.'

The principal provisions of Community law affecting legal relations between employers and employees relate to equal pay for men and women for equal work (Article 119 of the Treaty and the Equal Pay Directive 75/117); to equal treatment at work without discrimination on the ground of sex (the Equal Treatment Directive 76/207); to the protection of employment on the transfer of undertakings (the Acquired Rights Directive 77/187); and to pregnancy, insolvency of employers, collective redundancies and working hours, covered by a succession of other Directives.

General Comments

A significant number of employment cases illustrate Lord Wilberforce's perception of 'the intricate pervasiveness of the penetration of European Community Law into national systems'. Indeed, the impact of Community law on employment cases in English courts has been greater than on any other kind of case.

The growth and development of this case law over the last 25 years owes much to the efforts of specialist solicitors, barristers, and academic writers alert to the relevance of Community law points to employment disputes; to the expertise of industrial tribunals; to the initiatives of pioneering litigants and their supporters: the Equal Opportunities Commission, the Trades Unions and Employers' organizations; and to the changing social, economic, and political conditions which have stimulated the promulgation and application of Community law in many areas of employment.

General Principles

It is the general principles, not their detailed application, which fall for examination in this chapter. The leading employment cases of recent years are underpinned by three fundamental principles of Community law:

(1) *The principle of primacy.* Common law and statute law are liable to be displaced when incompatible with the paramount provisions of Community law. It is the duty of national courts to protect rights arising under Community law, to lift legal barriers obstructing the enforcement of those rights and to refuse to apply conflicting provisions of domestic law to the case.

(2) *The principle of purposive interpretation.* In the case of any field covered by a Directive, national courts are under a duty to interpret national law, whether made before or after the relevant Community law, to conform to the interpretation of the provisions of Community law by the European Court of Justice, where that can be done without distortion of the meaning of national legislation.

(3) *The principle of direct effect.* Provisions of Community law, if sufficiently clear, precise, unconditional, and not dependent on further legislation to implement them, may have direct effect in proceedings in national courts and be determinative of the rights and duties of individuals and of the state.

Some cases–the Principle of Primacy

This principle was applied by the House of Lords in a case of even greater long term constitutional significance than its immediate consequences for the employment rights of part-time workers. *R* v. *Secretary of State for Employment ex Parte Equal Opportunities Commission*[2] is striking in several respects. The proceedings were not brought in a tribunal by an employee with a particular complaint: they were initiated in the High Court by the

[2] [1994] ICR 317.

Equal Opportunities Commission seeking judicial review of legislation limiting employment rights to workers who had worked a minimum number of hours per week—sixteen or more hours a week in the case of those continuously employed between two and five years, and eight or more hours a week in the case of those continuously employed for five years or more. Workers who could not satisfy these minimum threshold requirements were not entitled to statutory protection against unfair dismissal or to redundancy pay.

The House of Lords held that:

1. The Equal Opportunities Commission's statutory duty to work towards the elimination of discrimination gave it the requisite standing to bring proceedings for judicial review on the basis of sex discrimination;
2. The threshold requirements were indirectly discriminatory on the grounds of sex, because more women than men were part-time workers and therefore unable to comply with the requirements;
3. A redundancy payment is 'pay' within the meaning of Article 119, which stipulates equal pay for equal work without discrimination on the ground of sex. Article 119 had already been held by the European Court of Justice in *Defrenne* v. *Sabena*[3] to be directly effective (from 8 April 1976) and enforceable between individuals in national courts, so that employees were able to rely on that Article for the disapplication of incompatible barriers to achieving equal pay in national legislation.

   Subsequent decisions of the Employment Appeal Tribunal support the view that 'pay' in Article 119 also includes compensation for unfair dismissal, though this has yet to be finally determined by the Court of Appeal or the House of Lords.
4. The threshold requirements for redundancy payments were contrary to the Equal Pay Directive and, in relation to unfair dismissal, contrary to the Equal Treatment Directive. As the provisions of that Directive are directly effective against the State (i.e., vertically, though not horizontally) part-time workers in the public sector could claim unfair dismissal against employers who were emanations of the state. It is a principle of Community law that a Member State defaulting in the full implementation of a Directive is thereby disentitled from relying on incompatible provisions of national law to defeat a claim based on Community law.
5. There was no objective justification for the indirect discrimination against women.

The effect of the declarations made by the House of Lords was that the threshold requirements in the Employment Protection (Consolidation) Act 1978 became unenforceable in proceedings between employees and

[3] [1976] ECR 455.

private and public sector employers, because the provisions were contrary to the directly effective paramount provisions of Community law. Employers could not rely on threshold provisions to reject or defend the claim for unfair dismissal or redundancy pay by a part-time worker.

The displacement of the statutory requirements was achieved without a reference of any question of interpretation to the European Court of Justice. It was a clear affirmation by the highest court in the United Kingdom of the primacy of Community law. Contrary to the views of some critics, the House of Lords were not challenging or questioning the sovereignty of Parliament. In fact, they acted in accordance with it and gave effect to it by applying the provisions of the European Communities Act 1972, which require courts in the United Kingdom to give effect to enforceable community rights.

In Employment law the important point was established that part-time workers enjoy protection under the same conditions as apply to full-time workers. This has now been recognized by amending legislation. The Employment Protection (Part-Time Employees) Regulations 1995 abolished all hours requirements regarding dismissals after 6 February 1995. The Employment Rights Act 1996 omits all mention of minimum hours of work as a condition of employment protection: Community law has prevailed for the benefit of the growing numbers of part-time workers, both men and women.

Following that change there is now before the House of Lords another case in which Community law is invoked, this time in the cause of short-term workers. Their complaint reflects changing conditions in the job market—a trend away from long term service with a single employer to short fixed term contracts and casual employment. In *R* v. *Secretary of State for Employment, ex Parte Seymour Smith*[4] a challenge had been mounted by female employees, with substantial success in the Court of Appeal, to the statutory requirement of two years continuous service for the acquisition of rights not to be unfairly dismissed and to redundancy pay.

The applicants' contention is that the two year requirement is indirectly discriminatory against women, certainly as at the date of dismissal of those applicants in May 1991, as more women than men then worked for continuous periods of less than two years. The Court of Appeal held that the two year requirement was (as at May 1991) in breach of the Equal Treatment Directive (though not in breach of Article 119) which has direct effect on the state and emanations of the state. It was discriminatory of women and was not objectively justifiable. The House of Lords have adjourned the appeal pending a reference to the European Court of Justice on the interpretation of the scope of Article 119.

[4] [1995] ICR 889 (CA); [1997] ICR 371 (HL).

Purposive Interpretation

Mrs Webb's case[5] exemplifies the methods of legislative interpretation used by the European Court of Justice and the effect of those methods on the interpretation of national legislation. The result of a reference by the House of Lords to the European Court of Justice on the interpretation of the Equal Treatment Directive was that Mrs Webb could succeed on a claim for sex discrimination which would have failed on the interpretation of the Sex Discrimination Act 1975 without regard to enforceable community rights.

Mrs Webb was employed to replace an import operations clerk absent on maternity leave. Her appointment was temporary, though it was anticipated that she would stay on after the return of the absent employee from maternity leave. After Mrs Webb had become pregnant she was dismissed. She could not claim unfair dismissal, as she had not been employed for long enough to acquire the statutory right not to be unfairly dismissed. She could not invoke the doctrine of direct effect of the Equal Treatment Directive, as that Directive only had vertical effect against the State. It was not horizontally effective between her and a private employer.

Her claim was for sex discrimination: she was dismissed because she was pregnant.

The employer's case, which found favour in the Industrial Tribunal, the Employment Appeal Tribunal, and the Court of Appeal, was that the reason for Mrs Webb's dismissal was not her pregnancy, but her anticipated inability to carry out the primary task for which she was employed (i.e., to cover for the absent employee) and that she was not treated less favourably than a hypothetical man, absent for a comparable reason (e.g., illness), would have been treated.

The House of Lords, in recognition of the principle that the 1975 Act should be interpreted to conform to the Equal Treatment Directive, made a reference to the European Court of Justice under Article 177 for the interpretation of the Equal Treatment Directive in the context of Mrs Webb's case.

The ruling of the European Court of Justice was that the dismissal of Mrs Webb for the reason given her employer was a dismissal for pregnancy. Her pregnancy made her incapable of performing her work. That was direct discrimination on the ground of sex. Comparison of her situation with that of a hypothetical man was impossible and irrelevant: pregnancy is a biological condition unique to women and it is not comparable to a pathological condition.

[5] *Webb* v. *EMO* [1993] ICR 175; [1994] ICR 770; [1995] ICR 1021.

In the light of that ruling, the House of Lords held that, in considering Mrs Webb's claim for sex discrimination under the 1975 Act, her pregnancy would be a relevant circumstance, which would not be a relevant circumstance in the case of a man. The result is that a woman may be regarded as treated less favourably than a man without the comparison of the treatment of a man required by the language of Section 1 of the 1975 Act.

The principle of purposive interpretation has also had important effects in cases brought under the Transfer of Undertakings (Protection of Employment) Regulations 1981 by employees claiming continuity of employment with a new employer following the transfer of the undertaking or part of the undertaking in which they were employed. The TUPE Regulations were made in 1981 to give effect to the Acquired Rights Directive, which has frequently been interpreted by the European Court of Justice. The rulings of the court have been on basic questions, such as the interpretation of 'undertaking' and of 'transfer'. The English Courts have given interpretations to the TUPE Regulations which they would not have given to the language of the regulations in the absence of the principle of purposive interpretation. A comparison with earlier decisions on the interpretation of TUPE and on the provisions relating to continuity of employment demonstrates the difference in approach to interpretation when English Courts are under a duty to give an effect to national law which accords with Community law, as interpreted by the European Court of Justice.

Direct Effect

Appropriately, in the birth of a new legal order, pregnant women have been pioneering litigants.

The doctrine of direct effect in its vertical form had interesting consequences in claims by thousands of women dismissed from the armed forces before 1990 on the ground that they were pregnant. Their claims in the Industrial Tribunals for compensation resulted in large awards in cases attracting widespread (often unfavourable and uninformed) publicity. There was less publicity for, and less public appreciation of, the legal basis on which it became possible to make those claims at all.

The applicants had no common law claims, such as wrongful dismissal: they had been engaged on the basis that, if they became pregnant, they would have to leave the services. They had no statutory rights under the national legislation, as the Employment Protection (Consolidation) Act 1978 and the Sex Discrimination Act 1975 excluded the armed forces from their application. They also set a ceiling on the maximum amount of compensation recoverable.

The validity of the claim based on sex discrimination was ultimately accepted by the Ministry of Defence, except for quantum of compensation. It was accepted that their right arose by the combined effect of the European Communities Act 1972, the Equal Treatment Directive, and rulings of the European Court of Justice. The Directive, addressed to and binding upon Member States and emanations of the state, guaranteed the same conditions of work without discrimination on the ground of sex. It did so unconditionally and in sufficiently clear and precise terms to be available to individuals in proceedings against the state in national courts. The state could not, on Community law principles, take advantage of its own failure to perform the obligation to implement the Directive fully into national law, i.e., the failure to amend the Sex Discrimination Act 1975 so as to accord with the Directive. The Directive neither excluded the armed forces from its application nor set an upper limit on compensation recoverable for breach of the rights conferred. As interpreted by the European Court of Justice, the Directive conferred a right to effective judicial protection for ensuring real equality of opportunity. There was a denial of that right as compensation subject to a ceiling fell short of full protection. All those rights and liabilities, remedies, and procedures arising under the Equal Treatment Directive became enforceable in English Courts by virtue of Section 2 of the 1972 Act.

Without Community law, the claims by the ex-service women would have failed. As it was, their claims succeeded without the need for a reference to the European Court of Justice under Article 177. It is a noteworthy feature of Community law, as applied in many employment cases, that there have been few references to the European Court. The Industrial Tribunals and higher courts have interpreted and applied Community law on the basis of earlier rulings on interpretation by the European Court.

Procedure and Time Limits

Important aspects of substantive law are sometimes uncovered in the solution of procedural questions. The procedure for enforcement of Community law rights in national courts highlights practical aspects of the relationship between Community law and the legal systems of Member States.

The cause of part-time workers has made an important contribution to the clarification of this aspect of Community law. In the *Equal Opportunities* case part-time workers succeeded in establishing in the House of Lords that their exclusion from employment rights was incompatible with Community law on sex discrimination. They were also successful in the European Court of Justice in establishing that their exclusion from access to membership of occupational pension schemes was contrary to Community law on equal pay.

The enforcement of those rights so recognized is for national courts. When individual part-time workers attempted to enforce those rights the national courts were faced with national legislation setting time limits for the institution of claims. If those time limits were applicable, the rights held to exist under Community law would not be enforceable in the case of many past claims.

For example, under the Employment Protection (Consolidation) Act 1978 (now the Employment Rights Act 1996) a claim for unfair dismissal must be presented to a Tribunal before the end of the period of three months beginning with the effective date of termination of employment. The tribunal has a residual discretion to extend that period for such period it considers reasonable. In order to exercise that discretion, the tribunal must first be satisfied that 'it was not reasonably practicable for the complaint to be presented before the end of the period of three months'. The impact of time limits on the enforcement of Community law rights was brought sharply into focus in the decision of the Court of Appeal in *Biggs* v. *Somerset County Council*.[6] Mrs Biggs was dismissed from her employment as a part-time teacher on 31 August 1976. She did not present her application to the tribunal for unfair dismissal until 1 June 1994, nearly eighteen years later. Under national law her claim was out of time. The question was: did that prevent her from pursuing her case under Community law? It was argued on behalf of Mrs Biggs that the statutory time limit did not prevent her from pursuing her case for three reasons: (a) her claim was based on Article 119 of the Treaty and national law time limits were not applicable to claims under that Article; (b) if, however, national law time limits were applicable to claims under Article 119, the tribunal should disapply them on Community law principles; and (c) if the national law time limits were not disapplied, the tribunal should extend the time for presenting the application, because it had not been reasonably practicable for Mrs Biggs to bring her claim within three months of her dismissal in 1976.

The Court of Appeal, like the Employment Appeal Tribunal, rejected all three arguments. Leave to appeal to the House of Lords was refused. The decision illustrates the relevance and application of two further principles of Community law:

(1) *The Principle of National Procedure*

In *Rewe*[7] and in subsequent decisions the European Court of Justice enunciated the principle that it is for the legal system of each Member State to determine the procedural conditions (including time limits) governing legal proceedings for the protection and enforcement of directly effective Community law rights. There are exceptions to and qualifications of this

6 [1996] ICR 364. 7 [1976] ECR 1989.

general principle: (a) there may be an express Community law provision on procedure and time limits. If there is, then it must be applied; (b) the national procedural conditions and time limits must not make it virtually impossible in practice for the Community law right to be exercised; (c) those conditions must not be less favourable than those relating to similar rights under domestic law. They must not be inferior and discriminatory.

In reliance on the principle of national procedure, fortified by the Community law principle of legal certainty, the Court of Appeal decided that the three months time limit was applicable to the claim for unfair dismissal by Mrs Biggs. Her claim was for unfair dismissal under the Employment Protection legislation of the United Kingdom. It was not a claim for equal pay or for sex discrimination under Article 119 or under a Directive. Her claim was not a Community law claim at all, for there is no Community right not to be unfairly dismissed. The relevance of Community law was its potential to displace provisions of national law of unfair dismissal (as well as other areas of law) where those provisions were incompatible with directly effective provisions of Community law. The Court of Appeal pointed out that, at the date of her dismissal, Mrs Biggs was entitled to invoke Section 2 of the European Communities Act 1972 and Article 119 of the Treaty of Rome for the disapplication of the restrictive effect of employment rights of part-time workers in the form of the threshold requirements of hours of work. She had not invoked that right. The fact that it was not until 1994 that the right was invoked successfully in the House of Lords did not make the time limits in the Employment Protection legislation incompatible with Community law or provide grounds for extending the time.

(2) *Principle of Default*

Mrs Biggs also invoked the principle established by the European Court of Justice in *Emmott* v. *Minister of Social Welfare*[8] that, as it is the duty of a Member State to transpose a Directive into national law, a Member State in default in so doing cannot rely on delay in instituting proceedings against it to protect the rights intended to be conferred by the Directive. In practice this principle means that a defaulting Member State cannot invoke a national time limit to defeat a claim against it. The time limit does not begin to run against the claim as long as the member state is in default of its obligation fully to implement the Directive.

If that principle applied to her case, as Mrs Biggs argued that it did, the three months time limit could not be relied upon by the Somerset County Council to defeat her claim; the Somerset County Council was an emana-

[8] [1991] ECR I–4269.

tion of a Member State and was affected by this principle. The principle of equal pay in Article 119 and in the Equal Pay Directive had not been transposed into domestic law until regulations were made in 1995 (which came into force on the 6th February 1995) following the decision of the House of Lords in the *Equal Opportunities* case.[9] It was only then that English law was brought into line with Community law on the principle of equal pay for equal work. Mrs Biggs had presented her claim before those regulations came into force.

This argument failed in the Court of Appeal. Article 119 was held not to confer any right to compensation for unfair dismissal where there was no sex discrimination. The three months time limit did not involve any element of discrimination on the ground of sex. The element of sex discrimination had been in the national legislation restricting the right to bring a claim for unfair dismissal. Mrs Biggs could have relied on Article 119 to displace those restrictions when she was dismissed in 1976. There was no legal barrier to her bringing her claim. The principle laid down in *Emmott* did not apply to her claim either under Article 119 or under the Equal Pay Directive. Article 119 was directly effective in the courts of Member States. No implementation by the Member State into national law was necessary. Article 119 was part of United Kingdom law, without any further act of implementation by Parliament in primary or secondary legislation. There was therefore no default in the implementation of the Treaty.

As for the Equal Pay Directive, that did not create any new or separate right from Article 119. It was only adopted to implement the directly effective principle in Article 119. *Emmott* did not therefore assist Mrs Biggs on that point.

Finally, Community law did not provide any ground for extending the period of three months. It was reasonably practicable in law for Mrs Biggs to bring her claim when she was dismissed. It would be contrary to the principle of legal certainty to allow a time limit to be extended because the law, as it had in existed in 1976, had not been fully explained judicially or fully understood until a later date. As appeared from the decision of the House of Lords in the *Equal Opportunities* case there had in fact been no legal impediment to Mrs Biggs invoking Article 119 to displace the restrictions on her right as a part-time worker to claim unfair dismissal.

In line with these principles, it has also been held by the Court of Appeal in *Barber* v. *Staffordshire County Council*[10] that where a claim for unfair dismissal had been withdrawn and then dismissed by consent, the principle of cause of action or issue estoppel operated to prevent an employee from starting a second set of proceedings based on his unfair dismissal, but

[9] *R.* v. *Secretary of State for Employment ex Parte Equal Opportunities Commission* [1994] ICR 317.

[10] [1996] 2 AER 748.

invoking Article 119 and the Equal Pay Directive instead of the national law of employment protection. The Court of Appeal decided that Article 119 did not create a right of action for unfair dismissal enforceable in an industrial tribunal, separate and apart from the right conferred by national legislation. The effect of Community law in this area was to lift barriers to or restrictions on a claim for unfair dismissal in so far as the barriers or restrictions were incompatible with Community law. Community law did not, however, have the effect of creating its own right of unfair dismissal.

More recently the Employment Appeal Tribunal and the Court of Appeal have applied the same principles to claims by part-time workers for the enforcement of access to membership of occupational pension schemes. It was held in test cases that the time limit in the Equal Pay Act applies for the enforcement of the right to equal treatment for pensions and that time limit is not incompatible with Community law: *Preston* v. *Wolverhampton Health Care NHS Trust*.[11] The House of Lords have referred to the European Court of Justice questions relating to the compatibility of national law time limits with principles of Community law.

The Employment Appeal Tribunal has held[12] that national time limits applied and that there were no grounds for disapplying them in relation to an application for leave to appeal out of time to the Employment Appeal Tribunal from the Industrial Tribunal, which had rejected a claim for unfair dismissal by a part-time employee. The principle in *Emmott* applied to the institution of proceedings, but not to the institution of an appeal against a decision. No principle of Community law was violated by the application of a national law rule setting a time limit for appealing.

Particular Areas of Substantive Law

It is impossible in this chapter to do more than skim the surface of developments in different areas of substantive employment law affected by the impact of Community law. Encyclopaedic works on Industrial Relations and Employment law devote much space to this topic. The interplay of principles of Community law with those of national law demonstrate the fundamental effects of Community law over a wide range of substantive employment rights and duties.

Transfer of Undertakings

At common law an employee only had employment rights against his employer with whom he had contract of service. If the employer transferred the business in which he was employed, the contract of service was

[11] [1996] IRLR 484; [1997] ICR 899 (CA); [1998] 1 All ER 528 (HL).
[12] *Setiyah* v. *East Yorkshire Health Authority* [1995] IRLR 348.

brought to an end. The employee might have a claim for breach of contract (e.g., for failure to give him contractual notice) but he had no right to continue his employment in the business in the hands of the transferee.

In 1981 the law of the United Kingdom was changed when the Transfer of Undertakings (Protection of Employment) Regulations (TUPE) were made to implement the provisions of the Acquired Rights Directive 77/187 by providing for automatic transfer of employment on the transfer of an undertaking in which the employees are employed.

The purpose of the Directive, as stated in its preamble, was to 'provide for the protection of employees in the event of a change of employer, in particular to ensure that their rights are safeguarded.'

The provisions of the Directive are not directly effective against a Member State as they are not sufficiently clear, specific, and unconditional in their terms. But that does not prevent the principle of purposive interpretation from being invoked in English courts. Decisions of the European Court of Justice on the Directive are frequently cited in support of interpretations of TUPE to ensure that TUPE is interpreted to conform to the provisions of Community law. An example of how far the courts will go to achieve a consistent interpretation of national law and Community law is the decision of the House of Lords in *Litster* v. *Forth Dry Dock and Engineering Co Ltd*.[13] TUPE applies for the protection of employees employed in the undertaking 'immediately before' the transfer. On a literal interpretation of that provision, which English principles of statutory construction would normally favour, protection could not be claimed by employees dismissed before the transfer, even if only hours before the transfer. In accordance with the principle of purposive interpretation the House of Lords held, following decisions of the European Court of Justice, that the relevant regulation in TUPE should be read as if it applied not only to employees employed immediately before the transfer, but also to employees 'who would have been so employed, if they had not been unfairly dismissed.' In an exercise of interpretation the House of Lords read into TUPE thirteen additional words to achieve a decision consistent with Community law.

The Acquired Rights Directive and decisions of the European Court of Justice have governed the result of other TUPE cases. For example, in its original form an 'undertaking' was defined in TUPE as excluding undertakings which were 'not in the nature of a commercial venture'. In infringement proceedings taken by the European Commission against the United Kingdom it was accepted that, in view of the decisions of the European Court of Justice on this point, the Directive was not limited to commercial ventures. Regulations were therefore made in 1993 which,

[13] [1989] ICR 341.

with effect from 30 August 1993, amended the definition of undertaking so as to include non-commercial undertakings.

In the interpretation of 'undertaking' and 'transfer' English courts and tribunals have reached conclusions which they would not have reached in the absence of decisions of the European Court of Justice giving a broad meaning to those expressions. These influences have been particularly strong in cases on the contracting out of services. On the authority of such cases as *Schmidt* v. *Spar*[14] the Court of Appeal and the Employment Appeal Tribunal have concluded that the contracting out of services may fall within the definition of a 'transfer of an undertaking', even to the extent of holding that there is a transfer of an undertaking when a first fixed term contract out of services has terminated and a second contract has been made, following a compulsory competitive tendering exercise[15]. In *Schmidt*, the European Court of Justice went so far as to hold that the employment of a single person to perform services (in that case cleaning services) could amount to an 'undertaking' and that a transfer could take place when those services were contracted out by the employer to a cleaning company. Even if there is no transfer of tangible or intangible assets, an undertaking may be transferred if the same or similar activities continue to be carried on in different hands and retain their identity. The European Court of Justice has, however, insisted that, in order to qualify as an undertaking within the meaning of the Directive, there must exist a 'stable economic entity'. Thus, in *Rygaard* v. *Stro Molle Akustik A/S*[16] the European Court of Justice declined to hold that there was a transfer of an undertaking when new contractors were brought in to complete an uncompleted building contract for a specific project initiated by a contractor who became insolvent. The recent decisions of the European Court of Justice in *Suzen* [1997] ICR 662 and of the Court of Appeal in *Betts* v. *Brinlet Helicopters Ltd* [1997] ICR 792 indicate a 'shift in emphasis' away from a 'transfer' in contracting out cases concerned with labour intensive activities.

The extent to which the Directive and the decisions on it may make serious inroads into traditional doctrines of English law became apparent in the case of *Wilson* v. *St Helens Borough Council*.[17] The Employment Appeal Tribunal felt bound by the decision of the European Court of Justice in *Foreningen* v. *Daddy's Dance Hall A/S*[18] to interpret TUPE so as to invalidate agreements made, on the occasion of a transfer, by employees with the transferee on different terms than those on which they had previously served with the transferor employer. The European Court of Justice had held in *Daddy's Dance Hall* that it was contrary to the public policy of the Directive for an employee to be free to vary his terms of employment on the transfer.

[14] [1994] ECR I–1311.

[15] *Dines* v. *Initial Health Care Services Ltd* [1995] ICR 11.

[16] [1996] IRLR 51.

[17] [1996] ICR 711; [1997] IRLR 505 (CA).

[18] [1988] IRLR 315.

The original terms remained in force, notwithstanding the agreement. The Court of Appeal reversed the decision of the Appeal Tribunal on other grounds. The result of the appeal to the House of Lords is awaited.

The principle of purposive interpretation produced a result which would not have been reached by an English Court guided more closely by linguistic considerations.

Equal Opportunities

In addition to the *Webb* case there have been decisions of the European Court of Justice leading to either the amendment of the Sex Discrimination Act 1975 and the Equal Pay Act 1970 or to an interpretation of national legislation in conformity with the interpretation of the European Court of Justice. The decision in *Marshall* v. *South West Hampshire Health Authority (No 2)*[19] led to the amendment of the Sex Discrimination Act 1975 to bring it in line with the Equal Treatment Directive by removing the upper limit (£10,000) on the quantum of compensation. The European Court of Justice held that the financial limit was incompatible with the requirements in Article 6 of the Directive that there should be effective judicial protection for the right to equal treatment conferred by Community law.

It remains to be seen whether the wide interpretation given by the European Court of Justice to the Equal Treatment Directive in *P* v. *Cornwall County Council*[20] will affect the interpretation and application of the Sex Discrimination Act. The European Court interpreted the Directive as covering not only discrimination between the male and female sex, but also cases of sexual orientation. The dismissal of a transsexual on notification of an intention to undergo a 'gender re-assignment' was held to be contrary to the Equal Treatment Directive which was directly effective against the respondent County Council, as an emanation of the State. It has yet to be finally decided by a court in the United Kingdom whether that interpretation affects the interpretation of the Sex Discrimination Act whose terms clearly require a comparison to be made of the treatment of one sex with the treatment of the other sex.

The interpretation of Article 119 and of the Equal Pay Directive has affected the Equal Pay Act 1970 as applied in English courts. On a reference determined by the European Court of Justice in 1993 a more flexible notion of indirect discrimination on the ground of sex emerged. According to the European Court in *Enderby* v. *Frenchay Health Authority*[21] it is not necessary under the Directive to show that there was a specific rule or criterion the application of which produced inequality. Indirect sex discrimination may occur if women are paid less than men in the same group for

[19] [1993] ICR 893. [20] [1996] IRLR 34. [21] [1993] ECR I–5535.

work of equal value. Further, the existence of separate collective bargaining machinery does not provide an objective justification for failure to observe the principle of equal pay. In the recent cases of *British Coal Corp.* v. *Smith* [1996] ICR 515 and *Barry* v. *Midland Bank plc* [1998] 1 All ER 805 the English Courts reached decisions on the Equal Pay Act 1970 without the need for a reference to the European Court of Justice.

Pensions

The decisions of the European Court of Justice on occupational pension schemes have far reaching consequences for part-time workers and their employers. Benefits under such schemes, though payable in the future after the cessation of the employment relationship, were held to be 'pay' within Article 119 and the Equal Pay Directive. It was contrary to directly effective Community law to discriminate on the ground of sex in the payment of pension benefits by employers or by the trustees of the scheme: *Barber* v. *Guardian Royal Exchange*;[22] *Coloroll*.[23] It was then held that Article 119 covered not just entitlement to benefit but also access to membership of such schemes and that the exclusion of part-time workers, who were predominently women, from them was discriminatory on the ground of sex: *Fisscher* and *Vroege*.[24] The English courts were then faced with procedural problems in the enforcement of rights to retrospective access to membership of pension schemes. The decisions on access, unlike those on benefits, were stated by the European Court of Justice to have retrospective effect: there was no cut-off date, such as the 17 May 1990, as in the *Barber* case. The position for the future was settled by statutory amendments (Pensions Act 1995 and the Occupational Pensions Schemes (Equal Access to Membership) Amendment Regulations 1995). It has been held that, for the past, the claims to access by part-time workers were subject to time limits in national legislation (the Equal Pay Act 1970), that those time limits were not incompatible with Community law and that neither public sector nor private employers were disentitled from relying on the time limits in defence to the claims: *Preston* and *Fletcher*,[25] affirmed by the Court of Appeal in February 1997, but since adjourned by the House of Lords pending a reference to the European Court of Justice under Article 177.

Claims for Damages against the State

Francovich v. *Italian Republic*[26] is better known as a landmark case on state liability for damages than as a decision on the rights of employees to guar-

[22] [1990] ICR 616. [23] [1994] IRLR 588. [24] [1994] ECR I–4541.
[25] [1996] IRLR 484; [1997] ICR 899 (CA); [1998] 1 All ER 528 (HL).
[26] [1991] ECR I–5357.

antee payments on the insolvency of their employers under the Insolvency Directive 80/987. As confirmed and elaborated by the recent decisions in *R* v. *Secretary of State for Transport ex p. Factortame* and *Brasserie du Pecheur* v. *Federal Republic of Germany*[27] the Francovich principle may render a Member State liable in damages to a person who can establish that he has suffered loss as a result of a serious failure of the state to perform its Community law obligation to implement a Directive, intended to confer rights for the benefit of individuals, fully into its national legal system. The principle is stated as follows in *Dillenkofer* v. *Federal Republic of Germany*:[28] 'Failure to take any measure to transpose a Directive in order to achieve the result it prescribes within the period laid down for that purpose constitutes per se a serious breach of Community law and consequently gives rise to a right of reparation for individuals suffering injury if the result prescribed by the Directive entails the grant to individuals of rights whose content is identifiable and a causal link exists between the breach of the state's obligation and the loss and damage suffered.' In *Mann* v. *Secretary of State for Employment*[29] the Employment Appeal Tribunal (later upheld by the Court of Appeal on this point) held that such a claim against the state for damages fell outside the jurisdiction of an industrial tribunal, which was confined to the determination of disputes between employers and employees. That restriction on competence was not incompatible with Community law under which questions of enforcement and procedure are for the national law, unless the national law makes it impossible in practice to enforce the Community law right or is discriminatory.

Conclusions

How will historians interpret the attempts of English courts to apply Community law in employment cases in the last quarter of the twentieth century? The economic historian will note the effects of fiscal policies on the changing pattern of employment; the conflict between the workers' quest for employment protection and job security and the promotion by the government of the United Kingdom of competition by deregulation and the creation of flexible labour markets; the employment consequences of compulsory competitive tendering and the contracting out of services; the decline of full-time, long-term employment; the increase in the numbers of part-time, short-term, temporary, and fixed-term workers and of self-employed workers.

The political historian will detect tensions among the Member States, and between them and the Community Institutions; increasing Community regulation of employment conditions; the political and social

[27] [1996] QB 404. [28] [1997] 2 WLR 253 at 290C–D. [29] [1996] ICR 197.

consequences of that regulation; and signs of the gradual emergence of a political order with federal characteristics. The social historian's interest will be caught by the reflection in legal decisions of fundamental changes in society: the effect of equal opportunities law on the growing prominence of women in the workplace; the consequent shift to the economic independence of women; the protection of rights of members of minority groups; the importance of the need to make provision for a private pension during a shorter working life for a longer period of retirement and old age in conditions of limited state provision, increasing costs of health and care services and risks of inflationary trends.

The historian of English law is familiar with a stable system of almost unbroken continuity evolving in slow motion, little influenced by the civil law systems of mainland Europe. He cannot fail to observe the impact of Community Law on the legal results achieved by its application in employment cases and also (more significantly) on legal concepts, methods, and reasoning: judicial review of primary legislation on the ground of incompatibility with Community laws of superior legal force; a shift in the relationship between Parliament and the Courts; purposive methods of interpretation and more liberal use of preparatory materials in relation to a very different style of legislative drafting; the novelty of directly effective measures emanating from a source other than Westminster or Whitehall; the radical notion of the state incurring liability to pay compensation for failure to enact legislation or for enacting defective legislation.

15

Community Intellectual Property Law in the English Courts

BY THE HON MR JUSTICE JACOB

It is not given to all to enjoy writing. But when Francis Jacobs and Mads Andenas ask, one does not have much choice. In part this is a chapter of personal reminiscence and in part a commentary on some bits of the law. It is a bit of a ramble. I hope it is not too idiosyncratic.

The Beginning

Intellectual property law has burgeoned since the early 1970s. Before then it was an unfashionable and rather dull area of law, typically involving half-hearted disputes in the patent office. The High Court was fairly moribund as far as IP was concerned.[1] But, just as we joined the Common Market (or just before) the sleeping giant awoke. People found they were able to turn to the law to prevent a variety of competition. Thus copyright entered the field of industrial design; copyright was used for the first time effectively to prevent copying of dresses and so on. IP lawyers began to devise new procedural remedies, first the Norwich order and, a few years later, the Anton Piller.

Thus IP law and Community Law were ready to meet when we joined the Common Market on 1 January 1973. And it was IP cases which featured most prominently in the UK courts so far as Community Law was concerned. I think the first time the Rome Treaty was referred to in any English Court was an IP case, *Lerose* v. *Hawick*.[2] It is now long-forgotten and of no importance save that it was the first. The case was heard on 29 November 1972, a month before the United Kingdom joined. The plaintiff sought an interlocutory injunction to restrain copying of a fabric design. The defendant argued that an injunction would have the same effect as an agreement not to use that design and that such an agreement would fall foul of Article 85. So there would be a defence after 1 January. At the time

[1] In 1963 Lloyd-Jacob J spoke of the 'somewhat exiguous list of the assigned judge', *Terrapin* v. *Builders' Supply* [1963] RPC 301 at 307. Only a handful of copyright cases were reported in the decade 1960 to 1970. And one only has to look at the thickening of volumes of the Reports of Patent Cases in 1972 to give an approximate date to the IP explosion.

[2] [1974] RPC 42.

I knew nothing about the Common Market. There was a very new junior in chambers who claimed he did and so, for the first time in my career I was given a junior. His name was H. I. L. Laddie. He was going to argue this point and was all full of enthusiasm and authorities. But Whitford J did not call upon us. He did not think an injunction was the same as an agreement and that was that.

Infringers' Defences

Lerose v. *Hawick* was a foretaste of what was to come. Defendants in IP cases began habitually to rely on the Treaty. Almost invariably such reliance was ultimately unsuccessful. I think it remains the case that even today, save in relation to goods put in free circulation in the Common Market by the IP right holder, no defence of Community Law has ever succeeded in the English courts. I do not find this particularly surprising since in most cases if there is no defence to an infringement claim apart from the Treaty, it is not self-evident that the Treaty should somehow come to the rescue.

I will trace this 'infringer's defence' through some of the cases. I think it was next tried (November 1974) in a passing off case, *Löwenbrau München* v. *Grunhalle Lager International*.[3] This was in the early days of 'foreign' beers. The plaintiffs, a large German brewery, were the only people to use the word *'Löwenbraü'* in the United Kingdom, though it was in fairly common use by others in Germany. Here, I suspect, only a few of those who knew the mark knew also that it meant Lion Brew, but no matter. The defendants wanted to use *'Grunhalle Löwenbraü'*. There was evidence that the name would deceive here, albeit not in Germany where there were a number of *Löwenbraü* beers, differentiated by additional names. The defendants were enjoined on an interlocutory basis. Graham J was able to distil from the existing community authority a doctrine of exhaustion but not a proposition that if the plaintiff cannot object in law to an act done in one part of the Community he cannot object anywhere. The only surprising thing about the case is that anyone ever thought the contrary might be arguable. Graham J also refused a reference under Article177. I think this was the first time anyone in the English courts had sought a reference,[4] again IP law leading the way.

[3] [1974] RPC 492.

[4] See *Van Duyn* v. *Home Office* [1974] 1 WLR 1107 at 1116: 'There appears to have been so far only one case in this country in which the court has been asked to make a reference, namely that of *Löwenbraü*' per Pennycuick J.

EMI v. *CBS*

At any rate Graham J certainly was not afraid to make a reference. He did so shortly thereafter (March 1975) in *EMI* v. *CBS*.[5] This was the second reference from the United Kingdom. Again a plain infringer tried to resort to the Treaty as an excuse. EMI held the registered trade mark, Columbia in all nine of the then members of the common market. But, as a result of history, CBS held the mark in the United States and some other countries. EMI sued in the United Kingdom, Denmark, and Germany to prevent US Columbia records from being imported or sold. Shortly before then the Court of Justice had given its (as we now know) erroneous decision in *HAGI*[6] to the effect that where a mark had become divided within the EEC, then even if there was no connection between the respective owners, neither could enforce its mark against the other.[7] CBS argued that this 'common origin' doctrine applied even where the mark had been divided between the EEC and some third country. A few years earlier the court had indicated a less than friendly attitude towards trade marks in *Sirena*.[8] CBS clearly hoped that the Court would have the same attitude towards the EMI rights. But it did not, holding that CBS should obliterate Columbia.[9]

I was the junior for EMI before Graham J. I was led by one T. H. Bingham QC. He suggested that another junior from his chambers be added to the team because that junior knew rather a lot about EEC law. I supported the idea with vigour because this was all a new world. Thus in the ECJ you will see that one Francis Jacobs was the first junior. I think this was his first active involvement in a trade mark case. The fundamental lack of logic of the common origin rule which we were up against in EMI clearly rankled with him: it was Advocate General Jacobs who wrote the opinion in *HAGII*[10] which led to the reversal of *HAGI*. That opinion is, in my view, essential reading for anyone concerned with trade marks. And it is a delight. I hope that if and when the ECJ comes to consider the 'extended' view of trade mark rights espoused by some (but not all[11]) in

[5] [1976] RPC 1.

[6] Case 192/73 *Van Zuylen* v. *Hag*, [1974] ECR 127.

[7] Even at the time I wondered who had really won the case. True it was that the Belgian plaintiffs could not enforce their mark against German HAG in Belgium or Luxembourg. But they got the right to enter Germany under the mark until, of course *HAGII*.

[8] [1971] ECR 69 at p. 82 para. 7: 'The exercise of a trade-mark right is particularly apt to lead to a partitioning of markets, and thus to impair the free movement of goods between States which is essential to the Common Market. Moreover, a trade mark right is distinguishable in this context from other rights of industrial and commercial property, inasmuch as the interests protected by the latter are usually more important, and merit a higher degree of protection, than the interests protected by an ordinary trade mark.'

[9] *EMI* v. *CBS* [1976] ECR 811.

[10] *CNL-SUCAl* v. *Hag GF*, Case C–10/89 [1990] 1 ECR 3711.

[11] As I know from discussion with some Dutch judges.

the Netherlands,[12] it will receive the same level of assistance. It would be a shame if the Court moves from the 'less worthy of protection' view of the 1970's to an 'over worthy of protection' view.

There are a couple of other reminiscences of the EMI case. The day before the hearing Tom Bingham wanted to go to the court room just to get the feel of where he would be the next day. It was nice to know he felt nervous. We got into the chamber and he stood at counsel's rostrum, just getting the feel. One of our party pointed out that the seats (upholstered and clad in white leather, or perhaps, more likely, imitation leather) for the parties and spectators were provided with ash trays. Tom said: 'Well if you take a job lot of aeroplane seats, you must take them as they come'. At the actual hearing there were counsel for the parties from both Denmark and Germany (whose courts had followed Graham J and made references in parallel cases). The Danes, fearing that interpreters would not render Danish into the other languages well, asked the leave of the Court to address it in English. Our side's Danish counsel's speech consisted of taking an LP in its sleeve, approaching the judges closely and showing how small obliterations of the mark, Columbia could be done. It worked—the decision was that CBS should obliterate. In retrospect, what was remarkable about the case was the real fear that the Court had such a down on trade marks that it would let the American Columbia in without any reciprocity from the United States.

Criteria for a Reference: *Bulmer* v. *Bollinger*

I return to IP law in the English Courts. It was in another IP case, *Bulmer* v. *Bollinger*[13] that the Court of Appeal first considered the criteria for making a reference to the Court of Justice under Article 177. The English makers of 'champagne cider' and 'champagne perry' sued the French champagne houses for a declaration that these names were lawful. The champagne houses counterclaimed for passing off. The action was proceeding when the United Kingdom joined the EEC. The champagne makers sought to add a claim to the effect that the use of 'champagne', except for the real thing, was contrary to EEC law. They also sought a reference. It was refused by Whitford J and by the Court of Appeal. Lord Denning

[12] See *Wagamama* v. *City Centre Restaurants* [1995] FSR 713; 'Back to the Dark Ages of Trade Mark Law', Kamperman Sanders, [1996] EIPR 3; 'Think before you Waga Finger', Prescott [1996] EIPR 315; and Kamperman Sanders, 'The Return to Wagamama' [1996] 10 EIPR 521. The signs are not that good. In *Puma* (Case C–251/95 [1998] RPC 199) the court sort of endorsed the *Wagamama* view. But the decision is not all that clear. More worrying is Jacobs AG's support for the protectionist view that trade marks applied outside the EU by the proprietor importing the goods into the EU (Opinion of 29/1/98 in *Silhouette* v. *Hartlauer*, Case C–355/96). Surely Kodak film means film of the Kodak company wherever it is made?

[13] [1974] Ch 401.

MR gave guidelines which concentrated on the word 'necessary': 'The point must be such that whichever way it is decided it is conclusive.' There was also great emphasis on deciding the facts first. Since then, it has generally been recognized that these guidelines were somewhat restrictive, but I think it fair to say that at least until recently our courts have been more reluctant than some continental courts to make a reference, perhaps because of this decision. It was in this case that Lord Denning spoke of the Treaty in graphic terms:

> When we come to matters with a European element, the Treaty is like an incoming tide. It flows into the estuaries and up the rivers. It cannot be held back . . . In future, in transactions which cross the frontiers, we must no longer speak or think of English law as something on its own. We must speak and think of community law, of community rights and obligations and we must give effect to them. This means a great effort for the lawyers. We have to learn a new system. The Treaty, with the regulations and directives, covers many volumes. The case law is contained in hundreds of reported cases both in the European Court of Justice and in the national courts of the nine. Many must be studied before the right result can be reached. We must get down to it . . . In the task of interpreting the Treaty, the English judges are no longer the final authority. They no longer carry the law in their breasts. They are no longer in a position to give rulings which are of binding force. The supreme tribunal for interpreting the Treaty is the European Court of Justice, at Luxembourg.

One sometimes wonders why it has taken some politicians so long to realize the truth of what Lord Denning said.

Diverting a little, it is worthwhile recording the ultimate fate of the champagne producers' plea. It failed.[14] And in due course the champagne growers got the regulations changed in their favour.

The Tin Can Litigation

Another 'first' for IP law is that it was in an IP case when the Court of Appeal considered the Treaty for the first time. The case was *Appln. des Gaz* v. *Falks Veritas*.[15] It was another infringer's defence case. Lord Denning began his judgment thus: 'This is the first case in which in this court we have had to consider the Treaty of Rome. It comes about because of a tin can.' In the early 1970s the power of copyright in industrial drawings was becoming widely appreciated. The plaintiffs were seeking to enforce the copyright in their drawing of the Camping Gaz tin to prevent the defendants making copies of their cans. The defendants sought to amend an existing defence which put copyright in issue and alleged estoppel by alleging breach of the Treaty. Both Articles 85 and 86 were relied upon. The judgment of Lord Denning

[14] *Bulmer* v. *Bollinger* [1978] RPC 79 at 110. [15] [1974] Ch 381.

contains a number of passages which in retrospect at least were too wide, for instance:

> In the ordinary way, the national courts of various member states can protect and enforce patents, trade marks, copyright and trade names by their own laws with their own remedies as they always have done . . . But the national courts should not enforce such rights in any case where such enforcement would impede the free movement of goods within the community between one member state and another.

Amendment was allowed, even though the Court recognized that there would be a large burden of discovery. This broad brush approach was, of course, an enormous invitation to infringers. Just pleading a breach of Articles 85 and 86 became a vogue. The difficulties of pleading were significant and they themselves became the subject of contests. The first of these was in the same case. The defendants had asserted a dominant position and its abuse in only general terms. Whitford J held the plea as it stood to be speculative and ordered proper particulars, *Appn. des Gaz* v. *Falks Veritas*.[16]

And the tin can managed to bother the Court of Appeal thrice more before it faded from view. First the plaintiffs, Gaz, seem to have been so concerned by the Eurodefences that they dropped their claim for an injunction and damages for infringements prior to UK entry into the EEC—and indeed for a slightly earlier period being that between the issue of the Writ (in mid-1972) and entry. They just claimed damages for past infringements.[17] On that basis they successfully sought to evade the need to give discovery concerning their alleged dominant position and breaches of Article 85. There was a bizarre argument in the Court of Appeal to the effect that somehow the Treaty was retrospective, but it did not wash. The decision of the Court of Appeal[18] is of no interest. What is of interest is the constitution of the Court, namely Viscount Dilhorne, and Lords Edmund-Davies and Scarman. I have never heard of an all-Law Lord Court of Appeal before or since. Maybe Lord Woolf should try borrowing some Law Lords now to help with the current backlog in the Court of Appeal.

Gaz, having got the Eurolaw out of their own claim, found the defendants wriggling by other means to get it back in. The defendants sued Gaz for breaches of Articles 85 and 86. Their first attempt was held wholly embarrassing,[19] a decision upheld by the Court of Appeal. They returned to the fray with a new Writ, joining in not only Gaz but Gaz's UK distributors, for whom I appeared. The pleading was complicated, prolix, and muddled,

[16] [1975] FSR 363.

[17] This may still have been a hefty claim, going back for some 6 years before the Writ and including the then permissible but outrageous claim for damages for conversion. If ever the claim had come to trial there would have been a beautiful point about whether the gas inside the cylinder, perforce of the shape of the cylinder, was an infringing copy.

[18] [1978] 1 CMLR 383.

[19] [1978] 1 CMLR 30.

with important allegations called 'particulars' buried away. Whitford J struck it out. However the defendants found a friendly Court of Appeal who allowed them to re-plead,[20] much to my annoyance—after all we had got the court to hold that the existing pleading was no good. As I recall it, even though they finally got a pleading allowed to go ahead, they ended up paying for the entire costs of the exercise. My submission to the Court on costs was 'if you get the Court of Appeal to draft your pleadings, you ought to pay.' The Court particularly went out of its way to say that it did not necessarily agree with Lord Denning in the first tin can case when he said:

> Articles 85 and 86 are part of our law. They create new torts or wrongs. Their names are 'undue restriction of competition within the Common Market'; and 'abuse of dominant position within the common market'. Any infringement of those articles can be dealt with by our English courts. It is for our courts to find the facts, apply the law, and use the remedies which we have available.

Again one sees the general view of the 1970s, that Euro-points should all be treated with care, avoiding deciding anything if at all possible.

The Courts Smell a Rat: 'Nexus' Arrives

I think the tin can litigation died thereafter, on what basis I do not know. It was left to other defendants in other cases to try to plead Euro-defences. The Courts started to be suspicious. In *British Leyland* v. *TI Silencers*[21] Walton J said of a pleading which in effect asserted no more than that an injunction would interfere with inter-State trade:

> These are really some of the most audacious allegations that I have ever seen, because what they amount to is a positive pleading that if the plaintiffs obtain the relief sought in the action, the defendants will be debarred from continuing to do a whole series of wrongful acts which they should never have been doing anyhow. Whatever else it is, the Treaty of Rome is not intended to be a pirate's charter.

In *ICI* v. *Berk*[22] the plaintiffs were suing in passing off. Their claim was that the exact imitation of their pills—pink pills—amounted to a misrepresentation. The alleged abuse was the charging of unfair prices which was said to affect trade between Member States. Sir Robert Megarry V-C struck the defence out. He said: 'The English courts must be ready to scrutinise a Euro-defence with care, notwithstanding any apparent complexity, and should not adopt the attitude, whether overt or covert, that because it is a Euro-defence it must at least be arguable.' He also said:

> I do not think it could be said that a person in breach of some statutory or other prohibition thereupon becomes an outlaw, unable to enforce any of his rights

[20] [1978] 3 CMLR 87. [21] [1979] FSR 591 at 598.
[22] [1981] 2 CMLR 91; [1981] FSR 1.

against anyone. If the plaintiffs are imposing unfair selling prices . . . I cannot see this breach of Article 86 means that the defendants are thereby set free from any liability to the plaintiffs if they, the defendants, commit the tort of passing off (or indeed, any other tort) against them . . . Further, if the defendants are right, the ability of the plaintiffs to sue them for passing off will exist and be destroyed in accordance with the prices which for the time being the plaintiffs are charging, coming and going as the plaintiffs charge a fair price or charge a price that is unfairly high or unfairly low, with all the problems that would arise from prices which are in a twilight zone of merely possible or arguable unfairness.

He particularly identified what he called (and has come to be generally called) the nexus point. He said that there was no nexus between the alleged overcharging (the alleged abuse) and the alleged passing off.

He further doubted whether there was an effect upon trade between member states and the alleged overcharging but did not base his decision on that ground. Jumping ahead, that is indeed a formidable ground on its own in an alleged overcharging case. It was the ground of strike-out in *Chiron* v. *Murex (No 2)*.[23] The plaintiffs had a patent on Hepatitis C testing kits. The defendants alleged abuse of Article 86 by overcharging and refusal to licence. It was not possible to point to a link between the allegedly high prices and an effect on inter-State trade, so the pleading failed. Other pleadings have suffered a similar fate on nexus.[24]

Article 177: Against what Court is there 'No Judicial Remedy?'

Incidentally, it was the *Chiron* case which highlighted a procedural problem about references under Article 177. What happens when the Court of Appeal finally deals with a Euro-point and refuses leave to appeal? Since the House of Lords may yet give leave to appeal one cannot say the decision of the Court of Appeal is that of the Court of final resort (i.e., in the language of Article 177, the 'court or tribunal of a member State against whose decisions there is no judicial remedy under national law'). The defendants in *Chiron* sought a reference from the CA but were refused. They went to the HL for leave to appeal, which was itself refused. They did not at that point ask for a reference. Instead they went back to the Court of Appeal and asked for a reference there. It was refused on the grounds that they were asking the wrong court, the Court of Appeal itself being *functus officio*. It may seem a pity that a procedural blunder defeated the application for a reference, but I do not think so.[25] I think the 'overcharging' defence ought to be no sort of defence at all. It is essentially hypocritical: what the defendant wants to do is charge just under the allegedly over-high price. He has no real interest in lower prices.

[23] [1994] 1 CMLR 410, CA.

[24] e.g., *Duracell* v. *Ever Ready* [1989] RPC 731.

[25] I try to disregard the fact that I was, for some time, including the initial successful strike out in the CA, counsel for *Chiron*.

What is an Unfair Price for Patented Goods?

Conceptually I think there are real problems with any allegation of 'overcharging' for patented goods. The whole point of a patent monopoly is to enable the patentee to charge more. Even in a context where overcharging is a statutory ground for a licence ('where a demand for the product in the United Kingdom is not being met on reasonable terms'[26]) it is extremely difficult to say a price is 'too much'. In *Research Corpn.'s Patent*[27] the patented drug cost eight times as much as an unpatented drug which was therapeutically equivalent. But the unpatented drug had terrible side effects which meant that the patient had to be an in-patient, whereas this was not so when the patented drug was used. In truth, using the patented drug was cheaper. Hoffmann J refused to find overcharging. In *Chiron*, as I recall it, the use of the test cost about two pounds per blood donation whereas other, unpatented tests for other diseases were about fifty pence. But the saving in increased medical costs alone from people who did not get hepatitis C as a result of the use of the test was some five times the cost of testing the blood supply for hepatitis C. It is too often easy, after the event, to say, as did the burghers of Hamlyn Town, 'A thousand guilders! Why, take fifty.' It is not uninteresting to note that so far as I know there has been no case decided anywhere (including direct complaints or action by the Commission) holding simply that a patentee has been overcharging and is thereby in breach of Article 86.[28] There may, of course, be cases of overcharging (Article 86 specifically contemplates 'imposing unfair . . . prices') but, absent some very extraordinary case, a claim of 'overcharging' should be regarded with very considerable suspicion.

The Current Status of 'Breach of Article 85 or 86 Defences'

Finally, I believe that there is a lot to be said for Staughton LJ's approach in *Chiron No 2*:[29]

> For my part, I consider that the time has come when these questions should be resolved, as they must be sooner or later. The nettle should be grasped now. Otherwise this and other cases concerned with intellectual property will be encumbered at trial with a great deal of evidence about market, dominant position and abuse which may be wholly unnecessary.

[26] Patents Act 1977, s. 48(3)(b)(i).

[27] [1990] RPC 663.

[28] In one of the few cases to go to trial on this point, *Hoover* v. *Hulme* [1982] FSR 565, Whitford J had no difficulty in rejecting the defence of overcharging, even though the plaintiffs' prices were higher than those of the defendants by quite a bit. The plaintiffs lost for other reasons, as I remember to my discomfort.

[29] [1994] FSR 187.

In the ordinary way, I consider that the remedy for abuses such as are alleged in this case is not to refuse relief to the holder of the patent against the infringer. That could be altogether lacking in proportionality . . . There are other remedies available.

However the majority of the Court in *Chiron No 2* did not support this, leaving it uncertain as to whether the ultimate legal position is as summarised by Hoffmann J in *Pitney-Bowes* v. *Francotyp-Postalia*:[30] 'It is sufficient that the existence of the intellectual property right creates or buttresses the dominant position which the plaintiff is abusing. The remedy contemplated by the court is that the plaintiff may have to be deprived of the means of maintaining his dominant position.'

It is certainly time that the courts decided the point: they may be guided by US experience where anti-trust defences, once all the rage, have largely faded away. Further, I have heard little of such defences even being raised, still less having any success, in other countries of the EC. This too is an important consideration. It is of course more attractive for a defendant to plead abuse here than on the Continent: it costs him little and he can put the plaintiff to enormous discovery.

Beyond the 'Subject-matter?'

I turn to another kind of Euro-defence. This is really an assault on the kind or width of an intellectual property right itself. The argument goes something like this: An IP right is a measure 'having equivalent effect' under Article 30. So unless Article 36 provides an exception, an IP right may not be used to affect inter-State trade. Article 36 provides for the 'protection of industrial and commercial property'. It is for Community law to decide the proper limits of this. It does so by the concept of the 'specific subject' of a right. If a national IP law purports to go beyond this, then to that extent it is not within Article 36 and the free circulation permitted by Article 30 prevails. For many years such arguments were tried. The leading English case rejected it at Court of Appeal level, *British Leyland* v. *Armstrong*,[31] Oliver LJ saying:

What the defendants have to say in this case is either that English copyright is not 'industrial or commercial property', or that the right which the statute confers upon the owner of artistic copyright to prevent copying by or from three-dimensional reproduction is not within the 'specific object' of the property rights. The former proposition is hopeless, having regard to the GEMA case[32] and, as regards the latter, the only argument which can be adduced to support is that the copyright owner does not have that protection in other countries of the Community. That appears to me to be a hopeless proposition, because the object of the property right can, as I see it, be judged only by the domestic law which creates it.

[30] [1991] FSR 72. [31] [1984] FSR 81 at 616. [32] [1981] 1 ECR 147.

And Fox LJ said:[33] 'It seems to me that, in the absence of any specific assumption or provision in the Treaty of Rome (and there is none) one can only ascertain the rights which constitute the specific subject-matter of copyright by looking at the national law.' A reference was refused and the point never got off the ground in the House of Lords because the House divined a defence under English law of a positive right to mend.[34] However I have always wondered whether the Court of Appeal was right.[35] I said so in *Kerly*,[36] where I particularly wondered whether the then rule that the holder of a Part A mark could prevent honest comparative advertising would stand up in the ECJ. It seems to me that the European Court of Justice must have the ultimate say in whether or not a right (or a particular aspect of a right) can properly be regarded as within Article 36. Thus in *BAT ('Toltecs')*[37] it was held that the taking of infringement proceedings under a dormant registered mark (permitted by national law[38]) was a misuse of rights. I am far from saying that the ECJ has a swinging power to cut back national IP rights. It plainly has not, and has refused to do so in a number of cases.[39] Only the *Magill* case[40] stands out as one where a national IP right was held as going too far.

Penneys

Next I go back to a little more reminiscence. What follows is not a pretty story. The youngest son of Garfield Weston (the chairman of the giant ABF

[33] p. 633.

[34] [1986] AC 577.

[35] And Whitford J went even further in *Parker Knoll* v. *Knoll Overseas* [1985] FSR 349 at 366. He held that even if Community law in effect modified what amounted to an infringement, that would be no defence to a defendant in a motion for contempt for breach of an injunction restraining infringement. The proper remedy would be to seek modification of the injunction. That can hardly be right, although the sensible course might well be to apply for modification before embarking on what would be a breach by the rules of national law.

[36] 12th ed. (1986) p. 221.

[37] Case 35/83 [1985] ECR 363.

[38] And so 'commercial or industrial property' by national law.

[39] e.g., *'Quattro'*, Case 317/91 *Deutsche Renault* v. *Audi* (question of confusion a matter for national law provided there is no arbitrary discrimination). Personally I rather wish something could be done about what seems the over-protective view of the German courts in respect of trade marks. Surely it is taking a dim view of the intelligence of the average German to hold that *Terrapin* is confusingly similar to *Terranova* (permitted by the ECJ, [1976] ECR 1039), or that *Racoon* and *Dragon* are deceptively similar, even if one assumes that Germans do not speak English [1996] GRUR 414? Other cases showing the reluctance of the Court to interfere with a national right are *Thetford* v. *Fiamma*, Case 35/87 [1988] ECR 3585, [1990] Ch 339 (UK rule, that older than 50 year patents do not novelty-destroy a patent, permissible even though other Member States do not have such a rule) and *Volvo* v. *Veng*, Case 238/87 [1988] ECR 6211. In the latter case (where I appeared for the defendants, though I was unable to get to the hearing), I thought there was a real chance that the ECJ might say 'hold on—50 years plus life of author for spare parts based on a copyright with no inherent artistic merit') but it did not. It is not surprising, after that, that the CA reaffirmed the *Leyland* decision in *Biotrading & Financing* v. *Biohit* [1998] FSR 109.

[40] *Radio Teleis Eireann*, Case T–69/89 [1991] II ECR 485.

food and other business group) set up a clothing store business in Ireland (where he lived with his Irish wife). He called it Penneys, I think innocently. The company prospered and was in its way to becoming the Marks & Spencer of Ireland. Penneys branched out to England and Scotland. The giant US store group JC Penney got to hear of the Irish Penneys. It had no shops in Europe but did have some slight use of its name on imported goods. It felt obliged to protect its name. It was almost certainly too late to sue in Ireland but it sued in England[41] and Scotland. I was the junior in the English case. JC also sued in Hong Kong (successfully claiming that a reputation among suppliers was enough for a passing off action[42]) and commenced various rectification proceedings against an assortment of ABF registered marks in an assortment of countries. In addition JC applied for a number of ABF marks in countries where ABF did not have registrations and these were opposed. Much money was spent on litigation which ultimately covered fourteen countries. There was a Scottish trial which lasted six weeks. Before judgment was given there the parties entered a settlement agreement. It was a simple deal: the Irish Penneys were to give up all use of the word on goods and all use of the word outside Ireland. They could carry on with the shop name in Ireland. And some money passed. Irish Penneys agreed never to attack JC's European trade mark registrations and, for ever outside Ireland, not to use the word as a trade mark or for shops. There were some worries at the time that this agreement might fall within Article 85(1). So the agreement was made conditional upon approval by the Commission. JC's US lawyers (who had a Brussels Office) said they knew what they were doing and arranged a meeting. We all polled up in the Commission building in Brussels (the one they had to pull down). We met the relevant official—I will not name him but he has long been a prominent member of DG4. He said there was a problem—the Commission will not give an exemption or negative clearance to agreements conditional upon approval by the Commission.[43] He added that otherwise he could not see a problem. We all went out to discuss the position. The discussion was over a Brussels lunch and involved myself and my solicitor, ABF's company secretary, JC's in-house European lawyer, and a lawyer from the Brussels firm representing them. By now we were good friends with JC and it was a good lunch. The JC in-house lawyer for Europe, having heard the assurance to the effect that there was no problem other than the fact that it was conditional said he would agree to make the agreement unconditional and ABF did likewise. We took the agree-

[41] The interlocutory proceedings are reported at [1976] FSR 367, CA.

[42] [1979] FSR 26.

[43] I have never seen any justification for this. I can understand the Commission not dealing with a purely academic agreement, but one that takes effect if approved is more than this. Parties ought to be able to avoid any risk of a violation of Art. 85(1) if they so wish.

ment back to the Commission in the afternoon and went home, thinking the job was done.

Nothing was heard for a couple of months and then a letter came raising objections to the agreement. Both we and JC were shocked. The objection was that it was anti-competitive because our side were agreeing for ever not to use Penneys outside Ireland. That this agreement was the result of a serious settlement of litigation counted for nothing. Nor did commercial reality impinge: if we were giving up Penneys then obviously we would be using a new name and mark and once that was in use, we would have no conceivable commercial interest in going back or attacking the JC registrations. We all went back to Brussels, JC including in their team Oliver Axter, a sixth generation patent lawyer from Dusseldorf with whom it was a pleasure to work. We went to see the official concerned, Oliver Axter and I representing the two parties, once enemies but now friends and facing a common enemy. The official refused to budge. It did not bother him that the agreement had been made unconditional on the basis of his promise that he foresaw no problem. We were given an appointment with another official. The alternative was for the parties to take the Commission to the ECJ—something the lawyers could not face taking to their management who thought this mad litigation had been settled. So we took up the further appointment and hammered out a modification to the agreement in an all day meeting with the Comission. It was JC which had to 'give way', losing ABF's agreement not to use the mark for ever. I had the idea of a five-year keep-out period, basing this on the period of five years non-use as a ground for removal of a registered mark which was the prevalent period in Member States, based on the Paris Convention.[44] The Commission bought this and gave a negative clearance.[45]

I think the costs of this perfectly pragmatic settlement were wholly disproportionate. It reflected no credit on the Commission at all. I heard that the JC man in Europe lost his job as a result of relying on the Commission's assurance. If true that was terribly unfair. It may well be that there ought to be an ombudsman to deal with maladminstration within the Commission. There is an interesting postscript: the new name used by the Irish Penneys was (and is) Primark. It has been successful and the view within the company later was that the new name helped contribute to the success by quite a way. For myself, I learned not to put my faith in Princes and to realize that the Commission had a lot to learn by way of fairness and by way of appreciating the true commercial significance of things like no-challenge clauses. I also learned that one had to be very careful in settling a case. I am glad to hear that in general the view is that things are

[44] Art. 5C(1). [45] [1978] FSR 385.

rather better now—certainly the rigid view of no-challenge clauses has gone. One other postscript is that JC, having got the rival Penneys out of the way, never did open up stores in the United Kingdom (nor, I believe, other European countries). And, of course, Irish Penneys never did attack any of the Penney registrations.

Free Movement

The last subject I wish to touch upon is free movement. By and large it was not the English courts which were involved in the cases leading up to the rule in *Merck* v. *Stephar*:[46] 'The proprietor of an industrial or commercial property right protected by the law of a Member State cannot rely on that law to prevent the importation of a product which has lawfully been marketed in another State by the proprietor or with his consent.'

As it happens I was counsel in *Merck*.[47] I thought (and still think) there was an injustice. The patentee had no Italian patent and sold there in competition with others, naturally at a reduced price compared with the price in countries where he had a patent. His goods, bought in Italy, were taken to Holland (where he had a patent) and sold there. The court, abandoning any fair notion of exhaustion of rights,[48] permitted this. I have always thought this was an unnecessary development of EC law. The rule went no further in the 1980s—for instance on an English court reference it was held that it did not apply to goods sold under a compulsory licence.[49] As a judge, I asked the Court to reconsider *Merck* in *Merck* v. *Primecrown*.[50] The Advocate-General recommended its reversal, but I was not altogether surprised to find that the Court thought it too late to do so.[51] I doubt whether, if the point had been new, the Court would have so held. It has developed a less hostile and more rational attitude to IP laws in the 1980s.[52]

By way of conclusion it is apparent that IP Euro-law in the English courts has been an active and fertile field. I believe we have contributed well to the general development of Community Law. I hope we can continue to do so in the future.

46 [1981] ECR 2063.

47 For the UK government, intervening.

48 There was no Italian right to be exhausted.

49 *Pharmon* v. *Hoechst*, Case 19/84 [1985] ECR 2281.

50 [1995] FSR 909.

51 Cases C–267–8/95, [1997] 1 CMLR 83.

52 Cf. the attitude in *Ideal Standard, IHT International Heiztechnik* v. *Ideal Standard* [1995] FSR 59, a case which surely would have gone the other way in the 1960s, 1970s and early 1980s, quite apart from the 'common origin' doctrine. I confess I was surprised by the result in any event. An assignment of a trade-mark for only some of the countries of the EC is bound to be market divisive and I would not have seen a lot of harm in saying it did not really work.

16

Judicial Attitudes to the UK Trade Marks Act 1994: Implementing the Approximation Directive

BY DAVID LLEWELYN, PARTNER, LLEWELYN ZIETMAN, SOLICITORS, LONDON; SENIOR VISITING FELLOW IN INTELLECTUAL PROPERTY LAW, CENTRE FOR COMMERCIAL LAW STUDIES, QUEEN MARY & WESTFIELD COLLEGE, LONDON

Introduction

It is now two and a half years since the commencement date of the 1994 Trade Marks Act ('the Act') which implemented the Approximation Directive[1] in the United Kingdom, a law which, in the words of Mr Justice Jacob 'greatly increases the importance of registered trade marks'.[2] Many of the assumptions of over a century of registered trade mark law in the United Kingdom were altered: a registered mark should be available unless excluded and the scope of protection for a mark once registered is broader than previously.

However, judicial attitudes to date suggest that some of the more enthusiastic wishes of trademark proprietors (and their advisers) are not going to be fulfilled. One of the government's aims[3] in introducing legislation on trade marks, to make it easier for businesses to register their trade marks, is not proving as straightforward as some had anticipated: even in considering an application made under the 1938 Act, Mr Justice Laddie commented in relation to a specification of goods covering computer software that such wide specifications 'may not be possible under the 1994 Act'.[4] Where infringement is concerned, the English judges have shown themselves unwilling to broaden the scope of infringement as far as some had hoped for.

[1] First Council Directive to approximate the laws of the Member States relating to trademarks, 89/104 EEC, OJ No. C351, 31.12.85 ('the Directive' or 'the Approximation Directive').

[2] Preface to Kitchin and Mellor *The Trade Marks Act 1994: Text and Commentary*, (1995).

[3] See *Reform of Trade Marks Law*, Department of Trade and Industry, Cm. 1203 (1990) at para. 10.

[4] *Mercury Communications Ltd* v. *Mercury Interactive (UK) Ltd* [1995] FSR 850.

The New Definition of a Trade Mark

The 1994 Act in section 1(1) has broadened the definition of a trade mark to include 'any sign capable of being represented graphically which is capable of distinguishing goods or services of one undertaking from those of other undertakings', adopting Article 2 of the Directive. This new definition non-exhaustively includes 'words (including personal names), designs, letters, numerals or the shape of goods or their packaging,'[5] but section 3 sets out the absolute grounds for refusal, which include in section 3(l)(a) signs which do not satisfy section 1(1) and in section 3(l)(b) the ground that the trade mark is 'devoid of any distinctive character'. In the AD2000 decision[6] the tribunal noted that underlying both the registrability and the infringement provisions is the basic principle that the protection afforded to registered trade marks 'is in particular to guarantee the trade mark as an indication of origin' (as stated in the tenth recital to the Directive). In this context, Mr Hobbs QC (sitting as the Appointed Person under section 76 of the Act) cited *Wagamama*,[7] *IHT* v. *Ideal Standard*,[8] *BMS* v. *Paranova*,[9] *Eurim-Pharm* v. *Beiersdorf*,[10] and *MPA Pharma* v. *Rhone-Poulenc*[11] to support his conclusion that 'there is nothing for such protection to attach to or bite upon when a sign serves only to designate characteristics other than origin'.

While the new definition of trade mark extends the scope for trade mark registrations, yet more important changes in the law have occurred concerning the new boundaries for infringement, similarity and confusion, and comparative advertising. In all these areas, the English courts have already had to interpret the new provisions.

Infringement—Section 10(1)

Section 10(1) provides for the most obvious case of infringement of a registered mark: identical mark on identical goods or services. This is classical trade mark infringement as it has been known in the United Kingdom since 1883. It should however be noted that now any use of the mark is caught, whether by graphical representation or otherwise, including by oral use.[12]

In *British Sugar*[13] Jacob J considered whether the defendant's 'toffee flavoured spread' fell within the plaintiff's specification of goods, 'dessert

[5] S. 1(1) the Act.

[6] *Allied Domecq's Application for AD2000*, unreported decision of Geoffrey Hobbs QC 3 Sept. 1996.

[7] [1995] FSR 713.

[8] [1994] ECR I–2789.

[9] Joined Cases C–427/93, C–429/93 and C–436/93, [1996] ECR I–3457.

[10] Joined Cases C–71/94, C–72/94 and C–73/94, [1996] ECR I–3603.

[11] Case C–232/94 ECR I–3671.

[12] S. 103(2).

[13] [1996] RPC 281.

sauces and syrups'. Despite the fact that the label on the back of the jar for the toffee spread stated that it was 'delicious at breakfast, with desserts or as a snack anytime', his Lordship found that it was not a dessert sauce, relying especially on evidence that all possible uses of the product other than as a spread amounted to less than 5 per cent of volume: 'When it comes to construing a word used in a trade mark specification, one is concerned with how the product is, as a practical matter, regarded for the purposes of trade.'[14]

Had his Lordship found that the defendant's use fell within the classification of goods in respect of which the plaintiff's mark was registered, he considered that the use of the sign 'Treat' as part of the defendant's mark 'Robertson's Toffee Treat' would have been the use of an identical mark to that registered (Treat) by the plaintiff. In other words, the absolute statutory protection accorded to registered trade marks remains unaffected by the many changes to UK law necessitated by the Approximation Directive and: 'Once a mark is shown to offend the user of it cannot escape by showing that by something outside the actual mark itself he distinguishes his goods from those of the registered proprietor.'[15]

Jacob J referred to his earlier decision in the *Origins* case,[16] in which he had stated that section 10(1), 'requires the Court to assume the mark of the plaintiff is used in a normal and fair manner in relation to goods for which it is registered and then to assess a likelihood of confusion in relation to the way the defendant uses its mark, discounting added matter or circumstances.'

On the use of 'Treat', his Lordship commented:

> one still has to identify the defendant's sign for the purposes of the comparison. In most cases there could be no difficulty. It is either there or not. However, it is possible for the sign to be hidden or swamped. No-one but a crossword fanatic, for example, would say that 'treat' is present in 'theatre atmosphere'. There is no question of this sort here, however. 'Treat' is there on the [defendant's] products for all to see.

In *Bravado Merchandising*[17] Lord McCluskey did not regard the actual typeface in which a particular word mark was registered to be an integral part of the mark unless there was a clear indication to such effect.[18] Although he expressed himself puzzled by the fact that one of the two marks in issue consisted of the words 'Wet Wet Wet' underlined in a distinctive way, he did not consider that this limited the registration to that particular formulation.[19]

[14] *Ibid.* Jacob J also referred to the fact that it was the Registrar's view that the defendant's product fell within Class 29 rather than Class 30 in which the plaintiffs mark was registered.

[15] Per Sir Wilfred Greene MR in *Saville Perfumery* v. *Woolworth* (1939) 43 RPC 147 at 161.

[16] [1995] FSR 280 at 284. [17] *Op. cit.* [18] At 215.

[19] The judge relied upon the case *of Morny Limited's Trade Marks* (1951) 68 RPC 131, decided under the 1938 Trade Marks Act.

Infringement—Section 10(2)

Section 10(2) goes much further and provides (following exactly the wording of Article 5(1)(b) of the Directive) that it is infringement of a registered trade mark for a third party to use a mark:

(i) identical with the trade mark . . . in relation to goods or services similar to those for which a trade mark is registered or

(ii) similar to the trade mark . . . in relation to goods or services identical with or similar to those for which the trade mark is registered

provided there exists a likelihood of confusion . . . which includes the likelihood of association with the trade mark.

In the *British Sugar* case,[20] Jacob J rejected the plaintiff's argument that if there is confusion then there must be similarity of goods because the product may be used for identical purposes:

> The sub-section does not merely ask 'will there be confusion?': it asks 'is there similarity of goods?', if so, 'is there any likelihood of confusion?'. The point is important. For if one elides the two questions then a 'strong' mark would get protection for a greater range of goods than a 'weak' mark. For instance, 'Kodak' for socks or bicycles might well cause confusion, yet these goods are plainly dissimilar from films or cameras. I think the question of similarity of goods is wholly independent of the particular mark the subject of registration or the defendant's sign.

This paragraph of the judgment is critical: it indicates clearly that the judge considered section 10(2) to be limited to objective similarity between the goods, regardless of the strength of the particular mark used by the plaintiff. Rather, the owner of a 'strong' mark will be able to avail himself of the extended protection under section 10(3) which may not be available to the owner of a 'weak' or 'unused' mark.

Thus, there now appears to be a hierarchy for protection of registered marks: the mark which has been merely registered but has not been used (and therefore has not developed any form of reputation) will only be protected against use on a relatively narrow range of goods, the goods or services covered by the specification and a 'penumbra' around it. On the other hand, a registered mark which has been used on a significant scale will be protected against use on *dissimilar* goods or services. It is suggested that this is a sensible and coherent way of approaching the scope of protection under the new Act, although it has its critics who consider that section 10(2) was intended to provide a wide scope of protection and that the definition of 'similar goods' should be a broad one.

His Lordship found that his conclusion on similarity of goods was supported by the recitals to the Directive, under which the issue of similarity

[20] *Op. cit.*

is separated in the recitals from the question of confusion. He considered that the recital which states: 'Whereas it is indispensable to give an interpretation of the concept of similarity in relation to the likelihood of confusion' does no more than state that in assessing similarity, 'one should bear in mind the fact that the purpose to be considered is trade mark purposes. It is not saying that goods are similar if there is confusion, no matter how dissimilar the goods may be. That is a matter for Article 5(2) (which is the basis of our section 10(3)).'[21]

His Lordship then proceeded to consider the question of similarity. First of all, he noted that the wider the scope of similarity, the wider the protection given to the mark would be:

'This suggests caution. Otherwise, however narrow a specification, the actual protection will be wide. In particular, this would be so in the important sort of case where a mark owner only got registration on the basis of actual distinctiveness for a narrow class of goods. It would surely be wrong that he should then in practice get protection for a wide range of goods. If a man wants wide protection he can always ask for it and will get it only if his claim is justified . . . I do not think the introduction of infringement for similar goods has vastly widened the scope of potential protection.'

It is interesting in this context to consider the case of *Mars* v. *Cadbury*,[22] where 'Treets' was registered by the plaintiff for chocolate flavoured confectionery, because it was only in relation to such a limited class of goods that the plaintiff had been able to persuade the Registrar that it had sufficient use to justify protection for such a quasi-descriptive mark. Such a case highlights the dangers of which Jacob J warns: if the actual protection given to the 'Treets' mark registered for chocolate-flavoured confectionery was wide, there would be little point in ever seeking a broad specification. One could avoid the problems of non-use by only having a registration in a narrow field and relying on 'similarity' to acquire protection over a wide range of goods.

While accepting that there was no intention in the new Act to adopt the concept of 'goods of the same description' used in the 1938 Act, Jacob J considered that 'the purpose of the conception in the old Act was to prevent marks from conflicting not only for their respective actual goods but for a penumbra and the purpose of *similar goods* in the Directive and Act is to provide protection and separation for a similar sort of penumbra.'

In making such an assessment, the judge suggested that the following factors would be relevant:

[21] The judge noted obiter that the circumstances of the Dutch case *Claeryn/Klarein*, 1.3.1975 NJ 1975, 472 may fall within s. 10(3) but would not fall within s. 10(2) because there would be no likelihood of confusion as to trade origin (and in this context cited the *Wagamama* case, *supra)*.

[22] *Op. cit.*

(a) the respective uses of the respective goods or services;
(b) the respective users of the respective goods or services;
(c) the physical nature of the goods or acts of service;
(d) the respective trade channels through which the goods or services reached the market;
(e) in the case of self-serve consumer items, where in practice they are respectively found or likely to be found in supermarkets and in particular where they are, or are likely to be, found on the same or similar shelves; and,
(f) the extent to which the respective goods or services are competitive and in this context it is useful to consider how market research companies classify the particular goods or services.[23]

However, his Lordship accepted that such a list could not be exhaustive and was for general guidance only and concluded: 'The fact is that the Directive and hence our Act has introduced an area of uncertainty into the scope of registration which in many cases can only be resolved by litigation.'

On the particular facts of the case before him, the judge considered that the two products had the same use to some extent but in the main had different uses; they were not generally in direct competition and they could be found in different places in supermarkets; their physical nature was different in that the plaintiff's product was poured while the defendant's needed to be spooned out of the jar; and market research regarded the two products as falling within different sectors. On the basis of these factors taken together, it was found that the defendant's spread was not *similar* to the plaintiff's dessert sauces and syrups.[24]

In the *Baywatch* decision,[25] it was held (adopting the two-part question set out in *British Sugar*)[26] to be unarguable that the defendant's use on encrypted TV broadcasts was use in relation to similar goods or services to the plaintiff's video tapes and discs. In *The European Limited* v. *The Economist Newspapers Limited*[27] Rattee J concluded in relation to section 10(2) that there was no similarity between the plaintiff's device mark 'THE

[23] With the exception of (e) and (f), these factors are those identified by Romer J in *Jellinek* 63 RPC 59 at 70 to be used in ascertaining what were 'goods of the same description' under the Trade Marks Act 1938.

[24] It is interesting to compare this analysis with the leading US authority of *Aunt Jemima Mills & Co* v. *Rigney & Co* 247 F 407 (1917), in which the US Second Circuit Court considered in relation to pancake batter and pancake syrup: 'that goods, though different may be so related as to fall within the mischief which equity should prevent. Syrup and flour are both food products, and food products are commonly used together. Obviously the public, or a large part of it, seeing this trademark on a syrup, would conclude that it was made by the complainant. In this way, the complainant's reputation is put in the bands of the defendant.'

[25] [1997] FSR 22.

[26] *Op. cit.*

[27] [1996] FSR 431. This decision is currently being appealed.

EUROPEAN' and the defendant's 'EUROPEAN VOICE' title on the basis that:

it is true that the word 'European' used as a noun is the most prominent part of the device registered as the plaintiff's trade mark. It does not, in my opinion, follow that the otherwise wholly different title of another newspaper is similar to the plaintiff's trade mark, whether visually or audibly, merely because it uses the common word 'European' in an adjectival sense to describe its contents, whether as the first or any other word in the title.[28]

Likelihood of Association

The notion of 'likelihood of confusion' contained expressly in section 10(2) (and Article 5(l)(b) of the Directive) is one which is familiar to trade mark practitioners in the United Kingdom, especially in passing off actions. But what do the words 'includes the likelihood of association' mean? Are they merely a sub-set of 'a likelihood of confusion' or do they go further?

There is no definitive answer. The EC Directive does not assist, as UK law has merely adopted the wording of Article 5(1)(b). However, Gielen[29] has pointed out that an EC Council Minute records that the concept of 'association' has been developed in particular under Benelux law which has had it since 1970. Benelux case law does not require confusion in order for a finding of 'association' and Gielen contends that the Minute, 'can certainly be used to say that the words "likelihood of association" originate from Benelux trade mark law and that there is more sense in studying how this notion is applied under Benelux law than there is, for example, under German law, where this concept also exists but with a different meaning'.[30]

On the other hand, the actual wording of section 10(2) (and the English-language version of Article 5(1)(b)) clearly requires a 'likelihood of confusion' in all cases[31] and 'likelihood of association' is included expressly as one of a number of circumstances which are likely to lead to confusion.

On this issue of 'likelihood of association', Laddie J in his landmark judgment in *Wagamama* v. *City Centre Restaurants*[32] concluded that:

It appears to me that any popular belief fuelled by articles in legal publications, that Article 5 of the 1988 Directive was intended to ensure that the domestic law of

[28] *Ibid.* [29] *European Trade Mark Legislation: the Statements.* [1996] EIPR 83.

[30] *Ibid.*, at 87. In his decision in *AD2000, op. cit.*, Geoffrey Hobbs QC commented. 'I am mindful that the burden of authority is against the use of such Minutes as an aid to the construction of Council directives' and referred to the observations of Laddie J in *Wagamama, supra* (even though by the time of the decision in *AD2000* the Minutes had been published in the Official Journal of the Office for the Harmonisation of the Internal Market).

[31] In the *Baywatch* case, *supra,* the judge noted that it 'is not sufficient if one mark merely leads to a likelihood of recall of the other mark' (at 28).

[32] [1995] FSR 713.

trade mark infringement in all Member States changed to that already adopted by the Benelux countries is open to question . . . It would be wrong to approach construction of the 1988 Directive and the 1994 Act on unverifiable rumours or Professor Gielen's certainty as to what was intended.[33]

In his view:

There are two possible constructions which may be placed on Article 5 of the 1988 Directive and section 10(2) of the 1994 Act. The rights of the proprietor against alleged infringers may be limited to classic infringement which includes association as to origin or, following the Benelux route, it could cover not only classic infringement but also non-origin association. In my view, the former construction is to be preferred. If the broader scope were to be adopted, the Directive and our Act would be creating a new type of monopoly not related to the proprietor's trade but in the trade mark itself. Such a monopoly could be likened to a quasi-copyright in the mark. However, unlike copyright, there would be no fixed duration for the right and it would be a true monopoly effective against copyist and non-copyist alike. I can see nothing in the terms of the Directive (or our Act), or in any secondary material which I could legitimately take into account, which would lead me to assume this was the objective. On the contrary, the preamble to the Directive seems to point in the opposite direction since it states: 'Whereas the protection afforded by the registered trade mark, the function of which is in particular to guarantee the trade mark as an indication of origin.'

Furthermore, there appears to be little commercial justification for any such extension of trade mark rights. If it had been the intention to make the Directive identical with Benelux law on this important issue it could have said so. Indeed, in view of the fact that to have done so would have been significantly to expand trade mark rights and thereby significantly restrict the freedom of competitors to compete, I would have expected any such expansion to have been stated in clear and unambiguous words so that traders throughout the European Union would be able to appreciate that their legislators had created a new broad monopoly. As it is, no such clear and unambiguous words have been used and the language of the Directive and the 1994 Act is consistent with the rights being restricted to classical infringement.[34]

The *Wagamama* decision has inspired fierce debate. Kamperman Sanders[35] expresses the view that the decision 'reduces the scope of the 1994 Act to the rigid confinements of the confusion rationale'.

He goes on to say that Laddie J's reasoning was flawed and says of his comments on the creation of a quasi-copyright (see above) that:

The further argument for dismissal of a non-origin based rationale on the basis that a broader scope of protection would create a new type of monopoly that can be likened to a quasi-copyright in the mark, but without a fixed duration, confuses the economic lifespan of a mark with that of an author or his or her heirs. It also

[33] [1995] FSR 713 at 728.

[34] *Ibid.*, at 731.

[35] *'The Wagamama Decision: Back to the Dark Ages of Trade Mark Law'* [1996] EIPR 3.

disregards the fact that, unlike many copyright works, trade marks require sustained investment and management in order to add value to the mark and to fend off both product and brand competition. Registration is only the first step in this process, for if the mark is not distinctive or strong enough, the 'association' criterion and certainly not (sic) the 'unfair advantage' criterion of section 10(3) will not be of help to the plaintiff in obtaining relief. It may be true that the 'association' criterion is a departure from the origin-based rationale, but this does not mean that it is a catch-all criterion. Benelux practice shows that action taken on the ground of the 'association' criterion does not automatically lead to a secure win. Other factors such as the reputation of the mark in question and the proximity of the products involved are measured in the same way as they are in 'classic' confusion cases. The consideration that unchecked monopolies are created does not therefore impress.

Kamperman Sanders concludes that the flawed reasoning stems from not examining the structure of the infringement provisions carefully. He states that:

From section 10(3) it is clear that the non-origin rationale forms the basis for protection . . . it is almost impossible to find a clearer legislative statement of intent on the expansion of the confusion rationale to the non-origin dilution rationale. Now that it is clear that expansion of the confusion rationale to the non-confusion rationale is applicable to the case of use of a sign on dissimilar goods, it is logically imperative that this is also true for similar goods, where the proximity of the products enhances the detrimental effect to the unique associative strength of the mark.

In reply to the article, Peter Prescott QC[36] first points out that section 10(3) is not mandated by EC law; the Directive states that Member States 'may' pass law to that effect. He goes on to say:

The reason 10(3) is confined to cases where the goods are dissimilar is that, if the marks are close enough to cause unfair advantage/detriment even where the goods are dissimilar, then the marks will be close enough to cause more than that; they will cause confusion, if the goods are similar . . . Thus, 10(3) was not extended to similar goods because it was not thought to be necessary to do so.

Prescott sums up his argument with: 'I should have thought that where a statute says that confusion *includes* a likelihood of association, then the latter must be a subset of the former. It must be that sort of association which involves confusion.'

It is difficult to see how a judge trained in the common law tradition could have come to any conclusion other than that reached by Laddie J in *Wagamama:* the wording of section 10(2) (and of Article 5(l)(b) of the Directive) is clear in its language as it expresses 'likelihood of association' as a particular circumstance within the concept of 'likelihood of confusion'. On the actual wording, to suggest otherwise would be to adopt the

[36] *'Think Before You Waga Finger'* [1996] EIPR 317.

tortuous reasoning that 'confusion' should be defined to include 'association'; in other words, one would need to define black as including white, a conclusion which is difficult to accept without, as Laddie J points out, an unambiguous statement to that effect and the Directive contains one neither in its terms nor its recitals.

Use on Dissimilar Goods or Services—Section 10(3)

Section 10(3) gives a remedy to the owner of a registered trade mark if there is use of an identical or similar mark in relation to goods to services which are *not similar* to those for which the trade mark has been registered. However, there is only infringement if the registered mark 'has a reputation in the United Kingdom' and the use takes unfair advantage of or is detrimental to the distinctive character or repute of the registered mark.

Reputation in the United Kingdom

The notion of 'reputation' is one with which the English courts have had difficulty: the law of passing off protects goodwill, it does not protect reputation. As Walton J in the *Athlete's Foot* case[37] so clearly analysed, a 'reputation' is something which English law has not protected: since the seminal decision of the House of Lords in *Spalding* v. *Gamage*[38] it has been firmly established that it is custom and sales ('the attractive force which brings in custom' per Lord MacNaughton in *IRC* v. *Muller's Margarine*[39]) which are protected in England: it is not something as ephemeral as a 'reputation' if there has been no business activity within the jurisdiction.

Similarly, UK law on the registration of trade marks has not required use of a mark before registration can be obtained: an intention to use has always sufficed.

What then is a 'reputation in the United Kingdom'? Of course, there must be some sort of use of the mark; section 46(1)(a) provides for revocation of a registration if there has not been 'genuine use in the United Kingdom' for a period of five years 'following the date of completion of the registration procedure' (presumably this means the date of application if the mark is registered, see section 40(3), although it is by no means clear).

But how much use is required in order to benefit from section 10(3)? It would surely not merely be use sufficient to prevent a successful revocation action under section 46: it must be something more, but how much more? Presumably, the more use, the more likely it is a court will find third party use to be detrimental to the distinctive character or repute of the registered mark. Up until now all marks have had to be distinctive, so 'distinctive character or repute' must mean something more than merely

[37] *Athlete's Foot Marketing Associates Inc* v. *Cobra Sports* [1980] RPC 343.
[38] (1915) 32 RPC 273.
[39] [1901] AC 217.

being capable of being registered as trade mark. Yet it cannot be so distinctive as to be 'well known' within the meaning of Article 6 *bis* of the Paris Convention because section 56 deals with such well-known or famous marks and, although the owner of a 'well known' mark falling within Article 6 *bis* could avail himself of section 10(3) if it is registered in the United Kingdom, the international character of the mark to be protected by Article 6 *bis* makes it unlikely that 'reputation in the UK' can be equated with 'well known' for the purposes of Article 6 *bis* and section 56.

It is in this area that continental notions of 'notoriety' may be imported into UK law. The percentages of awareness by the relevant public required for a mark to be found to be one of notoriety, as evidenced by either party-conducted or court-conducted market surveys, may become critical.[40]

But both academic literature and common sense suggest that surveying the public is an inexact science. It remains extremely doubtful whether English judges at least will arrogate to market survey organizations, no matter how independent, their right to conclude that a mark is 'distinctive' or not.[41] Rattee J in *The European*[42] observed that:

> The persons interviewed, most of whom had never seen a copy of *European Voice*, were asked, simply by looking at the top half of the front page of one issue, to speculate as to who published it—a question which they may well never have asked themselves or been concerned to know the answer to. This characteristic of the evidence is symptomatic of the artificiality of a survey of this type, in which members of the public are asked to speculate on the provenance of goods in a context quite outside the normal operation of the relevant market.

Detriment or Unfair Advantage

In one of the two judgments to date dealing with section 10(3), *BASF plc* v. *CEP (UK) plc*[43] the judge held that there was no arguable case of a relevant detriment in circumstances where the evidence did not disclose confusion. In the case, the second plaintiff was the registered proprietor of the mark OPUS for inter alia herbicides and fungicides and the defendants had announced an intention to distribute a new publication under the title 'Farming Opus', to be distributed free of charge to 25,000 of the largest arable and dairy farmers in the country.

[40] See Pagenberg, 'Beruhmte und bekannte Marken in Europa—Die Bestimmung der Verkehrsbekanntheit vor den nationalen und europaïschen Instanzen' in *Aktuelle Herausforderungen des geistigen Eigentums, Festgabe von Freunden und Mitarbeitern fur Friedrich-Karl Beier zum 70. Geburtstag*, ed., Joseph Straus, published by Carl Heymanns Verlag KG.

[41] See, for example, *Imperial Group* v. *Philip Morris Limited* [1984] RPC 293, in which Whitford J stated: 'Great importance inevitably attaches to the way in which the questions are cast. It is very difficult in connection with an exercise such as this to think of questions which, even if they are free from the objection of being leading, are not in fact going to direct the person answering the question into a field of speculation upon which that person would never have embarked had the question not been put.' (at 303).

[42] *Op. cit.*

[43] Ch D, unreported judgment of Knox J, 26 Oct. 1995.

In the judge's view:

The evidence shows that those who pay any significant degree of attention to what is written in the promotional literature or the finished product cannot fail to see what the defendant's goods in fact are: that is to say, a director of agricultural goods and services covering a very wide field both in terms of goods and services and in terms of their providers (the advertisers) even a cursory inspection shows that both arable, dairy and general farming is covered and the numerous suppliers, many in direct competition with each other, are included. Once the reader appreciates those not very subtle facts, he or she will not, in my view, be likely to be confused into thinking that the name 'Opus' indicates that this is a publication by the plaintiff . . .

At the other end of the scale there is a person who just looks at the outside and does not bother to go any further. I do not regard such a person as of any relevance because the impression made upon his or her mind by the process envisaged is necessarily so slight that it would not produce any significant confusion and also because I am unpersuaded that it would be right for the court to have regard to the reactions of such an inattentive reader.

In the absence of evidence of relevant confusion, the judge considered that there was no basis for finding that unfair advantage had been or threatened to be taken, contrary to section 10(3). In rejecting the arguments by counsel for the plaintiffs, the judge stated forcefully:

Unless it was possible to claim that any use of the plaintiff's mark in relation to any class of goods at all, when sold to persons who also deal with the plaintiff in the goods or class in relation to which there is statutory protection for the plaintiff's mark, was of itself necessarily detrimental to the distinctive character or repute of the plaintiff's mark, I am unable to see how in the case before the court there can be any such detrimental effect within the meaning of section 10(3). If the protection given by section 10(3) went that far, much of the effect of having classes of goods in relation to the registration of trade marks would disappear . . . Neither the distinctive character nor the repute of the plaintiff's mark is adversely affected when there is no risk of relevant confusion.

Michael Crystal QC, sitting as a Deputy Judge of the Chancery Division, expressed support for this view in the interlocutory hearing in *Baywatch Production Co. Inc.* v. *The Home Video Channel*.[44] In this case, the court was called upon to consider whether, contrary to section 10(3), the word, 'BABEWATCH' (an adult cable television programme) took unfair advantage of the reputation of the television series, BAYWATCH. The plaintiffs offered no evidence of confusion and the judge was unwilling to find that confusion was unnecessary in the application of this sub-section:

The use of the concept of similarity in section 10(3)(a) introduces in my judgment the ingredient of a likelihood of confusion on the part of the public into section

[44] [1997] FSR 22.

10(3) . . . It would, it seems to me, be illogical for section 10(3) to give a greater protection in relation to non-similar goods or services by dispensing with the ingredient of a likelihood of confusion than the protection afforded to similar goods under section 10(2).[45]

Thus, the judge concluded that section 10(3) only applies where there is use in relation to dissimilar goods or services of a sign which is similar to the trade mark (which must have a reputation in the United Kingdom) so that there is a likelihood of confusion on the part of the public. On the basis that he had found that the plaintiff had no arguable case under section 10(2) due to the lack of evidence of confusion, the judge was not prepared to find similarities between the two marks for the purpose of section 10(3).

These decisions, albeit at the interlocutory stage, highlight the unwillingness of certain English judges to accept the argument that the new Act has expanded the scope of protection for a registered mark beyond those circumstances where confusion has resulted or is likely to. On the other hand, in *British Sugar*[46] Jacob J appeared to accept that it would be possible for trade mark infringement to arise in circumstances where there was no relevant confusion when he cited the *Claeryn/Klarein* judgment in the Benelux.[47] However, it seems likely that it is only the unusual case, where there is a clear danger of a negative association between the plaintiff's mark and the defendant's (such as the unpleasant association of detergent with gin, as in *Claeryn*), in which the problem of a lack of confusion will be able to be surmounted.

Genuine Goods or Services: Comparative Advertising

Section 10(6) excludes from the infringement provisions any use of a registered trade mark by a third party 'for the purpose of identifying goods or services as those of the proprietor or a licensee'. But the sub-section does not excuse use in relation to genuine goods or services 'otherwise than in accordance with honest practices in industrial or commercial matters' if such use takes unfair advantage or is detrimental to the distinctive character or repute of the trade marks.[48] Thus, if there is 'unfair' comparative advertising (for example, by comparing 'apples and oranges' as in the *Compaq* v. *Dell* case,[49] or through the use of false statements) that would not be in accordance with honest practices and therefore constitute

[45] *Ibid*., at 30.

[46] *Op. cit.*

[47] Black, in *Baywatch: Sour Grapes or Justice* [1997] EIPR 39, notes that these obiter dicta were ignored by Mr Crystal QC in *Baywatch*.

[48] This formulation combines words from the Paris Convention ('honest practices in industrial and commercial matters') with some from Article 5(5) of the Directive which form part of s. 10(3) ('without due cause takes unfair advantage of, or is detrimental to the distinctive character, of the repute of the trade mark').

[49] [1992] FSR 93.

an infringement. If that is the case, courts may find litigants seeking to drag them into an arena they have been unwilling to enter: the arena of deciding between competing claims for products.

As stated clearly by Laddie J in *Barclays Bank* v. *RBS Advanta*,[50] a major objective of section 10(6) is to allow comparative advertising: 'As long as the use of the competitor's mark is "honest" then there is nothing wrong with telling the public of the relative merits of competing goods and services and using registered trade marks to identify them.' The proviso, that such use must be in accordance with honest practices, should not be construed in such a way as to effectively prohibit all comparative advertising:

> If the use is considered honest by members of a reasonable audience, it will not infringe. The fact that the advertising pokes fun at the proprietors' goods or services and emphasises the benefits of the defendant's is a normal incidence of comparative advertising. Its aim will be to divert customers from the proprietor. No reasonable observer would expect one trader to point to all the advantages of its competitor's business and failure to do so does not per se take the advertising outside what reasonable people would regard as 'honest'. Thus, mere trade puffery, even if uncomfortable to the registered proprietor, does not bring the advertising within the scope of trade mark infringement. Much advertising copy is recognised by the public as hyperbole. The Act does not impose on the courts an obligation to try and enforce, through the back door of trade mark legislation, a puritanical standard. If on the other hand, any reasonable reader is likely to say, on being given the full facts, that the advertisement is not honest, for example because it is significantly misleading, then the protection for trade mark infringement is removed.

As noted by Laddie J, section 10(6) is 'home-grown and is not based either on the Directive or on the Paris Convention, neither of which specifically permits comparative advertising'.

In *Vodafone Group plc and Others* v. *Orange Personal Communications Services Ltd*,[51] Jacob J found that a claim by Orange that their users would save on average twenty pounds every month compared with similar Vodafone tariffs did not constitute trade mark infringement falling outside section 10(6). The standard set for finding whether an advertisement was within honest practices was expressed: 'If a comparison is significantly misleading on an objective basis to a substantial proportion of the reasonable audience, it is not an "honest practice" within the section.' The judge agreed with Laddie J's conclusion in *Barclays Bank* v. *RBS Advanta*[52] that the qualifying words at the end of section 10(6)[53] 'in most cases add nothing of significance to the first part of the proviso'.

In the *British Sugar*[54] case, Jacob J commented on section 11(2) (which

[50] [1996] RPC 307. [51] [1997] FSR 34. [52] *Op. cit.*

[53] 'if the use without due cause takes unfair advantage of, or is detrimental to, the distinctive character or repute of the trade mark.'

[54] *Op. cit.*

implements Article 6(1) of the Directive) as it applies to comparative advertising:

I see no reason why the provision does not permit a fair comparison between the trade mark owner's goods and those of the defendant. The comparison had to be honest, but provided it was and was part of the genuine indication of, for instance, quality or price, I think it would be within the provision. Such honest comparative use might well upset the mark's proprietor (proprietors particularly do not like price comparisons, even if they are true) but would in no way affect his mark as an indication of trade origin. Indeed the defendant would be using the proprietor's mark precisely for its proper purpose, namely to refer to his goods. I can see nothing in the stated purpose of the Directive indicating that a trade mark monopoly should extend to the point of enabling a proprietor to suppress competition by use of his trade mark in this way.

In the recent decision of *British Telecommunications Plc* v. *A T & T Communications (UK) Ltd*[55] Mr Crystal QC, sitting as a Deputy Judge, set out the propositions for which *Barclays*[56] and *Vodafone*[57] are authority:

(a) the primary objective of section 10(6) is to permit comparative advertising;
(b) as long as the use of a competitor's mark is honest, there is nothing wrong in informing the public of the relative merits of competing goods or services and using registered trade marks to identify them;
(c) the onus is on the registered proprietor to show that the use takes unfair advantage of or is detrimental to the distinctive character or repute of the trade mark;
(d) there will be no infringement unless the use is not in accordance with honest practices;
(e) the test is objective: would a reasonable reader, upon being given the full facts, be likely to say that the advertisement is not honest?
(f) statutory or industry-agreed codes of practice are not a helpful guide as to whether a advertisement is honest for these purposes. This has to be gauged against what is reasonably to be expected by the relevant public of advertisements for the goods or services in question;
(g) the general public are used to the ways of advertisers and expect hyperbole;
(h) the 1994 Act does not require the courts to enforce a more puritanical standard than the general public would expect from advertising copy; and,
(i) an advertisement which is significantly misleading is not honest for the purposes of the sub-section.

[55] Ch D, unreported judgment of Mr Michael Crystal QC (Deputy High Court Judge), 18 Dec. 1996.
[56] *Op. cit.*
[57] *Op. cit.*

The judge added the further four propositions:

(j) the advertisement must be considered as a whole;
(k) at the interlocutory stage, the court should not hold words used in an advertisement to be seriously misleading unless on a fair reading, in context, against the background of the advertisement as a whole they can really be said to justify that description;
(l) a minute textual examination would not be embarked upon by a reasonable reader of an advertisement; and,
(m) therefore, the court should not encourage a microscopic approach to the construction of a comparative advertisement at the interlocutory stage.

It can thus be seen that the UK courts are going to be extremely unwilling to prohibit the comparative use of a registered trade mark unless there are compelling reasons to find such use 'not in accordance with honest practices'.

Conclusion

It can be seen that, absent a clear instruction from the European Court of Justice to the contrary, English judges are likely to view with disfavour attempts by trade mark owners to argue that the Directive has greatly broadened the scope of protection for registered marks. The touchstone of likelihood of confusion will remain at the core of trade mark infringement and some of the more esoteric (and arguable) forms of damage which constitute unfair competition in certain continental European jurisdictions are unlikely to be sufficient to persuade an English judge that harm has been done to the mark as 'an indication of origin'.

17

Community Law and Criminal Law

BY CONOR QUIGLEY, BARRISTER, BRICK COURT CHAMBERS

Enforcement of criminal law is primarily a matter for national courts and authorities on the basis of national criminal law provisions. European Community law itself does not as such provide for any criminal law, although Title VI of the Maastricht Treaty introduced provisions on cooperation in the field of justice and home affairs into the law of the European Union. Nevertheless, there are several ways in which Community law has an impact on criminal law practice and procedure. In this chapter, the following aspects of the interaction of EC law and domestic criminal law will be examined:

- the areas of EC and EU law with a criminal law aspect;
- special rules relating to the interpretation of EC directives;
- directly effective rights;
- penalties;
- the effect of invalid legislation.

Areas of EC/EU Law with a Criminal Law Aspect

For the most part, EC legislation is limited to setting out the substantive provisions of law which must be complied with. It is for domestic law to give full effect to these substantive provisions by providing for such procedural, administrative and enforcement rules as are necessary. This is equally the case with EC regulations as with EC directives. In particular, in the context of criminal enforcement measures, it is extremely rare for EC legislation to specify any particular steps which must be taken. Rather, if the EC legislation has any involvement, this will be limited, as in the Sixth VAT Directive,[1] to requiring the Member States to take such steps as are necessary for the correct levying and collection of the tax and for the prevention of fraud. One well-known exception to this general rule is to be found in the Money Laundering Directive, Directive 91/308/EEC,[2] which provides specifically that Member States must in particular determine the penalties to be applied for infringement of the measures adopted pursuant

[1] Council Directive 77/388/EEC, OJ 1977 L145/1 (as amended).
[2] OJ 1991 L166/77.

to the Directive. Note, however, that even in this case the Directive does not itself seek to determine the actual penalties.

In Title VI of the Treaty on European Union, Member States, without prejudice to the powers of the European Community, are to regard certain areas as matters of common interest. These include asylum policy, immigration policy, combating drug addiction, combating fraud, judicial co-operation in criminal matters, customs co-operation and police co-operation for the purposes of preventing and combating terrorism, unlawful drug trafficking and other serious forms of international crime. The Council may adopt joint positions and promote any co-operation contributing to the pursuit of the objectives of the Union, or it may adopt joint action in so far as the objectives of the Union can be attained better by joint action than by the Member States acting individually on account of the scale or effects of the action envisaged. A further alternative is for the Council to adopt conventions in these fields. Recent examples of measures adopted pursuant to the powers contained in Title VI of the European Union Treaty are as follows: Joint action 96/698/JHA[3] of 29 November 1996 on co-operation between customs authorities and business organizations in combating drug trafficking, Joint Action 96/699/JHA[4] of 29 November 1996 concerning the exchange of information in the chemical profiling of drugs to facilitate improved co-operation between Member States in combating illicit drug trafficking, Joint Action 96/750/JHA[5] of 17 December 1996 concerning the approximation of the laws and practices of the Member States of the European Union to combat drug addiction and to prevent and combat illegal drug trafficking, Council Resolution[6] of 29 November 1996 on the drawing up of police/customs agreements in the fight against drugs and Council Resolution[7] of 16 December 1996 on measures to combat and dismantle the illicit cultivation and production of drugs within the European Union.

The Money Laundering Directive and Joint Action 96/750/JHA provide a good example of the interaction between EC and EU law and national criminal law relating to the control of drug trafficking. Money laundering is defined in the directive as including the acquisition, possession or use of property, knowing, at the time of receipt, that such property was derived from criminal activity, in particular drug trafficking.[8] Under the Money Laundering Directive, Member States are required to ensure that money laundering is prohibited.[9] Similarly, pursuant to Joint Action 96/750/JHA, Member States are required to endeavour to approximate their laws to make them mutually compatible to the extent necessary to

[3] OJ 1996 L322/3. [4] OJ 1996 L322/5. [5] OJ 1996 L342/6. [6] OJ 1996 C375/3.
[7] OJ 1996 C389/1. [8] Council Directive 91/308/EEC, Art. 1.
[9] The bulk of the provisions of the Money Laundering Directive are, however, concerned solely with the use of the financial system for money laundering purposes.

prevent and combat illegal drug trafficking in the Union. In particular, Member States must ensure that under their legal systems the penalties imposed for serious drug trafficking are among the most severe penalties available for crimes of comparative gravity.[10] One issue which might arise is whether national criminal law prohibiting drug trafficking is to be appraised in the light of the Money Laundering Directive or by reference to Title VI of the Union Treaty. In particular, where those national measures might infringe the fundamental principles of the European Convention on Human Rights, might EC or EU law be applied in order to ensure their compliance with the Convention? Alternatively, are these national measures applicable in the national courts solely by reference to national law requirements of application and interpretation?

This issue is particularly important for the English courts where the ECHR is not as such directly applicable.[11] While English courts will normally interpret an Act of Parliament in a manner which is consistent with UK international law obligations, they cannot override the express wording of such an Act on the ground that it is incompatible with the Convention. On the other hand, EC legislation must be interpreted so as to comply with fundamental rights, such as the principles of the ECHR, otherwise it is invalid as a matter of EC law. Implementing legislation must, therefore, in order properly to implement a directive, equally be consistent with respect for fundamental rights. It follows, at least arguably, that UK legislation prohibiting drug trafficking must be interpreted and applied consistently with the principles as set out in the ECHR. Furthermore, even if the UK legislation is deemed to fall within the scope of application of Title VI of the Union Treaty, respect for the ECHR remains binding. First, Article F(2) of the Union Treaty states that the Union shall respect fundamental rights, as guaranteed by the ECHR and as they result from the constitutional traditions common to the Member States, as general principles of Community law. Whatever this might mean for the interaction of Community law and Union law remains to be seen, but at the least it would appear to require the Union to act in accordance with respect for fundamental rights. More importantly perhaps is the requirement in Article K.2(1) of the Union Treaty that the matters falling within Title VI must be dealt with in compliance with the ECHR, since this appears on the face of it to apply equally to action by the Member States as to action by the Community institutions. Indeed, it is the various matters, such as combating drug addiction, which must be dealt with in compliance with the Convention and not just the various measures adopted by the Council in accordance with Article K.3(2).

[10] Joint Action 96/750/JHA, Art. 4.

[11] See *Brind* v. *Secretary of State* [1991] AC 696.

Interpretation of EC Directives

It is by now crystal clear that, in the context of EC law, obligations can only be imposed on individuals by the EC Treaty or EC regulations or by national legislation implementing EC directives or giving further effect to EC regulations. Conversely, it is clear that EC directives cannot themselves impose obligations on individuals. Directives, however, must be taken into account in determining liability under national law. The issue of the interpretation of directives arises in two separate ways. First, since national law is to be applied in the light of and consistent with any directive governing the activity in question, it is necessary first to interpret the relevant provisions of the directive in order to determine the proper extent of liability as a matter of EC law. Secondly, the national law must be interpreted as far as possible consistently with the directive, with the proviso that the directive itself cannot be relied on to extend any notion of criminal liability under national law.

A good example of the use of directives to eliminate criminal liability is *Mol.*[12] Mol had sold amphetamines contrary to Dutch law on drugs. He was assessed by the Dutch tax authorities to value added tax on the profits from his drug selling activities. Mol applied for judicial review of the assessment on the ground that the transactions were not liable to value added tax because they were illegal. According to the Sixth VAT Directive, all supplies of goods and services are subject to VAT. No distinction is drawn between legal and illegal transactions. Similarly, no such distinction was drawn in the Netherlands legislation implementing the directive. The European Court of Justice looked to the context and objectives of the directive in order to determine whether it precluded the levying of VAT on narcotic drugs when they are unlawfully supplied. Since the harmfulness of narcotic drugs is generally recognized, there is a prohibition in all Member States on marketing them, with the exception of strictly controlled trade for use for medical and scientific purposes. Such drugs are, by definition, subject to a total prohibition on importation and marketing in the Community. Taking account of the fact that the purpose of the Sixth Directive was to promote the proper functioning of the common market, the Court of Justice concluded that the supply of illegal drugs could not fall within the scope of the Directive. Accordingly, the Netherlands legislation implementing the Sixth Directive also had to be interpreted and applied such that the supply of illegal drugs was not subject to VAT.

The use of directives to soften the application of the criminal law also arises in more unusual circumstances. For instance, in *Complaint against*

[12] Case 269/86, *Mol* v. *Inspecteur de Invoerrechten en Accijnzen* [1988] ECR 3627.

X[13] the Misleading Advertising Directive[14] was applied in the context of a criminal prosecution relating to the sale of imported cars. Richard-Nissan enjoyed an exclusive importation contract in France for Nissan vehicles. It made a complaint against the operator of a garage in Bergerac which placed display advertisements in the press with the words 'buy your new vehicle cheaper'. In fact these vehicles had been imported from Belgium and registered for import purposes although they had never been driven. They were cheaper than French dealer prices because the models sold on the Belgian market have fewer accessories than the basic models sold in France. French law prohibited untruthful and unlawful advertising. The Misleading Advertising Directive defined misleading advertising as any advertising which in any way, including its presentation, deceives or is likely to deceive the persons to whom it is addressed or whom it reaches and which, by reason of its deceptive nature, is likely to affect their economic behaviour or which, for those reasons, injures or is likely to injure a competitor. In the proceedings, the specific issues related to whether the advertising could claim that the cars in question were new and were cheaper. The Court of Justice placed emphasis on the great practical importance for the business of parallel importers of cars that advertising played. Parallel imports enjoy a certain protection in Community law because they encourage trade and help reinforce competition. Accordingly, applying these principles of interpretation to the Directive, advertising could not be considered misleading just because the cars were registered before importation. Rather, it is when the car is first driven that it loses its character as a new car. The claim that the cars were cheaper could only be regarded as misleading if it could be established that the decision to buy on the part of a significant number of consumers to whom the advertising in question is addressed was made in ignorance of the fact that the lower price of the vehicles was matched by a smaller number of accessories on the cars sold by the parallel importer.

While these two examples show that directives can be used to apply national legislation in such a way that the defendant benefits from a wider interpretation than might be obvious from the bare wording of the legislation, it is by now equally clear that a directive cannot be used on behalf of the state to aggravate criminal liability under national law. It is well established that the Member States' obligation to ensure proper implementation of directives applies equally, for matters within their jurisdiction, to the courts. It follows that, in applying national law, whether the provisions in question were adopted before or after the directive, the national court called upon to interpret it is required to do so, as far as possible, in the light of the wording and the purpose of the directive in order

13 Case C–373/90, *X* [1992] ECR I–131.

14 Council Directive 84/450/EEC, OJ 1984 L250/1.

to achieve the requisite result.[15] Indeed, when interpreting and applying national law, every national court must presume that the State had the intention of fulfilling entirely the obligations arising from the directive concerned.[16] However, the obligation on the national court to refer to the content of the directive when interpreting the relevant rules of its national law is limited by the general principles of law which form part of Community law and in particular the principles of legal certainty and non-retroactivity.[17] In particular, this obligation on the national court reaches a limit where the interpretation leads to the imposition on an individual of an obligation laid down by a directive which has not been transposed or, more especially, where it has the effect of determining or aggravating, on the basis of the directive and in the absence of a law enacted for its implementation, the liability in criminal law of persons who act in contravention of the provisions of that directive.[18] Advocate General Jacobs explored this issue in *Vessoso & Zanetti*.[19] He concluded that the rule of interpretation had the result that obligations may arise and be enforceable in civil proceedings between private parties which would not result from an interpretation of the national law taken in isolation. However, in criminal proceedings, an interpretation of national legislation could not be required by a directive so as to impose criminal liability in circumstances where such liability would not arise under the national legislation taken alone. To hold otherwise would run counter to the principle *nulla poena sine lege*. Advocate General Jacobs further opined that similar principles would apply where a Member State has introduced legislation to give effect to a directive but that legislation, although creating criminal liability, does not specify clearly and unambiguously all the circumstances in which that liability arises. In those circumstances, national courts could not be required to interpret the national legislation in the light of the wording and purpose of the directive where the result would be to impose criminal liability which would not otherwise exist.

Directly Effective Rights

Numerous examples could be given of reliance on directly effective rights so as to avoid criminal liability which would otherwise arise under national law. For example, in *Choquet*[20] the ECJ held that national rules

[15] Case 14/83, *Von Colson* v. *Land Nordrhein-Westfalen* [1984] ECR 1891; Case C–106/89, *Marleasing SA* v. *La Comercial Internacional de Alimentación SA* [1990] ECR I–4135.

[16] Case C–334/92, *Wagner Miret* v. *Fondo de Garantía Salarial* [1993] ECR I–6911.

[17] Case 80/86, *Kolpinghuis Nijmegen* [1987] ECR 3969, para. 13.

[18] Case 80/86, *Kolpinghuis Nijmegen* [1987] ECR 3969; Case C–168/95, *Arcaro* [1996] ECR I–4705.

[19] Cases C–206; 207/88, *Criminal proceedings against Vessoso & Zanetti* [1990] ECR I–1461.

[20] Case 16/78, *Choquet* [1978] ECR 2293.

relating to the issue of driving licences by the Member States exert an influence, both direct and indirect, on the exercise of the rights guaranteed by the EC Treaty relating to free movement of persons. However, such rights are not necessarily absolute. Thus, in *Skanavi*[21] a Greek woman was prosecuted for driving in Germany without a valid German driving licence despite the fact that she had been resident in Germany for over one year. She had a valid Greek licence and argued that she should be able to rely on her directly effective rights under the Treaty. German law recognized the right to drive on a foreign licence for up to one year, but thereafter required possession of a German licence. The ECJ held that such a requirement was not incompatible with her Treaty rights.

EC directives are equally capable of being relied on in order to establish directly effective rights against the State. In *Ratti*[22] Italy had failed to implement two directives relating to solvents. The defendant was prosecuted under Italian law for failing to indicate on the label of solvents the percentage of benzene and certain other substances. The Italian legislation ought at that time to have been amended so as to comply with the directives. Such amendment would have resulted in the repeal of the provisions of Italian law which the defendants were charged with infringing. The ECJ held that a Member State which has not adopted the implementing measures required by a directive in the prescribed periods may not rely, as against individuals, on its own failure to perform the obligations which the directive entails. It followed that a national court requested by a person who had complied with the provisions of a directive not to apply a national provision incompatible with the directive not incorporated into the national legal order must uphold that request if the obligation in question is unconditional and sufficiently precise. Accordingly, after the expiration of the period fixed for the implementation of a directive a Member State may not apply its internal law, even if is it provided with penal sanctions, which has not yet been adapted in compliance with a directive to a person who has complied with the requirements of the directive.

While the notion of direct effect is normally described as the means by which a provision of EC law grants an individual rights which the national court must protect, it should in fact be borne in mind, particularly in the context of the criminal law, that direct effect is more accurately defined as the quality attaching to a legal provision by which that provision can be applied by a national court. It is not actually necessary that the person relying on the directly effective provision personally receives individual rights. This is best illustrated by the case of *Stoeckl*.[23] Stoeckl was an executive of a company which was prosecuted in France for employing a

[21] Case C–193/94, *Skanavi* [1996] ECR I–929.
[22] Case 148/78, *Pubblico Ministero* v. *Ratti* [1979] ECR 1629.
[23] Case C–345/89, *Stoeckl* [1991] ECR I–4047.

number of women to work at night contrary to the French labour code. Council Directive 76/207/EEC provides that application of the principle of equal treatment with regard to working conditions means that men and women are to be offered the same conditions without discrimination on grounds of sex. The French labour code, however, provided that women, with some exceptions, could not be employed for any night work, in particular in plants, factories or workshops of any kind whatsoever. Needless to say, the same restriction on night work did not apply to men. The ECJ held that the prohibition on night work for women was contrary to the Directive. However, in the context of the criminal proceedings, it was not the women who were seeking to rely on the Directive to establish the individual right to non-discriminatory treatment. Rather, it was the employer who was seeking to rely on the Directive to establish that he should not be prosecuted for permitting women to work on the same terms as men regardless of French law.

It is, of course, well established that the direct effect of directives may not be relied on by the State as against an individual.[24] In *Arcaro*[25] the ECJ was asked whether a different approach could be taken where a directive required implementing legislation to impose certain obligations on individuals, but the national law contained additional provisions allowing the individual to avoid those obligations. The background to this case was that certain directives required the Member States to control the discharge of certain dangerous substances by means of a system of prior authorization. An Italian decree was adopted to implement the directives, but required authorization of discharges only if they came from new plants. No such limitation was provided for in the directives. Essentially, the question was whether Community law required the national court in those circumstances to disapply the additional provisions of national law so as to allow the application only of such provisions of national law as complied with the Directive. Tempting as this may be, the ECJ replied in the negative, holding that there was no method of procedure in Community law allowing the national court to eliminate national provisions contrary to the provisions of a directive which has not been transposed where that provision could not be relied upon before the national court.

Penalties

Where an EC regulation or directive does not specifically provide any penalty for an infringement of its provisions or refers for that purpose to

[24] Case 152/84, *Marshall* v. *Southampton and South West Hampshire AHA* [1986] ECR 723; Case C–91/92, *Faccini Dori* v. *Recreb Srl* [1994] ECR I–3325.

[25] Case C–168/95, *Arcaro* [1996] ECR I–4705.

national laws, regulations or administrative provisions, Member States are required to take all measures necessary to guarantee the application and effectiveness of Community law. This is yet another manifestation of the duty of co-operation referred to in Article 5 EC.[26] For that purpose, while the choice of penalties remains within their discretion, they must ensure in particular that infringements of Community law are penalized under conditions, both procedural and substantive, which are analogous to those applicable to infringements of national law of a similar nature and importance and which, in any event, make the penalty effective, proportionate and dissuasive.[27] This principle applies in the same manner throughout the field of EC law, whether relating to agricultural fraud, tax evasion, health and safety at work, environmental protection and so on. A typical example of enforcement provisions being required in order to ensure the proper application of EC legislation arose in *Siesse*.[28] Council Regulation (EEC) No 4151/88, dealing with customs matters, requires that a declaration for release of goods for free circulation or an application for assignment of another customs-approved treatment or use be submitted within a certain prescribed period. The regulation did not, however, provide for any specific administrative penalty in the event of infringement of this requirement. The ECJ held that the Member States were free to choose the penalties which seemed appropriate to them. It was quite compatible with the objective of the regulation that a surcharge be levied in the case of infringement, since such a penalty was intended to encourage traders to act within the time limits.

Normally, in accordance with the principle of non-discrimination contained in Article 6 EC, the rule is that the penalty applied must be similar to that applied in the case of analogous infringements of domestic law. For instance *Hansen*[29] involved Council Regulation (EEC) No 543/69 which set limits to the driving periods and rest periods which must be complied with by the driver of a vehicle involved in road transport. In order to enforce this, Danish law provided for a system of strict liability. Hansen & Son, an employer, was prosecuted in respect of infringements by drivers which it employed. The ECJ accepted that the introduction of strict liability corresponded to the system generally applicable in Denmark for protection of the working environment. On the other hand, there may be limits to the non-discriminatory approach. Council Directive 68/360/EEC imposes certain obligations on nationals of a Member State entering the territory of another Member State relating to the possession of an identity

[26] Case C–326/88, *Anklagemyndigheden* v. *Hansen & Son I/S* [1990] ECR I–2911.

[27] Case 68/88, *Commission* v. *Greece* [1989] ECR 2965; Case C–326/88, *Anklagemyndigheden* v. *Hansen & Son I/S* [1990] ECR I–2911; Case C–5/94, *The Queen* v. *Ministry of Agriculture, Fisheries and Food, ex parte Hedley Lomas (Ireland) Ltd.* [1996] ECR I–2553.

[28] Case C–36/94, *Siesse* v. *Director da Alfandega de Alcantara* [1995] ECR 3573.

[29] Case C–326/88, *Anklagemyndigheden* v. *Hansen & Son I/S* [1990] ECR I–2911.

card or passport. In *Sagulo*,[30] the ECJ accepted that such persons could not be put on the same footing as nationals of the host Member State. There was therefore no objection to foreign nationals being subject to different penal provisions from those applying to nationals of the host State who infringe an obligation to obtain certain identity documents.

In the exercise of their discretion, Member States may choose whatever sanctions they deem most appropriate and may, therefore, involve strict liability[31] or criminal liability[32] as long as the penalty is not disproportionate.[33] A penalty will not be regarded as disproportionate merely because it is more severe than penalties provided for by other Member States. It transpired in *Hansen* that Denmark alone had introduced a system of strict liability. The argument that strict liability was therefore disproportionate was rejected by the ECJ. Furthermore, it agreed that a system of strict liability may prompt an employer to organize the work of his employees in such a way as to ensure compliance with the regulation.

A penalty will be regarded as disproportionate if it interferes unduly with fundamental rights guaranteed by the EC Treaty. Thus, in *Messner*,[34] the ECJ held that non-compliance with formalities for establishing the right of residence of an individual could not be penalized by means of imprisonment, since this would be disproportionate to the gravity of the infringement and would be an obstacle to freedom of movement. In *Skanavi*, it was held that, although the requirement to obtain a German driving licence was compatible with EC law, nevertheless any penalty for an infringement of that requirement had to be proportionate. Treating a person who had failed to have a licence exchanged as if he were a person driving without a licence, thereby causing criminal penalties, even if only financial in nature, would be disproportionate to the gravity of the infringement in view of the ensuing consequences. For instance, a criminal conviction might have consequences for the exercise of a trade or profession, particularly with regard to access to certain activities or certain offices, which would constitute a further, lasting restriction on freedom of movement. In *Hansen* it was also argued that the imposition of strict liability by Denmark alone had the result that the risk of being penalized in Denmark was greater for undertakings established in that State so that competition within the common market was distorted. This argument was, however, rejected by the ECJ.

[30] Case 8/77, *Sagulo* [1977] ECR 1495.

[31] Case C–326/88, *Anklagemyndigheden* v. *Hansen & Son I/S* [1990] ECR I–2911.

[32] Case 50/76, *Amsterdam Bulb BV* v. *Produktschap voor Siergewassen* [1977] ECR 137.

[33] Case 299/86, *Drexl* [1988] ECR 1213; Case C–326/88, *Anklagemyndigheden* v. *Hansen & Son I/S* [1990] ECR I–2911; Case C–367/89, *Richardt* [1991] ECR I–4621; Case C–83/94, *Leifer* [1995] ECR I–3231.

[34] Case C–265/88, *Messner* [1989] ECR 4209.

Proportionality applies not just to a system of penalties but also to the individual imposition of a penalty. In particular, where a Member State has not enacted a specific penalty system to enforce any given EC regulation or directive but rather applies general provisions of law, the ECJ held in *Sagulo* that it is the task of the national court to use its judicial discretion to impose a punishment appropriate to the character and objective of the provisions of Community law the observance of which the penalty is intended to safeguard.[35] Also, in *Hansen* the ECJ, having determined that a system of strict liability was compatible with EC law nevertheless also drew a distinction between the imposition of a fine and the amount of the fine. It was not disproportionate to the objective pursued by the road transport regulation to impose a fine in cases of infringement. Nevertheless, the principle of proportionality might also be applied to the actual amount of the fine itself in individual cases.

Invalid EC Legislation

EC legislation may be declared invalid by the ECJ on grounds of lack of competence, infringement of an essential procedural requirement, infringement of the EC Treaty or of any rule of law relating to its application, or misuse of powers.[36] In this respect, a number of general principles of EC law have been recognized by the European Court including, in particular, respect for fundamental rights, proportionality, breach of legitimate expectations, legal certainty and non-discrimination. The legality of EC legislation may be challenged in an action commenced in a national court.[37] In those circumstances, the national court may refer the matter to the European Court of Justice for a preliminary ruling concerning the interpretation of the EC Treaty or the validity and interpretation of acts of the EC institutions.[38] However, in order to ensure the uniform application of EC legislation, the national court may not itself declare that acts of the EC institutions are invalid.[39]

The effects of a declaration of illegality of EC legislation are generally similar whether the proceedings involve civil law or criminal law. There are, however, certain circumstances in which criminal proceedings might be affected by illegality where similar civil proceedings would not be so affected. This was the case in *R* v. *Kirk*[40] which involved a prosecution of

[35] Case 8/77, *Sagulo* [1977] ECR 1495, para. 12.

[36] Art. 173 EC. See also Art. 184 EC.

[37] See, however, Case C–188/92, *TWD Textilwerke Deggendorf* v. *Germany* [1994] ECR I–833 which limits the ability to challenge in national courts EC decisions which could have been reviewed pursuant to Art. 173 EC.

[38] Art. 177 EC. See also Art. L EU.

[39] Case 314/85, *Foto-Frost* v. *Hza Lübeck-Ost* [1987] ECR 4199.

[40] Case 63/84, *R* v. *Kirk* [1984] ECR 2689.

a Danish fisherman in the United Kingdom for breach of the UK fishing legislation. This case involved a fascinating interaction between national law and EC law and the effect on both of the European Convention on Human Rights. By the Sea Fish Order 1982, the United Kingdom prohibited fishing within a twelve-mile coastal limit by any fishing vessel registered in Denmark. Kirk, the master of a Danish fishing vessel, was intercepted on 6 January 1983 while fishing within that limit and prosecuted by the British authorities. He argued that the Sea Fish Order was incompatible with EC law and therefore unenforceable. The ECJ examined the structure of EC law regulating fishing. It transpired that under the Act of Accession, the United Kingdom was given power to derogate from the general rules of EC law governing the common structural policy in the fishing industry by allowing a six-mile coastal limit for a period expiring on 31 December 1982. The general rule was to the effect that Member States could not discriminate against fishing vessels from other Member States and had to ensure in particular equal conditions of access to and use of fishing grounds situated in coastal waters. The Council had been asked by the United Kingdom to extend the derogation beyond 31 December 1982 but had been unable to agree by that date. It was only on 25 January 1983 that the Council adopted Regulation (EEC) No 170/83 establishing a Community system for the conservation and management of fishery resources, Article 6(1) of which retroactively authorized the United Kingdom, as from 1 January 1983, to retain the derogation for a further ten years and to extend the six-mile limit to twelve miles. In determining whether this retroactive legislation was valid or not, the ECJ referred to the ECHR. The Court specifically refrained from embarking on an examination of the general legality of the retroactivity of Article 6(1) of the regulation. Indeed, the normal approach would be to permit retroactivity unless considerations of legal certainty, including any breach of legitimate expectations, weighed in favour of a contrary approach. The United Kingdom had notified the European Commission of the Sea Fish Order on 22 December 1982 and the Commission had approved the Order provisionally pending adoption by the Council of definitive rules. However, given that the proceedings involved criminal liability, the ECJ stated that it was sufficient that retroactivity could not, in any event, have the effect of validating *ex post facto* national measures of a penal nature which impose penalties for an act which in fact was not punishable at the time at which it was committed. That was the case where the national measure at the relevant time was invalid and unenforceable because it was incompatible with directly applicable EC law. This analysis was justified by reference to Article 7 of the ECHR which precludes retroactive application of criminal liability.

18

Tax Law: Rules or Principles?[1]

BY JOHN F. AVERY JONES CBE

This is the year of simplification of tax legislation and I should like to add my thoughts to the debate. There is nothing new in complaining about the complexity of tax legislation. Every generation does it. To give two examples, the Codification Committee in 1936 looked back longingly to the early days of income tax:

> . . . the Statutes of 1842 and 1853 were relatively simple. The growth of legislation since 1907 and its increasing complexity have been in large measure due to the high rates of tax in operation . . . The space occupied by the provisions relating to such reliefs and exemptions is now prodigious, and contrasts with the comparative brevity of the earlier code . . . [2] Unhappily the actual language in which many of the statutory provisions are framed is so intricate and obscure as to be frankly unintelligible'.[3]

In 1955 the Royal Commission said much the same: ' . . . the law on the subject of income tax remains voluminous, complicated and obscure . . . [4] The history of earlier attempts [to simplify it], however, suggests that the problem may be in fact an intractable one, beyond the reach of recommendations'.[5] Looking back at the legislation as it was in either of those years we may wonder what they were worrying about, but it is continued inaction that has brought us to the really serious position we are in now. We have the Report from the Revenue[6] and the Interim,[7] and then the Final,[8] Reports of the Institute for Fiscal Studies Tax Law Review Committee to prove it. I am sure that we can all agree that tax legislation is complex.

I want in this chapter to build upon the proposals of Leonard Beighton in his Philip Hardman Memorial Lecture, The Finance Bill Process: Scope

[1] This is the text of the Annual Lecture delivered to the Institute of Fiscal Studies on 17 June 1996. It has also been published in *Fiscal Studies*, vol. 17, Issue no. 3. I am grateful to Prof. John Tiley for reading an early draft of this lecture and for making many useful comments.

[2] Report of the Income Tax Codification Committee, cmnd. 5131, para. 18.

[3] Para. 20.

[4] Royal Commission on the Taxation of Profits and Income, cmnd. 9474, para. 1080.

[5] Para. 1081.

[6] The Path to Tax Simplification, Dec. 1995 and Background Paper.

[7] Interim Report on Tax Legislation, Nov. 1995.

[8] Final Report on Tax Legislation, IFS, June 1996.

for Reform,[9] in which he put forward as a solution to the increasing complexity of tax legislation, the case for a more purposive interpretation by the courts thus enabling the legislation to be simpler, clearer, and more direct. One of the points he made was that . . . with the principles of European Law becoming increasingly important, and with the role of the European Court of Justice becoming ever more significant, we may find that the United Kingdom courts have in any case to move in that direction.' I intend to examine this influence of EC tax law in the light of the European Court's and our courts' interpretation of it. I shall put forward the suggestion that by following this route we can have legislation which is both simpler and more certain.

I. The Causes of Complexity

There is even quite a lot of agreement about the causes of the problem. The Tax Law Review Committee devotes a chapter of their Interim Report to it. First they refer to the tax base. It would be natural for an Institute for Fiscal Studies lecture to concentrate on this, but I shall not do so now. If policy makers listened harder to the Institute for Fiscal Studies something might be done, but I am sceptical. I used to think that if all gains and losses on gilds and bonds were taxed as income the system would be simpler, but after this year's Act I have my doubts. The Tax Law Review Committee refer also to the legacy of Addington's tax of 1803, the common law approach, the increasing sophistication of commerce, the desire for certainty, the need for legislation to prevent avoidance, the courts, political tinkering, the Parliamentary process, Parliamentary counsel, the lack of time. In other words our whole legal culture. The Revenue's report concentrates on four of them: tax reform (e.g., independent taxation and self-assessment), the increasingly global and sophisticated business environment (e.g., foreign exchange gains, manufactured dividends), changes in general legal framework (e.g., open-ended investment companies, demergers), and 'the increasing desire for tax law to be detailed and precise so that it is certain in its application'.[10] My impression is that the first (tax reform) and third (legal framework) are not too important (self-assessment does seem to cover a lot of pages but it has been beneficial in doing away with some of the complexity[11] as well), and that the second (sophisticated environment) and fourth (detail) are connected: while the

[9] [1995] BTR 33. See also his comment on the Tax Law Review Committee's Interim Report and the Revenue's Report at [1996] BTR 1.

[10] The Path to Tax Simplification, Report, para. 3.

[11] It has also caused some extra complexity, such as different Sched. A, rules for companies and individuals. More could be done to simplify the system for self-assessment. Do we, for example, need ss. 348 and 349 any more?

business environment is more sophisticated, it is not four times more so than in 1970 (swaps may be new but foreign exchange gains existed in 1970). That leaves the pursuit of certainty through more and more detail, which I suggest is now amply proved not to work. Detail and certainty do not necessarily go together. We all agree with Adam Smith about certainty. The desire for it results in more and more detail hoping to answer every question. As the Tax Law Review Committee rightly say, 'The possible permutations of facts are virtually infinite so that legislation cannot realistically aspire to answer every question. In this sense, complete immediate certainty is unattainable.'[12] The result is that tax legislation is more than four times as long as it was 25 years ago but I do not believe that we have achieved any more certainty, rather the reverse. The time has come to do something about it.

II. Rewriting Tax Legislation: Will it Cure the Complexity?

The Reports by the Revenue and the Tax Law Review Committee have suggested rewriting the legislation in plain English as the, or at least part of[13] the, solution. I have nothing against the draftsman writing in easier-to-understand English; indeed it will make my life easier. But, if that is possible, why is he not already doing so?[14] To be fair to the much maligned draftsman, the answer is that he operates under incredible time pressure usually drafting while the policy is being refined, whereas others take the draftsman's finished product and rewrite it in intelligible English at their leisure. It will take a great deal of resources to rewrite the whole of tax legislation while it is increasing at the current rate, and when it has been done I do not think we shall really be satisfied that the problem has been solved. Indeed, if the legislation is rewritten, it might in some ways make matters worse because I would expect the courts to look at the old and the new legislation in order to see the extent to which former decisions can be relied upon. The Australian draft legislation provides that if the rewritten Act appears to have expressed the same idea in a different form of words in order to use a clearer or simpler style, the ideas are not to be taken to be different just because different forms of words are used.[15] This seems to be not just an invitation to, but a requirement on, the courts to

[12] Interim Report para. 3.21. The reference to immediate certainty is to the Renton Committee Report, the Preparation of Legislation, cmnd. 6053, meaning having a clear and accurate legal effect without reference to the courts.

[13] See the end of s. III.B and s. V for comments on the other major recommendation of the Tax Law Review Committee.

[14] A simple point which might be considered is whether it is necessary for a sub-s. to consist of only one sentence; breaking it up into shorter sentences in itself would make ii easier to read.

[15] New s. 1–3.

look at both the old and the new legislation, so that they might as well just continue to look at the old, which does not appear to be a simplification.

My real objection to rewriting is that I do not find much of a connection between the causes of the problem and the proposed solution. The solution seems to me to be an implied acceptance that nothing can be done to remove the real causes of complexity which are deeply rooted in our whole legal culture. If you start with 6,000 pages[16] of gobbledygook you will end up with a number of pages (which may be greater or less than 6,000,[17] but will certainly be a large number of pages) of easier-to-read legislation, but will we all say that this is the end of complexity? Suppose we were all gathered here again in five years' time (assuming, contrary to Stanley Kubrick's vision, that judges have not been replaced by computers) when all the then-current tax legislation has been rewritten in an intelligible form in accordance with the wishes of the Tax Law Review Committee and the Revenue: do you think we shall all be saying of our tax legislation that everything is for the best in this best of all possible worlds? I do not believe so, and I think that a more drastic solution is needed. As an Australian, Professor Graeme Cooper, has rightly said 'a complex system may be clearly expressed and yet will remain a complex system. The complex rule remains.'[18]

III. Parliament and the Courts

Perhaps because I am a lawyer I see the problem in terms of Parliament and the courts. The stages through which tax law passes in the making starts with a Minister with an imaginary cartoon box above his head within which is written the 'Idea' (such as, 'let us have a 20 per cent rate of tax on savings income').[19] This is refined by the Revenue, subject to the Minister's approval, dealing with such matters as whether savings income includes income from land, annuities or payments from discretionary trusts. It is at this stage that all the detail is introduced, including such matters as the effect of the change on references to exemption from surtax in pre-1971 double taxation agreements (I assure you I am being quite

[16] See text at n. 23 for this figure.

[17] The Revenue say that there is no compelling evidence from existing attempts to rewrite legislation that will result in an overall increase or decrease in length, Background Paper. Annex 5, para. 84. An Australian writer has estimated that the rewrite will reduce the length of their legislation from about 6,000 pages to about 4,500 pages, see Richard J. Vann, Improving Tax Law Improvement: an International Perspective. Australian Tax Forum 1995, pp. 193–225.

[18] *A Rose is a Flower is a Plant—Tax Simplification South of the Equator*, 1995 Conference Report, Report of Proceedings of the 47th Conference, Canadian Tax Foundation.

[19] These stages are described in the Path to Tax Simplification. Background Paper, para. 1.8.

serious).[20] The Parliamentary draftsman puts the developed idea into legislative form, containing every conceivable detail identified by the Revenue in their instructions. The Parliamentary draftsman is unfairly blamed for all our problems but I do not believe that he is the person insisting on the detail being contained in his instructions. Indeed I expect the reverse is true, that he persuades the departments that some of it is unnecessary. Parliament debates it, at least in theory, and passes it. Taxpayers, aided by their advisers, act on it by, for example, deducting tax at 20 per cent instead of 24 per cent and taxpayers, again aided by their advisers, fill in tax returns and are assessed. Finally, if matters are not agreed, they come before tribunals and courts. What matters in the last resort is whether the whole process results in the most efficient way the court gives effect to the wishes of Parliament (more accurately meaning, the wishes of the Minister aided by the Revenue Departments). Put this way the important issue is the interaction between Parliament (which from my description above really means what the Revenue Departments feed into Parliament) and the courts. Parliament is addressing the judges.[21] What really matters is that the courts should come up with the right answers, not whether the rest of us have an easy time reading the statutes, though it would be nice if we could achieve both.

A. Tax Legislation Today

If we confine our attention to income tax, corporation tax, and capital gains tax, so that we eliminate the distortions of the introduction of PRT and the changes from estate due to capital transfer tax to inheritance tax and the increasing number[22] of double taxation agreements, since 1970 the legislation has grown from 1,297 to 4,580 pages[23] of primary legislation (a 253 per cent increase) and 171 to 1,444 pages of secondary legislation (a 744 percent increase), making a total increase of 310 per cent resulting in 6,024 pages. This is a compound growth rate of nearly 6 per cent per annum since 1970, over 8 per cent since 1988 and over 12 per cent since 1992. In five years time we shall have 8,000 (33 per cent more), 9,000 (50 per cent more) or 10,700 (77.5 per cent more) pages at the same respective rates of growth, assuming that the rewritten legislation is the same length (which, of course, makes it doubtful that all the legislation will in fact have been rewritten in simplified form in five years). Although we shall have come

[20] FA 1996, Sched. 6, para. 21.

[21] This is another objection to simplified drafting which is aimed at the man in the street or the ordinary adviser, most of whom never read it anyway. The target audience for tax legislation is commented on in the Tax Law Review Committee's Final Report, paras. 4–5 onwards.

[22] Which is a good thing.

[23] Taken from Table B in The Path to Tax Simplification, the Report itself. A page for this purpose is a Royal Octavo page as in the HMSO edition of the Taxes Acts.

to the end of the amendments necessitated by self-assessment, my prediction about the rate of increase particularly now that there is a new government is at the upper end of the range. There is no reason to suppose that the legislation will not continue to grow. In ten years from now we could be looking at 10,600, 13,500 or 19,000 pages at these rates of growth.

We should bear in mind that legislation is not the only measure of the volume of relevant materials. There are numerous statements of practice, extra-statutory concessions, published Revenue guidance, Tax Bulletins, etc., and now Hansard, to say nothing of cases in the courts (the decisions of the Special Commissioners are now also being reported) to be considered before answering any problem. Another factor to bear in mind is that most businesses do not deal only with the Inland Revenue, but also with Customs and Excise, where the VAT legislation now runs to 570 pages of primary and secondary legislation plus another 250 pages of European legislation and there is also some tertiary legislation contained in their booklets. We must not forget National Insurance as well. Tax Law is nasty, brutish . . . and long.[24]

By comparison, I read recently,[25] but I have not counted it myself, that France has about 450 pages of tax codes plus 400 pages of Annexes, and Germany has about 450 pages of tax legislation (200 on personal income tax, less than 50 on corporate income tax, and 200 of supplementary laws). The Tax Law Review Committee mention that the German constitution requires that its tax legislation should be written in clear and detailed terms, and German practitioners complain that it is becoming more detailed.[26] All things are relative. However misleading such comparisons may be, there must be some fundamental difference between these countries and ourselves which is surely worth exploring. I shall suggest that the main difference is that they are interested in principles while we think of tax law as rules. As an Australian, Professor Richard Vann, has pointed out: 'We suffer from tax rule madness, a disease that affects the advanced Anglo-Saxon countries generally with Australia having a particularly virulent form.'[27] It is no consolation to know that others are worse off, but tax rule madness is a good description of the problem here.

The Revenue's paper says it may well be thought that length alone is not an important measure, and the real measure should be how long it takes to find a particular legislative text and understand its meaning.[28] The Tax Law Review Committee say much the same: 'So the reality is not that users of tax legislation want that legislation to be as short as possible but that they need to be able to comprehend it in the shortest time possi-

[24] I wish I had thought of that variation on Leviathan. I think it was said of capital gains tax computations but I have been unable to trace the source.

[25] Vann (see n. 17) at 222.

[26] Interim Report. para. 3.11.

[27] Vann (see n. 17) at 222.

[28] Background Paper, Annex 5, para. 85.

ble.'[29] They do, however, make the point that length presents a serious difficulty for new practitioners becoming familiar with the whole tax field.[30] More importantly, the Tax Law Review Committee rightly draw attention to the spiral effect: 'Once a tax system has become complex, even a conceptually simple change may only be achievable by means of a complex provision because the new legislation has to fit into the conceptual framework and language of the existing body of law . . . In this way, this spiral may become self-perpetuating unless something is done to arrest it.'[31] While length in itself is clearly not the only measure of complexity, when we are dealing with direct tax legislation of over 6,000 pages I think the time has come to stop the spiral and think at least of slowing down the increase. If you want to cure tax rule madness you have to do more than treat the symptoms.

B. The Courts

So much for Parliament, I turn now to the courts. Sadly, as the Renton Committee concluded, the real reason why the mass of words has increased is because the judges could not be trusted to give effect to the ideas behind them, and so less and less leeway is given to them: 'The real problem is one of confidence. Would Parliament be prepared to trust the courts?'[32] The Renton Committee's conclusion was 'that interpretation of Acts drafted in a simpler, less detailed and less elaborate style than at present would present no great problems provided that the underlying purpose and the general principles of the legislation were adequately and concisely formulated.' Interestingly, the last words of the report were a quotation to the effect that Parliament's suspicions, that the judges could not be trusted, was wholly unfounded, taken from evidence by two Scots judges, whose tradition in pre-union statutes was much closer to the present European tradition.[33] It is clear from the increase in size of tax

[29] Interim Report, para. 1.18.

[30] Interim Report, para. 1.17.

[31] Interim Report, para. 3.15.21, good example is the recent consultative document on employee travel and subsistence which proposes substituting 3 pages of legislation for the 5 lines we have had since 1853 which were admittedly in some need of change, but does it really need all this detail?

[32] See n. 12, para. 19.41.

[33] Of the interpretation of old statutes of the Scots Parliament, Lord Dunedin (the Lord President) has said: 'Such statutes were passed under a totally different state of affairs, with a language that does not always fit modern life. The function of the Court in interpreting them is not that of modification. It is truly interpretation, but necessarily, in such a case, of the spirit and not of the letter.' *Heriot's Trust* v. *Paton's Trs* XLIX Scottish Law Reporter 858. This passage was cited in *Whatmough's Trustees* v. *The British Linen Bank* 1943 SC (HL) 51 in which Lord Thankerton stated at p. 57: 'The Act of 1696, like other old Scots Acts, has necessarily been the subject of much judicial construction and interpretation, and, as pointed out by Lord Dunedin (then Lord President), such interpretation is necessarily of the spirit and not of the letter . . . ' He also mentions that the English courts adopted the same approach to older statutes, such as the Statute of Frauds. I am grateful to Martyn Jones for his assistance

legislation since the committee reported in 1975 that the answer to Renton's question, 'would Parliament be prepared to trust the courts?' (which I suggest really means, 'would the Revenue Departments be prepared to trust the courts?') is no. We are therefore witnessing this ever-increasing spiral of legislation which, judged by my criteria of whether the judges are more likely to give the right answers, is completely and obviously doomed to failure.

One major reason for the mess that we are in, is that it was caused by the habit of the courts construing tax legislation as a matter of words. One of the earliest statements about how to construe tax legislation is that of Lord Cairns in *Partington* v. *Attorney General* in 1869:[34]

> As I understand the principle of all fiscal legislation, it is this: if the person sought to be taxed comes within the letter of the law he must be taxed, however great the hardship may appear to the judicial mind to be. On the other hand, if the Crown, seeking to recover the tax, cannot bring the subject within the letter of the law, the subject is free, however apparently within the spirit of the law the case might otherwise appear to be. In other words, if there be admissible, in any statute, what is called an equitable construction, certainly such a construction is not admissible in a taxing statute, where you can simply adhere to the words of the statute.[35]

These words are usually quoted out of context, Lord Cairns started the paragraph from which this quotation is taken by saying that he found for the Revenue both on the basis of form and substance, which he considers separately in his speech. Hubert Monroe in his Hamlyn lectures[36] discusses how Lord Cairns, who had himself been Solicitor General and Attorney General, came to deliver his guidance on the interpretation of fiscal legislation when in the same volume of the law reports he applies a purposive construction to the Land Clauses Consolidation Act. But whatever the reason, this approach was a fact for the next hundred years. The next quotation comes from another House of Lords case in 1980: 'A subject is only to be taxed upon clear words, not upon "intendment" or upon the equity of an Act. Any taxing Act of Parliament is to be construed in accordance with this principle.'[37]

But even so there has been a change. Lord Wilberforce continued: 'What are clear words is to be ascertained upon normal principles: these do not confine the courts to literal interpretation. There may, indeed should, be

over Scots law. Perhaps the Scots have had the advantage over the English that more of their law is found in older statutes and so their tradition has been able to survive better.

[34] A case on probate duty. This was before the courts started hearing cases about income tax in 1874.

[35] (1869) LR 4 E & E App HL 100.

[36] *Intolerable Inquisition? Reflections of the Law of Tax* by H. H. Monroe, Stevens, 1981

[37] Lord Wilberforce in *Ramsey* v. *IRC* 54 TC 101 at 184E.

considered the context and scheme of the relevant Act as a whole, and its purpose may, indeed should, be regarded.'

I am not sure that it is right to lump all courts together because the former minute scrutiny of words is primarily a Chancery Division habit, perhaps deriving from its role in construing documents. When the Queen's Bench Division first started on VAT their reaction was quite the reverse: in the very first case they refreshingly asked: 'what as a matter of substance and reality is the right answer?'[38]

Change is slow but it has been happening. Lord Justice Diplock, as he then was, said this in a lecture in 1965,[39] long before most of us thought there was a problem: 'Anyone who has decided tax appeals knows that most of them concern transactions which Members of Parliament and the draftsman of the Act had not anticipated, about which they had never thought at all. Some of the transactions are of a kind which had never taken place before the Act was passed: they were devised as a result of it.' And later:

> 'When an Act attempts, as this one [the Income Tax Act 1952 which most of us today would regard as part of the golden age of tax legislation when compared to the present] does, to deal specifically with every class of transaction which the draftsman can foresee, it becomes difficult indeed to extract from the mass of detail any principle which the Courts can say with confidence Parliament intended to be applicable to any class of transaction which the draftsman did not foresee. This is what drives the Court to adopt the narrow semantic approach. We cease to ask ourselves: What did the users of these words intend? and ask ourselves: What, as a matter of semantics, do the words they used mean? These are different questions and may result in different answers.

Ten years later he was to say in the course of a judgment: 'If one looks back to the actual decisions of this House on questions of statutory construction over the past 30 years one cannot fail to be struck by the evidence of a trend away from the purely literal towards the purposive construction of statutory provisions.'[40]

I am not sure that the effects of the change were being felt much in the tax field at the time. I think the turning-point in tax cases was caused by the realization by the judges that the narrow semantic approach led inevitably to tax avoidance. The courts were faced with lots of cases about tax avoidance schemes, which they alone had caused. Doctors have a word for it: iatrogenic, or doctor-induced, disease; my Greek is not up to it, but there should be a word for the judge-induced disease of tax avoidance, for that is what it was. The only way out of hearing an eternal diet of artificial tax avoidance cases was for the judiciary to invent a principle, a

[38] *Customs and Excise Comrs* v. *Automobile Association* [1994] STC 192 at 198.
[39] Presidential Address to the Holdsworth Club, University of Birmingham 1965, 122.
[40] *Carter* v. *Bradbeer* [1975)1 WLR 1204 at 1206–7.

principle so strong that it could overrule a previous House of Lords decision on the same facts.[41] *Ramsay* and then *Furniss* v. *Dawson*, by applying an extraneous principle to the interpretation of tax legislation, came as something of a shock.

Change has continued to the present. In a recent case, the first question Lord Nolan posed in the House of Lords after setting out the legislation and the taxpayers contention was: 'Was this the purpose that Parliament intended to achieve by the words used?'[42] Whether or not they are saying it, this is much more the approach being adopted by judges today. Unfortunately just as the courts have become much more interested in the idea behind the words, the words have increased in number, and it is more and more difficult to see any ideas behind the words. As recently as 1990, a judge in an oil taxation case said, and certainly could not have been criticized for saying: 'In reaching these conclusions I have not attempted to achieve any purposive construction of the detailed provisions of the Act since I am not sure what their purpose is.'[43]

The problem of the courts' new purposive approach is that there is little help available to the judges to answer what is clearly the right question: what was the purpose that Parliament intended to achieve by the words used? Consequently, as the Privy Council said in a recent appeal: 'Quite often the benefits of a "purposive" approach are illusory, since the purpose which is used as a point of reference merely reflects the contention of one or other of the parties about what the words ought to mean.'[44] The lack of any external materials from which the courts might find the purpose of legislation has changed, although only slightly, with *Pepper* v. *Hart*[45] according to which the courts may refer to ministerial statements in Hansard in cases of ambiguity or obscurity, and even now, that is a rule which is confined as far as possible. I was disappointed by the House of Lords' refusal in *Melluish* v. *BMI (No 3) Ltd*[46] to use Ministerial statements relating to other provisions of the same Act which might have given guidance on the construction of the provision in question, even when they agreed that it was ambiguous and obscure. On the other hand, the courts have been willing to relax the rule further when it comes to construing a statute based on European legislation in order to ascertain its purpose.[47] What advantage is it to require a judge to construe legislation, in other words, decide what Parliament meant, with one hand tied behind his back? No wonder foreigners think we are mad. I recently asked a Dutch tax lawyer what the first source was that he turned to in interpreting tax

[41] *Moodie* v. *IRC* [1993] STC 188 as it affects *Plummer* v. *IRC* [1979] STC 793.
[42] *ICI* v. *Colmer* [1996] STC 352 at 358b.
[43] *BP Oil Development Ltd* v. *IRC* 64 T.C. 498 at 532B.
[44] *Chan Chi-hung* v. *R* [1996] All ER 914 at 922b.
[45] [1992] STC 898.
[46] [1995) STC 964 at 978. See [1996] BTR 195 at 200
[47] *Three Rivers District Council* v. *Bank of England* (1996) 2 All ER 363.

legislation. His answer was their equivalent of *Hansard*. The reason was that he, like the Dutch courts, wants to know the answer to Lord Nolan's question: 'Was this the purpose that Parliament intended to achieve by the words used?'

The Tax Law Review Committee's recommendation favouring the use of explanatory memoranda[48] seems to me to be a logical extension of *Pepper* v. *Hart* and I support it as being a far more important recommendation than rewriting the legislation. What is in written form prepared in advance (which obviously must exist today), is surely more reliable than what the Minister says while on his feet when he may depart from his notes. We also have the odd situation today that, if the opposition do not ask for any explanation of a clause, in order to get through the day's business more quickly, the Minister will not even read out his prepared speech so we are all deprived for ever of this potential guidance. Publishing the memoranda and allowing their use by courts, and therefore by the rest of us, is a minor extension to *Pepper* v. *Hart* and is another way in which we can discover the statutory purpose. The Revenue's Report seemed much less favourable to explanatory statements but the Government has now come round to favouring them.[49]

C. *Out of Synchronization?*

So both the courts and Parliament have changed, but in opposite directions. Are we not today in the strange situation that Parliament (and, as I keep on saying, this really means what the Revenue Departments are feeding into Parliament) is still legislating for 1960s judges, who were adopting a narrow semantic approach, for whom the only answer was to put in more detail because they could not be relied upon to supply the detail that was not there? At the same time the courts are struggling to pay more attention to the purpose behind the words. We are giving the courts the material which they need in order to find the intention of Parliament, and we are talking about making further material available. But Parliament has not adapted to the change in the courts and has continued with its traditional method which was designed not to be used for purposive construction. To quote Atiyah and Summers:

> England has a long tradition of narrow, detailed drafting: the English draftsman has always (or at any rate for at least two centuries) tried to produce language which is capable of neutral, non-purposive interpretation. An English statute has traditionally been drafted in such detail that it can be said to be a catalogue of rules. It is not really a set of principles which the judges can be left to apply to a variety of situations, not expressly governed by the wording, or which they can be

[48] Interim Report, ch. 6 and Final Report, ch. 5.

[49] See the comments in the debate in the House of Lords on 27 March 1996 quoted in the *Tax Law Review Committees* Final Report, para. 2.8.

encouraged to build on, as though they were common law *principles*. By contrast America has a tradition (which goes back to Jefferson) of drafting in broader language, using legislation to state wide general principles, such as in the federal Constitution itself.[50]

They give some examples of the differences in approach generally, such as the one-section Sherman Antitrust Act compared to the UK detailed provisions on restrictive practices, or the one section in the Uniform Commercial Code dealing with unconscionable contracts. compared to the UK Unfair Contract Terms Act 1977.

The question facing us today is whether we can move the Revenue Departments, and thus Parliament, and the judges in the same direction at the same time. As with so much in tax, Malcolm Gammie has been here first. Discussing whether Parliament or the courts should make the first move, he said:

This chicken-and-egg situation may yet be resolved by the European cuckoo: as the influence of the European Union on our legislation grows, the different traditions of European law may force us to change our ways, to accept a greater use of statements of principle and to adopt a different interpretative approach. I do not underestimate the task involved in resolving the clash of English and European legal cultures—certainty versus the logical formulation of an idea. The latter may tell us the principle involved—or where the negotiation stopped but may give us little idea of the answer to a particular problem. Attempts by the English draftsman to provide the answer in detailed legislation may merely perpetuate the cultural differences or be doomed to founder in the European Court.[51]

My answer to the chicken-and-egg situation is that the European influence has already solved the problem. Our courts have already changed: perhaps less in their interpretation of internal law, but considerably in their approach to the interpretation of European Community law. The method of interpretation necessarily varies according to the nature of the material being interpreted. I want to consider what would happen if Parliament started to write tax legislation not merely in plain English, but in a manner which enabled judges to give effect to the intention behind the words, and at the same time gave them some material from which to find that intention? In almost any other situation we would carry out an experiment, but tax is too serious for that. I suggest that the application of European tax legislation, particularly in the field of indirect tax, has already carried out the experiment for us and our judges are now coping very well with it. All that remains is for the Revenue departments to follow the example of European legislation when they are instructing the Parliamentary drafts-

[50] *Form and Substance in Anglo-American Law* by Atiyah and Summers, Oxford, 1987, at 323.

[51] *Legislation for business: is it fit for public consumption?* 1994 Fiscal Studies 129 at 138.

man, rather than insisting that every detail is included, leaving it to the courts to apply principles to its interpretation.

IV. Principles

Could our tax legislation be rewritten so that it would be construed in accordance with principles rather than containing nothing but rules trying unsuccessfully to cover every eventuality?[52] Dworkin makes the distinction, which I think we are searching for here, between rules and principles.[53] The distinction is that rules are applicable in an all-or-nothing fashion, whereas principles are not. Principles can have exceptions, can conflict with one another; can, for example, apply only when conduct is reasonable; and they can give one guidance about how to deal with the points not expressly covered by the law. Rules do not conflict with each other (if they do, one of them must give and become a subsidiary rule). Principles do not conflict with rules. If a rule is clear, the rule applies and that is the end of it, even though it is an exception to the principle and therefore in conflict with it, But the real use for the principle is to determine what the rule means in the first place (and hopefully to reduce the amount of detail required in stating the rule), in which case there is no conflict. The difficulty about rules is that if something is not expressly covered by them there is no guidance about how to solve the problem, when you are told that only plain words will do. Being brought up on rules, we do not like principles. The Tax Law Review Committee quotes Bennion on Statute Law:[54] 'the pragmatic British are chary of statements of principle. They distrust them because they almost invariably have to be qualified by exceptions and conditions to fit them for real life. What is the use of a principle that cannot stand on its own?'[55] Atiyah and Summers say the same: 'Indeed, we believe that one reason why English judges seldom regard principles (as distinct from rules) as forms of law is that they tend to think that only rules (preferably hard and fast rules) can be *real* law.'[56] This is at first sight odd bearing in mind that the common law consists of nothing but principles and it does not bother judges that principles conflict and that the most suitable one is applied.

One might have expected, from the comparison of our method of legislating with that of the United States which I quoted above,[57] that shorter tax legislation would also be found in the United States where courts are more used to dealing with principles,[58] both in relation to the constitution

[52] Or are there no principles in tax law, as suggested by John Prebble in 'Why is Tax Law Incomprehensible?' [1994] BTR 380.

[53] *Taking Rights Seriously* by Ronald Dworkin, Duckworth, 1977, at 22.

[54] Interim Report. para. 4.18.

[55] Bennion on Statute Law, 3rd ed., p. 25.

[56] Atiyah and Summers (see n. 50), pp. 88–9.

[57] See n. 50.

[58] Atiyah and Summers (see n. 50), ch. 3.

and broadly-worded statutes, even in regulatory fields.[59] This is superficially true of primary tax legislation in the United States but it is not the whole story because all the detail is in Regulations. I do not have an answer to the reason for this unusual amount of detail in US tax law compared to other law but, as I shall comment later, we seem to be moving more in the European direction of placing greater reliance on accounting treatment and less in the US direction of having a self-contained tax system. In any case, Europe is bound to exert a greater influence on our tax system.

John Tiley has summarized the difference in approach between the traditional English way and the European way as one in which the European Court states the principle then works down to the facts whereas our courts do the reverse.[60] The European Court tends not to argue by considering what the position would be if the facts were different.[61] The real difference is that in the European sense principles are at a higher level of abstraction than our courts use when making arguments based on the facts. Bennion is right in saying that we are not yet happy to deal with a principle like discrimination, but a few years ago one might have said the same about legitimate expectation and unjust enrichment.

In this sense, the principle is something external to the rules which helps one to construe the rules, and, in consequence, enables the rules to be less detailed. As we have seen, *Furniss* v. *Dawson* expresses a principle of statutory construction which helps one to construe the rules in the statute in a way which prevents certain type of avoidance, which means that the statute does not itself have to contain so many, or possibly any, anti-avoidance rules. This principle is perhaps not the best example from my point of view to demonstrate that principles lead to more certainty, mainly because the nature of the principle was left to develop as an emerging principle. But now it seems to have stopped emerging, although it is still developing,[62] we have learned to live with it. The problem, particularly with tax, is that we do not have many such principles.

D. General Principles Drafting

There seems to me to be some confusion in the discussion about principles in tax legislation. Both the Tax Law Review Committee[63] and the

[59] Atiyah and Summers (see n. 50), p. 76. And see Judicial Anti-Tax Avoidance Doctrine in England: A United States Perspective by Professor Popkin [1991] BTR 283 at 285.

[60] The Law of Taxation in a European Environment, Cambridge Law Journal, 51(3) Nov. 1992, 451 at 469.

[61] An unusual example is the consideration by the AG of the effect of a sublease instead of a surrender in *Lubbock Fine* v. *Customs and Excise Commissioners* [1994] STC 101, considered below.

[62] *Whittles* v. *Uniholdings Limited (No 3)* [1996] STC 914.

[63] Interim Report, para. 4.5.

Revenue[64] use the expression, general principles drafting when they really mean less detailed drafting, such as the statute saying that profits of a trade are taxed, without defining either profit or trade. Describing such legislation as consisting of general principles suggests that it is different in nature from other legislation. The Revenue, however see all tax law as rules containing more or less detail: 'Like all legislation, whether in common law or civil law countries, and whether set out in general principles, or in extreme detail tax legislation consists of rules that have to be applied to particular facts.'[65] They see no difference, except of degree, between the scope given by general principles drafting (concepts like income, trade, etc.), and detailed drafting which, however detailed, still cannot cover every set of circumstances They conclude: 'All legislation must consist of a mixture of relatively general and relative detailed terms that are selected from the limited resources of language to fit the underlying policy as closely as possible to the potentially unlimited facts with which it must deal. [66] Naturally, they say, it follows from this approach to general principles drafting that, if there is less detail, there is more uncertainty, and so this is not a recommended approach.

When the Tax Law Review Committee and the Revenue speak of general principles drafting they are not really talking about principles; rather it is a matter of Parliament leaving it to the courts to invent the principles without much, if any, assistance from the legislation. To say that we tax profits of a trade without explaining either profits or trade does not seem to me to be a statement of principle; it is just a vague rule. It is the courts, not the legislature, which employs principles in explaining what is meant by profit or trade. Other examples of principles invented by the courts are the doctrine of source, the capital/income distinction and 'receivability without receipt is nothing'. In inventing those principles the courts operated in their traditional fashion working from case to case refining the principles. A good example can be seen in relation to retirement relief from capital gains tax over the question whether a farmer has disposed of part of a business or just an asset such as a field or milk quota.[67]

The Tax Law Review Committee quote the Renton Committee:[68] '. . . the traditional approach in Europe has been to express the law in general principles . . . Here, on the other hand, the traditional approach has been to spell out in the statutes themselves the precise way in which the law is to apply in differing circumstances.' The expression, general principles drafting was originally used by the Renton Committee in connection with

[64] Background Paper, Annex 5, para. 5.

[65] Annex 2, para. 7.

[66] Annex 5, para. 10.

[67] *Atkinson* v. *Dancer* [1988] STC 758; *Jarmin* v. *Rawlings* [1994] STC 1005; *Wase* v. *Bourke* [1996] STC 18.

[68] Interim Report para. 3.8, quoting from para. 9.14 of the Renton Committee (see n. 12).

European legislation 'which relies upon the courts and the Executive to fill in the details necessary to the application of the statutory propositions to particular cases, in the light of the general intention of the legislature expressed in preambles, recitals and other documents'.[69] The importance of the reliance on these further sources to point the way to the correct interpretation seems to have been ignored by the Tax Law Review Committee and the Revenue in drawing the conclusion that more detailed drafting is necessarily more certain.

V. The Tax Law Review Committee's Proposal in their Final Report

The Tax Law Review Committee Final Report, influenced by Leonard Beighton's criticism of the Interim Report,[70] puts forward the interesting suggestion of a two-tier system consisting of primary legislation expressed in general principles, supplemented by secondary legislation setting out the details.[71] This proposal is coupled with proposed changes in Parliamentary procedure enabling amendments to be made to statutory instruments during debate, and having a standing consultative committee of tax practitioners to comment on the drafts. Unfortunately, this proposal is not put forward for the rewriting of the existing legislation because of the need for these new Parliamentary procedures. The following benefits are claimed:

> Firstly, the primary legislation would be much shorter and more comprehensible and, consequently, it would be easier to see the right answers to cases at the margins where the application of the detailed rules is unclear—frequently a problem at present. Secondly and leading on from this, we believe that less elaboration would frequently be required than at present so that the total package of primary and secondary legislation would be smaller than the primary legislation typically is at present. Thirdly, Parliament would be able to concentrate on the policy merits of the primary legislation without the detail obscuring these. Fourthly, the legislation would be less cast in stone; the secondary legislation could more easily be amended if this became necessary.[72]

I fully agree with the first (more comprehensible primary legislation), third (Parliament concentrating on the policy) and fourth (ease of change)[73] of these, particularly the first, as it must help the court to see the wood from the trees, and therefore see great merit in the proposal. But I am concerned about whether the proposal really would achieve the second benefit and result in shorter overall legislation. With more time for consultation there could be more demand for detail in the secondary legislation, and a continuation of the current tax rule madness. This proposal

[69] See n. 12, para. 9.14.
[70] The Right Path to Tax Simplification [1996] BTR 1.
[71] Final Report, para. 3.12.
[72] Final Report, para. 3.6.
[73] Although too much change would make it difficult to find the law.

is essentially the US solution and, as we have seen, the experience there does not instil confidence that simplification will be achieved.

VI. A Modified Proposal

I should like to put forward a modification of the Tax Law Review Committee proposal, which looks in the direction of Europe rather than the United States. This is also a two-level solution, but the levels are different. At the top are more abstract principles corresponding to those found in the EC Treaty applying generally, and the more specific principles found in the preamble to Community legislation. The second level is the legislation itself which is interpreted with the aid of the higher level principles, as well as the explanatory memoranda. There is no third level of detailed legislation, but, of course, below the legislation is Revenue practice which is now published. The reason I put this forward is that one can demonstrate from Community legislation that this does reduce the amount of detail while at the same time still giving certainty.

The real choice, I believe, is not between detailed rules that we have today, and less detailed legislation, when detailed legislation wins on the ground of certainty; but between detailed rules, and less detailed legislation interpreted in accordance with principles, where less detailed legislation wins on the ground of certainty because the use of principles provides predictability. The Royal Commission said the same thing in 1955 but nothing came of it: it expressed '. . . a preference for clear statements of principle in a brief enactment over detailed attempts to cover by anticipation all imaginable evasions of it'.[74] The Revenue agree that countries which use less detailed tax legislation do achieve a reasonable state of certainty.[75] Among the reasons given are that civil law countries rely more heavily on accounting profits, that courts take a more purposive approach to statutory interpretation, and that practices such as rulings are more highly developed. As to the first (following accounting profits) we are seeing a shift towards more reliance on accounting treatment and a move away from the capital and income distinction for companies, as in the loan relationship provisions. The logical end result would be that we had two systems of taxation, one for individuals and the other for companies, in accordance with the European tradition; this, in itself, would be a simplification for many taxpayers.[76] The second reason (purposive approach by the courts) is interesting, because it again suggests that certainty is

[74] Royal Commission on the Taxation of Profits and Income, Cmnd. 9474. para. 1089(5).

[75] Background Paper, Annex 5, paras 23–6.

[76] See *The Finance Bill* 1996: *Keep it short, keep it simple* by Prof David Williams [1996] BTR 101, 103–4. As he points out, companies now have a different Schedule A, have a different scope to Sched. D, Cases I, III and VI, and Case IV does not apply to them all.

achieved by the courts being purposive, which leads to the question: how do the courts know what the purpose is? The answer presumably is that they have regard both to principles expressed in the legislation and to external materials, such as Parliamentary reports.

The reference to rulings is also interesting because we are in the course of discussing pre-transaction rulings in this country,[77] although personally I do not see much wrong with an expansion of the present system of informal rulings. But, if a more formalized system of rulings could be looked at, not in isolation, but together with a proposal for less detailed drafting, I am all in favour of it. The criticism is sometimes made that rulings place too much power in the hands of the Revenue. I am not sure that this is a serious objection; the power is already in the hands of the Revenue whenever they say how they will interpret legislation because most people do not want to take them on in the courts.

With less detailed legislation there appears to be more scope for Revenue interpretation, but such interpretation still has to be in accordance with the stated principles. The detailed form of our legislation may have been influenced in the past by the lack of any remedy for the taxpayer against Revenue discretions, with Parliament trying to reduce the discretion exercised by officials.[78] But there is now no lack of safeguards available to the taxpayer, from the Revenue Adjudicator to judicial review,[79] although the latter suffers from the problem of the taxpayer having to start separate proceedings in the High Court. One change which is, however, needed in this area is to give the Special Commissioners power to review exercises of discretions so as to prevent the need for the taxpayer to pursue two separate lines of appeal, often in relation to the same dispute.[80] The VAT and Duties Tribunal has powers to do this but only in some circumstances, which could usefully be extended for the same reason.[81] In many cases it is the existence of these remedies, not the need to use them, which provides the safeguard.[82] If there is a shift of power it is to the courts (including for this purpose the appeal tribunals).

[77] Pre-Transaction Rulings, Inland Revenue, Nov. 1995. These plans have since been dropped: IRPR 26 Sept. 1996.

[78] See David Goldberg's Philip Hardman Memorial Lecture, *Between the Taxpayer and the Executive: Law's Inadequacy: Democracy's Failure?* [1996] BTR 9.

[79] See Beighton (see n. 9) p. 45.

[80] See the author's Philip Hardman Memorial Lecture, *Tax Appeals: the Case for Reform* [1994] BTR 3.

[81] See FA 1994, Sched. 5 in relation to customs and excise matters and some examples in relation to VAT such as the provision of security.

[82] See the Report of the Keith Committee on Enforcement Powers of the Revenue Departments, Cmnd. 8822, particularly para. 1.5.1(d) and ch. 25.

VII. The Application of Principles to Tax Law in European Community Tax Legislation

One might think that, however beneficial it would be if we had less detailed legislation which we interpreted in accordance with principles, this could not happen without a revolution affecting the legislature, the courts, the Revenue Departments and tax advisers, that is to say, our entire legal culture. Indeed most of the Australian commentators despair of any change happening for this reason. I believe that such an attitude is wrong in the United Kingdom where, in relation to Community tax legislation, we are already doing what I am proposing. In Europe, and, more importantly, in the practice of the European Court when interpreting European Community legislation, which is just as much part of our legislation,[83] there is far more attention to principle, with, I suggest, the twin advantages that the rules can be less detailed, and the result is nevertheless still certain. The principles which the court uses are found in the preamble to European legislation, and there are some general principles which underlie all European Community law.[84] The Court is an interesting institution which seems to combine successfully the methods of civil and common law. We may still regard it as predominantly based on civil law, but elsewhere in Europe the way it follows its previous case law means that it is regarded as based on common law.

One objection to less detailed tax legislation made by the Revenue is that there is no clearly identifiable less detailed drafting style that the United Kingdom could take as a model.[85] The Revenue have had little to do with European legislation[86] and so they have probably not paid much attention to it, although their paper did make a passing reference to the civil law drafting of the Sixth VAT Directive.[87] I suggest that European Community tax and in particular VAT, legislation provides just such a model, although I would not put most of it forward as a model of good drafting. Although the amount of direct tax covered by European legislation is still small, there is a considerable volume in the VAT and customs fields. The Tax Law Review Committee recognizes the impact of European legislation

[83] In round figures the Inland Revenue collects £100bn in taxes, while the European based VAT and customs duties account for £50bn, so the part with a European base is not insignificant.

[84] For a discussion of the method of interpretation used by the ECJ generally, see the papers presented to a Judicial and Academic Conference, 27–8 Sept. 1976, Luxembourg 1976, particularly *The Case Law of the Court of Justice—A critical examination of the methods of interpretation* by F. Dumon.

[85] Background Paper, Annex 5, para. 32.

[86] The parent-subsidiary Directive, the mergers Directive, and, formerly, capital duty are their only fields of contact with European legislation apart from general principles like discrimination in the EC Treaty itself and the odd tax reference in other matters such as EEIGs.

[87] Annex 5. para. 5 of the Background Paper.

drafted predominantly for civil law jurisdictions[88] but they include this as one of the causes of complexity. This seems odd particularly when considering directly applicable regulations which are much less detailed than our legislation; it may have some truth in the absurd situation of directives where the taxpayer can argue his case either on internal law or European law, whichever suits him best, while the tax authority is restricted to arguing on the basis of internal law on the ground that it is the state's fault if this does not correspond to the Directive. Although directives require internal legislation it is not true to say that this is why there is less detail in them. A provision of a directive having direct effect is interpreted without regard to internal law. Have we nothing to learn from how they draft and interpret European Community tax laws?

Interpretation of European Community law is based on principles which assist in the interpretation and tell you how to deal with details not expressly covered. The point I want to make is that this gives more, not less, certainty when applied to less detailed drafting. I shall illustrate this with VAT. The European Court of Justice has now given a large number of decisions on the interpretation of the VAT directives, and so there is a body of law which can be analysed to see if it leads to certainty. As Farmer and Lyal[89] say:

> In interpreting the Community VAT legislation the court has relied heavily on the teleological method of interpretation. It has paid close attention to the description of the model system in Article 2 of the First Directive and to the considerations set out in the preamble to the Directive, in particular the aim of achieving a tax which is neutral in domestic and intra-Community trade. It has been conscious that neutrality depends first and foremost on its general application. Thus, concepts forming the basis for the tax such as 'supply' and 'taxable person' have generally been construed broadly; conversely, exemptions limiting the scope of the tax have consistently been construed narrowly.
>
> The court has employed the technique of giving independent Community law meanings to basic terms . . .
>
> The court has also laid great emphasis on the contextual or schematic method of interpretation. Individual provisions of the VAT legislation form part of a complex system of taxation, and their function is often best understood when they are read together with other provisions.

Let us look at a few cases and see how the court applies principles to the interpretation of the VAT directives and ask ourselves whether the result is less certain than with UK-style legislation? The principle is more important than the drafting as is illustrated by my first example. Taxable person is defined in the Second VAT Directive to mean any person who indepen-

[88] Interim Report, para. 3.48.

[89] *EC Tax Law* by P. Farmer and R. Lyal, Clarendon Press, Oxford, 1994, p. 89. See n. 83 on the methods of interpretation adopted by the court generally.

dently and habitually engages in transactions pertaining to the activities of producers, traders, or persons providing services, whether or not for gain. This case concerns a body which, in order to promote trade with another country, does not charge for its services.[90] The issue is whether it can recover VAT which it pays. Clearly it does not charge any tax because VAT is chargeable only where there is payment for services. Literally it is a taxable person. It is carrying on business though not for gain. The court approached the issue in this way. It first identified the features of VAT in the light of its purpose. The purpose was found in the preamble, the need to achieve harmonization of the tax as will eliminate distortion of competition. The court then looked for a principle, found this time in Article 2 of the First VAT Directive mentioned in the quotation above from Farmer and Lyal: that VAT involves the application to goods and services of a general tax on consumption exactly proportional to the price, whatever the number of transactions which take place in the production and distribution process. That principle requires deduction of tax paid at each stage from tax charged. When one has reached the end of the chain of production, tax is finally charged but is not deductible. That occurs here. The business, by not charging for its services, is in the same position as a final consumer. There is no distortion of competition in these circumstances; the business in question is providing services different in character from taxable ones. These considerations outweigh the literal interpretation of taxable person: 'Consideration of those two articles,[91] a literal analysis of which is not prima facie an appropriate way to resolve the issue as to whether or not an organisation which habitually provides services free of charge may be regarded as a taxable person, indicates that it would be advisable to identify the relevant features of the common system of value added in the light of its purpose.'

In the next case it is instructive that the court looked for the principle first and only turned to the ordinary meaning of the words after finding no guiding principle. It concerns whether the substantial repair of school books is the making of a book (low-rate in the Netherlands, or zero-rate here) or is it an ordinary service? The court said:

> . . . it must be stated that the other provisions of the Second and Sixth Directives give no indication of the meaning to be attributed to the word 'made' [context first]. Nor is any enlightenment to be gathered by looking at the purpose pursued by the Council in adopting the two directives [purpose next]. Their main objective is to determine the basis of assessment of value added tax in a uniform manner according to Community rules. That objective will be attained whatever meaning

[90] *Staatssecretaris van Financiën* v. *Hong Kong Trade Development Council* (Case 89/81) [1983] 1 CMLR 73.

[91] Second VAT Directive, Art. 2 providing that VAT was payable on services supplied against payment, and Art. 4 defining taxable person.

is given to the word 'made', provided that that meaning is identical in all the member states. In those circumstances the word made can only be interpreted by reference to common usage [ordinary meaning of words last].[92]

Much the same issue arose in a case in the English courts, whether pleating fabrics for girls' skirts was zero-rated as being the production of children's clothes.[93] The court went first, as English courts do, to the ordinary meaning of the word, 'produces', although it is fair to say that the court had been referred to the European court case and consequently may not have found it necessary to look at the context and purpose before turning to the ordinary meaning.

Another recent example where the European Court went behind the apparent ordinary meaning of the words was a recent case on whether VAT is charged on a payment of compensation made under Community legislation to a farmer for giving an undertaking to discontinue milk production as part of Community measures designed to reduce the over-supply of milk without reducing farmers' incomes.[94] A supply of services is defined to include obligations to refrain from an act.[95] The compensation payment was directly linked to the act of giving the undertaking to discontinue milk production which is a condition for the supply being for consideration. On the wording therefore VAT appears to be payable, as indeed the German and Italian governments argued; however, the court went behind the wording, basing its decision on the principles laid down in the First VAT Directive that 'the principle of the common system of VAT involves the application to goods and services *of a general tax on consumption*'. This is another example of the point made by Farmer and Lyal of the court paying close attention to the description of the model system in Article 2 of the First Directive. VAT is a tax on consumption but here there was no consumer. No benefit was received by the Community in return for the payment; it was merely acting in the common interest of promoting the proper functioning of the Community milk market. As the Advocate General said, the situation is quite different from an undertaking not to compete given on sale of a business, because in that case the purchaser obtains a direct benefit from the undertaking. This is an example of the principle being used to interpret the rule, which appeared to say the opposite when looked at in isolation. It is only by applying the basic principle that the meaning of the rule can be determined.

Another principle is that exceptions are construed strictly in European legislation. It used to be the case that the court's approach to exemptions was more like the plain words approach that the English courts tradition-

92 *Van Dijk's Boehuis BV* v. *Staatssecretaris van Financiën* (Case 139/84) [1986] 2 CMLR 575.
93 *Customs and Excise Comrs* v. *Ali Baba Tex Ltd* [1992] STC 590.
94 *Mohr* v. *Finanzamt Bad Segeberg* (Case C–215/94) [1996] STC 328.
95 Art. 6(1) of the 6th VAT Directive.

ally use to construe legislation generally,[96] but, even when applying a strict approach, principles are still applied. In contrast, in the United Kingdom there does not seem to be any distinction in approach between charging provisions and exemptions. The Sixth Directive exempts 'the leasing or letting of immovable property'.[97] Internal law in the United Kingdom originally interpreted this on the plain words approach to mean that the grant of a lease was exempt but the surrender of a lease, which is the opposite of letting, was taxable. The European Court decided otherwise.[98] If letting was exempt, so must any change in the contractual position of the parties be exempt. It was not necessary to spell out every detail in the legislation. The way in which the Advocate General reached this conclusion is interesting. He made three preliminary remarks. First, that exemptions are to be construed narrowly (in legislating the exemption the United Kingdom was following this principle, but was interpreting it too narrowly). Secondly, exemptions should have a uniform effect throughout the Member States. Thirdly, and most interestingly, he looked on property transactions as an economic cycle in which new buildings are subjected to VAT in the normal way but once a building had been occupied it had been consumed and future transactions were exempt, although because of the possibility of opting for taxation it could re-enter the economic cycle. He then turned to interpret the reference to leasing in the light of the context and bearing in mind the purpose and structure of the Directive. His reason is based on his third preliminary remark. Leasing transactions should either be in or outside the economic cycle and not partly outside on the grant of the lease and inside on its surrender with consequent distortions about whether the landlord could recover the tax charged. 'The coherent application of the Sixth Directive and respect for the principle of the neutrality of VAT demand that that should be so.'[99] We would have had difficulty in reaching this conclusion through our plain words approach, which goes to show that if our traditional approach can be too narrow when applied to exemptions, it must be far too narrow in relation to charging provisions. The case is a good example of how legislation can be shorter if one pays attention to the principle rather than the words.

The real benefit of principles is when one is dealing with something not expressly provided for in the legislation. My next example concerns a husband and wife, not otherwise carrying on business, who purchased a building under construction with a view to letting it as showrooms.[100]

[96] In *Committee of Directors of Polytechnics* v. *Customs and Excise Comrs* [1992] STC 873 at 884e Brooke J, in construing an exemption provision of the 6th Directive, said that the approach to the construction of the 6th Directive was very similar to the approach taken by English judges to the interpretation of English taxing statutes.

[97] Art. 13B(b).

[98] *Lubbock Fine* v. *Customs and Excise Comrs* [1994] STC 101.

[99] at 119b.

[100] *Rompelman* v. *Minister van Financiën* (Case 268/83) [1985] 3 CMLR 202.

This was deemed to be an economic activity for VAT as 'the exploitation of tangible or intangible property for the purpose of obtaining income therefrom on a continuing basis'.[101] The question arose whether they could recover input tax on the building work immediately or only when the exploitation took place on receipt of income. The Dutch government took the logical position that, if it was the exploitation that gave rise to its being within VAT, this started when income was received. The court had no difficulty in deciding that neutrality required that the input tax should be recovered immediately because otherwise VAT would be included in the expenses of the business. The point was taken one stage further in a recent case in which a company intended to carry on a business purifying sea water to turn it into drinking water.[102] It commissioned a feasibility study, the results of which put off the potential investors and the company was wound up before it had started business. Was the input tax, which had been correctly deducted on the basis of the previous case, now repayable? The Advocate General regarded the Dutch case as one of timing which did not apply when there was never any economic activity. So, as there was no economic activity, the company had no right to deduct input tax and was in the same position as a private consumer. The court disagreed with the Advocate General, a fairly unusual occurrence. It argued that the principle of neutrality applied in the Dutch case did govern this one. The input tax was correctly reclaimed at the time in good faith. It was contrary to the principle of legal certainty that later facts should change this. In addition, neutrality required that there should be no tax burden on a business. There should be no differences between businesses already carrying on business and those starting up. A genuine intention to carry on business was therefore as good as carrying on a business.[103] As before, a wide interpretation was given based on the principle of neutrality that businesses should not bear any VAT. The Advocate General had been too literal in not regarding it as a business. All that is shown by the disagreement between the Advocate General and the Court over which principle was more important is that nothing will ever be completely certain; the issue is whether it is more certain than our present methods in the United Kingdom.

VIII. Would it Work Here?

It is, of course, one thing to say that the European Court with its judges from each Member State can deal with European legislation; it is another

[101] Sixth VAT Directive, Art. 4(2).

[102] *Intercommunale voor Zeewaterontzilting* v. *Belgian State* (Case C–110/94) [1996] STC 569.

[103] Incidentally, the VAT Tribunal had come to the same conclusion in *Merseyside Cablevision* v. *Customs and Excise Comrs* (1987) VATTR 134.

to say that our own judges can do so. This is no longer an abstract question. Recently, we had the interesting spectacle of the Court of Appeal deciding on whether the English or Scots courts had jurisdiction in relation to a void interest swap transaction by a local authority, 'having regard to any relevant principles laid down by the European Court . . . and to any relevant decisions of that Court'.[104] In doing so they came to a different conclusion from the one that would have done under English law.[105] So far as tax is concerned, it is clear that the courts (in which I include the VAT and Duties Tribunal) are not only coping but by now have a great deal of experience of interpreting European tax legislation in accordance with principles particularly in the field of VAT. One could argue that the approach was not originally on the same lines as the European Court, but it certainly is now. As examples, last year the House of Lords confidently decided that a self-supply charge to VAT was inconsistent with the Sixth Directive without referring the question to the European Court.[106] This year, the House of Lords has upheld a provision of internal law as being consistent with the Directive, containing a clear example of Lord Slynn, a former Advocate General and then judge at the European Court, using the method of construing a derogation which the United Kingdom was permitted to make from the Directive in accordance with its objective of preventing avoidance or evasion, here meaning loss of revenue caused by the method of selling via agents who were below the registration limit, also without referring the question to the European Court.[107] Interestingly, this reversed the majority of the Court of Appeal who had, quite correctly, given the derogation a narrow interpretation but their interpretation was too narrow as they had not taken the purpose of the derogation into account. Again this year, the Court of Appeal decided a VAT case almost entirely on European law.[108] The High Court has just decided a case using the recitals to the Sixth Directive as the key to its interpretation.[109] In another case the High Court has had regard to the principle behind the Directive in deciding that input tax cannot be reclaimed by a trader if the supply to it was used in making supplies before the trader was registered, even though, under the statutory rule giving the time of supply as the date of invoice, this was after registration.[110] In the VAT and Duties Tribunal construing European legislation is a daily occurrence.

[104] *Kleinwort Benson Ltd* v. *Glasgow City Council* [1996] 2 WLR 655, applying Civil Jurisdiction and Judgments Act 1982, s. 16 (3).

[105] The decision was that an action for restitution of sums paid under a void contract was a matter relating to a contract.

[106] *Customs and Excise Commissioners* v. *Robert Gordon's College* [1995] STC 1093.

[107] *Fine Art Developments plc* v. *Customs and Excise Comrs* [1996] STC 246. See in particular 260h, 261e.

[108] *Nell Gwynn House Maintenance Fund Trustees* v. *Customs and Excise Comrs* [1996] STC 310.

[109] *Diversified Agency Services Ltd* v. *Customs and Excise Comrs* [1996] STC 398.

[110] *Schemepanel Trading Ltd* v. *Customs and Excise Comrs* [1996] STC 871.

The approach of the UK courts to the interpretation of European legislation is a moving target to which I cannot do justice in this chapter. I would like to put forward a suggestion for some further research. This is that the Revenue should take a closer look at the results of interpreting the legislation with which Customs and Excise deal, both in its interpretation by the European Court and more particularly by our own courts.

IX. Conclusion

I suggest that the answer to our problems can be found in how they do things in Europe. I predict that the result of the further research which I propose will show that courts in the United Kingdom can not only happily construe legislation which is far less detailed than our own in accordance with principles, but in doing so, achieve far more certainty than is currently the case with our internal law. If it works for Community tax law, let us try it for our own tax law. What we need is less detailed legislation construed in accordance with principles, not a continuation of the plague of tax rule madness.

I give the last word to a repetition of the conclusion of the Renton committee 'that interpretation of Acts drafted in a simpler, less detailed and less elaborate style than at present would present no great problems provided that the underlying purpose and the general principles of the legislation were adequately and concisely formulated'.[111]

[111] See n. 12, para. 19.41.

19

Some Points of Friction between English and Brussels Convention Jurisdiction[1]

BY ADRIAN BRIGGS, BARRISTER, 2 HARE COURT;
FELLOW & TUTOR IN LAW, ST EDMUND HALL, OXFORD

At one level it is possible to examine the impact of the Brussels Convention[2] on the jurisdictional rules of the English courts by comparing and contrasting points of detail with each other. But the purpose of this chapter is a little different: to examine three particular questions which raise the more general, or more obscure, question of how traditional jurisdictional principles of English law may have been affected, more or less indirectly, by the coming into force of the Convention. There is not a general theme or a moral which is sought to be drawn. But there are genuine puzzles, to which an open mind might find intricate enough to be worth giving serious thought.

The three topics to be covered are (a) the power of an English court to stay proceedings on forum non conveniens or on other traditional grounds; (b) the power to grant anti-suit injunctions, and (c) the exclusion of arbitration from the scheme of the Convention. The first two of these sub-divide into a number of particular examples, and this is how they will be examined here. We start with the first.

[1] This chapter, originally in the form of a paper, was delivered at a seminar at King's College London on 21 March 1997. I am grateful for the comments (even in the form of frowning and vigorous head-shaking) from those who attended, and especially from Lord Justice Evans, who chaired the seminar. Where I have chosen to persist in views which others may consider to be erroneous the responsibility is mine alone.

[2] Civil Jurisdiction & Judgments Act 1982, Sched. 1, contains the Brussels Convention in the form as acceded to by the United Kingdom. The most recent amendment appears as SI 1990/2591, made on the accession of Spain and Portugal. An accession Convention for Austria, Finland, and Sweden was signed on 29 Nov. 1996, but is not yet in force. In all material respects save the fact that the Court of Justice has no jurisdiction to interpret it, the Lugano Convention (Civil Jurisdiction & Judgments Act 1982 Sched. 3C, as inserted by Civil Jurisdiction & Judgments Act 1982 Sched. 1) raises the same points of law as are discussed here. Throughout this chapter, references to 'the Convention' are references to the Brussels Convention, but where there are textual variations as between the different versions, these are pointed out.

The Power to Stay Proceedings in an English Court on Forum Non Conveniens or other Traditional Grounds.

We are here concerned with a case in which the English court has jurisdiction in the sense that a writ has been served and an application for the setting aside of service under RSC Order 12 rule 8 has failed or will not be attempted. The result in either case is that the court has jurisdiction, and has had it ever since the moment the writ was served. The first question to examine is whether (and if ever, when) it will be open to the court to accede to an application by the defendant to stay proceedings in favour of their being resolved in the natural forum, which lies elsewhere. I will not consider the extent to which the Convention may allow for proceedings to be dismissed or stayed on the ground of litispendence,[3] but will examine just the general common law discretion to stay in conformity with *Spiliada Maritime Corporation* v. *Cansulex Ltd*.[4]

It is assumed that a number of points are uncontroversial. First, that an English court, when it stays proceedings, remains seised of them.[5] This is not an empty theoretical point. One of the main points of a stay is that if things turn out differently in the foreign court from what the English court had foreseen and expected, an application may be made to lift the stay, and proceedings may be resumed without the need for a fresh writ, without problems of limitation having cropped up in the meantime, and so on. Moreover, if the stay was imposed upon the basis of, or in return for, undertakings being extracted from the defendant, measures to enforce these may be taken within the context of the proceedings which are, ex hypothesi, still pending in England. At no stage, then, does the defendant ask the court to relinquish jurisdiction.

Secondly, the English doctrine of forum non conveniens was developed as an English[6] response to jurisdictional rules of inappropriate width. Had English rules on jurisdiction been more narrowly defined than by the simple fact of lawful service, this doctrine might never have developed. Now as the jurisdictional rules of the Convention are, in some respects at least, rather narrower than those of the common law, there is, to be sure, less of a need for such a doctrine to operate as a gloss on these rules.

Thirdly, there is an attitude of general continental hostility towards a doctrine of forum non conveniens[7]. This may be because they do not

[3] Arts. 21 and 22.

[4] [1987] AC 460.

[5] *Rofa Sport Management AU* v. *DHL International (UK) Ltd* [1989 1 WLR 902.

[6] Though, of course, there is an intellectual debt to the law of Scotland.

[7] For two striking examples, see the essays of Gaudemet-Tallon and Schack in Fawcett (ed.) *Declining Jurisdiction in Private International Law* (1995); reviewed by the writer at [1997] LMCLQ 172

understand it,[8] and are offended by their construction of a phantom which does not at all correspond to what English lawyers see as the point of the doctrine. On the other hand, continental lawyers comprise a large majority on the bench of the Court of Justice, and it will not be easy to reprogramme their minds to accept something which they believe was never part of the Convention. Certainly it must be true that when the original Convention was drafted, there was never any intention to have it accommodate a doctrine of forum non conveniens. Beyond this, the reasons for this hostility encompass a combination of things, including the following. A *judicial* discretion in the hearing of cases where the *legislature* has prescribed that jurisdiction exists may be thought to be a usurpation of function and an interference by the judges with the balance of political power. It may be thought that a litigant should be able to read the text of the Convention, and to deduce from it where he may sue without being torpedoed by *Spiliada*. Well, perhaps. This attitude may depend upon the relative degrees of respect accorded to judges and legislators. In France, where Napoleon was the legislator and the judicial function was very tightly controlled, this may seem natural. The conditions of the United Kingdom are very different indeed. Again, the plaintiff who has read the Convention may be understandably annoyed if he commences proceedings, only to discover that although the court has jurisdiction (as he rightly concluded) it will nevertheless decline to proceed to hear the case. Salt is rubbed in the wound if this conclusion emerges only after several thousands of pounds have been incurred in his own legal fees,[9] and the knife really is given a twist if an order for payment of the other side's costs is made against him for losing on the stay issue.

With those general points declared, let us look at the some of the areas, and some of the cases, in which the question may come up for analysis.

When the English court has Article 2 Jurisdiction[10] *and the Natural Forum is in a Non-contracting State*

Re Harrods (Buenos Aires) Ltd[11] established that, as far as the Court of Appeal was concerned, a stay could be granted in such a case. At the risk of losing accuracy through paraphrase, it was considered that where the

[8] *Cf.* Kennet [1995] CLJ 252.

[9] It is very different (although the plaintiff may not really see it) if the defendant challenges the jurisdiction by means of an application which does persuade the court that it has no jurisdiction at all, leaving the plaintiff to start over again, elsewhere.

[10] It need not be Art. 2 which applies. Any jurisdictional base in Arts. 2, 5 or 6 will raise the same issue.

[11] [1992] Ch 72. The House of Lords, to which an appeal was made, referred 6 questions to the Court of Justice, but the case settled and the reference was withdrawn. The possible impact of the case being one concerned with Article 16(2) of the Convention appears to have been missed by the lower courts but was taken (as I am informed by Alexander Layton, QC, whom I thank for the information) when the proceedings first came before the House.

dispute, or the jurisdictional choice, lay as between the United Kingdom and Argentina, an inter-european jurisdictional settlement had no application to the matter. It was not the business of the contracting states to interfere in questions which arose as between the United Kingdom and Argentina.

As a matter of *English* law as set out in *Spiliada*, this is all rather odd. Not least is the argument that it may be so unjust to despatch the plaintiff to the court of a non-contracting state that a stay will be refused, even though the natural forum is in that state. For if he wins in such a state, the plaintiff gets a judgment which will qualify for recognition[12] in England. But it may not be enforceable in England,[13] and whether or not it is, its subsequent recognition in England does not convert it into a contracting state judgment, capable of being recognized and enforced under Title III.[14] The second limb of *Spiliada*[15] may well militate against this result as a matter of English law, whatever the Convention may separately say.

But as a matter of *European* law, it is not obvious that the reasoning in *Re Harrods* is correct either. For in remaining seised of the case, the English remedy of a stay does prevent the plaintiff seeking to sue in another contracting state court: the English court remains seised, and Article 21 of the Convention will prevent another contracting state from accepting jurisdiction over the same cause of action.[16] That does lay the foundation for an argument that the effect of the remedy will impact directly and acutely on the courts of other contracting states, and that it cannot therefore be said that the question has no impact on other contracting state courts. Next, it amounts to just as much a waste of costs for the plaintiff, who has correctly interpreted the Convention, but who still fails to get a hearing from the contracting state court which he chose to seise. True, the plaintiff may seek leave to discontinue the proceedings if he does not like the interlocutory result which he finds he obtains, but this will not affect the costs objection, and it is not at all certain that all judges will permit a plaintiff to discontinue, in order to try again in another contracting state, just because he now regrets his original choice of jurisdiction to sue in England.[17] So it may not be quite as true as it is simple to say that there is no contracting state interest in this

[12] On the ground that the defendant will have submitted, or will have been required to undertake to submit, to the jurisdiction of the foreign court.

[13] Only final and conclusive judgments for a fixed sum of money will be capable of enforcement.

[14] *Owens Bank Ltd* v. *Bracco* [1994] ECR I–117.

[15] That is, that a stay may nevertheless be refused if it would be unjust to confine the plaintiff to a judgment from the natural forum.

[16] Consideration is given below to arguments which might be set against this; it is believed that, ingenious though some of them are, they are misguided.

[17] *Internationale Nederlanden Aviation Lease BV* v. *Civil Aviation Authority* [1997] 1 Lloyd's Rep 80.

factual matrix. Even so, it has to be admitted that, whatever the answer is, the text of the Convention does not proclaim it with clarity.

When the English Court has Article 4 Jurisdiction[18] *and the Natural Forum is in another Contracting State*

Here the arguments are quite different, even though as a matter of English authority the result is just the same. The original jurisdiction of the court is now based first on Article 4 of the Convention, and then, and by reason of Article 4, on the traditional rules of the common law. As a result, the *Spiliada* power to stay proceedings is brought in and incorporated by reference to Article 4 with the common law rules on jurisdiction; and if it is brought in, it must allow a stay to be ordered in favour of another contacting state. This conclusion has been adopted at first instance,[19] and also by the Court of Appeal.[20]

I can see the argument for this conclusion. It proceeds as if Article 4 represents a doorway out of the Convention, back into the outside world of unreformed and un-interfered with civil jurisdiction. As a result, the court can deal with the jurisdictional aspects of the case without the encumbrance of the Convention. If *Spiliada* is part of the common law on jurisdiction, its application will be in conformity with the Convention, not in opposition to it. But it is submitted that this picture of the Convention is misleading. For we know that Article 4 does not free the court from other aspects of the operation of the Convention. Along with Article 16, which is expressed to apply regardless of Article 4, it is still necessary to observe the Convention's rules on litispendence;[21] the rules on choice of court agreements may still apply.[22] And any judgment will, of course, be entitled to take advantage of Title III.

The trick is once again to separate, as the Court of Appeal did, internal *Spiliada* arguments from Convention ones. As to *Spiliada*, and the internal rules of *English* law, it first requires the defendant to identify a court having jurisdiction and in which the case could be heard more conveniently for the ends of justice. Now if the English court remains seised of a case it has stayed, this condition cannot obviously be satisfied. Any court in a contracting state will have no jurisdiction over the same cause of action because it will be second seised in relation to a cause of action of which the

18 That is, over a defendant not domiciled in a contracting state.

19 *The Xin Yang and the An Kang Jiang* [1996] 2 Lloyd's Rep 217; *Sarrio SA* v. *Kuwait Investment Authority* [1996] 1 Lloyd's Rep 650.

20 *Sarrio SA* v. *Kuwait Investment Authority* [1997] 1 Lloyd's Rep 113. As Evans LJ was the presiding judge, this aspect of the seminar was approached with some delicacy. The decision of the Court of Appeal was reversed by the House of Lords: [1997] 4 All ER 929, but on grounds not material to the present discussion

21 *Overseas Union Insurance* v. *New Hampshire Insurance* [1991] ECR I–3317.

22 For Art. 17 does not require the defendant to be domiciled in a contracting state.

English court was and remains seised.[23] It would be different if the English court had declared that it had no jurisdiction, had set aside the writ or service thereof, and had thereby dis-seised itself, but it has not done so; and for reasons spelled out earlier, it will not do so.

Nor is it, with great respect to some of those who believe differently,[24] any answer to say that the jurisdiction of the English court has not been 'established' within Article 21, for the very reverse is true. But the argument is alluring,[25] and needs to be rebutted carefully. Article 21, as now amended, allows a court which has been seised second to 'stay its proceedings until such time as the jurisdiction of the court first seised has been established', and once the jurisdiction of the court first seised has been established, to decline jurisdiction. This very minor amendment was intended to prevent a court seised second dismissing proceedings forthwith, only for the court first seised later to rule that it had no jurisdiction, and to dismiss the action brought before it. It simply does not permit it to be argued that the first court has jurisdiction but that this jurisdiction is not established, so that the second court may disregard it: 'not established' means nothing more than 'not yet adjudicated upon', nothing more.[26] Nor is it accurate to say that a stay means that an English court has irrevocably determined that it will leave the case to be heard in another contracting state, for the possibility cannot be wholly excluded that the stay may be lifted and the action allowed to proceed. For once that has happened, and perhaps before, the stay can be lifted, and the case will proceed.

[23] Article 21. Even if the plaintiff were to attempt to seise the other court with a different cause of action, it would presumable be related within the meaning of Art. 22, and may be dealt with by that article.

[24] Evans and Brooke LJJ in *Sarrio* would have been prepared to adopt this view had the facts called for it; and their conclusion would, if accepted by the other court as well, remove this objection to a stay.

[25] It may be said that the decision of when the jurisdiction of an English court is 'established' is a matter on which the English courts may declare and adapt to correspond with the basic assumptions of the Convention. This was done in relation to *when* an English court is seised in *Dresser (UK) Ltd* v. *Falcongate Freight Management Ltd* [1992] 1 QB 502; *The Sargasso* [1994] 3 All ER 180. But the analogy is, for the reason explained below, not close enough to adapt it to this case.

[26] See the Report of Jenard and Möller on the Lugano Convention, where this is given as the sole explanation for the textual amendment to Art. 21: 1990 OJ C189/57 at 78 (para. 64). The original text of Art. 21 stated that 'any court other than the court first seised shall of its own motion decline jurisdiction in favour of that court. A court which would be required to decline jurisdiction may stay its proceedings if the jurisdiction of the other court is contested'. There was nothing stated about the court first seised 'establishing' its jurisdiction: that court either had jurisdiction or it did not. If it did, the second court had no choice but to dismiss; if it did not, the court seised second would proceed to hear the case. There was no third option. The minor textual amendment simply deals with the possibility that the jurisdiction of the first court might yet be objected to but has not yet contested. It is therefore quite incapable of bearing the weight of the ingenious but erroneous interpretation placed upon it by the Court of Appeal in *Sarrio*.

Moreover, it may be difficult to persuade a court in another contracting state to conclude that it can take jurisdiction: after all, the issue is not so much whether an English court believes a foreign court should consider that it has jurisdiction, but whether that foreign court will believe that it has. Take *Sarrio SA* v. *Kuwait Investment Authority*[27] as an example. If the English proceedings had been stayed and the Spanish court resorted to by the plaintiff, what would have happened if that Spanish court had concluded, despite the opinion of the Court of Appeal, that Article 21 acted to deprive it of jurisdiction? The answer, presumably, is that an application would have been made for the lifting of the English stay. The fact that the application could be made, and the fact that it would be likely to be granted, would just go to demonstrate that the Spanish court had been right all along. The conclusion is that *Spiliada* itself militates against a stay as a matter of domestic *English* law, by reason of the indirect but inescapable effects of the Convention.

It is odd—indeed, the Court of Appeal in *Sarrio* appeared to regard it as impossibly odd—that the result would be different if the proceedings had been commenced under RSC Order 11. But in such a case, however, satisfaction of the *Spiliada* test is a precondition of the very existence of jurisdiction: if it is not satisfied, *Spiliada* itself stands as authority for the fact that service of the writ will be set aside, and the court will thereupon be without jurisdiction, dis-seised. Where RSC Order 11 is the jurisdictional rule relied on, it will be possible and will be correct to utilize *Spiliada*, for the identification of England as the natural forum for the litigation is an integral part of the original jurisdiction of the court where this is established under RSC Order 11. That is the state of English law; it may be odd, but it can hardly be gainsaid. And it may also go to explain why it is that service within the jurisdiction is mentioned in the second paragraph of Article 3, as a rule which may be invoked as of right in certain cases[28] but service out under RSC Order 11 is not.

As far as the *Convention is* concerned, it may be thought that it places no obstacle in the path of a stay in such a case. But even this is not so clear. For the objections to a stay are much the same as where jurisdiction had been founded on Article 2. The plaintiff will have read Article 4, but will now find he has lost time and wasted money in litigating in England. If the doctrine of forum non conveniens is objectionable on this ground, it is just and precisely as objectionable here as well. Moreover, the second paragraph of Article 4 appears to give the plaintiff a right to avail himself of the jurisdictional rules contained in the second paragraph of Article 3.[29] In other words, he has a *right* to avail himself of jurisdiction invoked by the service

[27] [1997] 1 Lloyd's Rep 113.

[28] As to which, see below.

[29] Where they are spelled out to establish that they may not be used against a defendant domiciled in a contracting state.

of the writ on a defendant within the jurisdiction. Now if the plaintiff reads the Convention and does that which he is said to have a right to do, he may think it is rather less than a right if he is told (i) that he may not get a hearing, and (ii) that must pay the costs of both sides, incurred in finding out what his right really added up to. For these reasons, it is suggested that the impact of the Convention may be more extensive (if insidiously so) than was acknowledged, and that *Sarrio* should not be the last word on this question.

When the English Court has Article 4 Jurisdiction and the Natural Forum is in a Non-contracting State

This may be thought to be an easy case: it is, after all, a combination of the previous two examples. But if that is so, the objections which could be put up to the imposition of a stay in this case are in fact a combination of those raised above. If an English court stays its proceedings, its order is, in effect, that the plaintiff may not now obtain a judgment from the courts of any contracting state, and that dramatic decision follows from the simple fact of his having commenced proceedings in England. Even if—contrary to the view preferred here—it is correct to say that the question has nothing to do with any other contracting state, the order made certainly does. Moreover, the plaintiff will have availed himself of the right conferred on him by the second paragraph of Article 4, to invoke the jurisdiction described in the second paragraph of Article 3. Once again, it is not clear why he should lose that right, and pay all the costs of finding out that the text of the Convention was a mirage. It may be that this is an unattractive conclusion to be forced to, but it does not appear to be difficult to derive from the text of the Convention; and it is not unthinkable that the Court of Justice could be persuaded to think it. The question may be asked as to what should be done about it; a modest suggestion will follow.

When the English Court has Article 2 Jurisdiction and the Natural Forum is in another Contracting State

This is said to be the easy case: no serious authority appears to support the view that a stay of proceedings may be granted here. *Re Harrods* took it as a settled point, but distinguished the case before it. Mance J, at first instance in *Sarrio* did the same. The hostility of Professor Schlosser[30] was to the operation of the doctrine as between contracting states; and there is no case for it.

But it is possible to play devil's advocate, and to ask whether this conclusion has to be accepted or can be responded to. For a start, it cannot be asserted that the effect of the Convention has been or is to prevent the

[30] OJ 1979 C59/71 at 97 (para. 78).

practice of forum shopping. It goes on all the time, as the law reports (in this country at least) amply reveal. Take a simple tort case. It may be possible to sue the defendant in England pursuant to Article 2, if the United Kingdom is the state of the defendant's domicile. But if the tort was committed in another contracting state, where all the witnesses were, and in the courts of which state the plaintiff would have done less well than he will in England, is this not traditionally to be seen as a blatant case of forum shopping? If it is, how can it be prevented? It can no longer be controlled by jurisdictional rules, and it cannot be controlled, so it is said, by the *Spiliada* doctrine. Nor, all too regrettably, can it be prevented by the operation of choice of law rules. For Parliament—short-sightedly, to be sure—has legislated to prevent an English court choosing to apply the law which the courts of the natural forum would have applied.[31] So there is now nothing which can be done about it? Is that what any thoughtful legislator should be seeking to achieve?

Why should *Spiliada not* be used? One answer is that Professor Schlosser does not approve. But what is his problem? Prominent among his published objections is the alleged waste of a plaintiff's money which attends a *Spiliada* hearing. But this objection may be made to go away: quite unexpectedly, an argument has arisen which may help. Recently the Court gave judgment in the odd little case of *Van der Linden*.[32] There, an application had been made to enforce a German judgment in Belgium. Unfortunately, as the respondent pointed out, the applicant for enforcement had failed to serve all the documents required by Articles 46 and 47; and, just as unfortunately, although Article 48 did make some provision for the cure of deficiencies in the documentation, it did not provide for deficiencies in the service of *those particular* documents to be cured. But, said the Court, there was nothing to prevent the court addressed applying its own procedural law to the question, and granting a procedural remedy of cure to the applicant. All that was required was that the applicant, who was seeking the procedural indulgence from the procedural menu of the court addressed,[33] 'bears all costs unnecessarily incurred'. This looked like common sense: the party who made the error, and who wanted relief the Convention did not appear to permit, had to pay all the costs wasted or otherwise thrown away in putting it right.

This is not so far from the *Spiliada* difficulty. What is wrong with the proposition that if the defendant wants to apply for a stay on forum non conveniens grounds, there is no reason why he should not have his relief, just so long as *he* pays all the costs unnecessarily incurred? If he seeks an indulgence which the Convention does not appear to foresee (but which it

[31] Private International Law (Miscellaneous Provisions) Act 1995 s. 9(5).
[32] [1996] ECR I–1393.
[33] And not, it is important to note, from the Convention itself.

does not textually preclude[34]), he should be required to pay for it. But if he does,[35] the sting is drawn from one of Professor Schlosser's main published objections. True, there is still the problem of the English court remaining seised, but even this may be capable of being overcome with a bit of imagination. The *Sarrio* solution was one such attempt; but this has been doubted above. But when applications are made under RSC Order 12 rule 8, writs are set aside by masters and judges, but even though the writ may have been set aside, appeals are still brought against their orders. It appears, therefore, that a decision that a court has no jurisdiction, and the consequent order, does not necessarily prevent further applications being made in those proceedings. The possibility may yet be held to exist that relief of the *Spiliada* variety could be applied for under RSC Order 12 rule 8, but granted in the form of setting aside the writ, but with explicit or tacit acknowledgement of the right to appeal against this order at a later date. If such a solution had the effect of dis-seising the court, it might be easier to justify the granting of a stay as being compatible with the Convention. At least, the arguments outlined above would be capable of being responded to; and that would be a start. Given the brilliance of the *Spiliada* doctrine,[36] it may be worth the effort of seeking to defend it in a way which is a little less blatant in its assertion that the Convention has no relevance and that there is therefore no more to be said.

When the English Court has Jurisdiction under the Convention, but as a Matter of Common Law would have no Subject-matter Jurisdiction at all

This is just a final postscript to the proposition that there really needs to be some very careful work done, both on the extent of, and the limits upon, the indirect impact of the Convention. Suppose a claim is brought in England—England having jurisdiction under the Convention—but over which the English law has previously established that there is no right for the municipal courts to adjudicate. Does the Convention make justiciable something which was not so before? The conclusion that it does have this effect was reached in an absolutely extraordinary judgment, recently handed down by Lloyd J in *Pearce* v. *Ove Arup Partnership Ltd.*[37] If it is true, as the judge found it was, that an English court had no jurisdiction at com-

[34] At this point, the arguments based on *Kongress Agentur Hagen GmbH* v. *Zeehaghe BV* [1990] ECR I–1845, that the Convention does not aim to harmonize national law rules on procedure, which continue to operate as long as the practical effect of the Convention is not impaired, may assist.

[35] All the more so if he *undertakes* to pay all such costs.

[36] Which has become more, not less, important in the light of legislative restriction of the power to utilize the doctrine of *renvoi* to reproduce in England the effect of a case being heard in its natural forum.

[37] [1997] Ch. 293; evidently approved on this point in *Coin Controls Ltd.* v. *Suzo International (UK) Ltd.* [1997] 3 All ER 45.

mon law to entertain a claim concerning foreign intellectual property rights, such as patent or copyright, did this change when the defendant was subject to the personal jurisdiction of the Court according to Article 6[38] of the Convention? He held that it did; and the fact that the issue had been seen as non-justiciable prior to the Convention was now overridden by the Convention. It is fair to say that this ascription of magical powers to the Convention[39] is as unexpected as it is wrong. The better (probably the only tenable) view is that justiciability is not a matter of civil jurisdiction but of substantive law, of the outer limits of the powers of municipal courts. It cannot be argued, surely, that an English court must now be prepared to determine title to land in a non-contracting state, just because the defendant happens to be domiciled in England? It cannot be argued, surely, that if a defendant would be entitled to state or sovereign immunity, the action must now be allowed to proceed against, say, the President of the French Republic, just because it arises out a statement alleged to be defamatory of an English plaintiff? It cannot be argued, surely, that a claim should be capable of being brought by or against an unincorporated association, just because the claim would appear to fall within the text of a Convention rule and in some other contracting state with jurisdiction in the individual case, the action would be permitted to proceed? Yet *Pearce* may open the door to arguments of this difficult kind.

But if that was a surprise, there was even more in store. The judge took the view that to the extent that the choice of law rule—the common law rule of double actionability[40]—which would be applied meant that the plaintiff would lose, this choice of law rule was a measure having equivalent effect to a jurisdictional barrier to the claim. One hopes that this breathtaking approach, which cannot be confined by logic to the choice of law rule in tort, or to choice of law rules at all, come to that, will not last long. Even so, it reveals that there is need for a careful and thorough thinking through of the indirect effects claimed for the Convention, in a way which the high pressure of particular litigation may not be able to accomplish. If there is to be a defence of English rules on jurisdiction, and of the English rules on the conflict of laws rules as these have developed over the years, this is an urgent task.

The Power to Restrain Proceedings in another Contacting State

We now to turn to something more sharply controversial, and certainly more offensive: the power of an English court to issue anti-suit injunctions

38 Although the particular Article is not important to the argument.

39 For this happy form of words I am indebted to Mr Layton, QC.

40 The claim arose out of events preceding the coming into force of Part III of the Private International Law (Miscellaneous Provisions) Act 1995, and was therefore unaffected by it. The judge plainly thought that the claim did, however, fall within the subject matter scope of the Act.

against respondents who are pursuing litigation in the courts of another contracting state. We know that the courts have this power as a matter of English law.[41] We also know that there appears to be a growing enthusiasm for granting such orders, at least where the foreign proceedings are seen as having been brought in breach of contract. It is not always clear that an English judge should apply English perceptions of oppression or vexation in respect of parties and/or litigation which may have nothing to do with England at all, save for the fact that the respondent may be ensnared by the jurisdictional rules of English law. These matters may indicate that there needs to be some sorting out of the domestic law on when and why injunctions are granted.[42] But the impact of the Convention is a different point altogether. What *is* the relevance of the fact that the proceedings which are to be interfered with are, or may be brought, in the courts of another contracting state? Does this impinge on the willingness of the courts to order injunctions?

It does not often appear that it does. Indeed, the high water mark of the granting of injunctions has, oddly enough, come where the proceedings were brought in another contracting state: in *Continental Bank NA* v. *Aeakos Compania Naviera SA*,[43] in Greece; in *The Angelic Grace*,[44] in Italy; and in *Bankers Trust International* v. *RCS Editori SpA*,[45] also in Italy. The Admiralty judge has summarized this jurisprudence as meaning that where the proceedings are brought in breach of contract, there has to be shown a good reason why an injunction will not go to restrain the respondent from committing it.[46] In *The Angelic Grace*, it was nearly said openly, and is certainly said by implication, that the Italian court might well be grateful that proceedings, which it should not have been troubled with, have been prevented from making a nuisance of themselves by the prompt police action of the English courts. Well, possibly. What ought the answers be?

Two points will need to be considered and kept well apart. There needs to be personal jurisdiction over the respondent, for an anti-suit injunction is likely to arise in a civil or commercial matter; and if it does, the Convention may confer, but may also remove, jurisdiction in personam. Quite separately, if there is personal jurisdiction over the respondent, it has to be asked (i) where there is a private law right to it, and (ii) whether

[41] For the best single statement of the basis of the law, see *Societe Nationelle Industrielle Aérospatiale* v. *Lee Kui Jak*]1987] AC 871.

[42] See [1997] LMCLQ 90, 413.

[43] [1994] 1 WLR 588.

[44] [1995] 1 Lloyd's Rep 87.

[45] [1996] CLC 899.

[46] *A/S D/S Svendborg* v. *Wansa* [1996] 2 Lloyd's Rep 559. It should be noted that the Court of Appeal in *Alfred C. Toepfer* v. *Cargill* (25th October 1997) expressed caution and referred two important questions to the Court of Justice. But it is understood that the case has settled and the reference will not be proceeded with. The status of *Toepfer* v. *Cargill* therefore remains uncertain.

there are other reasons, more naturally seen as part of comity or as part of public international law, why the remedy ought nevertheless be withheld. But we will first look first at the jurisdictional question, and at the possibility that the Convention removes from the court personal jurisdiction over the respondent. It can arise in a number of ways; two may be taken as representative.

When the English Court is Seised Second but Believes it has a Superior Form of Jurisdiction to that of the Court Seised First

This may arise, for example, where the English court believes that there is a choice of court agreement which Article 17 would regard as giving exclusive jurisdiction to the English court. What happens if the respondent appears to defy that agreement by launching proceedings as plaintiff in another contracting state? Assuming that Article 17 would have given jurisdiction to the English court, does Article 21 of the Convention nevertheless remove it, on the footing that the same cause of action was commenced in another contracting state, first in time?

It is well known that *Continental Bank*, *The Angelic Grace*, and *Bankers Trust International* deny this. They take the view that Article 17 confers exclusive jurisdiction on the nominated court, and that, as a result, the English court alone should be hearing the case. The conclusion is then hard to resist: the proceedings in another contracting state are therefore brought in a court with no jurisdiction. But although that may be the conclusion, it is not clear that it is for the English court to reach it: it may be the correct analysis, but it is not clear that it is open to the English court to propound it and to grant orders in consequence of it.

Take the two points. As to personal jurisdiction over the respondent, there is room for disagreement. Article 17 would appear to give it, but Article 21 to take it away again. As the other court was seised first; and as *Overseas Union Insurance* leads to the conclusion that it is not open to a court seised second (i) to conclude that the court seised first should not have been seised at all, and (ii) thereupon to proceed to hear the case, some may think that it is even less open to the court seised second to reach that conclusion and grant the order of an anti-suit injunction. This conclusion is persuasive; but it may be gainsaid. Article 21 applies only if the two courts are seised of the same cause of action; and a claim in the first court for damages for breach of contract is not, usually at any rate, the same cause of action as the claim in the second court for an anti-suit injunction. If so, Article 21 does not apply after all, and the English court is not deprived of personal jurisdiction over the respondent. It might be different if the English proceedings had been brought for substantive relief on the merits, and the anti-suit injunction was merely an incidental application within the course of those proceedings. But that was not the case in *Continental Bank*.

Even if there is personal jurisdiction over the respondent, and even if there is breach of a legal right not to be sued, is there any reason not to enjoin the respondent? It is submitted that there is. First, if the foreign contracting state court has considered the point and has made a ruling that it has jurisdiction, and that Article 17 has not taken it away, there is no obvious reason why that decision should not itself be recognized as determining the application for an injunction. Secondly, if it has not yet done so, the position is only a little different. There will be no judgment to recognize, but one will be coming, from a court with jurisdiction to give it. Is it really right, as a matter of the scheme of comity between contracting states, for an English court to do this for itself? Article 17 is central to the jurisdiction of both courts.[47] I do not believe it is right. The mutual trust between courts, which has been legislated for by the Convention and whether we like it or not, does not allow for this; and (as one might say, if we are talking equity here) *qui prior est tempore potior est jure*. The reason to withhold the remedy is not because there is no private legal or equitable right at stake, but because there are reasons almost of public interest or public law why it is inappropriate for an English court to assume the right to answer the question and dish out the orders. What would happen, for example, if an attempt were made to enforce the anti-suit injunction under the Convention in the foreign contracting state? Are the consequences really something which should be contemplated with calm?

After all, it is far from clear that a foreign court will see that its attitude should be one of gratitude that the Court of Appeal has saved it from having to rule on its own jurisdiction. It is evident that some states take the view that their citizens[48] have a constitutional right of access to the courts. Will it then be welcome for an English court to override this constitutional guarantee? Perhaps not. A brilliant example of this emerged in *Philip Alexander Securities & Futures Ltd* v. *Bamberger*.[49] A German court had refused to allow service of English interlocutory anti-suit injunctions on this very ground; the fact that it had done so led the Waller J, and the Court of Appeal, to conclude that it would be wrong to order final injunctions to interfere with proceedings in the German courts. As a counterweight to the aggressive policing exemplified by *The Angelic Grace* this is a welcome piece of reasoning. There is no difficulty with it if one acknowledges that the granting of an injunction involves both private law and public law interests; and that even if there is jurisdiction to do it, and even though there is a private right to relief, it may not be in the public interest to interfere with proceedings in another contracting state. If this view is not taken,

[47] To confer jurisdiction in the one case, to remove it in the other.
[48] Presumably a privilege extended to nationals of other Member States as well.
[49] [1997] ILPr 73.

the working out of the consequences will be very complicated, will lead to much recourse to public policy as a ground withholding recognition,[50] and will, in the end, not allow the courts to develop their own view about where the limits should lie.

It cannot be overlooked that although there may be personal jurisdiction over the respondent, and although there may be oppressive or vexatious or unlawful conduct on behalf of the respondent, it may not be for the English court to police it. This may be part of the broader problem that the way anti-suit injunctions operate within the conflict of laws is not fully understood; but in the context of the Convention, it is hard to believe that it was meant to allow for these to be granted. Here, therefore, the indirect impact of the Convention may be easier to predict.

When the English Court is Seised Second but Believes it has Ordinary[51] Convention Jurisdiction and the State Seised First does not have Jurisdiction at all

This may appear to be a weaker case for an injunction. On the other hand, the conclusion will be that the foreign contracting state court has no jurisdiction over the defendant, and that it is therefore a breach of the applicant's legal rights conferred by the Convention for him to be sued in that court. As a result, the prospect of obtaining an injunction ought to be just the same. There will still need to be personal jurisdiction over the respondent. Article 17 cannot be relied on for this, now, but other bases may be; and if it is argued that Article 21 prevents this, the response will again be that it is inapplicable as the causes of action are not the same. As the violation of a statute conferring jurisdictional privileges looks very much like violation of a legal right not to be sued, there may be no reason why the logic which led to *Continental Bank* and its progeny does not apply so as to justify an injunction here as well.

Indeed, this widening conclusion is hinted at in a splendidly robust judgment of the Court of Appeal in *Airbus Industrie GIE* v. *Patel*.[52] Though the actual injunction went to restrain proceedings, which should have been brought in India, from being prosecuted in Texas, the Court set about telling a few home truths about the rights and wrongs of litigating against European defendants in Texas with enthusiasm. One point, said Hobhouse LJ, helped the applicant demonstrate its legitimate interest in obtaining an injunction: it was domiciled in France, and therefore had an interest in being sued only in the French courts. There are reasons to dissent from this conclusion, not least because the theory underpinning of

[50] Art. 27(1).
[51] Such as Art. 2.
[52] [1997] 2 Lloyds Rep 8; under further appeal. Personal jurisdiction over the respondent was not an issue, and is not discussed here.

Re Harrods, that the Convention is irrelevant in relations with non-contracting states, was evidently overlooked. But Hobhouse LJ did say what may have been suspected: that if the Convention gives rights to applicants to sue and not to be sued, breach of any part of the Convention may be enough to establish a legal right not to be sued. If a case such as this one were to form the factual basis for the first reference to the Court of Justice on this point, it would present too inviting a target for the Court of Justice to miss. It may be prudent for the English courts to clip the wings of this remedy before it flies too near the sun and destroys itself. Even if this is done, there is no guarantee that the Court will be persuaded that the Convention is not being subverted. It may be that the logic of *Overseas Union Insurance*, that there is no permissible second guessing of the jurisdiction of courts before which proceedings are pending, is inexorable, and that any remedy which is predicated upon the power of an English court to do this is itself contrary to the implicit scheme of the Convention.

Where the Respondent is not Domiciled in a Contracting State and Personal Jurisdiction over him is Based on Article 4

It might be thought to follow in some loosely intuitive way that if the person suing a defendant in another contracting state is not domiciled in a contracting state either, so that personal jurisdiction over him as respondent may be taken under Article 4,[53] then he is, or this is, a case to which the Convention has no application. The conclusion sought to be drawn might be that the power of the court to issue an injunction should not be limited or restrained by considerations of the sort sought to be extracted from the Convention, as just described. Alternatively, it may be contended that the power to order anti-suit injunctions is, just as was claimed for the *Spiliada* power to stay proceedings, an integral part of the jurisdictional scheme of English Common law, the application of which is mandated by Article 4. This would be a very difficult argument to accept. If it is incorrect to see Article 4 as constituting a door leading out of the Convention, then the usual internal restraints of the Convention must continue to operate. Moreover, if the impact of the injunction is going to be that proceedings in a civil or commercial matter in a contracting state are interfered with on the essential ground that an English court believes that the foreign court should dismiss the proceedings on jurisdictional or other grounds, the offensive quality of an injunction is just the same as before, and the reasons for not granting it are just the same as before. Such a case may help add weight to the proposition that it is rather too simplistic to say that jurisdiction under Article 4 has nothing to do with the Convention. It is not obvious that it can be put better or more clearly than that; the argument is almost irresistible.

[53] *Overseas Union Insurance* would still insist that Art. 21 was applicable in principle; but the point about the causes of action not being the same will still apply.

The Exclusion of Arbitration from the Scope of the Convention

The third area I wish to look at, if only briefly, is a case where the text of the Convention is clear in what it excludes, but the conclusions which might be thought to follow from this have not always been accepted as enthusiastically as they might have been. We have already touched on one aspect of this, when considering the enforcement of arbitration agreements by injunction.[54] The concern now is not the enforcement of contractual promises to arbitrate at the moment of breach, but the exclusion of arbitration from the Convention by the sub-paragraph (4) of the second paragraph of Article 1. It is clear that the Convention does not apply as part of English law in relation to arbitrations governed in any way by English law. It is also clear, as is shown by *Marc Rich*,[55] that it does not apply either to judicial proceedings which are part of the setting up, regulating, or policing of an arbitration agreement.

So far, so good. Now we know that the Convention excludes arbitration from its scope. We also know that if subject matter is excluded from the Convention, that exclusion is not to be collaterally undermined by the obligation to consider something which does fall within the scope of the Convention as being governed by it. A brilliant example of this is found in *Hoffman* v, *Krieg*,[56] a case which deserves to be better and more widely read.

Maintenance falls within the scope of the Convention; questions of divorce and status in general do not. In *Hoffman*, a German decree of maintenance had ordered a husband to support his wife. A Dutch court then pronounced a decree of divorce, and deduced that it should refuse to recognize the maintenance order. It was held by the court that it was right to do so. The reasoning of the court is simplicity itself: as status and divorce fall outside the Convention, the Dutch court was free to take its own view of the status of the parties. This freedom was not cut down or contradicted by the fact that there had been a judgment in respect of something which did fall within the scope of the Convention. The second paragraph of the ruling said that, 'A foreign judgment whose enforcement has been ordered in a contracting state pursuant to Article 31 of the Convention, and which remains enforceable in the state in which it was given must not

[54] This was the factual context of *The Angelic Grace*, *Bankers Trust*, *Philip Alexander*, and *Toepfer* v. *Cargill*.

[55] [1991] ECR I–3855. The case is an especially good read for anyone wishing to see how scornfully thorough, and thoroughly scornful, was the AG's evaluation of the evidence given in the litigation by Professor Schlosser. It is a real connoisseur's piece.

[56] [1988] ECR 645. The point is supported, though less conspicuously, by *Van den Boogaard* (Case C–220/95; [1997] 3 WLR 284), dealing with maintenance (which falls within the Convention) and rights in property arising out of a matrimonial relationship (which does not: Art. 1, sub-para. (2) of the second para.).

continue to be enforced in the state where enforcement is sought when, under the law of the latter state, it ceases to be enforceable for reasons which lie outside the scope of the Convention.' That, it seems, is plain enough. If the Dutch law on status was incompatible with the foreign judgment, the foreign judgment was not to be recognized: not for reasons which fell within the Convention, but because the subject matter did not do so at all. So, therefore, if the English law on arbitration[57] is incompatible with the foreign judgment, the foreign judgment should be denied recognition for exactly the same reasons.

Yet certain of the judiciary have been unaccountably resistant to this conclusion. In *The Heidberg*,[58] Judge Diamond QC appears to have had this argument put to him, and rejected it. In a more thoughtful judgment in *Philip Alexander Securities & Futures* v. *Bamberger*,[59] Waller J saw the point which Judge Diamond had not accepted. Though he would have been prepared to deny recognition of the foreign judgment on grounds of public policy,[60] a ground which is internal to the Convention, he did not appear to accept that the basis for non-recognition lay outside the Convention as *Hoffman* had suggested. He nevertheless saw the difficulty of this: if a judgment from another contracting state court declaring that there was no binding arbitration agreement would fall outside the Convention, surely the same had to be true of a judgment which decided this and went on to award damages on the merits. Given that, it may be wondered whether he should not have concluded that where recognition of a judgment would involve the court disregarding its private international or other law of arbitration, the judgment itself fell outside the recognition provisions of the Convention.

Two reasons have been given for not applying *Hoffman* according to its terms. One is that the result in *Hoffman* could also have been based on Article 27(4), which is a basis for the withholding of recognition which is internal to the Convention. It is undeniable that Article 27(4) is problematic, for it will often be redundant. But the Court did not decide the case on the basis of Article 27(4). It reached its conclusion in paragraph 15 of the judgment, and went on to say that its conclusion was 'confirmed by Article 27(4) of the Convention . . . ' Article 27(4) was not, therefore, the basis of the decision.

A second basis is that Civil Jurisdiction & Judgments Act 1982, section 32(4) states that the non-recognition of a judgment on the ground that it was obtained in breach of what *English* law saw as breach of a binding

[57] Such as is found in Civil Jurisdiction & Judgments Act 1982 s. 32.

[58] [1994] 2 Lloyd's Rep 287.

[59] [1997] ILPr 73. The aborted reference in *Toepfer* v. *Cargill*, n. 46, would have examined this question.

[60] Art. 27(l); the learned judge made generous reference to a lecture given by the present writer which had raised this possibility.

agreement to arbitrate does not apply where the Convention requires recognition of the judgment. But the proper conclusion to draw from *Hoffman* is that English law does not require recognition of the judgment; and there is therefore no reason why the judgment, obtained in breach of a promise to arbitrate, should be recognized.

It remains a mystery why it is that *Hoffman* is not taken to be the firm and clear basis for the non-recognition of judgments obtained in violation of an arbitration agreement which is itself outside the scope of the Convention. The unimpressive analysis in *The Heidberg* does not deserve to linger much longer in the books.

But more than this, the question is yet another example of the way in which the interfaces between the Convention and national law—many of which were evidently wholly unsuspected by the drafters of the Convention—have not been worked out. To a considerable extent, the failure should be blamed on the academic commentators, even though it is frustrating that at times they appear to be writing only for the advantage of themselves and for no one else. To some extent our system of judicial precedent may have had the effect of giving judgments a wider impact than is properly warranted. To some extent the problem is that the people who have the last word on this question are the judiciary of the Court of Justice who, it may be suspected, know little and care less about the subtle and complex rules of English jurisdiction and civil procedure, and who harbour the suspicion that the United Kingdom is always trying to slip past them something which will eat away at the European Union from within. But whoever is to blame, the indirect impact of the Convention upon our rules of civil procedure, which has little to do with what the text says, and a lot to do with the unregulated powers of the Court of Justice, is a menace which few of us saw coming at the time. This chapter is not meant as a call to vote for the Referendum Party. Many of us have got a lot of fun, and expect to get a lot more fun, out of the Convention and its unexpected side-effects. But on a personal note, if I were to wake up tomorrow to discover that it had all been a bad dream, and that the Convention had never been enacted in this country, I doubt if my state of gloom would last beyond elevenses.